D1347579

"Norman attended nearly every meeting of the Convention and interviewed almost all its leading protagonists, and within a few months of its conclusion has produced what is sure to prove the definitive account of its work. In less skilled hands, such a book could have proved as dry as dust, but Norman has produced a lively and entertaining read."

Dick Leonard, a former Brussels bureau chief of the Economist, in The Bulletin

"Mr Norman is at his best when offering rare glimpses of what went on behind the open Convention scene – in the places where the public had no access."

Lisbeth Kirk in the EUobserver

"It's a thorough, detailed and readable account of the Convention's 16-month journey from the end of February 2002 to July 2003. As a historical record of the Convention, it will probably be unsurpassed."

The European Voice

"Peter Norman's 'The Accidental Constitution' is a masterful, reliable account of the Convention's official proceedings and of the off-the-record discussions that took place. It is an impressive and unique book. I admire Peter Norman for his ability to provide such vivid insight of those events, as they unfolded. I consider it an ideal guide for a thorough understanding of the Convention's historical significance and results."

Lamberto Dini, former prime minister of Italy,
and member of the Convention

The

Accidental Constitution

Second Edition

To Janice

The

Accidental Constitution

The Making of Europe's Constitutional Treaty

Peter Norman

EuroComment • Brussels

Published by
EuroComment
Avenue Général Eisenhower 28
1030 Brussels
Belgium

For further information regarding any aspect of this publication, please contact: info@eurocomment.be

ISBN 90-77110-08-9

Cover photograph provided by A/P Reporters

Table of Contents

PART III
Changing Dynamics: From Skeleton to Early Draft Articles

Preface to the Second Edition

When, early in 2002, Peter Ludlow suggested I might like to write a book about the Convention for EuroComment, his new publishing venture, neither of us realised that the Convention and the European Union's constitutional treaty would keep us busy for the following three years.

This is the second edition of *The Accidental Constitution*. The first edition, which was published by EuroComment in November 2003, was the story of the European Convention and the draft constitutional treaty negotiated by the Convention's 207 members, and handed over to EU governments in July 2003.

This book takes the story further. It includes a chapter on the negotiations among EU member states during the Intergovernmental Conference (IGC) of 2003 and 2004 that produced the text, which was signed by the EU's 25 member states in Rome at the end of October 2004. It also looks forward to challenges surrounding the ratification of the treaty, which form the next stage of the story. It deliberately pays special attention to the situation in the UK, which, at the time of writing, seems to be the member state most likely to reject the Constitution.

According to the treaty, all 25 member states have to approve the text by 1 November 2006 if it is to enter into force as planned. Whether the European Union can move on to become more efficient and democratic now depends on the decisions of the national parliaments of the EU's member states, and on voters in those countries, including Britain, which are holding referendums.

This book has set out to be more than just a chronicle of the Convention and the IGC that followed it. I have also tried to explain and analyse these events in the broader context of a Union that increasingly affects the lives of the citizens of its member states, old and new, for better or worse.

I hope this will give the book a relevance that endures. Because I believe strongly that one of the EU's great failings is its inability to explain its purpose and its actions, I have tried to write a book that can reach out to the lay reader. I originally took my cue from the Convention's president, Valéry Giscard d'Estaing, who said he wanted the outcome of the Convention to be understandable to an educated teenager. While I am not sure that Giscard achieved his goal, I am encouraged by the reactions to the first edition of *The Accidental Constitution* to believe that this book can appeal to a wider readership than the priesthood of EU specialists who work in and with the Union's institutions inside the Brussels beltway.

I have also tried to write a book that is ideologically neutral. This is no easy task when writing about the EU and I often thought how much easier my life would be if I were to tackle the themes of the Convention from an extreme europhile or eurosceptic viewpoint. Because it is so complex and bewildering, the EU invites commentaries from all manner of zealots who can run amok with the truth, confident that generally well-informed opinion-formers lack the knowledge or resources for reasoned rebuttal. I will be content if this book spreads some understanding, especially in the United Kingdom, as the referendum on the constitutional treaty approaches.

That said, neutral is not the same as neutered. I have views on the EU and it is only right that the reader knows my underlying position before embarking on this book. I am a British citizen. I consider myself a European, albeit one who regrets some aspects of the European Union as it exists today.

Having lived and worked during the past 37 years at different times in Britain, Germany and Belgium, and spent altogether roughly the same length of time in each of these countries, it probably could not be any other way. But, in writing this book, my aim has been to put my opinions to one side. I have tried to treat the facts as sacred. I hope the judgements are measured. They are, however, my own.

This book differs in some respects from the first edition of *The Accidental Constitution*. To accommodate the account of the IGC, some detail of the early history of the Convention has been trimmed but without subtracting from the significance accorded to that unique body. There is no longer a documentary annex. The original documentary annex included the articles, with brief comments attached, of the first 'constitutional' part of the draft treaty agreed by the Convention and other selected articles from the Convention text. These texts have been overtaken by the treaty agreed by member states in June 2004.

Thus when discussing draft treaty articles in detail, this edition refers the reader, by the use of square brackets, to the constitutional treaty text as agreed by the member states in the IGC. This text has been published in full in the EU's official journal and is readily available at no cost. A note on sources explains how it can be accessed in several places via the EU's 'Europa' web portal.

The note on sources appears after this preface. However, in connection with this edition of *The Accidental Constitution*, I would like to thank Fiona

White, for her quiet professionalism while editing this book and Peter Ludlow, for his guidance. Special thanks go to my wife, Janice, to whom this book is dedicated, for her continuing support, encouragement and patience.

Peter Norman
London
27 February 2005

Note on Sources

The negotiation of the European Union's constitutional treaty generated a vast amount of material, much of which has informed this book and which is readily accessible for readers who want to discover more.

The EU's leaders decided at their December 2001 summit in Laeken that the European Convention's discussions and all related official documents would be in the public domain. Similarly, the official documents used in the Intergovernmental Conference (IGC) that followed the Convention have been published.

One of the first acts of the Convention secretariat was to set up an internet site, http://european-convention.eu.int, which is a treasure trove of information. More than 850 documents were posted on it in a series labelled CONV. Many of these documents are cited in the text of this book and acknowledged in the footnotes.

These documents include background notes of the Convention's secretariat and Praesidium draft articles, the contributions of individual Convention members, the various versions of the constitutional treaty and the draft that was submitted to the Italian presidency of the EU on 18 July 2003. The site also carries material that informed the discussions in the Convention's working groups, the 6,000 or so amendments to draft articles that were submitted during the process of crafting the Convention draft between February 2003 and July 2003, and speeches, including several by the Convention president, Valéry Giscard d'Estaing. When the Convention ended in July 2003, it was decided that the internet site should remain unchanged and open for at least five years. The archives of the Convention have also been deposited with the secretariat of the Council.

From April 2002, the European Parliament started to publish verbatim accounts of the Convention's debates in the language used by the individual speakers. Six months later, the parliament began to produce summaries of the debates. Together these proved an invaluable checking tool. They can be read on http://www.europarl.eu.int/Europe2004/index_en.htm, the Future of Europe Page on the parliament's website, under the heading 'Debates at the Convention'.

The constitutional treaty, as agreed by the member states in June 2004, was signed on 29 October 2004 in Rome. The full text, which is cross-referenced in square brackets from chapter 12 onwards, is available in the 20 official EU languages and Gaelic. Perhaps the most user-friendly version is that published in the Official Journal of the European Union, C310 of 16 December 2004 (ISSN 1725-2423). This text, which also includes all annexes, protocols and declarations attached to the treaty, is accessible free of charge via special Constitution pages on the EU's 'Europa' portal (http://europa.eu.int/constitution/) and at the EUR-Lex website, which provides access to European law (http://europa.eu.int/eur-lex/lex/). The Europa portal also provides easy access to the EU's Futurum website and other sites containing more information about the constitutional treaty and its negotiation.

The IGC also generated a fair number of documents, although fewer than the Convention. They are identified by the prefix CIG and are accessible via the Council website (http://ue.eu.int) in the section dedicated to the Constitution. Many are cited in this book.

Attending all but two plenary sessions of the Convention gave me access to the conventionnels, their assistants, other followers of the Convention, press conferences and briefings. While the documentary sources cited above provided the bones of the story, personal contacts added the flesh.

The Convention press service was always helpful beyond the call of duty, particularly after I moved from Brussels to London during the life of the Convention. I am greatly indebted to Nikolaus Meyer-Landrut and Christine Priol. I am also grateful to Jo Mulcaire of the *FT*'s Brussels office for helping to keep me in touch with events after my move.

I consulted the websites of governments, foreign ministries, the European political party groups, broadcasting organisations and newspapers, and references to these can be found in the footnotes. Where articles or interviews in newspapers have served as primary source material, they are acknowledged in footnotes. By way of background, the *EUobserver* website (http://euobserver.com) has proved an increasingly helpful guide to events in Brussels and the EU's national capitals. The briefing notes produced by Peter Ludlow, EuroComment's founder and the publisher of this book, provided some extremely valuable insights into the IGC.

I owe special thanks to many people who cannot be named or more closely identified who helped me understand the Convention and the IGC. Although the Convention was an exercise unique in its openness, many of the most interesting developments took place away from public scrutiny: in the Praesidium, in bilateral discussions among the protagonists and in national capitals. I owe much to the help and candour of many people who were kind enough to give me their time and trust. A final acknowledgement and word of thanks must go to former colleagues in the Brussels press corps, who, in the traditions of the place, were typically generous in sharing information during my researches into the negotiations on Europe's constitutional treaty.

Part I

Setting up the Convention

CHAPTER 1
A New Way to Reform the Union

The tall, elderly gentleman was working the room. Elegant in an immaculately tailored, slate grey suit and sober maroon tie, he appeared unconscious of the video cameramen who jostled around him.

But a light application of stage make-up showed that Valéry Giscard d'Estaing had prepared for a moment in history. The former president of France, voted out of office some 20 years before, was back – and in charge of a great experiment that could change the destiny of Europe.

The 76-year-old elder statesman was preparing to preside over the first constituent assembly of a continent uniting after a century of carnage and division. Around him, in the packed plenary hall of the European Parliament in Brussels, were another 206 members of a Convention that had been called to consider the future of the European Union and its relationship with 28 present and future member states.

No one knew, on that last day of February 2002, what the Convention would produce. Men and women from the 28 democracies were gathered in Brussels because the leaders of the European Union's member states had determined that Europe was 'at a cross roads'.[1] They wanted the Union to be more democratic, transparent and efficient, and to this end had created a novel assembly of 105 full members and 102 alternates to ponder its constitutional future for more than a year.

The Convention was a first. Never before had the European Union been subject to such intense scrutiny from such a large and diverse group of people. The 'conventionnels,' as Giscard called them, were representatives of an area stretching from Finnish Lapland, north of the Arctic Circle, to the toe of Italy in the south, and from the Portuguese Azores far to the west of the European mainland to Turkey's eastern frontier with Iraq, close to the cradle of civilisation.

Never before had EU governments gone so far in sharing the tasks of plotting constitutional change as in the Convention. Hitherto, preparing

---

[1] The Laeken Declaration, December 2001.

reform of the EU was the jealously guarded preserve of member state administrations, whose ministers and senior officials negotiated behind closed doors in 'intergovernmental conferences'. For the first time, the representatives of national leaders would discuss proposals for change with national parliamentarians from 15 present and 13 applicant states of the European Union, and members of the European Parliament and the European Commission. The great majority of conventionnels were elected representatives of Europe's citizens with delegates from the 28 national parliaments making up more than half of their number.

The members of the Convention met in unprecedented open conditions. Its plenary sessions were held in public and broadcast on the Union's satellite television channel. A vast number of documents were posted on the Internet. Inevitably, the Convention was not quite as open as many would have liked. The discussions in the Praesidium, the 13-member body charged with pushing the Convention forward, took place behind closed doors and the minutes released after the Convention's close were – intentionally – not particularly illuminating. Published information gave only occasional insights into the negotiations in the back rooms and corridors away from the Convention hall, while Giscard and his aides sought to draw a veil over his bilateral talks with Union leaders in his travels around the capitals. But compared with past intergovernmental conferences – and that which was to follow it – the Convention was remarkably transparent.

A counterpart to diversity and openness was unpredictability. When the Convention started, it was far from clear that it would discuss, let alone draft. In its early months, it was open whether it would result in a written Constitution, a constitutional treaty, a series of treaty amendments or just recommendations. There were many, mainly concentrated in national capitals, who thought it would be no more than a high-level talking shop. There was a widespread expectation that it would, at best, come up with a series of options, which would allow the governments in the intergovernmental conference, or IGC, that would follow the Convention largely to ignore its results and carry on as before.

Two years, eight months and one day after Giscard opened the Convention, the heads of government and foreign ministers of a greatly enlarged EU gathered in far more ornate surroundings in Rome to sign a 'Treaty establishing a Constitution for Europe'.

The ceremony took place in the Palazzo di Conservatori on the Capitoline Hill. The new treaty was signed in the room where, in 1957, representatives of six western European states signed the first Treaty of Rome setting up the European Economic Community, the forerunner of today's EU. Signing the constitutional treaty on 29 October 2004, were the leaders and ministers of 25 member states with a combined population of 450 million. Also on hand to add their signatures to the 'final act' that accompanied the treaty were the leaders of Bulgaria, Romania and Turkey. The three candidate countries had shared in the work of the Convention during its 16 and a half months and sent observers to the IGC, in which the member states carried forward the negotiations between October 2003 and mid-June 2004.

As is often the case in the European Union, the mood at the signing ceremony did not quite match the hoped-for grandeur of the occasion. Overshadowing the event, and weighing on the minds of many present, was a separate political row over who should be members of the new European Commission, the executive body of the EU that would take office in November. But there was no denying the significance of the occasion. The signing, said Bertie Ahern, the Irish prime minister and engineer of the final compromise on the constitutional treaty that completed Giscard's work, proved Europe could function effectively. 'The agreement on the Constitution provides convincing and irrefutable evidence that the EU of 25 can take important decisions for the future of our people.'

The next step is for the constitutional treaty to be ratified by all 25 EU member states so it can enter into force. Its future will depend crucially on the citizens of countries that are putting it to a referendum. In February 2005, the Spanish electorate approved the treaty by a large majority but on a low turnout. Nine other countries are committed to referendums. Those in the UK, France, Poland, the Czech Republic and the Netherlands are subject to a greater or lesser degree of risk.

This book tells the story of how Europe's constitutional treaty came about. It explains the issues addressed by the Convention and the Intergovernmental Conference that followed it. It provides the background to the debates over ratification of the treaty in the EU's member states. The book tells what to expect from 1 November 2006, when Europe's constitutional treaty will take effect, provided all member states have approved it by that time.

Knowing 'how' the European Union's draft constitutional treaty came about is crucial to understanding the 'what' of its contents. This book sets out to describe the process of 'how' and consider the 'what' of the constitutional treaty that the Convention and IGC produced. It is a tale of people and policies but above all, of the unexpected. That is why the book is called *The Accidental Constitution*.

CHAPTER 2
Pressure for Change

2.1 THE UNCERTAIN GIANT

The European Union entered the 21st century plagued by doubts. Viewed in the broad sweep of history, it was a huge success. In the 50 years since Robert Schuman, the French foreign minister, proposed the creation of a European Coal and Steel Community on 9 May 1950, it had brought peace and prosperity to countries previously hell-bent on mutual destruction in two world wars. It had grown from 6 to 15 member states and was negotiating entry terms with another 12 candidates – 10 of which would become members on 1 May 2004. Its changes of name reflected growing ambition, from the European Economic Community of 1957, through the European Communities of 1965 to the European Union of 1992. Internal borders between member states had disappeared throughout most of its area. It was the world's biggest trading entity. It aspired to a common foreign and security policy. Its common market acted as an engine for integration, involving ever more Union decisions in the lives of the citizens of its member states whether they liked it or not.

The Union had formidable and historic tasks in hand. Its prospective enlargement to include the former Communist countries of central and eastern Europe would put a line under the post-Second World War division of Europe by the Iron Curtain. The recognition, in 1999, of Turkey as an applicant amounted to a promise to bridge ancient divisions that had split Europe since the fall of Constantinople to the Turks in 1453. Among the existing 15 member states, 12 were engaged in an unprecedented and bold experiment to create a single currency, the euro, without first achieving political union or harmonising their economic and fiscal policies. All 15 were committed to forging a single market for goods and services. The Lisbon European Council in March 2000 added the target of creating 'the most competitive and dynamic knowledge-based economy in the world' by 2010.

Yet as the Union hatched ever greater ambitions and became ever more important in the lives of its citizens, it failed to develop its full potential on the world stage or find a place in peoples' hearts.

Member state	Date of membership	Population ^{P}
Germany*	1958	82.5
France *	1958	59.6
Italy*	1958	57.3
The Netherlands*	1958	16.2
Belgium*	1958	10.4
Luxembourg*	1958	0.4
United Kingdom	1973	59.3
Denmark	1973	5.4
Ireland*	1973	4.0
Greece*	1981	11.0
Spain*	1986	40.7
Portugal*	1986	10.4
Sweden	1995	8.9
Austria*	1995	8.1
Finland*	1995	5.2
Poland	2004	38.2
Czech Republic	2004	10.2
Hungary	2004	10.1
Slovakia	2004	5.4
Lithuania	2004	3.5
Latvia	2004	2.3
Slovenia	2004	2.0
Estonia	2004	1.4
Cyprus	2004	0.7
Malta	2004	0.4
Candidate countries		
Romania	2007+	21.8
Bulgaria	2007+	7.8
Turkey	N	70.2
Croatia^	N	4.0
^{P} In millions. Source: Eurostat, status 1 January 2003.		
* member of the euro.		
+ expected accession date.		
N accession negotiations due to start in 2005.		
^ participated in neither the Convention nor the IGC. Population data: Croatian government.		

Table 1: The European Union after successive enlargements

The Union's weak international profile partly reflected collateral damage
from its two great projects of the 1990s: the euro and the single market. Both

were motors of greater integration and intended to advance the EU. But they required large-scale adjustment of rules, legislation and habits at the Union and national levels. The EU therefore looked inwards in the decade after the collapse of communism, when pressures mounted for it to play a bigger global role. The gap between the Union's economic strength and ambitions and its ability to project power outside its territory was cruelly exposed in the wars of the Yugoslav succession, where the resolution of conflict in Bosnia and Kosovo required US intervention. The Union began to address these deficiencies at its December 1999 European Council in Helsinki with plans for a 60,000-strong rapid reaction force. But the world did not stand still to let the EU catch up. The terrorist attacks on New York and Washington on 11 September 2001 and their effect in turning the US, the world's sole superpower, into a still more assertive force on the global stage, stepped up the challenges facing Europe as it tried to develop its foreign and defence policies.

The Union's rapport with Europe's citizens was weak. Voter participation in the June 1999 European Parliament elections dropped below 50% for the first time and fell further in the enlarged EU of 25 member states in the elections of June 2004. A Danish referendum on whether to join the euro in September 2000 and an Irish referendum in June 2001 on adjustments to the Union's governance in the Treaty of Nice resulted in damaging defeats for supporters of more integration. These setbacks were to continue, as when Sweden voted in September 2003 to stay out of the euro. In national politics, far right politicians, such as Jörg Haider in Austria and Jean Marie le Pen in France, made gains on platforms that included hostility to the Union. The regular meetings of member states' leaders in the European Council sometimes became an excuse for riots, stirred up by a small hard core of anarchist-inspired anti-globalisation protesters and hooligans. Eurobarometer surveys in spring 2000 and 2001 showed overall support for the EU in its 15 member states dip below 50%. The fractured relationship between Union and citizen was not helped by a sense of institutional malaise in Brussels. The mass resignation of the European Commission, headed by Jacques Santer in March 1999, amid allegations of mismanagement, nepotism and fraud tainted the image of what headline writers called 'Brussels'.

Beneath the surface, the ideas of what constituted the Union were in flux and had been for some years. In the 1950s, the original six members embarked on a federal project to create 'an ever closer union among the peoples of Europe'. This was swiftly balanced in the following decade by the vision, made flesh in France's president, Charles de Gaulle, of a Europe anchored in the nation-state. Very much the goal of the continental west-European post-war elite, federalism reached its provisional climax with agreement in the 1992 Maastricht Treaty to pool sovereignty over monetary policy and create the single currency. However, in that same treaty, the member states set political limits to integration elsewhere by placing the new areas of foreign and security policy and justice and home affairs in separate 'pillars', where they would decide actions by cooperating among themselves on an intergovernmental basis.[1]

This ambivalence towards integration continued through the 1990s as a younger generation of politicians in EU member states took over and began to question the 'top down' prescriptive approach towards the Union's development adopted by the European Community's founding fathers and the 1980s generation dominated by Germany's chancellor, Helmut Kohl, and French president, Francois Mitterrand. Not that they rejected the Community out of hand. When it was found that the intergovernmental methods failed to deal with a sharp increase in the numbers of asylum seekers and illegal immigrants, the leaders decided at their June 1997 Amsterdam summit to gradually bring these parts of the justice and home affairs pillar under the community umbrella. But the 'Community method' of conducting affairs through specially designed European institutions was only one of several ways forward. When the leaders met in Lisbon in March 2000 to relaunch the single market, they relied on an elaborate system of benchmarking national policies, dubbed the open method of coordination, to push the project ahead.

Little wonder, therefore, that the Union developed complex structures as it grew. It was far from being a classic federation. There was no central elected government or any great central bureaucracy, as in the US, to manage foreign policy, defence, justice or macroeconomic policy. These remained the responsibility of the member states. Instead, the Union was entrusted with exclusive competences in remarkably few areas and which reflected its origins as a 'common market' or 'European Economic Community'. These were competition rules in the internal market, a common commercial policy, the customs union, the conservation of fish stocks under the common fisheries policy and, from 1999, monetary policy for those member states which adopted the euro. In most areas of economic and political activity, the Union and the member states worked together, following many and varied rules that had been devised and modified over decades, in the course of complex and frequently confused negotiations.

The differing levels of engagement of Union and member states were reflected in its institutional structure. There was an 'institutional triangle',

---

[1] These were the second and third pillars respectively, which became titles V and VI of the treaties of Maastricht, Amsterdam and Nice. The first pillar embraced the existing European Communities and detailed Community policies and institutions.

comprising a Commission of appointed officials, a Council of Ministers[2] with a secretariat, which represented the member states, and a directly elected European Parliament. These institutions secured the Union's objectives in the areas of pooled sovereignty that constituted the European Community. The Commission, representing the European interest, had the right to propose legislation. The Council, consisting of ministers from member states meeting in various different formations, and the Parliament, representing Europe's citizens, would approve, amend or reject the legislation in the process known as the 'Community method'. Also part of the Community structure were the Court of Justice, which enforced Community law, and the independent, Frankfurt-based European Central Bank running monetary policy.

Giving strategic direction to the three participants in the Union's 'institutional triangle' was the European Council of heads of state and government, which met at least twice a year and frequently more often. It was chaired by a different national leader every six months under a system of rotating presidencies that applied also to the Council of Ministers. The European Council grew greatly in importance as member states resorted increasingly to coordinated national policies to obtain their objectives in the Union rather than pool sovereignty using the Community method.

The Union's relatively simple architecture was greatly complicated by the decision in the Maastricht Treaty on Union to develop a common foreign and security policy and cross-border initiatives in justice and home affairs without pooling sovereignty in the traditional Community manner. The resulting two intergovernmental pillars had their own decision making practices alongside the traditional Community structure. Ironically, given its name, one of the main objectives of the Maastricht Treaty on Union was to keep the pillars apart.

The European Union was therefore a hybrid with two sources of political legitimacy: the Community and the member states with the citizen

---

[2] The Council of Ministers, as an institution, is easily confused with the European Council, mentioned in the next paragraph, and the Council of Europe, which is an intergovernmental body based in Strasbourg and which has nothing to do with the European Union. The references in this book to the Council of Ministers, the Council and the Council secretariat identify the same institution, or elements of it, representing the Union's member states in the 'institutional triangle'. The European Council is defined as a separate institution in the constitutional treaty and is given its full title when it appears in this book. However, there are some quotations where the speaker says 'Council' when meaning 'European Council'. In these cases, either the word 'European' is inserted in parentheses or an effort has been made to put the quotation in a context that makes it clear the speaker is referring to the European Council.

represented in both. The inbuilt tension between those parts in which sovereignty was pooled and decisions reached through the Community method, and those parts in which the member states retained their sovereignty and cooperated on an intergovernmental basis, spawned a quasi-religious divide among their respective adherents. Having grown a structure unlike any other in history, the European Union spent much of the 1990s trying to make it work more effectively.

Complex negotiations aimed at changing or augmenting the Union's founding treaties became frequent. The Maastricht Treaty was followed after five years by the Treaty of Amsterdam, which made modest progress, notably in extending citizens' rights and in prescribing the transfer of asylum and immigration policies to the Community pillar. Just three months after the fall of the Santer Commission, the European Council in Cologne decided to give the Union a more human face by bringing together the fundamental rights applicable at Union level into a Charter. This task was entrusted to a novel body comprising government representatives, European and national parliamentarians plus one commissioner, which called itself a Convention.

But important issues relating to the Union's institutions went unresolved and there was an unmistakeable sense that as far as reforming the Union was concerned, the law of diminishing returns had set in, just as it was facing the unprecedented challenge of enlarging to the east.

As the 21st century dawned, it became clear that the remedy in the planning stage – another intergovernmental conference of the member states that would be held in 2000 and conclude in Nice in December that year – lacked the breadth and ambition necessary to tackle the accumulation of challenges facing the Union. The IGC that culminated in the Nice Treaty of December 2000 had the narrow brief of tackling technocratic 'leftovers' from the previous attempt at revising the Union's founding treaties at the Amsterdam summit of June 1997.

The Nice negotiation had the laudable aim of avoiding a paralysis of decision making caused by institutional gridlock in an EU that was now set to grow to 25 or more member states. But the issues seemed paltry compared with the historic tasks the Union had taken on. The Nice agenda was all to do with the distribution and use of power among the member states as a preliminary for the enlargement to encompass the former communist states of eastern and central Europe and the Mediterranean island states of Malta and Cyprus. The main points of contention were the future size and composition of the European Commission, the weighting of member states' votes in the Council of Ministers and the possible extension of votes by qualified majority in place of unanimity. During the course of 2000, the member states added 'enhanced cooperation' to the list. Enhanced cooperation, by which a small number of member states could forge ahead with integration in specific areas of policy, was emblematic for the Nice agenda. It was a policy that was approved at Amsterdam, with a purpose that its title left unclear, that had never been used, and which stirred strong passions inside the Brussels beltway. It had zero resonance with voters in the Union.

Those politicians who listened to the people found Europe's voters were not necessarily hostile to the Union playing a bigger role in the world. When asked, voters in most member states wanted what the 2002 Spanish EU presidency defined as 'more Europe' to tackle problems that individual member states were no longer powerful enough to deal with or which had cross-border ramifications. Their concerns included aspects of foreign and defence policy and such intra-Union problems as cross-border organised crime or the movements of asylum seekers and illegal migrants, environmental disasters, food safety and, because epidemics had never respected national boundaries, the spread of diseases of humans and animals. It appeared early in 2000 that the ordinary voter had a better idea about the future demands on the Union than many politicians.

2.2   A NEW DEBATE ON EUROPE'S FUTURE

In this environment, Joschka Fischer, Germany's foreign minister, launched the debate on Europe's future through a speech at Humboldt University in Berlin on 12 May 2000.[3] Speaking, so he claimed, as a private individual, Fischer set out ideas to allow the Union to continue integrating while doubling its membership through enlargement. His prescription was to transform the EU from a union of states to a 'lean federation', which would be 'capable of action, fully sovereign yet based on self-confident nation-states' and which citizens would understand. It would be a federation in which people would retain their national identities. The nation-states would have 'a much larger role' than the states or *Länder* in the federal republic of Germany.

To achieve these goals, Fischer proposed a transition 'to full parliamentarisation as a European federation'. This would mean 'nothing less than a European Parliament and a European government which really do exercise legislative and executive power within the federation'. To avoid a

---

[3] 'From Confederacy to Federation: thoughts on the finality of European integration.'
Available on the German foreign ministry website www.auswaertiges-amt.de

strong centralised federation, he spoke of integrating Europe on the basis of a division of sovereignty between Europe and the nation-state, drawing on the concept of subsidiarity[4] by which political decisions should be taken as closely to the citizen as possible. He thus proposed a second chamber of the European Parliament, which would contain elected members of national parliaments. He left open whether Europe's government should be developed from the intergovernmental European Council or the Commission, the agent of the community approach, to which he would add a directly elected president 'with far-reaching executive powers'.

Fischer broached the idea of a Constitution quite late in his speech. Europe, he said, would have to be 'established anew with a Constitution', which would be centred around 'basic, human and civil rights, and equal division of powers between the European institutions and a precise delineation between European and nation-state level'. The division of sovereignty between the Union and nation-states would be the 'main axis' for the European Constitution. Fischer also pondered what might happen if not all countries wanted more integration. He suggested that a majority, or failing that, a small group of member states constituting an *'avant-garde'* might want to push ahead with political integration, rather than face standstill by clinging to a federation of states. Whatever happened, no European project would succeed 'without the closest Franco-German cooperation'.

Fischer's message came almost 50 years to the day after Schuman launched what would become the European Union. His speech was skilfully timed and, although hedged with ambiguities, lifted the debate on Europe's future to a new level. It provoked a wide range of responses, with two of the most significant coming from the French president, Jacques Chirac, and Britain's prime minister, Tony Blair.

Chirac's vision, outlined before the Bundestag in Berlin on 27 June 2000, was less federal than Fischer's but the two were close on a large number of points. Chirac put stronger emphasis on the nation-state and Europe's international role than Fischer did, telling the German parliament that neither France nor Germany was 'envisaging the creation of a super European state which would supplant our national states and mark the end of their existence as players in international life'. According to Chirac, Europe's nations were 'the source of our identities and roots' and 'for the peoples who come after us, the nations will remain the first reference points'.

---

[4] Subsidiarity was first written into the 1992 Treaty of Maastricht but was rarely obeyed.

But he also wanted to see Europe 'as a world power' with strong institutions and an effective and legitimate decision making mechanism, 'in which majority voting is the rule and which reflects the relative weight of the member states'. To ensure that Europe retained a capacity for greater integration after enlargement, he suggested that interested countries should forge a 'pioneer group' with Germany and France and, using the enhanced cooperation procedures agreed at Amsterdam, start in 2001 on improving economic policy coordination, strengthening defence and security policy, and join together in fighting organised crime.

Chirac looked beyond the negotiation that would end in Nice in December to the 'first European Constitution'. He proposed to prepare this new push for reform by way of an open discussion involving the member states' governments, the candidate countries and Europe's citizens through members of the European and national parliaments. Bringing the idea of a Convention into the debate on Europe's future, Chirac added: 'There are several possible ways of organising, ranging from a committee of wise men to an approach modelled on the Convention which is drafting our Charter of Fundamental Rights.'

Tony Blair chose to outline his vision of Europe in Warsaw, capital of Poland, the biggest of the states negotiating to join the Union, and a memorial to a people's proud struggle to keep alive a national identity through more than two centuries of foreign oppression. Speaking just after the Danish 'no' vote on the euro, he was anxious to underline that Britain's future was 'as a leading partner in Europe'.[5]

On the federal nation-state spectrum, Blair was further towards the nation-state vision of Europe than Chirac, but he was also adamant that Europe should be more than just a free trade area.

> Europe is a Europe of free, independent sovereign nations who choose to pool that sovereignty in pursuit of their own interests and the common good, achieving more together than we can achieve alone. Europe will remain a unique combination of the intergovernmental and the supranational. Such a Europe can, in its economic and political strength, be a superpower – a superpower but not a superstate.

Blair looked at the European reform agenda by asking the question: what do the people of Europe want and expect it to do? He outlined goals including completing the single market, reform of the common agricultural policy,

---

[5] On 6 October 2000. Speech to the Polish Stock Exchange available on www.number-10.gov.uk

fighting organised crime, obtaining a more coherent foreign policy, restoring full employment and protecting the environment, and stopping Europe from interfering in what it should not do.

Blair's chosen instrument for promoting these aims was the European Council. It should set an annual agenda for the Union. The Commission, through its president, would play a role in this process and remain the independent guardian of the treaties. But 'we', meaning the European Council, 'would have clear political direction, a programme and a timetable by which all the institutions would be guided'.

Blair's government was open to reforming the way individual Councils worked. He also cast doubt on whether the Union's six-month rotating presidency could survive enlargement. He was sceptical whether a single Constitution could emerge out of the Union's existing treaties and, invoking Britain's lack of a written Constitution, invited other countries to realise that 'a constitutional debate must not necessarily end with a single, legally binding document called a Constitution for an entity as dynamic as the EU'. But he did urge 'a statement of principles' to determine what would best be done at the European and national levels.

Like Fischer, Blair called for a second chamber of the European Parliament, involving national parliamentarians. But it would have a controlling function. Its most important job would be to review the Union's work in the light of the statement of principles: in effect subjecting subsidiarity to political review. This, Blair said, would be preferable to judicial review of formal constitutional provisions through a European constitutional court.

These visions of European leaders broadly mirrored political conditions in their respective home countries. But while Europe's leaders were mulling over the Union's future, the negotiations leading up to the planned end of the IGC in Nice were going from bad to worse. In October 2000, about two months before their close, they were punctuated by a spectacularly bad-tempered row between big and small member states at a special European Council meeting in Biarritz. The final conference of EU leaders in Nice was a gladiatorial cliff-hanger of unusual bitterness that lasted four days and ended just before dawn on a December Monday morning.

Nice finally achieved messy compromises on the issues facing the intergovernmental conference: the Commission's size, reweighting votes in the Council of Ministers, the allocation of seats in the European Parliament, the rules of enhanced cooperation, and a limited extension of qualified majority voting in the Council to some 30 treaty articles where previously unanimity applied. Although Jacques Chirac, the summit host, closed the proceedings with a prediction that Nice would go down 'in the history books as one of the great summits because of the extent and complexity of the issues settled', the leaders recognised more would be needed. Blair spoke for nearly all the participants when he said, 'As far as Europe is concerned, we cannot do business like this in the future.'

CHAPTER 3
Setting up the Convention

3.1   THE NICE AND LAEKEN AGENDAS FOR EUROPE

It was fortunate that before tempers really became frayed at Nice, the assembled EU leaders agreed a 'Declaration of the future of the Union'. It called 'for a deeper and wider debate' about the EU's future development that would lead to a new intergovernmental conference (IGC) in 2004. They also proclaimed as a legally non-binding document, the EU Charter of Fundamental Rights that had been drawn up during 2000 by the EU's first ever convention.

The debate was to address four important issues absent from the Nice agenda. These were:

- 'How to establish and monitor a more precise delimitation of competences between the EU and the member states, reflecting the principle of subsidiarity.'
- 'The status of the Charter of Fundamental Rights of the EU proclaimed in Nice, in accordance with the conclusions of the European Council in Cologne.'[1]
- 'A simplification of the treaties with a view to making them clearer and better understood without changing their meaning.'
- 'The role of national parliaments in the European architecture.'

The agenda defined in Nice was a reaction to the debate on Europe's constitutional future triggered by Fischer's Humboldt University speech of May 2000 and picked up some of the points made later by Chirac and Blair. The declaration also took note of widespread disenchantment with the workings of the EU by identifying 'the need to improve and to monitor the democratic legitimacy and transparency of the Union and its institutions, to bring them closer to the citizens of the member states.' Although the four points made no reference to a Constitution, they would, if eventually transposed into the EU treaties, give the Union a governing architecture with

---

[1] The Cologne summit of June 1999 decided to consolidate the fundamental rights applicable at Union level into a charter and said that, once proclaimed, it would 'have to be considered whether and, if so, how the charter should be integrated into the treaties'.

many aspects of a Constitution such as a bill of rights and a clear definition of who does what.

The competences question, or 'who does what' in Europe, was politically important in the light of a widespread feeling that faceless bureaucrats in Brussels were acquiring ever greater powers and usually by stealth. The wish to involve national parliaments more in EU affairs was the obverse side of this coin and linked to awareness that the European Parliament, by itself, could not plug the EU's widely perceived democratic deficit. Simplification of the treaties was pure common sense, as anyone opening the existing 1,045 pages of jumbled and often incomprehensible articles, protocols and declarations[2] could testify.

That the Charter of Fundamental Rights should be placed back on the EU reform agenda, while being proclaimed in Nice, recognised that its newly established status was unsustainable. In Nice, the Charter was proclaimed as a political declaration only because of British objections. The UK insisted it should not have legal status for fear that the social rights included among its 54 articles might become enforceable through United Kingdom courts. Germany, backed strongly by France, Italy and the Benelux countries, wanted the Charter incorporated into EU law as a bill of rights, which would distinguish the Union as a community of values.

2001 was a year of definition in which two 'c' words, 'constitution' and 'convention', gradually gained acceptance. Guy Verhofstadt, the restless, young Belgian prime minister and holder of the Union presidency in the second half of the year, played a key role in pushing forward the debate. A strong advocate of the Community method of decision making, Verhofstadt was the first Union leader to highlight the need for simpler and more transparent policy instruments.[3]

One year on from Nice, the European Council in Laeken agreed a declaration that combined soul-searching over where Europe had gone astray with a welter of possible remedies. Europe, the Laeken declaration said, was 'at a cross roads'. It needed to become 'more democratic, more transparent and more efficient'. In doing so, it must resolve three basic challenges:

- 'How to bring citizens, and primarily the young, closer to the European design and the European institutions.'

---

[2] European Union: Selected instruments taken from the treaties. Book I, Volume I.
[3] Speech to the 7th European Forum Wachau in Göttweig, Austria, 24 June 2001, filed among the speeches of the prime minister on www.premier.fgov.be

- 'How to organise politics and the European political area in an enlarged Union.'
- 'How to develop the Union into a stabilising factor and a model in the new, multipolar world.'

To flesh out these challenges, the Laeken declaration added more than 50 detailed queries to the issues raised in the earlier declaration of Nice. The text was at times repetitive and confused, and bore all the hallmarks of a difficult political compromise between proponents and opponents of greater integration.

However, it spelled out issues that were to be important for the Convention. It called for a better division and definition of competences in the EU, in particular between those exclusive to the Union, those of member states and those shared by the Union and member states. It asked whether there needed to be any reorganisation of competences, suggesting this could 'lead both to restoring tasks to the member states and to assigning new missions to the Union'. It delved into the nitty-gritty, posing questions such as *whether* the EU should have a more integrated approach to police and criminal law cooperation, and *how* it should develop a more coherent foreign and defence policy or improve economic policy coordination. It raised the question of simplifying the instruments used by the Union to implement its policies and asked, for example, whether there should be fewer ways of passing laws and whether to have a distinction between legislative and executive measures.

The declaration wondered how to increase the democratic legitimacy and transparency of the EU's three big institutions: the Commission, the Council and the European Parliament. Should the Commission president be elected, and, if so, by whom? Should Parliament be involved more in EU law making by extending cases where it has equal rights with the Council through the process known as 'codecision'? Should citizens have better access to documents and should the Council of Ministers' meetings be in public, at least when it was making laws?

It looked at the possible future role of national parliaments, asking whether they should be represented in a new institution in Brussels or whether they should focus on policing subsidiarity.

When dealing with decision making and the EU institutions, Laeken went back over some of the ground covered at Nice and asked whether more decisions should be taken by qualified majority voting. It put a question mark against the Union's six-month rotating presidency and the role of the various Council formations. However, it made no reference to the Nice decisions on the future composition of the Commission and European

Parliament, or the complex sharing out of votes among present and future member states to determine a qualified majority in the Council, implying that, one year on from Nice, the leaders at Laeken wanted these questions left alone.

Noting that the Union's objectives, powers and policy instruments were spread over four treaties (covering the Coal and Steel Community, the European Communities, Euratom and the European Union), the declaration asserted that simplification was essential to achieve greater transparency. It therefore wondered whether 'without changing their content' the distinction between the Union and the Communities should be reviewed.

It posed the question, 'What of the division into three pillars?' Picking up on preliminary work by the European University Institute in Florence, the declaration asked whether the treaties should be reorganised into a 'basic treaty', akin to a Constitution, that would be separated from other, more technical, treaty provisions. This prompted the question whether the technical part should be subject to different, less rigorous, amendment and ratification procedures than those in force, which required the ratification of each member state.

The Laeken declaration asked whether the Charter should be incorporated into the basic treaty and whether the Union should accede to the European Convention on Human Rights.

The issue of a Constitution was raised with a notable degree of caution. The headline 'Towards a Constitution for European citizens' gave the clearest indication of where the text wanted to go. However, the declaration implied that a Constitution was something for the distant future.

'The question ultimately arises as to whether this simplification and reorganisation might not lead in the long run to the adoption of a constitutional text in the Union,' it said. Then pondering its contents, it added in the haziest of terms, 'What might the basic features of such a Constitution be? The values which the Union cherishes, the fundamental rights and obligations of its citizens, the relationship between member states in the Union?'

These questions, and any answers, were to be mulled over by a Convention. This would be made up of 'the main parties involved in the debate on the future of the Union'. It would start on 1 March 2002 and draw up a final document in preparation for the 2004 IGC agreed at Nice.

The Convention would meet in Brussels. In marked contrast with the practice of IGCs, all its discussions and official documents would be in the public domain. The Convention could either produce different options, or recommendations if it could achieve a consensus. However, the leaders at Laeken made clear that its final document would provide no more than a starting point for discussions in the IGC set for 2004, which would 'take the ultimate decisions'.

Nonetheless, Verhofstadt saw a vital role for the Convention. There must be 'no taboos'. It must address questions not normally asked by the member states in the Council of Ministers or their summits. It must consider fundamental reform of the treaties.

Britain, a late convert to ideas of constitutions and conventions, said it would not stand in the way of the project, although it had reservations. 'If it is a question of clarifying a tangled web of treaties which are unintelligible, then we are up for that. But if it is a question of renegotiating some sort of framework for a superstate, then No,' was how Peter Hain, Britain's minister for Europe, interpreted the message of Laeken.

3.2 THE CHOICE OF A CONVENTION

The decision to entrust preparation of the IGC to a Convention had emerged over the previous 12 months.

Following Jacques Chirac's passing reference to the Charter convention in his speech to the German Bundestag in June 2000, Paavo Lipponen, Finland's prime minister, floated the idea[4] that a convention should launch a 'constitutionalisation process' for the Union, which would include the candidate states. Thereafter, similar proposals began to appear in speeches on Europe's future.

The Union's first ever convention, which in 2000 drew up the Charter of Fundamental Rights, was deemed a success – particularly when compared with the shambles of the Nice IGC and summit. During 2001, there was growing pressure from the European Commission and the Parliament for a Convention to be set up. The UK, a long-term sceptic about its merits, accepted the idea during the summer. Goaded on by Louis Michel, Belgium's foreign minister, the General Affairs Council agreed in October

---

[4] In a speech to the College of Europe in Bruges 10 November 2000, filed under EU Speeches on the Finnish government website, www.government.fi

2001 that a Convention should meet in 2002 to take forward the tasks set down at Nice and to be refined in Laeken. Its structure would be similar to the Charter convention, with the important innovation that candidate countries would participate.

Some vital decisions about the Convention were left for Laeken, however. The most important was who should be its chair. There were two main candidates: Wim Kok, the widely supported and soon-to-retire prime minister of the Netherlands, and the former French president, Valéry Giscard d'Estaing. To the surprise of many and the unconcealed dismay of Verhofstadt, Giscard was chosen. The odds on the summit appointing the septuagenarian elder statesman had been narrowing in the days ahead of the Laeken meeting. But the clever tactics of President Chirac and the unwillingness of Kok to push himself forward clinched the deal.

Giscard's appointment was the first of many surprises that would characterise the history of the Convention. It had one very positive, unforeseen consequence. Acting on the spur of the moment, Verhofstadt decided Giscard should have two deputy chairmen and obtained the summit's agreement to appoint two members of the 'Laeken Group', a small, top-level team of advisers to the Belgian prime minister in the months ahead of the meeting. One of the two, Giuliano Amato, Italy's left of centre prime minister at the time of Nice, had also been a contender for the chairmanship of the Convention until Silvio Berlusconi, the centre-right incumbent in Rome, pulled back from supporting him. The other, Jean-Luc Dehaene, was Verhofstadt's predecessor as Belgian prime minister and, as a Christian Democrat, balanced Amato by coming from the centre-right.

The leaders at Laeken then agreed the Convention would be composed of 15 representatives of the heads of state or government of the member states (one per member state), 30 members of national parliaments (two per member state), 16 members of the European Parliament and two Commission representatives.

The 13 candidate countries (including Turkey, which was not yet negotiating membership) would be fully involved in the Convention's proceedings and represented, like the member states, with one government representative and two national parliament members each. The only restriction was that the candidates would be unable to prevent any consensus that might emerge among the member states.

The Convention would have a Praesidium composed of the chairman, the two vice-chairmen and nine members drawn from the Convention. Because of the two vice-chairmen, the Praesidium ended up bigger than originally planned. The nine included representatives of Spain, Denmark and Greece, which held the six-month rotating presidencies during the Convention's life. In addition, there were two representatives each of the national parliaments, the European Parliament and the Commission.

The inclusion of two Commission representatives reflected another late decision of benefit to the Convention. The Commission's representation was doubled to two, so that Antonio Vitorino, the commissioner for Justice and Home Affairs, joined Michel Barnier, the commissioner with the institutional reform portfolio, in the Convention and the Praesidium.

The Praesidium would be assisted by a Convention secretariat, provided mainly by the Council Secretariat. The Convention members would have alternates, to be designated in the same way as the full members. The Laeken text stipulated that members could only be replaced by alternates if they were not present.

There would be 13 observers: six representing the regions, six the Economic and Social Committee and the 'social partners', and the European Ombudsman. To continue the wider debate on Europe's future, there would be a Forum, representing civil society, defined as 'the social partners, the business world, non-governmental organisations, academia, etc.', which would receive regular information on the Convention and 'serve as an input to the debate'.

EU leaders would be informed of developments through oral progress reports from the Convention chairman at subsequent European Council meetings.

3.3   THE CONVENTION TRIUMVIRATE

Giscard was a controversial choice as chairman. The press immediately fastened on his age and his patrician ways and wondered if he was quite the man 'to bring citizens, and primarily the young' closer to Europe. Those with long memories recalled his injudicious acceptance of a gift of diamonds from the self-crowned 'Emperor' Jean-Bedel Bokassa of Central Africa that helped bring about his defeat by Francois Mitterrand in the French presidential election of 1981. Others suggested Giscard's nomination was a ruse by Chirac to remove a long-standing rival and potential critic from France's 2002 presidential election campaign.

But Giscard's credentials for presiding over the Convention were impressive. His spectacular and rapid rise to the pinnacle of French politics bore witness to a powerful intellect. His personal history gave him an emotional commitment to Europe. Although often branded as haughty, he could be extremely charming, particularly when talking to an attractive woman. While his tall slender frame, domed head and elegant suits signalled aristocratic aloofness, a pair of twinkly eyes indicated a lively sense of humour below the surface. Dismissive of those he considered his intellectual inferiors, Giscard could be a remarkably good listener, provided the speaker was making sense. But as some members of the Convention would learn to their cost, Giscard was quick to spot and squash logical inconsistencies and verbal infelicities. A stickler for correct procedure, he displayed remarkable powers of concentration and stamina during the Convention's lengthy plenary sessions and expected the same from the 'conventionnels', as he called Convention members. Accustomed to power, Giscard soon exercised authority over the 200 very different egos of the conventionnels and their alternates.

In the weeks following his appointment, Giscard made frequent reference to America's 1787 Philadelphia Convention. His comments showed he was doing his homework and looking back at historical precedents. They gave him an opportunity to remind critics that Benjamin Franklin, one of the fathers of the US Constitution, was 81 when the Philadelphia Convention met.

Giscard was born on 2 February 1926 in Koblenz, Germany, the son of a French official in the French-occupied Rhineland. He fought for France in the Second World War. Elected to the French National Assembly in 1956, he was General de Gaulle's finance minister between 1962 and 1966, when he balanced the budget for the first time in 30 years. Blamed for causing a recession, he was sacked and went on to found his own right of centre party, the Républicains Indépendants. He returned to the finance ministry between 1969 and 1974 during the presidency of Georges Pompidou and then became the fifth republic's third president after winning the first of his contests with Mitterrand. When appointed to head the Convention, he was the last active member of that generation of European politicians whose support for European integration was rooted in their own experience of war. This alone guaranteed him a certain prestige among the conventionnels.

His practical contributions to the European Union were also considerable. As French president between 1974 and 1981, Giscard, in partnership with West Germany's chancellor, Helmut Schmidt, helped to both sustain the European Communities and promote European economic integration through the difficult years that followed the inflationary oil shock and recession of 1973. He was founder of the European Council, although it was unclear whether creating this exclusive 'club' of Union leaders gave him any extra leverage with the present members. He had also promoted the first direct elections to the European Parliament in 1979 and was an MEP between 1989 and 1993. With Schmidt, he founded the European Monetary System of semi-fixed exchange rates in the late 1970s, so starting the process of economic and monetary integration that culminated in the euro.

However, there were areas where his vision was more restricted. He was not particularly interested in the Court of Justice or the European Central Bank. He was surprised, on meeting top businessmen a few months after the Convention started, to find that they regarded the Commission as a positive force that protected their interests in an integrated market rather than as an encroaching Brussels-based bureaucracy.

In the 1950s, Giscard was influenced strongly by Jean Monnet, one of the founding fathers of today's EU. But by the time he was appointed to the Convention, his enthusiasm for a federal approach to Europe's future had waned. Early in 2002, he told the French daily *Le Monde* that neither a federal Europe nor the intergovernmental approach, based on negotiation and cooperation among the member states, would work in the soon to be enlarged Europe of more than 25 member states. The Union would instead develop as a hybrid, as a 'union of states with federal competences'.

Giscard had no blueprint for reforming the Union. But he had a compass and he knew how to change course as circumstances dictated. As the founding father of the European Council, he was by experience and instinct more a Council than a Commission man. But he had concluded that the European Council in its existing format would not work with 28 member states, partly because there would be so many small member states in the enlarged Europe.

He took a dim view of the Commission and the ambition of its president, Romano Prodi, for it to be the 'government' of Europe. He argued that the European Council had a much clearer vocation to be the EU's executive power. 'We would not be able to have a government with the present composition of the Commission,' he sniffed.

In February 2002, before the Convention started, Giscard outlined two institutional priorities. He told Lamberto Dini, the former Italian prime minister and representative of the Italian senate on the Convention, that he wanted a stable presidency for the European Council and a smaller Commission. Around the same time, Giscard suggested in a conversation with MEPs that the Commission had served its purpose in establishing the single market. He made the same point to commissioners Vitorino and Barnier at their first lunch together. When he met the Parliament's constitutional affairs committee at the end of March 2002, he was rather more diplomatic: he said the EU needed both the Commission and the Council with 'perhaps a more original cooperation between them'.

Twice prime minister of Italy and, as such, a veteran of Nice, Giuliano Amato was also a distinguished professor of constitutional law. Whereas Giscard oozed authority, Amato earned it through his knowledge, ingenuity and intellect. Amato had a subtle mind: indeed, it was so subtle that Tony Blair once told the British Labour party Convention members that trying to work out what Amato stood for was like trying to follow a single strand from beginning to end in a dish of spaghetti. Aged 63 when the Convention began, Amato approached it as a pragmatic integrationist. In a response to Fischer's Humboldt speech, he had described the Union 'as still a bold joint venture between partner states: a Union which moves ahead by successive adjustments, combining integration and cooperation, common structures and classic intergovernmental compromises, standards to be achieved, authorities acting as umpires and mutual monitoring'. It summed up his undogmatic view of the Union.

Amato was keen to see national parliaments play a bigger role in EU affairs. But he was cautious as to whether the Convention would produce a Constitution.

As a chairman of two working groups in the Convention, Amato was to find ways of solving two of the Union's most confusing constitutional conundrums. He made possible the creation of a single legal personality for the Union, getting rid of the three-pillar structure in the process, and greatly simplified the Union's ultra-complex systems of legislating. He also became head of the Socialist 'political family' in the Convention. He was more successful in the Praesidium and Convention plenary than in his party role where some brute political power would have come in useful. During the Convention, the conventionnels belonging to the Party of European Socialists (PES) were less disciplined than those of the Liberal and centre-right European People's Party caucuses.

Amato was feline. Giscard's other deputy, the 61-year-old Jean-Luc Dehaene, was a bulldozer of a man. Stocky, with a deal-maker's rough and ready charm, Dehaene was Belgian prime minister and the country's pre-eminent political fixer from 1992 until 1999, when he lost office in a general election to Verhofstadt's 'rainbow' coalition of liberals, socialists and greens after a spate of judicial, administrative and political scandals.

Dehaene was a keen federalist, who nonetheless always knew when to temper passion with pragmatism. He was in line for the presidency of the European Commission in 1994 until his candidacy was blocked by John

Major, the UK prime minister at the time, who feared the Belgian was too federally inclined and too close to the German chancellor, Helmut Kohl. One of Giscard's early decisions was to ask Dehaene to organise the 'forum' linking the Convention to civil society. As chairman of the working group on 'external action',[5] he was to make an important contribution to the draft Constitution. His finest hour came in the Convention's closing weeks, when, thanks to his negotiation prowess, he ended a split in the Praesidium and restored it as an effective decision making body. As the arch-federalist who knew when to accept a less than perfect deal, Dehaene pointed the way for others to embrace the final compromise.

Relations between Giscard, Amato and Dehaene were not easy at first. The three were very different personalities, and Verhofstadt had contrived to foster suspicion among them. With the wry comment, 'He's well supported', Verhofstadt at Laeken had let slip that he saw the appointment of the two vice-chairmen as a way of circumscribing Giscard's power. It took time for reservations to die away, but when they did, the three proved to be a very effective team.

3.4   THE PRAESIDIUM FORMS

Michel Barnier and Antonio Vitorino, the Commission's conventionnels, were the two other Praesidium members confirmed at Laeken. Vitorino had a fine legal brain and was to emerge as one of the Convention's key problem solvers. Fluent in several languages, his interventions in the plenary usually drew applause even though sometimes listeners would be hard pressed afterwards to explain the point he was making. He had the important skill, in a body that was to operate by consensus, of knowing when to defer the resolution of a difficult issue to the point where it would gain general acceptance. Born in Lisbon in January 1957, Vitorino's politically formative period coincided with the dying years of the Salazar dictatorship and Portugal's 1974 Carnation Revolution. A socialist, he rose high in Portuguese politics to be deputy prime minister and defence minister before moving to Brussels in 1999 to take over the newly upgraded justice and home affairs portfolio in the Commission. Having been the Commission's representative in the earlier Charter convention, Vitorino was to take the chair of the Convention working group handling the Charter of Fundamental Rights.

---

[5] Convention jargon for all aspects of foreign affairs except defence.

Michel Barnier, who doubled as commissioner for institutional affairs and regional policy, was another veteran of Nice and had been French minister for Europe during the Amsterdam Treaty IGC. Born in January 1951, Barnier had built his political power base in the Savoie region of France in the Alps above Lake Geneva. With the looks of a 1950s matinee idol – and often underestimated because of this – Barnier was never really part of the French European establishment. Unlike Giscard and many of the top French officials in European institutions, Barnier was not an *énarch,* a former student of the prestigious École Nationale d'Administration. His domestic political allegiance was to Chirac's brand of centre-right French politics, which added to coolness in his relations with Giscard. Nonetheless, Barnier turned down a senior French government post to stay in the Convention after Chirac's presidential election victory in 2002, and became an unexpectedly successful chair of the Convention working group on defence.

Both Commission representatives were to contribute significantly as individuals to the eventual success of the Convention. However, their roles could have been more impressive had they been given coherent support by the rest of the college of commissioners.

The next Praesidium members to be confirmed were those of the European Parliament. Because of a deal between the European Parliament's two big political families, the Spaniard Inigo Méndez de Vigo of the European People's Party (EPP), Parliament's biggest political group, and the German Social Democrat, Klaus Hänsch, were widely tipped as the MEPs' representatives on the Praesidium even before the Laeken summit met.

Born in 1956, Méndez de Vigo was another politician whose formative years coincided with the end of dictatorship. But unlike Vitorino, Méndez de Vigo built his career on the centre-right as a member of the Partido Popular of Spain's prime minister José Maria Aznar. A lawyer by training, Méndez de Vigo was charming, affable and ambitious. He chaired the Parliament's delegation to the Charter convention and won his spurs early in Giscard's Convention as chairman of a working group that devised rules for the more effective application and control of subsidiarity. A skilful behind-the-scenes operator, Méndez de Vigo organised a discreet but influential dining club of 'movers and shakers' that would meet in the Brussels Hilton during each plenary session.

Hänsch, 63 when the Convention started, was a former president of the Parliament and the only German national in the Praesidium. It was his misfortune to chair one of the Convention's more difficult and, therefore, less successful working groups – that on economic governance. He nonetheless had his moments in the plenary. Ever inclined to see a glass half full rather than half empty, Hänsch was particularly useful for Giscard in rallying his fellow conventionnels behind the president's perception of consensus. His ability to sum up positively, powerfully and cogently some of the more crucial twists and turns as the Convention developed would elicit a muttered 'bravo' from Giscard high on the dais in the plenary hall. Both Hänsch and Méndez de Vigo were to come in for criticism from their fellow MEPs in the Convention as being too willing to succumb to Giscard's blandishments.

The three governments with places in the Praesidium opted for Brussels insiders. The result was a steering body including four MEPs, two commissioners and a former commissioner with an inherently integrationist bias.

Spain's prime minister, José Maria Aznar, chose MEP Ana Palacio, chair of the European Parliament's human rights and justice and home affairs committee, to be his representative. Palacio, who was 53 when appointed, had been a centre-right MEP since 1994 and was widely admired, not least because of the brave way in which she had seen off an attack of cancer earlier in the parliamentary session. She quickly became one of the Convention's most active and charismatic members. 'I'm really what the Convention is about,' she once said, 'taking different allegiances and making one project'. She proved so successful that in July 2002, Aznar appointed her foreign minister: a promotion that unfortunately meant she would have less time for the Convention and which prompted her to swap places with Alfonso Dastis, her alternate, in 2003. Although Spain was to suffer setbacks as the Convention's work developed, she remained an enthusiastic supporter of the Convention method of preparing EU reform. In particular, she praised its openness as a vital response to contemporary media democracy. The idea of changing EU treaties behind closed doors in an intergovernmental conference was 'a 19th century diplomatic approach unsuited to the 21st century'.

Denmark, which was to hold the rotating presidency in the second half of 2002, appointed Henning Christophersen, a former minister of finance and foreign affairs and a vice-president of the Commission between 1985 and 1995. The Praesidium's only liberal, Christophersen was a Brussels-based consultant when, at aged 62, he joined the Convention. He was given the difficult task of trying to make sense of competences and came in for much criticism when he reported his conclusions, which left all confused except Christophersen himself. He was more effective later when addressing budgetary questions.

Greece's representative on the Praesidium was another MEP, George Katiforis. A stalwart of the Party of European Socialists in the Parliament, Katiforis had twice been head of the economic office of Andreas Papandreou, the Greek prime minister, before being elected to the Parliament in 1994. Katiforis, who was 66 when the Convention first met, had spent many years as an academic economist: an experience reflected in his often discursive interventions. His last major publication, *An Introduction to Marxist Economics* was published in 1989, which was unlucky timing as that year the Berlin Wall came down. Katiforis's good humour and interest in social affairs came to the fore when he chaired a working group on 'Social Europe' shortly before ceding his Praesidium place to George Papandreou, the Greek foreign minister and son of his former boss, in 2003.

The last Praesidium members to be named were those representing the diffuse, and initially badly organised, group of conventionnels from national parliaments.

Gisela Stuart, a British Labour MP, was one of two national parliamentarians elected to the Praesidium on 22 February by parliamentarians from the member states. As one of the minority of women members, and German-born to boot, the 46-year-old Stuart appeared an ideal choice for an important role in the Convention to the spin-obsessed government in London. She symbolised the pro-European ideals of Tony Blair's New Labour party when she won the English constituency of Birmingham Edgbaston in the 1997 landslide election victory from Dame Jill Knight, a fierce Conservative populist. A former junior health minister in Blair's government, Stuart brought a legal training to the task of representing the British House of Commons in the Convention. The Convention, she once confided, was simply 'the most important job I've ever done', although at times it seemed more a chore than a pleasure. She was to chair a working group, which made some modest suggestions on how to enhance the role of national parliaments in the Union. But, perhaps because she was so wedded to the ways of Westminster, she never properly came to represent the very diverse group of conventionnels from national parliaments.

Stuart's task in the early months was made no easier by the distractions of her right-of-centre stable mate, John Bruton. As a member of the parliament in Dublin, the former Irish prime minister had to contend with a general election and looming referendum on the Nice Treaty at home. Once free of these preoccupations, Bruton, who was 54 at the start of the Convention, proved an effective member of the Praesidium. He chaired a successful working group, which dealt with the Union's 'area of freedom, security and justice' – the policy area dealing with asylum, immigration, police cooperation and the fight against internationally organised crime. His role was crucial in brokering the final Convention compromise over France's demands that a national veto should be retained over trade policies covering cultural and audio-visual services. Bruton would occasionally remind the Convention of its need to connect with the citizens and raise important – but hardly constitutional – issues such as the looming threat of global pandemics. This commendable effort, however, could not save him from falling into the same trap as Stuart and failing to represent sufficiently the concerns and enthusiasms of the group of the national parliamentarians to the triumvirate heading the Convention.

The 12-strong Praesidium defined in the Laeken declaration was expanded in April to 13, with the addition of Alojz Peterle, the representative of the Slovenian parliament. Peterle's appointment, first as a 'guest' and eventually as a full member, followed heavy lobbying by the candidate countries which complained that they had no one in the Convention's decision making body. Peterle, who was 53 when the Convention started, had risen from a poverty-stricken childhood to be Slovenia's first democratically elected prime minister between 1990 and 1992. As the representatives of the candidate countries decided not to form a distinct group in the Convention, Peterle's power base in the Praesidium was even more nebulous than those of its other two national parliamentarians. Politically, he was part of the EPP caucus, where he found a mentor in Méndez de Vigo, who proved a valuable ally when Giscard tried to bully Peterle in the final session of the Praesidium.

3.5   BUILDING THE SECRETARIAT

Throughout January, Giscard was searching for someone to head the Convention secretariat. He later said everyone he asked told him to take the best person available. He found his man in Sir John Kerr, who was named secretary general on 24 January, a month before his 60th birthday and just days after retiring as head of the British foreign office.

Kerr was no stranger to the European Union. A resourceful man and a wily and tough negotiator, he performed the now legendary feat of hiding under the table when officials were banished from the conference room during the closing hours of the Maastricht summit, so that he could continue advising his prime minister, John Major, on the British opt-out from the single currency.

He was also used to surviving difficult situations over longer periods. He was Britain's permanent representative to the EU between 1990 and 1995, when London's relationship with its European partners came under

increasing strain as Major's government succumbed to the power of the
Conservative party's eurosceptics. Yet, perhaps because he was Scottish
rather than English, Kerr always believed in the importance of a constructive
UK approach to the EU.

As the Convention's *eminence grise*, Kerr was seen and not heard. He would
sit next to Giscard on the dais, whispering in his ear, writing pencilled notes
to be passed to individual conventionnels, making, whenever possible, a
show of interest in the remarks coming from the plenary hall, and
occasionally slipping down into the plenary to cut a deal or negotiate away a
perceived misunderstanding. To the inevitable charges that he was Blair's
'mole', Kerr would quietly reply that he was appointed to serve the
Convention as a whole – a claim frequently validated in later months by
expressions of frustration about his activities from British officials. He
defined the secretariat's task as providing logistical support for Giscard, his
deputies and the Praesidium, and drawing up documents. In the
Convention's early months, these would synthesise the debate over Europe's
future: later they would be the drafts, first preliminary and later refined, of
the constitutional treaty.

Kerr was quickly ensconced, with a trademark ashtray at hand, in the
functional, sparsely furnished offices provided by Pierre de Boissieu, deputy
secretary general of the Council, in the EU Council of Ministers building in
Brussels. An important early appointment was Nikolaus Meyer-Landrut as
the Convention spokesman. He was a career diplomat from the German
foreign ministry and previously the spokesman in Brussels for the German
permanent representation to the EU.

Giscard and Kerr recruited a blend of talents from different backgrounds to
form the secretariat. There were lawyers, diplomats, administrators and
academics of UK, German, French, Spanish, Portuguese, Swedish, Belgian,
Dutch and Polish nationalities.

It was Kerr's job to turn the eager, young recruits into a team. This he did by
making them all sit round a table, two days a week, and discuss the
successive versions of the draft analytical papers that fuelled the
Convention's debates in its early months. The same technique was applied
later when the secretariat began to prepare the draft articles. The resulting
brainstorming allowed Kerr to learn the individual strengths of the
secretariat staffers, enabling him to allocate the right people to assist the
various working groups. The secretariat members learned to work with each
other, creating a team spirit that paid off as the pressure of work mounted.

The secretariat became the powerhouse of the Convention. After the very last session of the Convention, Giscard paid a handsome tribute to Kerr, describing him as 'one of the most brilliant men I have ever met'. Typically, Kerr declined to respond.

3.6   THE CONVENTIONNELS

The Convention gradually constituted itself during the early weeks of 2002. It was a big enterprise. There were 105 full members (including Giscard and his two deputies) and 102 alternates, making it bigger than many parliaments. Because of the involvement of the candidate countries, it was larger than the previous EU convention that agreed the Charter of Fundamental Rights. It was much bigger than the Philadelphia Convention, which agreed the US Constitution in 1787.

Not only had the Union's national leaders been willing for the first time to involve others in mapping the EU's future, they had set up a body in which government representatives would be in a minority. Leaving the triumvirate at the top to one side, there were 56 national parliamentarians, 28 government representatives, 16 MEPs and 2 commissioners, with an alternate for each of these. Although far more broadly based than any previous body charged with reforming the Union, the final assembly was not representative of the EU's population. As Giscard was wont to lament, there were too few women. Although the government conventionnels of Sweden, Finland, Poland and (later) Latvia were women, their low representation at the Convention (17 women members and 23 female alternates) provided a poor advertisement for the EU's policies of equal rights and 'gender mainstreaming'. The Union's eurosceptics, who were a substantial force in the UK, Denmark and Sweden, were still less well represented. Led by Jens-Peter Bonde, a veteran Danish MEP, and David Heathcoat-Amory, a British Conservative member of the House of Commons, they numbered just four conventionnels and four alternates.

By contrast, the European Parliament's presence was bigger than its official contingent of 32 full members and alternates. Like Greece and Spain, Luxembourg chose to be represented by an MEP – Jacques Santer, its former prime minister and the Commission president from 1995 to 1999.

There were other former national leaders besides Giscard, Amato, Dehaene, Bruton, Peterle and Santer. One of the most influential was Lamberto Dini, the Italian senator, who would become a decisive figure in the frantic politicking of the Convention's final months. By contrast, Lennart Meri, the former Estonian president and a national hero, was appointed to represent his country but failed to appear after April 2002.

Among serving ministers were Peter Hain, the British minister for Europe, and Pierre Moscovici, his French counterpart. Moscovici was to be replaced in November 2002 after the Socialists' defeat in the French presidential and National Assembly elections by Dominique de Villepin, the foreign minister. Hain stayed the course, despite promotion, first to be minister for the UK principality of Wales (which, bizarrely, was a position of cabinet rank in Britain, unlike minister for Europe), and later to be leader of the House of Commons. Louis Michel, the Belgian foreign minister who played a big part in securing member states' acceptance of the Convention, was to be a spasmodic attendant, reflecting the pressure of work to which all foreign ministers were subject and the growing demands of Belgium's 2003 general election.

Several governments appointed academics, reflecting in some cases a belief that the Convention would be little more than a talking shop. Finland was represented throughout by Teija Tiilikainen, an EU expert from Helsinki University. Until autumn 2002, Gerhard Schröder's representative was Peter Glotz, a thoughtful 62-year-old Social Democrat professor for media and societal studies at the Swiss University of St Gallen who had quit German politics in 1996. He was to be replaced by Joschka Fischer, Germany's foreign minister, in a move which signalled Berlin's realisation that the Convention was a serious business. Fischer's arrival prompted other countries, including France, Greece and Slovenia, to follow suit, turning the Convention into a body that no government could afford to ignore.

CHAPTER 4
Early Days

4.1   DIFFICULTIES AFTER LAEKEN

Many predicted at Laeken that the Convention would be little more than a talking shop that would rapidly sink from view. In the first months of 2002, it appeared more a forum for squabbling with a capacity to generate negative headlines.

In mid-January, reports began to circulate in Brussels that Giscard wanted paying for the job of chairman and expected the going rate: around 20,000 euro a month, similar to the gross income of Commission president, Romano Prodi. Also on his wish list were a luxury suite of rooms in a top Brussels hotel and a hand picked team of 10 to 12 people to help him perform his task.

At first sight, Giscard's requests seemed like pure greed. Here was a man who had not only pushed himself forward for the job. He was well endowed with pensions and emoluments as a former president of France, deputy in the National Assembly and president of the regional council of the Auvergne. Moreover, Roman Herzog, the president of the EU's previous convention on the Charter and a former president of Germany, had been happy to draw expenses only. Giscard's demands were a blow for Pierre de Boissieu. Despite an extremely tight budget, the Council's deputy secretary general had moved fast to create space for the Convention's staffers, clearing a floor in the Justus Lipsius building of the Council of Ministers for its use. It looked as if he had invited a cuckoo into the nest.

The issue was not quite as clear-cut as Giscard's critics claimed. The Laeken declaration was silent on the issue of payment for the Convention president and his deputies. It was assumed that the other conventionnels would be paid by their respective institutions. But unlike Herzog, who was appointed to the Charter convention by the German government and then elected its president by his peers, Giscard had been appointed by the summit to act in the interests of the Union, its members and the applicant countries. An international elder statesman like Giscard would clearly need bodyguards. He also needed to sleep somewhere in Brussels. Was it appropriate for him to carry these costs himself? Should France, the country that put him forward, foot the bill or would that not subvert his independence? If there was a risk of the latter, should not the EU foot the bill somehow?

The issue was closed after Giscard issued a statement from his office[1] in the French National Assembly, as deputy of Puy-de-Dome, acknowledging his work would be unpaid. Rather than deny the reports, Giscard said his only request was that the payments should be 'appropriate and in line with the norm of the European institutions' because he had wished 'to position the Convention at a good level *vis-à-vis* other institutions'. COREPER, the forum of EU ambassadors, agreed and foreign ministers, meeting in the General Affairs Council of 28 January, confirmed that Giscard and his two deputies would be paid expenses but no salary. Giscard would receive 1,000 euro a day, which would be expected to cover his accommodation in Brussels and that of two bodyguards. Amato would receive 750 euro per day, while Dehaene, who was mayor of Vilvoorde, near Brussels, would be entitled to 200 euro daily.

Another demand of Giscard was easier to solve. The Laeken declaration said the Convention should start on 1 March, a Friday. Giscard reasoned – correctly – that he would get more media coverage if the launch was moved forward to 28 February. He lobbied Spain, the new holder of the EU's rotating presidency, which consulted its partners and agreed.

In a third area of controversy – the rules of procedure – Giscard was at odds with the Convention as a whole. His early thoughts[2] envisaged a very powerful Praesidium with the sole right to draw up agendas for the Convention and even more muscular Convention president.[3] One draft of 27 February, for example, would have allowed Giscard to 'arrange the order in which items are to be taken, determine the length of discussion on each item, decide who is to speak, and apportion and limit the length of each intervention'. Giscard was also determined not to have the decisions of the Convention subject to votes and insisted at first that the alternates should play a very limited role in the Convention's proceedings.

Giscard's antipathy to the alternates partly reflected concern that the full Convention members would be less than diligent in attending the plenary sessions, and so fail to develop the necessary *esprit de corps*, if the alternates were practically their equivalents. But restricting the alternates posed real

---

[1] Dated 25 January 2002.

[2] The difficult issues are still apparent in CONV 3/02 dated 27 February 2002, which brought the problems into the public domain on the Convention website after several weeks of drafting and discussion between designated Convention members and the secretariat.

[3] During 2002, the titles 'president' and 'vice-president' gradually supplanted the terms 'chairman' and 'vice-chairman' used in the English version of the Laeken text and will be used henceforth in this account of the Convention.

problems for national parliaments with more than one chamber and some of the smaller political groups.

The British parliament, for example, had decided that its two full members of the Convention should come from the House of Commons and their alternates from the House of Lords. Curbing the alternates would have meant an inadequate participation in the Convention for the Lords, which was a chamber with a high level of constitutional expertise. It would also have put the UK Liberal Democrat party at a disadvantage *vis-à-vis* the Labour and Conservative parties because its representative among the national parliamentarians was Lord Maclennan of Rogart. Giscard's proposals would also have left Sir Neil MacCormick MEP, an authority on legal and political theory and the only Scottish Nationalist Party member in the Convention, unable to do his job properly.

The disputes over the rules of procedure were not resolved by the opening of the Convention on 28 February. They rumbled on until the Praesidium produced revised proposals[4] on 14 March. By the time the issue came to the Convention floor in the 22 March plenary session, not only had Giscard made concessions, but most members were anxious to get on with the real business of the Convention. As Hänsch declared: 'The duty of the Convention is to draft a constitutional treaty, not rules of procedure.'

There was a tacit agreement between the Parliament representatives and Giscard that rules should be interpreted with some flexibility as the Convention bedded down. After an animated debate, Giscard uttered the two words *'Je constate',* which roughly translates as 'I determine that ...' before announcing there was a consensus. He declared the rules accepted and the squabbling subsided.

Although the wrangling appeared arcane, the row over the rules of procedure was an important episode. It showed to the Convention rank and file that Giscard could change his mind when presented with firmly presented and well-argued counter proposals. The compromise over the rules of the game also helped lift some of the mistrust with which the conventionnels viewed the Praesidium. The format and half the members of the Praesidium had been designated by heads of government. Yet it had served as the conduit for bringing the objections of the conventionnels to Giscard's attention.

As for Giscard, he came away from the dispute with a vitally important prize. The Convention had accepted that its decisions would be established

---

[4] CONV 9/02.

by consensus and not by votes. Giscard had made clear in January that he would not accept voting, because the Convention did not reflect European demography and its component parts were of very different orders of magnitude. Consensus, on the other hand, was a wonderfully vague concept and as long as it was Giscard who determined consensus in the Convention, he had great power. Consensus was Giscard's secret weapon and it stayed under his control until the Convention's final day.

4.2   THE OPENING CEREMONY

The body, which first met on 28 February, was a bold departure from the previous tradition of EU institutional reform behind closed doors. The Convention opened in the plenary hall of the European Parliament building in Brussels, with its proceedings open to the public, broadcast live on EBS – the EU's satellite broadcaster – and carried on the Internet.

The grumbles and doubts of recent weeks were replaced by a bustle of excitement as the 105 members and 102 alternates came into the hall and found their seats, with conventionnels at the front and alternates behind. Then respectful silence as they sat through a ceremonial opening with speeches from José Maria Aznar, the Spanish prime minister and president in office of the European Council; Romano Prodi, Commission president and Pat Cox, the recently elected president of the European Parliament. The massed ranks of suits testified to the lack of women among the Convention's members. The kilted Scottish Nationalist alternate, Sir Neil MacCormick MEP, in his Maclaine of Lochbuie tartan, provided a rare flash of colour amidst the grey.

Giscard took the floor last. For once, the Convention president did not mention Benjamin Franklin or the 1787 Philadelphia Convention. Instead, Giscard launched the Convention with a speech that invited the conventionnels to 'dream of Europe'.

He was both inclusive and emotional. After beginning with 'Ladies and Gentlemen' in the 11 official languages of the Union, and adding the Polish 'Szanowni Panstwo', he offered the Convention members a stark choice between the 'yawning abyss of failure' or the 'gate to success'. Failure would see what had been created in Europe over the previous 50 years 'reach its limit and be threatened with dislocation'. If the Convention failed, 'each country would return to the free trade system. None of us – not even the largest of us – would have the power to take on the giants of the world. We would then remain locked in on ourselves, grimly analysing the causes of our decline and fall.'

Success, 'if we agree to propose a concept of the European Union, which matches our continental dimension and the requirements of the 21st century', would allow the conventionnels 'to leave here and return home, whether you are Italo-European, Anglo-European, Polish-European – or any of the others – with the feeling of having contributed, modestly but effectively, to writing a new chapter in the history of Europe'. Europe needed to overcome its shortcomings in its own interests and those of the world.

> If we succeed, in 25 years or 50 years – the distance separating us from the Treaty of Rome – Europe's role in the world will have changed. It will be respected and listened to, not only as the economic power it already is, but as a political power which will talk on equal terms to the greatest powers on our planet, either existing or future, and will have the means to act to affirm its values, ensure its security and play an active role in international peace keeping.

Giscard mapped out three phases for the Convention's work. First would be a phase 'of open, attentive listening' when the Convention would ponder what Europeans wanted of the Union at the start of the 21st century. The second 'study' phase would examine the questions raised at Laeken, the organisation of European institutions resulting from the Treaty of Nice and the various ideas put forward for the future of Europe. Only after this examination would the Convention, in its third phase, be able to draw up recommendations or a proposal for the IGC, scheduled for 2004.

He reminded the Convention that it was neither an IGC nor a parliament. It was a unique opportunity – 'the first occasion since the Messina Conference in 1955'[5] – with both the resources and time to examine in detail the future of the EU.

There was only one spontaneous burst of applause, when, to the surprise of all, he urged the Convention to 'achieve a broad consensus on a single proposal' for a constitutional treaty 'which we could all present' to the IGC. Consensus, he said, would 'open the way towards a Constitution for Europe'.

In a schoolmasterly manner, he told the members of the Convention's four components they 'must not regard themselves simply as spokespersons for those who appointed them'. The Convention could not succeed if views remained entrenched. 'It needs to become the melting-pot in which, month by month, a common approach is worked out.' In short, it needed to create a 'Convention spirit'. Giscard sought to calm those who feared most of the work would be carried out in the Praesidium. Declaring that 'for me, the

---

[5] Which paved the way for the EEC and Euratom treaties.

Convention is the Convention', he explained that the Praesidium would prepare and organise the Convention's proceedings but 'everything else' would depend on the Convention members and their contributions.

It was a confident performance, executed with charm and energy and designed to allay many of the suspicions and doubts that had surfaced since the Laeken summit. He lavished compliments on the previous speakers, and slipped occasionally from French into heavily accented English and German. His remarks, while generating respect rather than excitement, showed he was determined to be a strong leader. He was ambitious, with a real determination to leave his mark on history, and not just for a few years, but for the first half century of the 21st century at least. His aim for the Convention to 'achieve a broad consensus on a single proposal for reform' showed he would not accept a lowest common denominator outcome. Whereas the Laeken declaration included the possibility of the final document containing different options, Giscard wanted to present the IGC and subsequent European Council with a proposal that would be very difficult to turn down. And to back up this drive for consensus, Giscard had already, in his own mind, ruled out the idea of votes in the Convention.

He wanted to develop an *esprit de corps*. The year-long Convention should not be the place for negotiations among member states or EU institutions. Unremarked at the time, his reference to rethinking the organisation of European institutions, resulting from the Treaty of Nice, hinted at radical proposals to come.

4.3   THE LISTENING PHASE

Giscard appealed in the opening ceremony for the conventionnels to show enthusiasm for their mission. They did. Their meetings in the European Parliament building in Brussels were well attended, unlike most plenary sessions of the Parliament. Between 70 and 80 speakers would take the floor in each of the working sessions as the conventionnels demonstrated a strong desire to get down to serious business.

But there were problems. The MEPs, playing on their own turf and steeped in the mysteries and jargon of the EU, were impatient with Giscard's listening phase. Aware of the huge volume of work ahead, they wanted to get on with drafting texts. This created friction with some of the national parliamentarians who needed time to feel their way in unfamiliar surroundings, and complained of being underresourced and underinformed. The applicant countries' conventionnels made little impact for several months as their governments focused on the enlargement negotiations. The member states' representatives also tended to be reticent, with some notable exceptions such as Spain's Ana Palacio and Britain's Peter Hain.

The high British profile in the Convention was one of the more striking phenomena of its early months. Hain impressed many pro-integrationists when he stated in March that the Convention's task was 'nothing less than the creation of a new constitutional order for a new Europe'. Although this was coupled with a warning that Britons 'only want Europe to act when it genuinely has something extra to add', the UK approach still appeared a refreshing change. Hain's faithful attendance and assiduous lobbying of fellow Convention members, notably from the applicant countries, showed Blair's government had learned its lessons from the EU's fundamental rights convention of 2000 when it was out of sympathy with the proceedings and became isolated.

The Convention's early months saw its organisers try to reach a broader public through two days of hearings with 'civil society' in June and a special Youth Convention in July. Looking back a year later, a Convention official described the civil society forum as a 'gallant failure', which pleased the Brussels-based lobbies but failed to get through to the general public.

The Youth Convention was a pet idea of Giscard's, which he had mentioned in his speech during the opening ceremony. Plans were made for 210 young persons (aged between 18 and 25) to come to Brussels between 9 and 12 July and hold a Convention to be modelled as closely as possible on the Convention proper. The Youth Convention members were chosen by the conventionnels, who were asked to ensure an appropriate diversity as far as sex, occupation and geographical background were concerned. They complied in terms of gender, with the result that half the Youth Convention were female. The young delegates were invited to join the proper Convention on 11 and 12 July and report their findings to it.

'You are here to enlighten us. We need your fresh ideas and your freedom of thought,' Giscard told the Youth Convention's opening session. He was to be disappointed. The Youth Convention proved to be far more acrimonious than the senior Convention, and even had its own mini-scandal when a candidate for the chair was found to be over 25. It agreed a strongly federal text (including the idea of a 'welfare Europe' with 'common legislation in the fields of social policy and equal opportunity'), which was supported by three-quarters of its delegates. A minority report, signed by 51 eurosceptic and disenchanted rank and file members, accused the Youth Convention of 'limited legitimacy' and said it had been conducted 'in a manner that was unrepresentative, undemocratic and too concerned with vested interest and political factions'.

The concerns were shared by some members of the grown-up Convention. Johannes Voggenhuber, an Austrian Convention member, complained that the Youth Convention was an assembly of young bureaucrats, 'many of whom were already practiced in the clichés, jargon and fixed ideas of the parties that sent them'. He had hoped, perhaps tongue in cheek, that it would be a forum 'where the young Spanish seamstress might confer with the Finnish electrician, where the Hungarian engineering student might meet the Irish social worker'. Instead, the politics student from Paris met the politics student from Berlin. 'It is not European youth that has come to Brussels, but the future bureaucrats of the EU institutions.'

Whatever their failings, the hearings of civil society and the Youth Convention showed how the Convention was turning into a much bigger enterprise than expected. The numbers in and around the Convention hall grew from month to month, swollen by advisers and assistants making up the sophisticated support systems on hand for MEPs and government representatives. Adding to the buzz were officials, diplomats, journalists, lobbyists and members of the NGOs that made up civil society.

This burgeoning activity obliged the members of the Convention to become enthusiastic networkers. Their plenary meetings – held on an afternoon and the following morning, usually once and sometimes twice a month – would be only part of their activities. The mornings, before each plenary session, began early and were spent caucusing in various overlapping groups. The evenings would be filled with more networking and working dinners. The ballooning workload of Convention members put a premium on able assistants, who were soon forming networks of their own.

The political families were of crucial importance in providing structured links between the members of the various component groups and would usually meet early on the first day of a plenary session. Benefiting from their relatively small numbers, the Liberal Democrats organised quickly and developed a cohesive caucus, headed by Andrew Duff, a British MEP. The PES or socialist group, under Amato, was less easily organised, in part because a shambolic selection of PES representatives for the Convention's group of MEPs excluded some of the more talented PES constitutionalists from the Convention. A baffling omission was that of Richard Corbett, a British Labour MEP, who was an authority on the parliament. By contrast, Elmar Brok, the long-serving German Christian Democrat MEP and Convention member, turned the centre-right EPP members of the Convention into a formidable block.

Other fora cut across party lines. The conventionnels met in groups of *composantes* – as representatives of the component governments, national parliamentarians and European Parliament, usually after the meetings of the political families before each plenary session. There were also meetings of national contingents, eurosceptics, working dinners of the small to medium-sized member states and 'federalist breakfasts'. While the federalist breakfasts petered out, the 'Hilton dinners' were an enduring institution.

The Hilton dinners were organised by Méndez de Vigo, with the financial support of Pat Cox, the European Parliament president, and modelled on informal dinners that Méndez de Vigo had arranged during the Charter convention. A group of 'movers and shakers' met on the 26th floor of the Brussels Hilton after the first day of each two-day plenary session to test ideas on a totally informal basis across the traditional demarcation lines of political party and component group without officials present. Regulars were Hain, Hänsch, Brok, Bruton, Dini, Barnier and Vitorino, and Poland's Danuta Hübner. As the government representatives of France, Germany and Spain came and went, so the *placement* changed. Pierre Moscovici handed his place to Pascale Andréani,[6] Peter Glotz to Hans Martin Bury[7] and Ana Palacio (although staying in the Convention as an alternate) to Alfonso Dastis. Jacques Santer, for the Luxembourg government, attended occasionally; Jean-Luc Dehaene and the Netherlands' Gijs de Vries attended when institutional issues dominated the agenda towards the end of the Convention. Hannes Farnleitner, the Austrian conventionnel and one of the most outspoken representatives of the small member states, was invited once.

4.4 MOVERS AND SHAKERS

The Convention in its listening phase was dominated by a strong cohort of federal thinkers who emerged alongside the members of the Praesidium as its early movers and shakers. Most of them were MEPs, who had the advantage of operating in familiar surroundings and with familiar material.

One key figure was Elmar Brok, the leader of the conventionnels of the European People's Party. The EPP had a problem in that the 55-year-old cigar-chomping Brok and Méndez de Vigo cordially loathed each other and this sometimes got in the way of efficient communication with each other. But Brok, a political protégé of former German chancellor Helmut Kohl with a girth to match, was a tireless and effective operator with sharp political

---

[6] De Villepin's visits to the Convention were too brief to allow attendance at the Hilton dinners.
[7] Similarly, Joschka Fischer's attendances at the Convention were limited in time.

judgement who welded the EPP's national parliamentarians and MEPs into a cohesive body. In the Convention's final months, Brok emerged as one of its key power brokers and deal-makers.

Also from the EPP, Alain Lamassoure, a French MEP and former speechwriter for Giscard, was a constant and thoughtful contributor to the debates. A one-man ideas factory, Lamassoure, 58, played an important part in the early debates on who should do what in the EU as the author of an influential parliamentary report on delimiting competences between the Union and member states.

Andrew Duff, the leader of the Liberal caucus, was another prolific producer of ideas and proposals. Duff was a rare combination of UK citizen and convinced federalist, and was not afraid to provide the grit for the Convention's oyster. The 51-year-old Liberal Democrat MEP for the east of England was described by one admirer, 'a good little Socrates in the system'. Duff was so enthusiastically federalist that a UK diplomat was once heard proposing that he should be tried for treason. Duff had served in the Charter convention. Impatient with the protracted listening period, Duff was the first to start submitting his own draft constitutional treaty texts to the Praesidium.[8]

Seated next to Duff was another conventionnel who enjoyed creating a stir. Olivier Duhamel, 51, a French Socialist MEP, was the Convention's 'blogger', producing an entertaining diary of its happenings on the World Wide Web.[9] In the plenary, he saw himself as a picador, whose job it was to goad Giscard into candour. Because Duhamel's father was once a political ally of Giscard, Duhamel was able to maintain a good-humoured relationship with Giscard that transcended age and party affiliations.

The fully paid-up member of the Convention's awkward squad was Johannes Voggenhuber, the Austrian MEP and one of the few Greens in the Convention. Voggenhuber, 51, a keen federalist and outspoken critic of Giscard's manner and methods, was one of the very few conventionnels who would openly take the president to task in a plenary session. Sometimes, however, he would lose control of his rhetoric, as when he once disparagingly compared the proceedings to an 'Italian bazaar'. Giscard showed his skill as a chairman by delivering a mild rebuke to Voggenhuber before immediately handing the floor to Lamberto Dini. A former Italian prime minister and foreign minister, Dini then fulfilled his patriotic duty by

---

[8] CONV 22/02.
[9] Obtainable on Duhamel's page via www.d-s-f.net

upbraiding Voggenhuber in the most outspoken terms, leaving the hapless Green temporarily isolated from his supporters.

At 70, Dini was older than most of the Convention's influential players. He had spent much of his life as a senior monetary official, first at the International Monetary Fund in Washington and later at the Bank of Italy. He moved late into politics in 1994 when he was appointed Treasury minister in Berlusconi's first, short lived, coalition government. In 1995–96 he was caretaker prime minister of Italy. Dini was elected a member of the Italian parliament in 1996 and served as foreign minister from 1996 until 2001 when he became a member of the senate. A member of the Convention's Liberal caucus, he impressed in the early sessions with his thoughtful interventions while building up links with Duff and other conventionnels that would enable him to play a key role in the Convention's final stages. Dini, a supporter of greater integration, carried an iron fist in a velvet glove and knew how to pull the levers of power.

Erwin Teufel, 62, was another influential national parliamentarian. As prime minister of the southwest state of Baden-Württemberg, he was the senior representative in the Convention of Germany's opposition Christian Democrats and represented the Bundesrat, Germany's second chamber, where the CDU and their Christian Social allies from Bavaria held the majority. While German government approval would be a necessary condition for the Convention's success, its conclusions would also need the support of Teufel and the German states or *Länder* that he represented. This put Teufel in a strong political position. He also had a clear agenda as an advocate of a catalogue of competences. He represented a traditionally Catholic region and, like many in Germany's southwest, had close ties with France. He was Germany's cultural representative under the Franco-German partnership from 1995 to 1998. Giscard made a point of establishing and maintaining good relations with Teufel. One of Giscard's early keynote speeches outside Brussels was in Stuttgart, the capital of Baden-Württemberg in May 2002.

One of Giscard's most frequent complaints was about the poor representation of women in the Convention. Anne Van Lancker, a Belgian MEP, compensated through hyperactivity. The 47-year-old Flemish Socialist was a tireless advocate of a federal 'Social Europe'. Another problem was the relative lack of prominence of applicant country representatives, especially in contrast to the well-informed and assertive phalanx of MEPs. Going some way to redress this imbalance was Danuta Hübner, state secretary for European integration in the Polish Foreign ministry who represented the Polish government. A former academic, Hübner, 53, prized the Convention because it gave the applicant countries a sense of ownership in the soon to be enlarged EU.

Britain's Peter Hain had the highest profile of the government representatives during the first half of the Convention. Hain, 51 when the Convention started, was a rising star in Blair's government. As minister for Europe, he was in his fourth government job since the election of 1997. Born in Nairobi, educated partly in South Africa and a notable campaigner against apartheid, he had a Commonwealth rather than an EU hinterland. But he was a fast learner, naturally outward going, willing to speak his own mind and (unusually for a government representative) at times prepared to indicate to the plenary that he might be willing to shift policy. He was rapidly on first name, back-slapping terms with a large number of his fellow conventionnels. That was just as well. He had to work harder than most Convention members because the British government had much it wanted to protect. A significant cohort of Convention members calling for greater European engagement in social and economic affairs posed a threat to the UK position on the Charter as adopted at Nice. The UK was deeply suspicious of any moves to 'communitarise' foreign and defence policy. Hain also had to consider a sceptical public and largely hostile eurosceptic press at home.

The eurosceptics in the Convention were a very small group that had to make up for their lack of numbers by prominence in the plenary. They were led by the president of the 'Group for Europe of Democracies and Diversity', the 53-year-old Jens-Peter Bonde, a maverick Danish MEP since 1979 who was consequently well-versed in the ways of Brussels. British Conservative David Heathcoat-Amory, 52 at the start of the Convention, was an articulate advocate of the need to boost the EU's democratic credentials.

4.5   THE LISTENING PHASE: AN EVALUATION

The listening phase enabled the 105 Convention members and their 102 alternates to learn to work together – an important matter in such a diverse body. It also set down some important markers. It moved the debate about Europe's future very decisively in the direction of a constitutional treaty, to be based on just one proposal for reform. This goal was unclear before Giscard's announcement at the Convention's start on February 28.

The Convention rejected the idea of a strict catalogue of competences, as urged by the German *Länder* ahead of Nice, because of the inflexibility this would entail. But, as Giscard made clear when he reported to EU leaders at their June 2002 European Council in Seville, there was a consensus on the need to clarify who does what. The debates suggested the EU should focus on core issues with better policing of subsidiarity. These discussions matured in plans for national parliaments to be more engaged in EU affairs.

While there was no strong demand for the Union to have new competences, the early debates uncovered a strong wish for a more effective common foreign and security policy (CFSP) and more effective ways of combating cross-border crime, as well as support among some conventionnels for greater coordination of economic policies. The Convention was less clear in its early months over whether there should be more European involvement in social policy. Public services, culture, social security and – for the most part – education were areas where speakers generally wanted the member states to stay in charge.

Giscard himself highlighted the need for simplification, stressing that the Convention must produce proposals to reduce the mind-boggling complexity of the Union's systems, procedures and treaty texts so these could be easily understood by its citizens. He considered that the abstruse nature of decision making was a major cause of popular disaffection with the Union. Things had reached the stage where experts no longer knew what was going on, let alone the citizens.

The hearing of civil society in June revealed strong support among NGOs and conventionnels for incorporation of the Charter in the treaties. But as Dehaene made clear, there was little enthusiasm among the Convention's leaders for any rewriting of the Charter.

The Convention was far from revolutionary. And Giscard seemed determined to keep it that way by steering it towards incremental reforms that maintained the Union as a unique hybrid with both 'Community' and intergovernmental characteristics. Yet while there was no sign it would spawn a European 'superstate', there were clear differences between those who wanted a more integrated or federal Europe, and those who saw political control resting primarily with Europe's nation-states.

The choice was brought to the fore through the contrasting visions of the British, French and Spanish governments on the one hand and the Commission on the other. The British and French wanted to strengthen the role of the member states through beefing up the European Council and the Council of Ministers, and getting rid of the six-month rotating presidencies of the EU. The UK favoured a semi-permanent president of the European Council elected by member states. The Commission, in a document published in May, set out its case for a stronger 'Community method' of running the Union. It said the system used for single market legislation of having the Commission propose legislation, which was then amended by the

Council of Ministers and European Parliament using majority voting, should be greatly extended, with some modifications, to foreign and economic policy. The Commission also wanted the post of EU high representative or foreign policy supremo, created in 1999, brought into the Commission itself.

These opposing views would not be discussed in the Convention for many months. But they were among Giscard's preoccupations as he engaged in the less visible part of his job – that of consulting with the heads of government who had appointed him.

4.6   GISCARD'S BILATERAL DIPLOMACY

Giscard's bilateral contacts with Union leaders started early in January 2002 when he met José Maria Aznar, the holder of the EU's rotating presidency. Before the Convention's opening ceremony, he visited Silvio Berlusconi in Rome, Gerhard Schröder and Joschka Fischer in Berlin, Tony Blair in London, Wim Kok in The Hague and Göran Persson and Swedish parliamentarians in Stockholm. By the time of the June 2002 Seville summit, there had been follow-up visits to Blair, Schröder and Aznar, and two meetings with Romano Prodi, the Commission president.

There was a general perception that Giscard preferred to deal with the big member states. This was not strictly true. In the early months, he also conferred with Wolfgang Schüssel, the Austrian chancellor, and regional leaders including Teufel and Edmund Stoiber, the Bavarian prime minister and German opposition contender for the chancellorship in the 2002 national elections.

While the proceedings of the Convention were open to all, Giscard's bilateral meetings were not transparent. There was no schedule of his forthcoming talks on the website and no comment after the meetings. However, it was clear that potential problem countries, such as the UK or Austria, were high on his list of priorities.

Giscard's travels to the member states were geared towards securing consistency between the outcome of the Convention and the expectations of the governments that would eventually pass judgement on its work in the 2004 IGC. Institutional reform was on the Convention's agenda and Giscard needed, in particular, to know leaders' views about the future of the European Council and the Council of Ministers. In the early months, there was a need to brief heads of government about the unfamiliar creature they had created in Brussels, while towards the Convention's close Giscard himself was anxious to discern any 'red lines' which would prevent his interlocutors accepting a compromise.

In some cases, where he deemed it necessary to establish a rapport with a key figure, the meetings would be restricted in a small group with key advisers. This was the pattern of his visits to Blair, which took place in the flat above 10 Downing Street and where, on the first such occasion, Giscard nearly tripped over baby Leo Blair's toys. In other cases, such as his visits to Finland, Luxembourg, the Netherlands and Ireland, he would travel to a capital and make a point of meeting not just the country's leader, but ministers, parliamentarians and the country's conventionnels on their own turf.

4.7   GISCARD'S EARLY PERFORMANCE

Giscard's performance had been better than many expected or feared by the time the listening phase ended after the summer of 2002. He had the advantage of starting from a low base, after the damaging publicity over his demands for a salary and luxury accommodation in Brussels. But, in the Convention's plenary sessions, he proved an alert, attentive and firm chairman, who was nonetheless willing to accept innovation.

The election of Peterle to the Praesidium and the provision of translation facilities for the candidate country representatives pointed to some flexibility. His introduction of a 'blue card' scheme, by which members of the Convention could catch his eye and make short responses or pose questions, injected more life into the proceedings, which otherwise would have been dominated by set piece statements, and showed a commitment to making the Convention work. It was not easy for the conventionnels to extract concessions from him and there was much muttering about his performance in the corridors. But very little dissent crystallised in the Convention chamber itself. In fact, a lot of steam was blown-off in the preparatory meetings before the sessions.

Giscard had established his authority. In part, this reflected an instinct for power, exemplified by his approach to the rules of procedure, and in part, his enormous knowledge and experience of the Union. Another factor was the relative feebleness of the Praesidium – a weakness that he did little to counter as he built up the secretariat with Sir John Kerr.

A third factor was the clear will of most of the conventionnels to move ahead and make the Convention work. By July, the listening phase was coming to an end. Giscard had agreed in May that working groups of

Convention members should be set up to tackle issues in greater detail. It was time for the Convention to move up a gear.

CHAPTER 5
Working Groups and Constitutions

5.1   SETTING UP THE WORKING GROUPS

The Convention was in full transition from the listening to the study phase during the summer of 2002. One sign of the shift was the Praesidium's decision in May to set up six working groups. This 'first wave' got down to business in June with the aim of reporting during the autumn. Plans for four others to meet later in the year were announced in July before the summer break.

Each working group was chaired by a member of the Praesidium and had up to 30 members. Of the six early working groups, five focused on constitutional issues while the sixth, on economic governance, was policy related. Three of the four 'second wave' working groups were policy related, covering justice and internal security, the EU's external relations and defence. A working group on simplifying the Union's legislative procedures rounded off the constitutional agenda. The second wave groups were asked to report in late November or early December. In November, a reluctant Giscard agreed to set up an additional policy related working group, on social Europe, to report early in 2003. The working groups with details of their tasks, chairpersons and reports are summarised in Table 2.

The topics of the working groups generally reflected the conclusions drawn by Giscard and the secretariat from the early months of the Convention. The groups were instructed not to draft articles. Their aim was to look at legal and technical issues and not to reach political conclusions. However, the assumptions behind the groups were highly political. For example, Vitorino in drawing up the mandate for the group on the Charter simply assumed that 'the major political questions', of whether the Charter should be incorporated or whether there should be accession to the European Convention on Human Rights (ECHR), would 'meet with a positive political response' in the Convention.

The secretariat's enthusiasm for the subject matter varied. The group on economic governance was set up against the better judgement of the secretariat in response to the wishes of many Convention members. Giscard and Kerr then fought a long rearguard action before conceding a working group on social policy.

Task	Chair	Report
Subsidiarity, including its more efficient application and control	Inigo Méndez de Vigo	CONV 286/02 of 23 September 2002
The EU's Charter of Fundamental Rights and its incorporation into the treaties, plus the issue of EU membership of the European Convention on Human Rights	Antonio Vitorino	CONV 354/02 of 22 October 2002
The EU's legal personality and whether a single legal personality would contribute to simplifying the treaties	Giuliano Amato	CONV 305/02 of 1 October 2002
The role of national parliaments in the EU architecture, including studying best practice among parliaments	Gisela Stuart	CONV 353/02 of 22 October 2002
Complementary competences or areas where the Union would support actions at national or regional level	Henning Christophersen	CONV 375/1/02 of 4 November 2002
Economic governance and increased cooperation in economic and financial matters following the introduction of the euro and a more social Europe	Klaus Hänsch	CONV 357/02 of 21 October 2002
External action, including achieving better consistency of policies, investigating whether community methods can be applied, reviewing the role of the high representative and achieving better external representation of the EU	Jean-Luc Dehaene	CONV 459/02 of 16 December 2002

Defence, including tasks, capabilities, speeding up decisions, exploring the possibility of enhanced cooperation and improving arms procurement and R&D	Michel Barnier	CONV 461/02 of 16 December 2002
Simplification of legislative procedures, including reduction of procedures, extending QMV in step with codecision, simplifying the EU budget process and giving legal instruments clearer names	Giuliano Amato	CONV 424/02 of 29 November 2002
Freedom, security and justice, including improvements needed to treaties and instruments, improving judicial cooperation on criminal matters and adjusting treaty wording on asylum and immigration	John Bruton	CONV 426/02 of 2 December 2002
Social Europe, including the possible modification of Union competences and reduced resort to unanimity in decision making	George Katiforis	CONV 516/1/03 of 4 February 2003

Table 2: The working groups - their tasks, chairs and reports

With the working groups getting down to business, the Praesidium began in July to consider the outlines of the eventual Constitution. The activities of the working groups and the Praesidium were to be linked. Amato described the job of the working groups as 'preparing the building blocks for the final product'. The subjects investigated by the first five working groups, as well as that on simplification, went far to sorting out issues that needed clarification before embarking on the detailed drafting of the constitutional treaty. But only two groups – those on subsidiarity and the Union's legal personality – had reported by the time Giscard unveiled the first 'skeleton' Constitution on 28 October.

5.2   THE PRAESIDIUM PONDERS CONSTITUTIONAL OPTIONS

The Praesidium's decision to consider the content and structure of a constitutional text partly reflected pressure from Convention members. In June, a group organised by Maria Berger, an Austrian MEP and alternate, signed a motion[1] demanding that the Praesidium ask the European Commission to prepare a draft constitutional treaty for discussion by the Convention at its meeting scheduled for end-October. Although signed by only 18 conventionnels, the request was considered by the Praesidium, which decided unanimously not to take up the proposal 'since it would imply that the Convention would shirk its own responsibilities'.[2]

But there was still great uncertainty inside the Praesidium over what the Convention should aim for. Discussions in the Convention left unclear whether it should ultimately produce a 'basic' treaty, which was one option in the Laeken declaration, a constitutional treaty, as mooted by Giscard at the opening ceremony, or a fully-fledged Constitution.

An internal email, that was released by accident in July to the member states' permanent representations, pointed to a *'chapeau'* solution by which the Convention would agree new texts for a first, constitutional, part of a new treaty, which would be superimposed on the existing Union treaties. The document, while causing a stir, turned out to have no official status.

Sir John Kerr at this time was inclined to opt for a short, basic treaty, which would include the most important 'constitutional' elements of the existing treaties. In his view, the Convention should then sum up the remaining, more mundane contents of the existing texts as a set of principles, which would be handed to the legal services of the Union's institutions to be turned into treaty language after the Convention had disbanded. Meanwhile, Hervé Bribosia, a secretariat member who had previously worked for the European University Institute in Florence, had produced a draft paper, which examined the complexities of simplifying and merging the existing treaties.

At the beginning of August, Kerr visited Giscard at his main country home, north of Tours in France, to discuss the contents of a revised version of Bribosia's paper before heading to a holiday on the Atlantic coast. Giscard in turn went to Paris for a lunch with Amato and Dehaene, to bring them up to speed on developments. Kerr began drafting a text at the seaside.

---

[1] CONV 181/02.
[2] Summary of Conclusions: Praesidium meeting of 10 July 2002, filed under Praesidium documents on the Convention website.

After six revisions, a paper based on Bribosia's work contained the outlines of a basic treaty. After a preamble, the treaty would address such classic constitutional issues as the nature, structure and values of the Union; citizenship and the rights of Union citizens; the Union's general objectives; its institutions and decision making procedures; and the Union's policies before rounding off with the final provisions, which appear in all EU treaties, and deal with such issues as accession of new members and revision procedures.

But the paper also suggested making the basic treaty part of a broader reorganization and simplification of the two main EU treaties: the Treaty establishing the European Community (TEC) and the Treaty on European Union (TEU). Texts not included in the basic treaty would comprise 'part two' of the restructured product. This approach, the paper argued, was preferable to producing a new basic treaty and simply superimposing it on the existing treaties without adapting them. A *'chapeau'* treaty of this type, with the old and new systems coexisting, could pose a threat to legal certainty and 'might well prove a permanent source of conflict'.

The paper was destined for the Praesidium. But it was sent to all Convention members in September when an official clicked the wrong e-mail icon. Its substance was eventually published by the secretariat on the website.[3]

Giscard too had been busy gathering his thoughts over the summer and had emerged with about a dozen detailed proposals, which were presented to the Praesidium. All this activity left the Praesidium less than enthused. Some members felt 'bounced' by the developments and were wary of some of Giscard's enthusiasms.

When the Convention met after the summer on 12–13 September, Giscard felt able to report some progress. The Praesidium would present the structure of a constitutional treaty to the Convention during its 28–29 October meeting. His own preference was for a single text containing a constitutional section and a section on policies (part two), possibly to be supplemented by protocols.

Whatever the form, it was imperative that the Convention's work should be understandable to intelligent secondary school pupils.

---

[3] CONV 250/02.

5.3   THE SKELETON

On 28 October, eight months to the day after the start of the Convention, its members received their personally addressed copies of a 'preliminary draft constitutional treaty'.[4]

Advance briefing – notably by Amato – had aimed at scaling down expectations. In the event, the skeleton turned out to be a rather more substantial document than the Praesidium's news management techniques implied. This positive surprise was one reason it was well received. Hailing the draft as a 'significant step', Giscard explained to a packed plenary session that the text built on the broad consensus reached in the early October plenary in favour of a single legal personality for the EU. This opened the way for a merger of the EU and EC treaties in a single text, which in turn marked a 'fundamental step' towards the simplification of the treaties demanded by public opinion.

The skeleton had some eye-catching features. It floated the idea of a strong executive for the Union in the form of a stable president of the European Council. It signalled that the Charter would be incorporated and included, for the first time, the right of secession from the Union. It comprised three parts. The first laid down the EU's constitutional and institutional architecture while the second dealt with the Union's policies and action. The third would consist of general clauses, covering such issues as territorial application, language regime and rules for ratification and revision, as well as the provisions normally found in constitutional acts to ensure continuity with past treaties.

The first part, comprising 10 titles with 46 articles, was outlined in some detail. This, Giscard said, should be 'especially clear and incisive', should have 'some power and even some lyricism' and be 'comprehensible to all'. The aim of the text was to create a more ordered framework for the Convention's discussions. Some of the provisions, Giscard stressed, were derived from previous plenary debates. Others were proposals for debate. Some ideas made their way into the draft simply because they were pet ideas of the president. Other articles, including optional proposals for Council presidencies, touched on issues that had not been raised in the Convention.

After a preamble, 'title I' of part one set down in four articles the definition and objectives of the Union, the values and goals that brought the member states together and recognised the Union's single legal personality. Title I

---

[4] CONV 369/02.

got the draft off to a headline grabbing start – for Britain's eurosceptic press, at least. The first article didn't duck the 'f' word: the EU would be 'a Union of European States which, while retaining their national identities, closely coordinate their policies at the European level and administer certain common competences on a federal basis'.

It offended some Convention members by failing to refer to the EU as a Union of peoples. It also opened up the possibility for a change of name by mentioning 'European Community', 'United States of Europe' and 'United Europe' as possible alternatives to 'European Union'. The mere possibility of a name change helped secure the skeleton treaty a good deal of publicity, especially after Giscard indicated his preference for 'United Europe'. This name translated 'simply and strongly' in the different languages of the EU, he claimed.

Title II established and defined Union citizenship, stipulating that every citizen would enjoy 'dual' European and national citizenship and be free to 'use' either. A second article in this title incorporated the Charter of Fundamental Rights, although leaving details to be fixed in the light of the conclusions of the Charter working group.

Title III covered the Union's competences and actions in seven articles. It established the principle that any competence not conferred on the Union by the Constitution rested with the member states. It also stated in black and white that Union law enjoyed primacy in the exercise of competences conferred on the Union. Title III set out the principles of subsidiarity and proportionality, promised rules for their effective monitoring, and indicated the areas of exclusive Union competence, shared competence with the member states, and areas where the Union supported or coordinated action by the member states.

Title IV on the institutions also stirred controversy. Its observation that the Union 'has a single institutional structure' signalled an end to the second and third pillars with their different rules for common foreign and security policy and justice and home affairs, created in the Maastricht Treaty. It broached the issue of separate presidencies for the European Council and Council of Ministers well in advance of the discussion on such potentially divisive matters in the Convention. Outside the Convention, Britain, France and Spain had already proposed having a long-term president of the European Council to give the EU strategic direction. As was to become clear in later months, this 'ABC' idea (propagated by Prime Ministers Aznar and Blair, and President Chirac) was to establish a dividing line in the debate on the institutional future of Europe as the Commission and some small member states construed it as a move to concentrate power in a 'directory' of big member states.

Title IV (comprising ten articles and three optional articles) would allow the European Parliament to introduce a motion of censure on the activities of the Commission and would detail 'the procedure and consequences' of such a motion. It also raised the possibility of a Congress of the Peoples of Europe even though this pet idea of Giscard's was given a consistently unenthusiastic reception in the Convention itself.

Title V, setting out how to organise implementation of EU action, listed the various instruments and procedures available to the Union's institutions for exercising their competences. The nine articles would also include implementing procedures for common foreign and security policy (CFSP) and defence policy, and conditions for undertaking enhanced cooperation – that is allowing certain member states to move ahead of others on specific policies within the framework of the treaty.

Introducing a new title compared with previous treaties, title VI outlined in five articles the principles of the democratic life of the Union, with emphasis on equality and transparency. The EU's institutions were to ensure a high level of openness, allowing citizens' organisations to play a full life in the Union. The Parliament would be elected by a uniform procedure of direct universal suffrage in all member states. The debates in the Council, when legislating, would be public.

In three articles, title VII would detail the rules for the EU's finances, including the principles that the EU budget should be fully financed by the Union's own resources and kept in balance. Title VIII, in article 41, would set out who represents the Union in international relations, leaving scope for the Convention to define the future role of the high representative for CFSP. Title IX, article 42 was to define a privileged relationship between the EU and its neighbouring states.

In four articles, title X would set out the terms for EU membership, including the procedures for suspension should a member state violate the EU's principles and values. Article 46 would mention for the first time the possibility of voluntary withdrawal of a member state from the Union and the institutional consequences of withdrawal. Giscard said it was logical to include a right of secession because the constitutional treaty would probably have an unlimited life. This provision attracted considerable media attention, even though an exit clause had featured in other draft Constitutions, including Duff's outline constitutional treaty of September.

While part one was explained in some detail, parts two and three of the skeleton simply listed headlines. The draft explained that part two, detailing Union policies and their implementation, would contain the legal bases and in each area specify the type of competence (outlined in title III of part one) and the acts and procedures (title V of part one) to be applied.

As internal EU policies, part two listed the internal market (free movement of persons and services and goods); economic and monetary policy; policies in 'other specific areas' (nine, ranging from competition policy to research and development); internal security; and areas where the Union might take supporting action (employment, health, industry, culture and education). External action formed a second cluster of policies, and grouped together commercial policy, development cooperation, external aspects of internal policies, CSFP and conclusion of international agreements. Defence formed a separate category of policy. So too did institutional, procedural and budgetary provisions grouped under a general heading of the functioning of the Union.

According to Giscard, some 205 of the 414 articles making up the existing treaties would remain unchanged; 136 would be altered slightly while 73 would have to be substantially rewritten or regrouped.

The skeleton received a strong initial welcome from the conventionnels of the European Parliament. Hänsch hailed it as a document of 'courageous realism' that identified the most important elements of the future EU. Duff, while regretting the absence of a reference to the people in the first article, nonetheless pronounced it a 'splendid basis' for future work. 'It allows for a radical re-foundation of the EU along explicitly federal lines – entrenching the community system, clarifying objectives and strengthening parliamentary democracy at the European level.'

Britain's Peter Hain managed to sound both enthusiastic and sceptical. The text was a 'good start' and 'an important step towards settling our Constitution for a generation or more'. Hain took issue with the idea of changing the Union's name. 'The European Union is a successful brand name, a name we are all proud of.' The United States of Europe and United Europe were unacceptable. 'United States of Europe implies a superstate. United Europe looks to me like a football team.' Giscard, however, was in no mood to let United Europe drop.

Publication of the skeleton gave a palpable boost to the Convention's proceedings and structured the subsequent discussions. It defined the form of the eventual constitutional treaty, although this was to have four rather than three parts after the Convention decided that the Charter should be included in full as its part two.

The skeleton was felicitously timed – and that was thanks to pressure from rank and file conventionnels. Kerr originally wanted to delay production of an outline treaty until the start of 2003. Had that been the case, the story of the Convention and its constitutional treaty could have been very different. Unknown to Giscard, Commission president, Romano Prodi, had commissioned a small group of officials to produce a full draft treaty in July. The Commission document – code-named Penelope – appeared in December, and, because of a bungled launch, never had the influence that the Commission president hoped for or the draft deserved. Had Penelope pre-empted the skeleton, she would have dominated the subsequent debate.

Part II

Issues and Working Groups

CHAPTER 6
The Issues: Broad Constitutional Questions

Publication of the skeleton proved an important turning point for the Convention. The text mapped out clearly the route it had to follow and threw the issues that had arisen during the eight months since the Convention's launch into sharp relief. Some of these – but not all – were clarified by the efforts of the working groups which, reporting during the autumn of 2002, added flesh to the skeleton's bones.

The issues, although often overlapping, can be categorised in four groups: broad constitutional issues; competences and their implementation; new or expanding policy areas, and the Union's institutions.

6.1   A CONSTITUTION OR A CONSTITUTIONAL TREATY?

One of the uncertainties surrounding the Convention was whether its goal was to draft a Constitution or a constitutional treaty. Giscard had muddled the terms in his speech at the Convention's opening ceremony. Consensus on a single recommendation would 'open the way towards a Constitution for Europe', he declared, only to add, 'In order to avoid any disagreement over semantics, let us agree now to call it a 'constitutional treaty for Europe.'

The two terms – Constitution and constitutional treaty – were bandied about without clear distinction throughout the life of the Convention. Clarification was important because it reflected on the nature of the Union. A Constitution implied a structure with independent sovereignty in the form of a self-sufficient source of political power deriving from the people and was thus the goal of federalists and keen integrationists. A constitutional treaty was agreed and ratified by the member states, which conferred powers on the Union. It was therefore a goal that could appeal to conventionnels more rooted in the nation-state.

Drawing the distinction was not easy, however, because of the Union's unique hybrid nature. The EU was clearly not a state, lacking such attributes as a large budget, the resources to implement Community law and the traditional means of coercion in the shape of an army or police. But the treaties went far beyond the normal parameters of international treaties. They provided for institutions with substantial powers and established a rule of law with a Court of Justice, which had established the primacy of Union law from an early stage.

The skeleton shed limited light on the problem. On the one hand, it made clear the Convention's goal was to draft a constitutional treaty. But it also promised many of the attributes of a Constitution, by outlining a first part that would detail the Union's values and objectives, a bill of rights in the shape of the Union's Charter of Fundamental Rights, powerful institutions, the division of powers and political procedures, including elements of accountability and democracy.

It left unclear key issues that needed to be defined if the final draft was really to be a constitutional treaty rather than a Constitution. One such issue was the conferral of powers. The skeleton never mentioned that the member states conferred power on the Union. Other important issues were the procedures for ratification and revision of the eventual draft. The skeleton gave no details of what it called part three[1] the 'general and final provisions', which would include these procedures.

Future amendments were an area of importance for distinguishing between a Constitution and a constitutional treaty. A normal feature of Constitutions with independent sovereignty was inclusion of the power of amendment among their political procedures. The position, as regards future amendments in the skeleton, was unexplained and remained unclear until the Convention's end because there was insufficient time to achieve a consensus before the June 2003 European Council in Thessaloniki, and no mandate afterwards to finish what by then had become Part IV of the constitutional treaty.

The final text, as presented to the Italian presidency, took over existing treaty provisions,[2] which stipulated unanimous agreement and ratification by all member states 'in accordance with their respective constitutional requirements'. This result was a constitutional treaty, as Amato elegantly underlined after the Convention finished. Asked just after the 13 June agreement on part I, whether he was proud of his 'baby', Amato replied 'Yes. I am proud. But I wanted a girl, and we have given birth to a boy.' As he elaborated in an article for *Il Sole 24 Ore*, 'Constitution' in Italian is a feminine noun while 'treaty' is masculine.

---

[1] Part IV in texts from May 2003.
[2] TEU Article 48.

6.2   THE UNION'S VALUES AND OBJECTIVES

The Convention's first task in its listening phase was to debate what was expected of the European Union and the missions it should undertake.

The Union's values and objectives were important questions. Its values would set standards for membership. Its objectives would justify its existence to exercise certain powers at the European level and would therefore shape its constitutional identity. In this respect, the Union differed from a nation-state where a Constitution would exist to describe how the state should function. The way the Union's values and objectives were defined was also important if the Convention were to produce a constitutional treaty, which would be easy to understand and so help bridge the gap between the Union and its citizens.

In the skeleton, the outline of article 2 set out as Union values: human dignity, fundamental rights, democracy, the rule of law, tolerance and respect for obligations, and for international law. Giscard was at pains to draw a distinction between the values in article 2, which were based on those in article 6 of the Treaty on European Union, and those in the Union's Charter of Fundamental Rights. This was because the values in article 2 could be used to initiate procedures for sanctioning member states for 'serious breach' of the Union's principles and values under article 45 of the skeleton.[3] For this reason, the article had to concentrate on core essentials – a point taken on board by the Praesidium when it set about turning the skeleton into the constitutional treaty's first draft articles early in 2003.

Article 3 of the skeleton outlined 'general objectives' and listed just eight. These were:

- protection of the common values, interests and independence of the Union
- promotion of economic and social cohesion
- strengthening of the internal market, and of economic and monetary union
- promotion of a high level of employment and a high degree of social protection
- a high level of environmental protection
- encouragement for technological and scientific progress
- creation of an area of liberty, security and justice

---

3 Corresponding to article 7 of TEU.

- development of a common foreign and security policy, and a common defence policy, to defend and promote the Union's values in the wider world.

The idea was that article 3 should give general objectives rather than a vast laundry list of all the Union's policies. The treaty's second part, which was presented in the skeleton in headline terms only, would appear later and present the objectives and their legal bases in far more detail than most Constitutions. But because, when introducing the skeleton, Giscard stressed the important role that the objectives had in defining the Union, the conventionnels proposed a mass of additional objectives after the Praesidium presented its first draft articles three months later. The lists of values and objectives were tweaked further in the Intergovernmental Conference that followed the Convention.

6.3   RELIGION AND THE CONSTITUTION

The skeleton was silent on the role, if any, of God in the constitutional treaty. But the issue of religion had surfaced in the debates on the Union's missions and values and was to prove a contentious subplot in the life of the Convention and the IGC that followed it.

There were heated exchanges in the previous Charter convention over proposals to include a reference to Europe's religious heritage in the Charter's preamble.[4] Various factors conspired to make religion a big issue in the discussions on the constitutional treaty. One was the participation of strongly Catholic Poland in the Convention. Convention members from the German Christian Democrat and Christian Social parties, like their predecessors in the Charter convention, also considered the issue of key importance. There was extensive lobbying of the Convention from religious groups, especially during the hearing of NGOs in June 2002. The lobbying went to the highest levels, as Giscard found when he met Pope John Paul II in Rome three days after the publication of the skeleton. Earlier that month, the Pope had underlined the importance of Europe's Christian roots and God's role as the author of life, human dignity and human rights.

On the other hand, there were strong arguments against. Europe was not just home to Christians. It was home to millions of Muslims and members of

---

4 The issue of whether religion should be mentioned in a reference to Europe's 'spiritual and moral heritage' was only solved by a translating sleight of hand by which the word 'religious' was dropped from the phrase in ten of the EU's languages while the German text said 'spiritual-religious [geistig-religiösen] and moral heritage'.

other faiths. Concentrated among the Socialist, Liberal and Green political families and among the French conventionnels, the supporters of the secular tradition in European politics were equally vocal and determined that God should have no place in the Constitution. Giscard gave an indication of his own position in his speech to the Convention's opening ceremony. He painted a picture of European history in which religion, and more specifically Christianity, was notable by its absence. 'Let us not forget that from the ancient world of Greece and Rome until the age of the Enlightenment, our continent has made the fundamental contributions to humanity: reason, humanism and freedom', he declared. These sentiments were echoed more than a year later when he wrote the first draft of the constitutional treaty's preamble – with the issue of God and the Constitution still unresolved.

6.4   THE LEGAL PERSONALITY AND THE END OF THE PILLARS

There was no hedging in the skeleton when it came to the Union's legal personality. Settling the issue once and for all, it said it would have 'explicit recognition'. The preliminary draft of 28 October was so clear because the working group on legal personality reported on 1 October[5] and came out in favour of a single legal personality for the Union in unambiguous terms.

One of the more pronounced oddities of the existing European treaty structure was that the Union had no explicit legal personality while the three communities that it encompassed (the European Communities, Euratom and the now defunct European Coal and Steel Community) did. This legacy of the Maastricht Treaty on Union meant the EU, unlike its three sub-units, could not represent Europe, sign treaties, go to or be summoned by a court, become a member of international organisations or accede to international conventions, such as the European Convention on Human Rights.

The group on legal personality was chaired by Giuliano Amato. Working swiftly and effectively, it demonstrated how clever chairmanship could extract the most from a modest brief and expressed views, which pointed to how the eventual constitutional treaty should look. The group was asked to examine the consequences of explicit recognition of an EU legal personality and its merger with that of the European Community, and whether these moves would help simplify the treaties.

---

[5] CONV 305/02.

Amato's report concluded the EU should have its own explicit legal personality, with only William Abitbol, the French eurosceptic MEP, objecting. The single personality, the group argued, would boost the EU's effectiveness, create legal certainty and transparency, and give the Union a higher profile *vis-à-vis* foreign states and its own citizens. The Union would become a 'subject of international law' and as such could engage in all types of international action.

Consideration of the EU's legal personality triggered quite wide-ranging thought about the final shape of the constitutional treaty. Amato's report foreshadowed the skeleton by expressing a preference for a new treaty that would combine the existing treaties into a 'single constitutional text'. This would be sub-divided into two parts – a basic part comprising constitutional provisions and a second part that would codify and reorganise all other operational and policy provisions in the existing Union and Community treaties. It also concluded that a single legal personality should mean abandoning the EU's pillar structure, which would look anachronistic in the new circumstances.

6.5   THE CHARTER OF FUNDAMENTAL RIGHTS

A list of human rights is part of most constitutions but was missing from the EU treaties. Protecting fundamental rights, however, had gradually grown as an issue in Union affairs. Article 6 of the Treaty on European Union pledged that the Union would respect fundamental rights as guaranteed by the European Convention on Human Rights (ECHR), and as they resulted from the constitutional provisions of the member states. Since the 1970s, the Court of Justice had built up case law, deriving from the principle that fundamental rights formed an integral part of the general principles of EU law. During the same period, the European Parliament and Commission tried on several occasions to strengthen the protection of fundamental rights in the Union.

The Charter of Fundamental Rights was drawn up by the EU's only previous convention in 2000. Consisting of a preamble and 54 articles, it was presented to EU leaders at their informal European Council in Biarritz in October 2000 and solemnly proclaimed in Nice two months later. Both the Nice and Laeken declarations raised the question of incorporating the Charter in a new EU constitutional treaty. The Laeken declaration also urged consideration of whether the Union should accede to the ECHR.

Incorporation of the Charter was an important goal for integrationists. It would supply the constitutional treaty with its bill of rights and give the

Charter legal force. In addition, as the European Parliament pointed out,[6] an enhanced status for the Charter would help put fundamental rights at the heart of integrating the Union's old and new member states.

Accession to the ECHR would reinforce the position of the Union as a community of human values. It had been debated for more than 20 years and while a secretariat study detailed plenty of technical issues there seemed to be nothing that political will could not overcome, especially with the issue of the Union's legal personality apparently resolved.

However, the Convention had to overcome one big political issue: Britain's fears that the Charter, if incorporated, could be used by the Court of Justice or the Commission to extend Union competence to the UK's industrial and social legislation.

Despite its non-binding character, the Union's legal authorities had started to take account of the Charter following its proclamation at the Nice summit. There were several cases of an advocate general at the Court of Justice using the Charter to identify fundamental rights in the Union. The Court of First Instance had invoked articles of the Charter as confirmation of the constitutional traditions of member states. From March 2001, the Commission had decided to subject proposals for legislation to a Charter compatibility check.[7]

On the other hand, the Charter, as proclaimed, contained so-called 'horizontal clauses' (articles 51 and 52) intended to block it from being used to change laws in member states where the Union had no competence. Britain feared the horizontal clauses might not apply to several of the Charter articles, which dealt mainly with social and 'aspirational' issues and which were based neither on the EU treaties nor the ECHR. London wanted the horizontal clauses tightening. The British position was summed up by UK prime minister, Tony Blair, in a speech on the future of Europe on 28 November in Cardiff, the capital of Wales.[8]

> Though we welcome, of course, a declaration of basic rights common to all European citizens and have ourselves incorporated the European Convention on Human Rights directly into British law, we cannot support a form of treaty incorporation that would enlarge EU competence over national legislation. There cannot be new legal rights given by such means, especially in areas such

---

[6] CONV 368/02.
[7] See footnotes on page 4, CONV 116/02.
[8] 'A clear course for Europe', filed under speeches on the Downing Street website www.number-10.gov.uk

as industrial law where we have long and difficult memories of the battles fought to get British law in proper order.

Although the UK eventually agreed to incorporation of the Charter, formal acceptance came only after securing additional assurances.

Britain's reservations about the Charter had a bearing on discussions over how it might be incorporated in the constitutional treaty. The issue was left open in the October skeleton. The options ranged from simply 'attaching' it to the treaties as a solemn declaration; through making reference to the Charter, either indirectly or directly, in the new text or its preamble; to annexing it to the planned constitutional treaty as a protocol; to insertion in full of the Charter's 54 articles. Positioning was important because it would influence the Charter's legal value. According to the secretariat, a legally binding quality for the Charter could only be assured through direct reference to its text in the constitutional treaty text, annexation as a protocol or the Charter's full incorporation in the final treaty.

When Vitorino's group reported[9] in late October, it decided that the Charter should be incorporated in the constitutional treaty and that the Union should be able to accede to the ECHR, while leaving the modalities unclear in both cases. Vitorino stressed the group's decisions would give no new competences to the Union. There would be no change to the Charter, save some editorial tweaking to make it fully compatible with the treaty. Even if the Charter were legally binding, the group said jurisdiction in action relating to it would lie principally in the courts of the member states.

The group recognised that it would be up to the Council of Ministers to decide unanimously on the separate issue of the EU acceding to the ECHR. But it gave the idea powerful backing by stating that accession would highlight the moral and ethical commitments of the EU and give citizens the same degree of protection of fundamental rights at EU level as they enjoy in their own countries.

Discussion of the Charter was closely bound up with the issue of Union citizenship. The skeleton referred ambiguously to 'dual' European and national citizenship where the individual would be 'free to use either, as he or she chooses, with the rights and duties attaching to each'. However, the Convention eventually settled for the option in force since the Maastricht Treaty, which made Union citizenship additional to national citizenship and conferred a series of rights. These were the right to move and reside freely

---

[9] CONV 354/02.

within the territory of the member states; the right to vote and stand as a candidate in European Parliament and local elections in the citizen's state of residence; the right to the protection of any member state in third countries where a citizen's own country of nationality is not represented; the rights of petition to the European Parliament and access to the Ombudsman, and the right to correspond with EU institutions and advisory bodies in any of the then 11, and later 20, official EU languages

CHAPTER 7
Who Does What and How?
Competences and their Implementation

7.1   COMPETENCES: THE RESPECTIVE ROLES OF UNION AND MEMBER STATES

That there was a need for clarification of competences was clear. Citizens and politicians, as Giscard told the Convention, needed to know the responsibilities of the EU and the member states. They had to plough through hundreds of articles in two treaties to do this. This complexity resulted in misunderstandings and weakened the EU's credibility.

The issue of competences was put on the EU reform agenda, largely at German behest. Ahead of the December 2000 Nice summit, the German Länder had threatened to refuse to ratify the resulting treaty unless there was progress towards a definition or 'catalogue' of competences to curb what they considered unwarranted intrusion into their affairs by 'Brussels'. Although other governments, including the UK and France, supported Germany, it was mainly at the instigation of Gerhard Schröder, the German chancellor, that the Nice conclusions asked 'how to establish and monitor a more precise delimitation of powers between the European Union and the member states, reflecting the principle of subsidiarity'.

The Laeken declaration, a year later, asked the Convention to consider how the division of competences could be made more transparent, whether any reorganisation of competence was needed and how to avoid any new division of competences leading to a 'creeping expansion' of Union powers at the expense of the member states. The Laeken summit even raised the possibility of the Union restoring some powers to member states.

Competences were a big issue early in the Convention. An important stimulus was a European Parliament report drawn up by Alain Lamassoure, the French EPP MEP and Convention member, and agreed in April 2002. With the benefit of hindsight, the Lamassoure report[1] was a prescient document. Its suggestions included merging the treaties into a single text,

---

[1] 'Report on the division of competences between the European Union and the member states', European Parliament consitutional affairs committee. On the Parliament's website: refs A5-0133/2002 and PE 304.276.

which would have two parts – one constitutional and the other relating to carrying out policies – and giving the Union a single legal personality. The Lamassoure report shied away from rigid lists. It pinpointed the competences shared between the Union and member states as the biggest difficulty and called for ground rules in this 'grey area' that would conform with the principles of subsidiarity and proportionality.[2]

A plenary discussion on competences in April appeared to put paid to the idea of a specific catalogue of competences. When Erwin Teufel, representing the German Länder, floated the idea of two catalogues that would clearly define the respective roles of the Union and the member states, it was rejected by representatives of several governments, including Germany, France and the UK. Britain's Peter Hain warned that a catalogue would create 'a rigid, static, legalistic body of rules,' which would lack flexibility.

In May 2002, a background paper[3] from the secretariat acknowledged the existing treaties were 'complex and impenetrable' on the issue of competences. It also highlighted criticisms that the Union had used articles 94, 95 and 308[4] of the European Communities Treaty to act in areas where it was not competent and so infringed the member states' powers.

The October skeleton signalled a hybrid solution, which would include both principles and detailed or indicative lists of different type of competence. Article 7 set out the principles of Union action, stating that this must be carried out in accordance with the treaty, within the competences conferred by it, and in compliance with the principles of subsidiarity and proportionality. Article 8 outlined the rules following from the principles. These blended a federal tone[5] with a promise to involve national parliaments in the rules for 'effective monitoring of subsidiarity and proportionality'. The skeleton promised that article 9 would list the categories of Union competence; article 10 the areas of exclusive Union competence; article 11 the areas of competence shared between the Union and member states and article 12 the areas in which the Union supports or coordinates action by

---

[2] Subsidiarity will be discussed in detail later in this chapter. Proportionality meant that the content and form of a given Union action should not exceed what was necessary to achieve the desired objective.

[3] CONV 47/02.

[4] Articles 94 and 95 detailed the rules for 'approximating' laws to achieve the internal market. Article 308 was the so-called 'flexibility clause', which allowed the Council, deciding unanimously, to take steps not specified in the treaty to achieve an objective of the Union in the course of operating the 'common market'.

5 Thus 'any competence not conferred on the Union by the Constitution rests with the member states'. (Emphasis added.)

member states, but has no competence to legislate. Article 13 promised to deal with common policies subject to specific rules, such as the common defence and foreign and security policies, and the policy on police matters and crime.

Shortly after publication of the skeleton, work on competences hit trouble. The complementary competences working group, chaired by Henning Christophersen, produced a confusing report,[6] which was very badly received. Admittedly, Christophersen faced problems. The focus of his group was difficult to define and seemed tangential to the 'grey area' of shared Union and member state competences identified by Lamassoure. There was initially no clear definition of complementary competences, although Christophersen described them as covering 'areas in which intervention by the community is limited to supplementing, supporting or coordinating the action of member states' and where the power to adopt legislative rules remained with the member states. That meant education, vocational training, youth, culture, health protection, industrial policy, employment policy, the supervision on national budgets, civil protection, tourism and sport.

But faced with what might have been a narrow brief, Christophersen chose to give his appointed task the widest possible interpretation. He saw the working group's job as clarifying the respective responsibilities of the member states and the Union. He then proceeded to tread on various toes. To some he appeared to be trying to reintroduce the catalogue of competences through the back door. His attempt to rechristen complementary competences 'supporting measures' provoked fury when it was explained that in normal circumstances, these would not be legally binding. Several conventionnels noted that such a position would have prevented the launch of some very popular Union policies, such as the Erasmus student exchange programme. Many federalist delegates were further angered that his group suggested a rewording of the expression 'an ever closer union' in article 1 of the treaty on Union.

Speaking for the EPP members of the Convention, the normally mild and courteous Lamassoure brutally rejected the report and, to loud applause, said its conclusions were useless: 'They cannot be explained to the public and they are of no use to decision makers'. Klaus Hänsch, for the PES group in the European Parliament, said some of the conclusions would make the Constitution more complex and would undermine the powers of the European Parliament.

---

[6] CONV 375/1/02, 4 November 2002.

At the end of a difficult plenary session for Christophersen, it was announced that the Praesidium would return to the issue in the future. To rub salt in the wounds, Dehaene told the press that the report's problems may have resulted from Christophersen leaving its drafting to his own (Danish) assistant rather than to the Convention secretariat. The report marked the most striking failure of the idea of delegating important preparatory work to working groups.

The discussion over competences took another twist towards the end of the study phase when the Commission, in its Penelope text[7], took an entirely different approach. Instead of classifying competences, the Commission's Penelope document of December highlighted various gradations of responsibility given to the Union. The Union's internal policies would thus be classified in terms of principal policies, flanking policies and complementary actions and so avoid any rigid classification of powers, which, as the Commission had explained in its May 2002 submission to the Convention[8] 'would have the disadvantage of artificially straitjacketing the Union's capacity for action'. This confusion made the task of the Praesidium all the more difficult once it started drafting articles on competences.

7.2   SUBSIDIARITY AND ITS MONITORING

As the Nice declaration and the skeleton made clear, subsidiarity was closely bound up with the issue of competences. Nevertheless, the Convention made good progress at clarifying the issues surrounding subsidiarity.

Subsidiarity was originally a principle of the Catholic church. It was introduced into Union law in the Maastricht Treaty, which ruled, that in areas outside the EU's exclusive competence, it should take action 'only if and insofar as the objectives of the proposed action cannot be sufficiently achieved by the member states and can therefore, by reason of the scale or effects of the proposed action, be better achieved by the Community'. Application of the subsidiarity principle was defined in a protocol attached to the Amsterdam Treaty, which bound the Union's institutions to compliance. It said Community action should be as simple as possible and that the Community should legislate only to the extent necessary. The Commission was enjoined to consult widely before proposing legislation and justify the relevance of its proposals with regard to subsidiarity.

---

[7] Working document at http://europa.eu.int/futurum/comm/const51202_en.htm
[8] COM 2002 247 final.

But the Laeken declaration clearly indicated something was amiss when it spoke of citizens not wanting 'European institutions inveigling their way into every nook and cranny of life'. One problem, as Jean-Claude Piris, the head of the Council's legal service, told the subsidiarity working group,[9] was the word 'better' in the Maastricht Treaty article, which meant subsidiarity was 'an essentially political and subjective principle'. The Court of Justice, which monitored compliance, had never annulled an act on the grounds of infringement of subsidiarity.

The working group, chaired by Inigo Méndez de Vigo, thus had to ask how subsidiarity could be monitored in the most effective manner possible, whether a monitoring mechanism or procedure should be established, and whether this should be of a political or legal nature.

The group, which was the first of the initial six working groups, completed its work around the middle of September and presented its findings to the 4 October plenary session.[10] It agreed to what amounted to a module of a constitutional treaty in readiness for the skeleton that would come from the Praesidium later that month. The group demonstrated that the Convention could move swiftly and pragmatically to produce concise and easily understandable political results.

The group managed successfully to bring together the interests of the Convention's federalists and its national parliamentarians, the component that had, hitherto, proved difficult to integrate into the Convention's proceedings. That was largely because Méndez de Vigo avoided a narrow partisan approach when chairing the group, although he was criticised for this during the 4 October debate by fellow MEPs who thought his proposals were too generous to national parliaments.

The working group concluded that subsidiarity could be both applied and monitored better. But it came out against the creation of any new monitoring body or the creation of a 'Mr or Mrs Subsidiarity' in the Commission. Instead, it set out ways in which the Commission should take greater heed of subsidiarity in drafting legislation (including a 'subsidiarity sheet' in each draft law) and set in motion measures to strengthen the protocol on subsidiarity.

More significant, it proposed the creation of an 'early warning system' allowing national parliaments to join in the monitoring of compliance with

---

[9] Working group document WD 04 WG 1.
[10] CONV 286/02.

the principle of subsidiarity. Thus, the Commission would have to tell each national parliament (and each chamber in bicameral parliaments) of its legislative proposals at the same time as the Council and European Parliament. Using a football metaphor, national parliaments could then raise a yellow card within a six-week period and object to the presidents of the Commission, Parliament and Council if the proposal appeared to contravene the subsidiarity principle. Depending on how many parliaments raised objections, the Community legislator (the Council of Ministers and the European Parliament) would decide what to do. If the legislator received a 'significant number of opinions from one-third of parliaments', the Commission would re-examine its proposal and, on the strength of the re-examination, might decide to maintain, amend or withdraw it.

Should these political steps yield no results, the aggrieved parliament could refer the matter to the European Court of Justice (ECJ). In a move that would give new power to the hitherto obscure Committee of the Regions, the working group suggested that it, too, could turn to the Court in certain cases. That would be when the Committee had been consulted and found that a piece of legislation was against the principle of subsidiarity and yet where the Council and Parliament had carried on regardless. The working group drew the line at giving similar rights to regions with legislative capacities, such as the German Länder.

The debate in the plenary and the concerns of MEPs prompted some further reflection in the Praesidium about aspects of the early warning scheme. The worries centred on the scale of national parliament involvement and whether one-third of national parliaments was sufficient to require the Commission to re-examine a proposal. Another concern was whether each chamber in bicameral national parliaments should be treated equally.

But broad support for the idea showed how different elements of the Convention – MEPs, member states, national parliaments and the Committee of the Regions (which was an observer) – could achieve a result with something for all and which avoided creating a new bureaucracy.

The subsidiarity group's final report hailed the early warning system as 'innovative and bold' and trumpeted it as 'the first time in the history of the European construction' that national parliaments would be involved in the EU legislative process. Although the criticisms of the MEPs took some of the shine off that hyperbole, the report's conclusions represented a useful step forward.

7.3   THE ROLE OF NATIONAL PARLIAMENTS

The role of national parliaments in EU affairs was a matter of concern for at least a decade and closely bound up with the debate about bringing the Union closer to the citizen. Much national legislation in the economic and social spheres resulted from Union directives, raising questions over whether national parliaments were consulted in an adequate and timely manner and whether they exercised sufficient scrutiny over developments in 'Brussels'. These issues became more pressing with the Union becoming increasingly involved in 'new' policy areas such as police and judicial cooperation, economic policy coordination, and the common foreign and security policy.

The member states had annexed a declaration to the Maastricht Treaty on the role of national parliaments, which called for a 'stepped up' exchange of information between the European Parliament and national parliaments. In it, governments promised to ensure that national parliaments received Commission proposals 'in good time' for information or examination. To enhance the opportunities for scrutiny, a protocol was attached to the Amsterdam Treaty, which specified that a six-week breathing space should elapse between the publication of legislative proposals and their being placed on the Council agenda for adoption as either an act or a common position of the Council.

But worries that national parliaments were insufficiently involved with the Union persisted. During 2000, Joschka Fischer in his Humboldt speech and Tony Blair in his Warsaw speech urged for an enhanced EU role for national parliaments, in each case suggesting they send representatives to a second chamber in Brussels. One of the four major points of the Nice declaration was the 'the role of national parliaments in the European architecture'.

The Laeken declaration asked whether national parliaments should be represented in a new institution alongside the Council and the European Parliament, whether they should act in EU areas where the European Parliament had no competence, and whether they should engage in the issue of competences by the preliminary checking of compliance with the subsidiarity principle.

In turn, the Convention's national parliaments working group was asked to look at their current role in the Union, the national arrangements that functioned best, and whether any new mechanisms or procedures were required at national or European level. Chaired by Gisela Stuart, the German-born British Labour MP, the group proceeded to look at national scrutiny arrangements to assess whether benchmarking or measuring best practice might do some good. It set out to examine if the Amsterdam protocol had improved information flows or whether an absence of transparency in the Council obstructed scrutiny by national parliaments of EU legislative procedures. Also on its agenda was the idea of a second chamber and whether this should focus on monitoring subsidiarity, or even foreign policy and justice and home affairs, which were largely intergovernmental. It worked closely with the subsidiarity working group.

Stuart was unlucky in that the important issue of subsidiarity had been already successfully handled by the working group chaired by Méndez de Vigo. Her group, moreover, soon became the battleground between supporters of an additional parliamentary chamber and MEPs who were determined – successfully as it turned out – to protect the legislative prerogatives of the European Parliament. When the group finally reported,[11] it was difficult to avoid a sense of anti-climax. Thinly disguised criticism came from the highest level – Giscard – when he summed up the 28 October plenary debate on Stuart's report. Hinting at a lack of ambition in the group, the president twice warned the Convention needed to be imaginative and must go beyond simply improving existing treaties.

Stuart's report reinforced the main findings of the subsidiarity working group by underlining that national parliaments should play a key role in monitoring the principle of subsidiarity. It added its voice to calls for the Council to enact all legislation in public and other activities 'with open doors as much as possible'. It recommended that the Amsterdam protocol be strengthened. The idea of possibly incorporating the Convention method in the planned treaty for preparing future amendments was innovative. The suggestion that COSAC – the Conference of Community Affairs Bodies of the Parliaments of the European Community – could become a forum for exchanging ideas of best practice in monitoring EU policies was modest but sensible, and would give greater purpose to a little-known talking shop.

The report's broad conclusions were worthy rather than gripping. It rejected any new institution. But the group's suggestion that the Convention should examine the desirability of periodic meetings of national parliaments and the European Parliament to debate important and strategic issues helped keep alive Giscard's unpopular idea of a Congress of European and national legislators. For that, the president was grateful.

---

[11] CONV 353/02.

7.4   THE EXERCISE OF POWER

The question 'who does what?' usually invites the supplementary queries 'and how?' and 'with what effect?' It was therefore inevitable that attempts to clarify competences and subsidiarity should lead to questions about the way the Union exercised its powers.

But other factors made a thorough examination of the Union's instruments of power imperative. The Laeken declaration put the highly political issue of extending qualified majority voting (QMV) in the Council of Ministers at the expense of unanimity on the Convention's agenda. For many conventionnels, the Union's prospective enlargement to 25 or more member states spelled blockage unless the QMV issue was reopened less than two years after heads of government agreed a limited extension of majority voting at the acrimonious Nice summit.

In pondering how to increase the democratic legitimacy and transparency of the Union's institutions, the Laeken declaration asked whether the EU should extend 'codecision', the procedure which gives the European Parliament equal powers in legislating with the Council of Ministers, and which had been extended in the Amsterdam and Nice treaties. Another issue was whether the codecision procedures could be simplified and speeded up.

Enlargement also prompted questions over what to do when small groups of member states wanted to move ahead with policies for greater integration which not all Union members could accept. The history of the Union was full of expedients for dealing with such cases, such as the British opt-out from the single currency. The Amsterdam and Nice summits had first created and then improved a mechanism known as 'enhanced cooperation', by which groups of countries would be permitted to move ahead without destroying the Union's spirit of solidarity. But enhanced cooperation was fearsomely complicated and remained untried throughout the life of the Convention. One of the tasks of the Convention was to make enhanced cooperation more user-friendly.

The inventiveness of past Union policy makers added to the challenges facing the Convention. What should be done with new policy instruments that were not properly embedded in the treaties? One such instrument was the 'open method of coordination', adopted with gusto at the March 2000 Lisbon summit as the way to boost the Union's economic performance, and based on the principle of member states tailoring their policies in response to a system of benchmarking and policy targets.

The Nice declaration merely nibbled at these problems. Reflecting Verhofstadt's interest in simplification, the Laeken declaration was less circumspect. After noting that 'successive amendments to the treaty have on each occasion resulted in a proliferation of instruments', it concluded that 'the key question is therefore whether the Union's various instruments should not be better defined and whether their number should not be reduced'.

The dreadful complexity of the Union's legal instruments was exposed in a detailed note from the Praesidium,[12] published in June 2002. This recalled that, according to article 249 of the European Communities Treaty (TEC), the Council, the Parliament and the Commission could 'make regulations and issue directives, take decisions, make recommendations or deliver opinions'. Of these, the two most important instruments were regulations, which were uniform laws applied with binding force throughout the Union, and directives, which were also binding, but where it was left to the member state to decide the form and methods necessary to achieve the desired result.

However, this relatively simple categorisation of policy instruments had long been supplemented by 'specific instruments of diverse scope and nature, the legal effects of which are often difficult to pin down'. These included 'guidelines', 'framework programmes' and (more) 'decisions'. One of the more bizarre qualities of the EU treaties was that policy instruments would share the same name but have different characteristics. In some cases, they would be in different parts of the treaties, in other cases not.

A further complication was that the Treaty establishing the European Union (TEU) included instruments specific to the areas of foreign policy and justice and home affairs, which also had their own names and characteristics. In implementing foreign policy, the EU would resort to 'principles' and 'guidelines', 'common strategies', 'joint actions', 'common positions' or such mouthfuls as 'enhancing systematic cooperation'. The justice and home affairs field could boast 'common positions', 'framework decisions', (yet more) 'decisions' and 'conventions'.

That was not all, however: there was no clear system of assigning powers to the various Union institutions. Oddly, in a Union so influenced by France, the EU treaties had escaped the influence of Montesquieu, the 18th century French political philosopher, who first enunciated the principles of the separation of powers, which came to be incorporated in much constitutional law. 'Legislative power is not defined by the treaties; they merely define, on

---

[12] CONV 162/02.

a case by case basis, the respective roles of the institutions involved,' the Praesidium observed. As a result, these roles were exercised 'via a very large number of procedures'. There were, for example, nine different ways in which the Council and Parliament, acting together as the Community legislator, could pass legislation.[13] A later paper from the Praesidium,[14] which took account of the involvement of other institutions, found more than 22 different decision making procedures in the TEC for adopting legislative acts.

Inconsistencies abounded, often as a result of political compromises aimed at circumventing or mitigating blockages created by unanimous decision making. As a general rule, codecision meant QMV in the Council but articles 42, 47 and 151[15] of the TEC specified codecision with unanimity. In some articles, such as article 18 on freedom of movement, some provisions required QMV and others unanimity. Other articles[16] contained 'bridges' or *passerelles* which allowed issues to move from unanimity to QMV at a point in the future. Although one of the Convention's goals was to simplify procedures, it would resort to new *passerelles* for several issues as a way of loosening the stranglehold of unanimity over future policy actions.

A further problem was that the treaties made no distinction between legislative and executive acts, leaving the whole area of secondary legislation in limbo. There were also questions about the quality of EU legislation. Because political compromises often made matters very complicated, legislation sometimes took years to pass, leaving the Union ill-placed to adapt to a complex and fast changing world, especially in the economic sphere.

The October skeleton at least held out the promise of coherence with its plan to group nine articles covering the instruments and procedures to implement Union action in title V of the planned constitutional treaty.

The working group on simplification was chaired by Giuliano Amato, who had earlier successfully sorted out the Union's legal personality. As he took

---

[13] Qualified majority with codecision; qualified majority with cooperation; qualified majority with assent; qualified majority and straight opinion; qualified majority without involvement by the Parliament; unanimity with codecision; unanimity with assent; unanimity with a straight opinion and unanimity without participation by the Parliament.

[14] CONV 216/02.

[15] Article 42 covered social security for migrant workers; article 47 the implementation of directives coordinating professional qualifications and article 151 incentive measures for encouraging cultural cooperation.

[16] For example, article 67 on visa, asylum and immigration.

control, he commented: 'Nothing is more complicated than simplification.' Amato was not resigned, however. He believed simplification was vital for encouraging democracy and faith in EU institutions. If citizens could not understand the system, how could they 'identify its problems, criticise it and ultimately control it'. His working group came up with proposals[17] that simplified both legislative procedures and instruments and significantly fleshed out the constitutional skeleton. Giscard described them at the Copenhagen summit as 'audacious but reasonable'. In the 5 December plenary debate on simplification, Alain Lamassoure said Amato had 'earned the stripes of a founding father of Europe'.

On procedures, it produced two profoundly important recommendations:

- Codecision, by which the Council of Ministers and Parliament are equals in legislating, 'should become the general rule for the adoption of legislative acts'. There would be exceptions, as in cases of great political sensitivity for the member states. But to underline the significance of codecision, it should be known as the 'legislative procedure' in the constitutional treaty.

- QMV in the Council and codecision should automatically go hand in hand. This recommendation transformed the debate over the group's reports from the technical to the political, and drew the plenary into discussion over whether the EU should retain unanimity at all. Britain, Ireland and Sweden were swift to insist on its retention for tax policies. Speaking for France, Dominique de Villepin insisted codecision should not apply to farm policy.

Amato's group took the bewildering array of EU legal instruments – which he put at 15 – and proposed cutting them to *six*, giving them more understandable names in the process.

There would in future be two key, binding legislative instruments: *European laws*, which would correspond to existing regulations and therefore be acts of general application, binding in their entirety and directly applicable in all member states; and *EU framework laws*, equivalent to existing directives, which bind member states as regards the results to be achieved, but leave the choice of form and implementation to national authorities. In addition, there would be binding, non-legislative acts, to be known as *decisions*. These might be directed at specific addressees, as in the case of appointments or state aid decisions. The EU would also have two acts of non-binding force:

---

[17] CONV 424/02.

recommendations and *opinions*. The new names would apply to the instruments of the common foreign and security policy as well as the classic community instruments, although foreign policy decisions, for example, would be known as *CFSP decisions*.

Notwithstanding this simplification, there would still be scope for so-called non-standard acts, such as resolutions, conclusions and declarations. These are not covered by treaty, are technically non-binding and yet, as the example of European Council conclusions shows, can still be extremely important. Most of Amato's renamed instruments found an enthusiastic consensus in the Convention. Problems arose, however, in connection with a sixth type of instrument he suggested. These would be delegated acts, which, the report suggested, could in future be known as regulations.

Delegated acts would kill two birds with one stone. First, they would play an important part in clarifying the boundary between matters falling to the legislative and executive arms of the EU institutions and tackle the EU's failure to live up to Montesquieu's precepts for a proper division of powers. Introduction of delegated acts would solve a second problem: the absence of any provision in the EU's treaties for secondary legislation in the EU.

To deal with the division of powers, Amato's group proposed a clearer 'hierarchy of legislation' in which laws and framework laws would be categorised as legislative acts. These would be adopted on the basis of the treaty and generally adopted by codecision of the Council of Ministers and the Parliament. The delegated acts or regulations would form a second category of acts and normally be adopted by the Commission to flesh out or amend legislative acts in line with rules set by the Council and Parliament in their joint capacity as legislator. A third category would be implementing acts, which would put into force legislative or delegated acts. Implementing acts would normally be enacted by member states although the group mooted the possibility of giving regulatory authorities the right to adopt some implementing acts.

The need for secondary legislation became clear in 2000 and 2001 when the EU's ambitious 'action plan' to complete the single market in financial services was falling badly behind schedule, in part because of the extremely technical nature of the material that was beyond the ken of most Euro-parliamentarians. The EU was forced back on a complex, committee-based process of accelerated decision making, devised by a group of 'wise men' chaired by Alexandre Lamfalussy, a former Belgian central banker and one of the fathers of the euro. This was eventually introduced in 2002 after a year-long delay caused by an institutional tussle involving the Commission, the Council of Ministers and the European Parliament, at the heart of which lay parliamentary concerns over the ceding of democratic control to executive institutions.

Amato's group suggested control mechanisms, such as a parliamentary 'call back' to bring delegated acts back into the power of the legislator or 'sunset' clauses to force a review of the acts' operations if necessary. But, in a re-run of the controversy that prompted Parliament to hold up the Lamfalussy method of passing financial services legislation, the plenary debate revealed some concern that delegated acts might represent a shift in the EU's institutional balance. As a result, Giscard called for more detailed proposals covering delegated acts to be submitted to the Convention at a later date.

The 'open method of coordination' also proved controversial, even though it had been adopted in large measure at the March 2000 Lisbon summit. The group said the open coordination method should be given constitutional status – an approach backed by the economic governance and Social Europe working groups. But some MEPs – notably the UK liberal Andrew Duff and the Austrian Green Johannes Voggenhuber – opposed the idea. Voggenhuber warned that open coordination could bring intergovernmental practices 'by the back door'.

Amato's report contained some other important recommendations. It said EU institutions must sit in public when legislating. It touched on the need for better quality legislation, raising the issue of improved consultation at all stages of the process. Poor consultation had been a serious impediment to drawing up financial services legislation.

Stimulated by Amato's fertile mind, the group considered some issues outside its mandate, which were listed in an annex to its report. One is worthy of note here because it foreshadowed important issues to be tackled by the Convention in 2003. A 'large number' of group members proposed that the existence of a qualified majority in the Council should be determined by a double majority system – which would reflect a majority of states and a majority of populations – rather than the complex voting weights negotiated at Nice and liable to revision with each addition or subtraction of a member state.

7.5   THE UNION'S FINANCES

The Union's budget had been the cause of epic struggles among the member states in the 1980s, when Britain's Margaret Thatcher battled to reduce the UK's net contributions and vowed never to accept 'half a loaf'. The power of the European Parliament to sign off on the Union's budget provided the constitutional lever for Parliament to force the mass resignation of the Commission in 1999.

But, in general, the Union's budget had dropped out of the headlines through the 1990s. Agreements between the main institutions on budget discipline, and the introduction of multi-year financial perspective, had taken much political heat out of the annual setting of the Union's revenues and expenditure, which, in global terms, were tiny at a fraction above 1% of the Union's gross domestic product. Although there were ongoing problems of fraud against the Union – highlighted each year by highly critical reports from the Union's Court of Auditors – these were not really constitutional issues.

The problems surrounding the Union's finances that faced the Convention were far more prosaic and boiled down to improving procedures for agreeing the budget, which were baroque in their complexity and bewildering to all but the most dedicated of experts. An allied issue was to determine the proper role of the democratically elected European Parliament, which had no control over revenues and control over only half of the Union's spending. This limited power over spending reflected a distinction between obligatory spending (on farm guarantees) over which Parliament had no control and non-obligatory spending, which covered such outlays as the structural and regional funds, where Parliament had the main say.

Amato's group on simplification urged a streamlining of the annual EU budget process, so that setting expenditure would be a similar procedure to codecision between the Parliament and Council. The Commission would submit a preliminary draft budget to the Parliament and Council. Amato's group proposed the Council would decide by a qualified majority while Parliament would have the last word, or special provisions to prevent a stalemate.

In a move that would increase Parliament's influence, Amato's group called for an end to the distinction between compulsory and non-compulsory spending. It recommended that the Union's various budgetary principles, such as the need for a balance between revenue and spending, should be grouped in one article, rather than dotted around in separate articles as in the existing treaties. A further useful proposal was that the multi-annual financial perspective should be included in the constitutional treaty to give it more weight.

The revenue side of the budget was potentially more controversial because of pressure from some conventionnels, notably the Commission and Belgium, for the Union to be able to raise its own taxes in place of other funds known as 'own resources' that financed the budget. There were four categories of own resources. Two – agricultural levies and duties from the common customs tariff – were relatively transparent but of declining importance. The others, a percentage of notional value added tax revenues and a levy linked to GDP, were impenetrable once the Union's methods of calculation had been applied.

The advocates of the Community tax claimed not to want a source of higher revenues but instead a revenue stream that would be transparent and allow Europe's citizens to know how they were contributing to the Union. Taxes have never been popular. But, through the centuries, they have done wonders for creating political awareness. A Union tax or a system by which the Union might take a share of national taxes could help promote a European demos. For this reason, it was a step too far for the less integrationist governments, such as the UK, Sweden and Denmark.

The plenary discussion on Amato's report revealed consensus on the need to list the main budgetary principles of the Union but discord on other issues. Giscard concluded that the group's ideas for reform of procedure needed more study, with the result that the EU's finances remained unresolved until fairly late in the Convention.

CHAPTER 8
New or Expanding Policy Areas

The Convention met to consider more than just the constitutional aspects of Europe's future. It was also a response to the perception that the EU was punching below its weight in a very complex and dangerous world, made all the more perilous by the 11 September terrorist attacks on the US. Opinion polls showed strong support across the Union for a more effective European foreign policy and action to combat what Chris Patten, the European external affairs commissioner, called the 'dark side' of globalisation: organised crime, terrorism and trafficking in drugs and human beings. The successful introduction of euro notes and coins on 1 January 2002 in the 12 member countries of the euro-zone gave heart to those who wanted more integrated economic and social policies to balance the very lopsided construction of Europe's economic and monetary union with its federal monetary policy and decentralised fiscal policies. Discussion of the new and expanding policy areas of foreign and defence policy, economic and social policy and justice and home affairs crystallised differences between conventionnels over how far the constitutional treaty should promote greater integration. In particular, the process highlighted the UK's special position. Justice and home affairs apart, the conclusions of the working groups in these areas contrasted with the UK's predominantly intergovernmental approach and pointed to fundamental differences between the Blair government's vision of Europe and the strong integrationist group of conventionnels.

8.1   COMMON FOREIGN AND SECURITY POLICY

The European Council in Laeken made sure that Europe's global role was one of the main issues on the Convention's agenda. Among the three main challenges it identified was 'how to develop the Union into a stabilising factor and a model in the new, multi-polar world'. Europe's citizens, the Laeken declaration noted, wanted to see Europe more involved in foreign affairs, security and defence.[1] These were new areas of policy, compared with trade and development where the Union was long established as a powerful global operator.

---

[1] An assertion backed by opinion polls. Eurobarometer 58, conducted in autumn 2002, reported that 67% polled were for 'one common foreign policy among member states' and 73% for 'a common defence and security policy'.

But while there was general agreement that Europe should be more effective on the world stage, there was a profound disagreement about how best to go about it. On the one hand, the Commission and integration-minded member states such as Belgium, favoured an extension of the Community method into foreign policy. For the more sovereign-minded countries, which at Maastricht had negotiated that foreign and security policy should be intergovernmental, it was anathema to consider giving the Commission the right of initiative and using qualified majority voting in the Council. As was to become all too clear when the member states split over Iraq, the Union was also liable to deep divisions on the substance of specific policies.

The Union's external relations covered a very broad front indeed, with strikingly different responsibilities and policy instruments.

- The European Community always had responsibility for trade and development cooperation. It had grown to become the world's largest trading bloc and its largest provider of development aid, giving the Commission (and the commissioners for external relations, trade and development assistance) a very important say in external affairs.
- The Community and member states had a shared responsibility where internal Union policies had international ramifications. Thus the Commission, Council and member states would share the management of the external aspects of monetary policy, research and the environment, and where international agreements were needed to achieve internal Union objectives.
- Since the Maastricht Treaty, the common foreign and security policy (CFSP) existed to safeguard the Union's interests and values, strengthen peace and security, and promote international cooperation, democracy, the rule of law and human rights. This 'second pillar' of the Maastricht Treaty on European Union was the preserve of the member states and had its own intergovernmental procedures and policy instruments. To increase the effectiveness of CFSP, the member states agreed in the Amsterdam Treaty negotiation to create a high representative for foreign and security policy to assist the Council. Javier Solana, the first incumbent, began operating in 1999.

As Solana pointed out, a common foreign policy was not a single policy. The Union did not aspire to replace 15 national foreign ministries and 15 sovereign policies with a single policy run from Brussels.[2] The aim was to identify common ambitions and ways of pursuing shared aims that gave 'real added value'.

The common foreign and security policy was, therefore, what the member states chose to make of it. As the Praesidium[3] observed, within CFSP 'there are no limits to the potential scope and intensity of foreign policy. The decision whether and how far to use the existing options provided for in the treaty depends entirely on the political will of the different actors involved.' The rub was that common political will implied consensus and was therefore extremely difficult to achieve.

The important actors in CFSP were very different to those in the Community method of decision making. The European Council decided principles and general guidelines while the Council of Ministers (in its General Affairs and External Relations formation) developed common policies on the basis of the guidelines. There was the high representative, often deployed in trouble-shooter role, and the member state holding the six-month rotating presidency. The Commission was accorded only a minor role in CFSP although it had responsibility for managing the CFSP budget, which at 30 to 40 million euro a year was very small. It amounted to less than 1% of the Union's 6 billion euro external relations budget and was insignificant compared with the 70 billion euro[4] spent annually on external action by the member states.

The Laeken declaration had great expectations for the Union in the world. It couched its future role in high moral tones. Europe needed 'to shoulder its responsibilities in the governance of globalisation'. It would be 'a power resolutely doing battle against all violence, all terror and all fanaticism, but which also does not turn a blind eye to the world's heartrending injustices'. Europe wanted to change the course of world affairs to benefit the poorest as well as rich countries. It was 'a power seeking to set globalisation within a moral framework, in other words to anchor it in solidarity and sustainable development'.

But Laeken provided only a few detailed ideas on how the Convention should approach external affairs. The declaration twice asked how to develop a 'more coherent' common foreign policy and wondered whether

---

[2] Solana speech in Stockholm, 25 April 2002, filed as S0078/02 in the Secretary General's archived speeches on the Council website, www.ue.eu.int
[3] In a background paper CONV 161/02.
[4] According to Pierre de Boissieu in a hearing organised by the working group on external action on 15 October 2002.

the Petersberg tasks,[5] which defined the Union's commitments in crisis management, should be updated. In the section on institutions, it asked how to strengthen the synergy between the posts of high representative for foreign and security policy, held by Javier Solana, and the external affairs commissioner, Chris Patten, and whether to extend the EU's external representation 'in international fora'.

The end-October skeleton also made only a few references to 'the Union's external role. Article 3 listed among the objectives of the Union 'development of a common foreign and security policy, and a common defence policy, to defend and promote the Union's values in the wider world'. In title V on the implementation of Union action, there was a promise that articles 29 and 30 would set out the respective implementing procedures for the common foreign and security and the common defence policies but no details.

Near the end of the skeleton were two other provisions. Entitled 'Union action in the world', title VIII consisting of article 41 would deal with whoever represented the Union in international relations and define the role and future rank of the high representative, while taking account of competences already exercised by the Community. Dubbed 'the Union and its immediate environment', title IX, consisting of article 42, 'could contain' provisions to define a privileged relationship between the Union and its neighbouring states, should a decision be made to create such a relationship.

It was the job of Jean-Luc Dehaene, the former Belgian prime minister and vice-president of the Convention, to put flesh on these bones as chairman of the external relations working group. He set out to answer five very practical questions:

- How should the interests of the Union be defined and formulated?
- How should the consistency of Union activities be ensured, taking into account all the instruments at its disposal (including trade policy and development aid)?
- What should be done to speed decision making, giving attention to the possible extension of the Community method or easing unanimity?
- What were the lessons learned from creating the Solana post?
- What changes in the Union's external representation would boost its international influence?

---

[5] Listed in article 17.2 of the TEU and named after the German government guesthouse and conference centre outside Bonn where they were agreed.

Dehaene came to the Convention in the plenary session of 20 December with a substantial report on external affairs.[6] It was a skilfully drafted work that glossed over divisions inside the group. The report was studded with references to 'large consensus', 'high degree of support', 'significant numbers in favour of' and 'a large trend' that spoke of less than full consensus. But as the power of the written word tended to outweigh protests in the plenary, this technique allowed ideas to go forward to the Convention and influence later discussions.

The group started from a general acknowledgement that the EU needed to be a strong and effective player on the world stage in political as well as economic terms. 'The central question,' the report stated, 'was therefore not whether the Union had a role to play but how it should organise itself in order effectively and coherently to promote fundamental values, defend common interests and contribute to the overall objective of global peace, security and sustainable development.'

Dehaene stressed the inclusive nature of his work. The group, he said, focused on 'how to coordinate and consolidate' the two different channels of EU decision making – the Community and the intergovernmental. It was not changing competences or powers, but trying to improve the coordination of policies to ensure the Union's common action was truly common.

CFSP, he added, would stay 'intergovernmental in character'. It would remain the job of the European Council to define EU strategic objectives and interests and establish parameters to guide EU and member states' action. But there were areas where the EU's internal policies, determined by the Community method, impacted on the world stage. Here the working group suggested that the eventual constitutional treaty make explicit the competence of the EU to conclude external agreements on issues which lay in its internal competence and for the Council to use qualified majority voting (QMV) in such cases.

The group reported 'a high degree of support' for separating a distinct External Action Council from the General Affairs and External Relations Council. A 'significant number of members' wanted the high representative to chair the External Action Council, while not having a right to vote. There was also strong support for a 'focal point', possibly a vice-president, within the Commission to coordinate all external issues. The group went on to consider ways of linking the posts of high representative and external affairs

---

[6] CONV 459/02.

commissioner and set in motion ideas that would result in a proposal for a European foreign minister.

One of the distinctive features of Dehaene's report was the support it gave to more QMV in foreign policy. Later in the life of the Convention, there would be wide differences between a large majority of integrationists wanting more QMV in CFSP and the wishes of intergovernmentalists, among whom the UK government was a notable supporter of unanimity.

Advancing an idea that would surface in the draft articles on external action, Dehaene's report suggested creating 'joint initiatives' of the high representative and Commission. Several group members suggested these should be approved by QMV in the Council because, by definition, they would represent 'a common EU interest'. In a passage that would resonate in the Convention's final days, Dehaene reported 'a high degree of support' in the working group for QMV in all areas of commercial policy, including services and intellectual property.

Dehaene's report agreed that 'maximum use' should be made of the existing, very limited provisions for QMV in foreign policy and recommended that the treaty should allow the European Council to extend (on the basis of unanimity) the use of QMV in CFSP. This was the first mention in the Convention of bridge or *passerelle* articles designed to eliminate the need for future treaty changes (with the attendant problems of ratification by all member states) for specific cases of moving from unanimity to QMV.

Surprisingly, the UK's Peter Hain disclosed in the plenary session of 20 December, that he, as a member of the group, had proposed the bridging clause 'to facilitate flexibility and the evolution of a stronger foreign policy'. At the same time, however, Hain appeared to be having second thoughts about QMV in foreign policy. He claimed it could expose internal fault lines in the EU's decision making to the outside world and he ruled out majority voting for operations under the European security and defence policy (ESDP). 'I do not think we should go any further on QMV at the moment,' Hain declared.

It was not the message that a majority of conventionnels wanted to hear, least of all Joschka Fischer. In the plenary, Fischer called for a 'bold fundamental decision' that all decisions in external affairs, apart from those on security and defence, should be taken by QMV. He argued that QMV was a way of achieving consensus rather than an instrument for voting down individual member states. 'We are not facing a decision in the enlarged Union between QMV and unanimity but between QMV and total lack of importance.'

Hain, however, bluntly ruled out 'communitarisation' of foreign policy and warned against reducing external representation to one EU seat in international bodies from 15, as suggested in the report. His remarks, together with other sceptical comments about the defence document, were a warning that broad agreement or consensus in working group or Convention did not exclude stiff opposition from powerful member states.

While Hain appeared to be drawing lines in the sand against communitarisation, others felt Dehaene did not go far enough. Typical was Alain Lamassoure, the French centre-right MEP. Dehaene, he noted, had, single-handed, achieved as much as an intergovernmental conference. But the documents lacked ambition: 'We have advances of 100 metres when we should be covering a kilometre.'

Lamassoure's downbeat assessment underestimated how influential the Dehaene working group would be. The report's significance lay in the way it maximised partial agreement in the working group to push an integrationist agenda. Its conclusions were a synthesis between the community and intergovernmental methods of running an area of policy where, in the previous ten years, considerations of national sovereignty had meant little movement away from the system agreed at Maastricht. As such, it was an important pointer to future developments in the Convention.

8.2   DEFENCE

Defence was supposed to be one of the first European projects, following the agreement of the European Coal and Steel Community in the early 1950s. But a treaty on a European Defence Community, negotiated among the original six member states, foundered after its ratification was rejected by the French National Assembly in 1954.

The issue slipped into the background, as the EEC, and later the European Communities and the EU, integrated along economic lines. However, the Maastricht Treaty provisions on the common foreign and security policy (CFSP) said it 'shall include all questions related to the security of the Union, including the eventual framing of a common defence policy, which might in time lead to a common defence'.

The Amsterdam Treaty gave the European Council the right to decide on the adoption of a common defence and made provision for cooperation on armaments 'as member states consider appropriate'. It also incorporated the so-called Petersberg tasks, which it said, 'shall include humanitarian and rescue tasks, peacekeeping tasks and tasks of combat forces in crisis management, including peace making'.

A key development came unexpectedly in December 1998 when the EU's two most powerful military nations – Britain and France – agreed in St Malo that the Union 'needs to be in a position to play its full role on the international stage'. Defence moved rapidly up the agenda thereafter, with the European Councils of Cologne and Helsinki in June and December 1999 agreeing on the principles and modalities of a rapid reaction force. Nice in December 2000 created decision taking bodies: a political and security committee to provide political oversight and strategic direction of crisis management operations; a military committee to direct military activities and a military staff, which would supply the necessary expertise. The Laeken Council decided the EU was 'now able to conduct some crisis management operations' and would be in a position to take on more demanding operations as its assets and capabilities developed.

But there was no clear guidance to the Convention on defence from the Nice or Laeken declarations or from the skeleton. It was left to the working group chaired by Michel Barnier to fill in the gaps. As a commissioner, Barnier was, in many respects, an unexpected choice to chair the defence group. Kerr wanted Lamberto Dini in charge, until it was pointed out that this could provoke ructions among other conventionnels outside the Praesidium who had fancied themselves as working group chairs. But Barnier, perhaps because the Commission has no realistic aspirations to get involved in defence policy, produced a report that won widespread approval from the pre-Christmas plenary session and even attracted some kindly words from Giscard, who was no friend of the French centre-right politician.

If anything, Barnier faced an even more difficult task than Jean-Luc Dehaene. Defence was a recent arrival in the panoply of EU policies and as his working group's report[7] noted, a 'special policy' at both national and European level. 'By nature it belongs to the most sensitive areas of sovereignty and calls upon essentially national resources.' It was for this reason that a defence working group, separate from that on external relations, was set up.

There was no denying the complexities posed by the very different commitments, capabilities and constitutional provisions covering member states' and applicant countries' defence policies. As the report noted, 11 member states were NATO members and 10 of these were also members of

---

[7] CONV 461/02.

the Western European Union (WEU), and so bound by collective defence clauses. Four member states were neutral, while special opt-out provisions applied to NATO member and non-WEU member, Denmark. The applicants included NATO members, NATO candidates, WEU associates and aspirants and, in the cases of Malta and Cyprus, two non-aligned countries.

But while committing forces (and, by implication, taking responsibility for casualties) should remain a matter for national governments and parliaments, the report staked out a claim for greater EU involvement following the events of 11 September 2001. The European security and defence policy (ESDP) now had to cope with global insecurity and new risks including international terrorist organisations and weapons of mass destruction. 'A purely national framework is no longer enough. At the same time, public opinion is calling more than ever for security and protection and appears to be very much in favour of European defence.'

Barnier decided to make a virtue out of necessity and not seek to produce a truly consensual report. The main recommendations, he said, 'received large support … A fully consensual report could only have reflected a minimalist agreement.' This approach at least enabled him to ask some important questions. Going to the heart of divisions over EU policies on defence, he asked:

> 'Should or should not an enlarged Union with some 30 member states allow certain member states to cooperate more closely? Is it acceptable for all the member states to have to align themselves with the least committed states? Must the Union abandon some policy aspirations, which are not shared by everybody?'

His report proposed a two-pronged approach in response to this problem. The EU should 'go as far as possible down the road travelled since Maastricht and Amsterdam of commitment by everybody to common goals'. In practice, this would mean expanding the existing Petersberg tasks of crisis management and peace enforcement with additional tasks such as conflict prevention; joint disarmament operations; post-conflict stabilisation and support for third countries combating terrorism, should they request it – an idea that was strongly supported in the 20 December plenary debate on defence.

To cope with the diversity of views and capacities among member states in an enlarged Union, some members of the working group suggested greater flexibility in decision making and action. This could mean a form of 'enhanced cooperation', sometimes described as a 'Eurogroup for defence', which would enable member states that so desired and had credible enough forces to cooperate more closely. If the willing states were brought into the orbit of 'enhanced cooperation' along the lines set out in the Treaty of Nice, they could operate within the institutional structures of the Union rather than outside. Conversely, countries which did not want to join a mission would be encouraged not to oppose it in a unanimous vote, but to abstain under a procedure known as 'constructive abstention' and thereafter not participate in decisions relating to the execution of the mission.

Barnier's report also spoke of the need to boost the role of the high representative (HR), although with a somewhat different emphasis to the discussion in the Dehaene report. The HR would have 'a right of initiative in crisis management matters' and be empowered in urgent cases to take decisions. But he or she would be very clearly reporting under the authority of the Council and in permanent contact with member states' representatives in the political and security committee (PSC). The report spoke of 'majority support' for a fund to cover costs in the early stages of a crisis management operation.

The plenary debate revealed widespread support for the idea of a collective defence clause in the treaty, which would provide for the mobilisation of both civil and military means to help member states deal with the new threat of terrorist attacks within the EU. There were sharp divisions, however, on extending such solidarity to a general collective defence clause. This idea was opposed in the working group by conventionnels from neutral states and advocates of collective defence as a matter for the NATO alliance, such as the UK.

However, there was strong support for an armaments and strategic research agency to be set up on an intergovernmental basis. Industrial policy was partly behind this idea, which had Giscard's backing. Barnier pointed out that the EU invested 10 billion euro in military research each year against 53 billion euro in the US, with the gap increasing rather than falling. 'This has important consequences not only on the military industry but also quite clearly on the civilian sector,' he said. 'In the medium term, thousands of jobs in the civilian sector will be threatened by the under-investment in leading-edge technologies which would never be developed for purely commercial civilian purposes.'

The agency might also spur member states towards meeting their obligations to supply capabilities for the 60,000 strong rapid reaction force pledged at the December 1999 Helsinki summit. The working group report listed several 'critical shortcomings' in meeting the Helsinki goal, notably in the areas of command, control and communications; strategic intelligence and the surveillance of troops in the field; strategic transport by air and sea and effective engagement capacity.

It is easy to be cynical about the armaments agency idea, given the past failure of EU member states to achieve much in the way of rationalising procurement, despite cooperative arrangements. But Barnier believed it had potential: he summed up the debate by comparing it to the European Coal and Steel Community in the early 1950s, which was the forerunner of the EU.

Barnier's report said 'most' working group members wanted to move from unanimity to other decision making procedures in defence 'relying more on consent and a culture of solidarity among member states'. One Convention member who did not was Peter Hain of the UK. Speaking for one of only two EU members with a rising defence equipment budget and for the country with arguably the most effective and mobile military forces in Europe, he reminded the Convention that 'only national governments have the right to commit their armed forces where they might risk their lives'.

The discussion on defence was 'at the limits of our ambition', Hain warned. It was dealing with national sovereignty in a situation where only a few governments committed soldiers. Speaking for the UK, he added, 'We are only going to do that if we have a decisive say.' He urged the Convention to realise the 'realities of power', that 'foreign policy has to be serious' and could not be based on European Parliament resolutions that could not be implemented. Hain was signalling there were limits to what the UK would accept. Three weeks before, in a speech in Cardiff, Tony Blair had also pointed to difficulties ahead. 'To achieve a unified European foreign policy, we need to decide what we are unifying around. In matters of defence and security, they are so fundamental to a nation's sense of itself, there is no institutional fix that can overcome a genuine difference of view.'

8.3   THE AREA OF FREEDOM, SECURITY AND JUSTICE

The collapse of the Soviet Union, the bloody break-up of Yugoslavia, the failure of states in Africa and Asia and the globalisation of crime posed new challenges to Europe's internal security in the 1990s, with which the Union had difficulty keeping pace.

Justice and home affairs (JHA) made a first appearance in the Maastricht Treaty in the form of intergovernmental cooperation to deal with 'matters of common interest'. These were listed as policies on asylum, border controls, immigration, combating drug addiction and international fraud, judicial cooperation in civil and criminal matters, customs cooperation and police cooperation to prevent and combat terrorism, drug trafficking and international crime. The new area of activity was covered by rules different to those applied in the European Community and the common foreign and security policy. In its original form, this 'third pillar' of the European Union was to prove largely ineffective because of its reliance of unanimity, with the result that it was subject to a major overhaul in the Amsterdam Treaty.

The Amsterdam Treaty cut back the third pillar by 'communitarising' the policies on immigration, asylum, border controls, visas and judicial cooperation in civil matters and transferring these to the 'first' community pillar. But again, progress proved disappointing, largely because the treaty stipulated that unanimity must apply for five years, after which the Union might move to qualified majority voting – provided all member states agreed. There was thus remarkably little effective follow-through to the October 1999 European Council in Tampere, Finland, which agreed an ambitious programme to breath life into the Union's 'area of freedom, security and justice'. However, in the judicial field, the shock of the 11 September attacks, backed by pressure from the European Council, provided the necessary impetus for justice and home affairs ministers to agree a European arrest warrant and a framework decision on combating terrorism.

The Laeken declaration noted 'frequent public calls for a greater EU role in justice and security, action against cross-border crime, control of migration flows and reception of asylum seekers and refugees from far-flung war zones'. Opinion polls suggested public support for Union involvement in securing increased internal security was greater even than that for heightened involvement in foreign and defence policy[8]. Article 3 of the skeleton included 'creation of an area of liberty, security and justice' among the Union's objectives while it was promised that article 31 would set out implementing procedures for policies on police matters and against crime.

It was therefore natural that the Tampere summit programme should be taken up by the Convention and, in the light of the slow progress achieved towards meeting the Tampere goals, that a working group should be set up to see how best to improve matters. Chaired by John Bruton, the plain speaking, former Irish prime minister, the group concluded[9] that the battle against crime was 'an area in which the EU can demonstrate its relevance to its citizens in the most visible way'.

---

[8] Eurobarometer in April 2002 found nine out of ten of a representative sample of EU citizens thought fighting organised crime and drug trafficking should be policy priorities for the Union.
[9] CONV 426/02.

'We are dealing here with crimes that affect people directly, such as threats of terrorism, illegal immigration, organised crime, drug trafficking, trafficking in human beings, crime using and abusing the Internet and the laundering of money and the associated international fraud,' Bruton told the plenary session of December 6. 'These are issues that need a response at European level.'

Bruton's group proposed sweeping changes, which – should the constitutional treaty ever be adopted – will be those that the average citizen is most likely to notice.

The group gave a push to existing plans for a common European asylum system by recommending that qualified majority voting and codecision be applied in the Treaty to legislation on asylum, refugees and displaced persons. It urged that a common policy on immigration be enshrined in the constitutional treaty and that the Union be allowed to provide incentive and support measures to integrate legally resident nationals of third countries, with QMV and codecision in these areas. QMV and codecision should also be applied to all measures needed for a common visa policy.

Turning to the third pillar, the group said the principle of mutual recognition of judicial decisions, where the judgements of one member state are recognised by the authorities of another, should be enshrined in the treaty. This was one of the main Tampere recommendations. To make this possible, it urged measures to 'approximate' certain areas of the member states' criminal law where there was a cross-border dimension. There should be minimum rules, defining the constituent elements of crimes and penalties in particularly serious cases[10] or where the crime was committed against an EU policy (such as counterfeiting the euro). There would also have to be approximation of some elements of criminal procedure and of rules organising police and judicial cooperation between the authorities of member states.[11]

The group reached a 'broad consensus' that subjecting cooperation in criminal matters to unanimity could not survive enlargement. As a result, a majority of the group's members called for QMV and codecision for legislation fixing the minimum rules for dealing with very serious cross-border crimes and those against common Union policies. As a balance to mutual recognition, QMV and codecision should also apply for setting

---

[10] Tampere mentioned among others, drug trafficking, trafficking in humans and the sexual exploitation of children.
[11] For example, in the area of arrest warrants.

common minimum standards to protect the rights of individuals in criminal procedure and for some common rules on aspects of criminal procedure, such as admissibility of evidence throughout the Union. In civil law, the group called for the principle of mutual recognition of judicial decisions to be enshrined in the treaty and covered by QMV and codecision.

These far-reaching steps in the direction of the Community method were hedged somewhat. The group proposed continued unanimity for pooling certain core functions of member states, such as the creation of Union bodies with operational powers (Europol and Eurojust, for example). To the annoyance of Commissioner Vitorino, the group suggested the Commission should share its right of initiative in 'third pillar' issues with member states, so that a quorum of one quarter of states could take an initiative.

The group also sought greater involvement of national parliaments in JHA issues, particularly in the definition of strategic guidelines by EU heads of state. It favoured more operational powers for Europol, the nascent EU police body, and Eurojust, the cooperation forum for public prosecutors, but was divided over whether to back the creation of a European public prosecutor. This hotly debated issue was a policy goal strongly supported by backers of a more federal Europe and the Commission.

Bruton's report received broad-based support in the plenary debate, prompting Giscard to hail its findings as 'important and visible progress' towards a homogenous European justice system which would be more simple, clear and efficient. The president observed that suppression of the third pillar might appear banal after nine months of the Convention, but few had considered such a development would be so easy at its start. Although there were many detailed objections to the group's report and some candidate countries were concerned about the shift to QMV and codecision, there was little sense that the problems raised in connection with the freedom, security and justice agenda could become deal breakers in the further negotiations on the constitutional treaty.

8.4   ECONOMIC GOVERNANCE

Developments in the EU economy at the time of the Convention's launch were justification enough for it to take a hard look at the Union's economic governance. The successful launch of euro notes and coins – the culmination of more than ten years planning and preparation – coincided with growing strains in the single currency zone. In the two months between the Laeken summit and the Convention's launch, the Commission called Germany and Portugal to account for threatening to breach the excessive deficit rules of the euro-zone's stability and growth pact, which limited national budget deficits to 3% of gross domestic product. Although a fudged settlement solved these problems for the time being, the episode focused attention on economic policy coordination in the Union. The Laeken declaration had asked: 'How can economic policy coordination be stepped up?' Pressure from the Convention, supported by Giuliano Amato and Klaus Hänsch in the Praesidium, led to the creation of an economic governance working group. Hänsch's reward was to be given the chair.

The Convention was straying into a difficult area, however. Economic and monetary policy was in the hands of well-entrenched forces. While the European Commission was always keen to boost its coordinating role, neither the European Central Bank nor the member states' finance ministers were inclined to change the status quo.

Hänsch set his group a number of questions.

- Did the introduction of the euro justify transferring competence for some aspects of economic policy to the Community?
- Was the stability and growth pact operating effectively?
- Should there be additional measures to help strengthen economic policy coordination?
- Should social and employment policies be considered of 'common concern' and require coordination in the same way as economic policy?
- Did the euro's introduction affect arguments for or against fiscal harmonisation and should some procedures for deciding tax issues be changed?
- Were responsibilities properly shared out in managing the euro?
- Should the informal 'Eurogroup' of finance ministers from the euro-zone be given a formal status, to take account of enlargement, when the number of euro-zone countries would fall from a big majority to less than half of Union members?
- Should the euro be better represented in international fora and, if so, how?

He ran into trouble. The working group was soon badly split between left and right on a host of issues. Some were very familiar, such as an impasse over whether decisions on taxation should be taken unanimously or by qualified majority voting. Others centred on the wish of many Convention members (about a fifth) to inject a greater social component into EU economic policy making. Hänsch had hoped to finish the group's deliberations in September 2002. Instead, his final draft (replete with plenty of square brackets indicating discord) attracted comments from group members running to 66 pages. The discussion on the report[12] in the plenary did not take place until 7 November.

On the big issue of competences, the group backed the status quo, leaving the monetary policy of the euro to be exercised by the ECB as a competence of the Union and economic policy the responsibility of member states.

It put its weight behind maintaining the Eurogroup and called for stronger euro-zone representation in international organisations. The Eurogroup received even greater support during the plenary discussion when more than a dozen conventionnels said it should have a stronger institutional position in the Union. Pierre Moscovici, the soon to be replaced French government representative, presciently proposed that it should be mentioned in the eventual treaty (possibly in an annex) with the Eurogroup president being appointed for an extended period of two years.

But the group split several ways over how to improve economic policy coordination, although some of its ideas garnered sufficient support to resurface later in the life of the Convention. There was strong but not unanimous support for strengthening the role of the Commission in policing the EU's broad economic policy guidelines (BEPG), which constituted one of the main tools of economic policy coordination, and the stability and growth pact. The group was 'inclined to propose' that the Commission should be able to issue warnings directly to member states not complying with the BEPG or running an excessive deficit against the stability pact's rules. Given that Commission president Romano Prodi had recently denounced the stability pact as 'stupid', the group's inclinations were quite an endorsement of the Commission's economic watchdogs and their commissioner, Pedro Solbes.[13]

There were predictable divisions in the group and the plenary over tax harmonisation, with the UK leading the Convention members who rejected more qualified majority voting in this area. Britain's Peter Hain was supported by government representatives, Lena Hjelm-Wallen of Sweden, Dick Roche of Ireland and Henrik Hololei of Estonia.

However, in a re-run of the debates before the Nice summit of December 2000, there was widespread support in the working group for QMV for tax measures that would further the single market. Again this idea met fierce

---

[12] CONV 357/02.

[13] Shortly after President Prodi's remarks, his predecessor Jacques Santer, Luxembourg's representative in the Convention, observed during the 7 November plenary session that: 'The arrangements of the pact are not always as stupid as those who read it.'

resistance from the UK. But Giscard, in his account of the Convention to December's Copenhagen European Council, said it was 'nevertheless gaining ground'. Poland, for example, generally supported unanimity in tax matters but was prepared to accept QMV for single market measures. The idea was wholeheartedly endorsed in a joint Franco-German paper on economic governance published just before Christmas.

The economic governance group also divided along party lines between right and left on whether the treaty should take more account of 'Social Europe'. After protests by more than 40 conventionnels and alternates, a reluctant Giscard accepted the creation of a new working group on Social Europe to take this debate further and report by early February. At the end of the debate, Giscard noted various majority positions but decided these fell short of consensus. 'Consensus does not mean unanimity. But it does mean more than a majority', he declared.

8.5   SOCIAL EUROPE

If proof were needed that the Convention had a mind of its own, it came with the insistence of a vocal group of more than 40 Convention members and alternates for thorough discussion about the place social policy should have in the planned constitutional treaty.

For its many advocates, 'Social Europe' was an essential part of European integration. They could point to the European Community Treaty's article 2 on the EU's tasks, which mentioned promoting 'a high level of employment and social protection' and 'economic and social cohesion' among the member states. Social policy was in the treaties from the beginning in 1957 while the first regulations covering the coordination of social security of workers had been adopted by the Council in 1958. The Union's involvement in what was a shared competence grew substantially in the intervening years with social policy being given a prominent place in the Treaty of Amsterdam. The Laeken declaration asserted that 'citizens want results in the fields of employment and combating poverty and social exclusion' and asked how the EU could intensify cooperation in the field of social inclusion.

Yet it rapidly became clear that Giscard had little time for social policy. He turned a deaf ear to calls for a working group on the issue during the listening phase. The Convention secretariat feared that, as a single issue topic, Social Europe would trigger a left-right split in the Convention and also spawn demands for other working groups (on the regions or agriculture, for example) that would deflect the Convention from its core constitutional preoccupations.

However, neither Giscard nor Sir John Kerr had reckoned on the stubbornness of the social policy supporters, who ranged behind Anne Van Lancker, a Belgian socialist MEP. With two other MEPs – Johannes Voggenhuber, the Austrian Green and Sylvia-Yvonne Kaufmann of Germany's former Communist PDS party – Van Lancker gathered 45 signatures in September 2002 to demand a debate and a working group on 'Social Europe'. During the October 3–4 plenary session, more than 40 members and alternates spoke up in support of these demands. Of the 20 or so speakers who rose to debate the matter on 3 October, only Lamassoure opposed the idea, arguing that the Convention should confine itself to constitutional rather than policy issues.

After some backstage negotiations between Kerr and Van Lancker, the dissidents settled for coverage of the social issues in the Hänsch working group and a debate on social matters in the November plenary discussion on the report. It proved only a temporary respite, however. Following the debate on 7 November, Giscard gave way and preparations were made for a 'Social Europe' working group. The group was to be chaired by George Katiforis, the Greek government representative and Praesidium member. Cynics interpreted its large size, with 60 members or twice the level of the previous groups, as a ploy by Kerr to limit its effectiveness.

The mandate[14] for the working group harked back in part to the skeleton and asked whether article 2, on the values of the Union, and article 3, setting out its objectives, properly reflected Social Europe. Among other points, it asked whether competences in social matters should be modified and how far QMV and codecision should replace unanimity.[15]

By the time the group reported to the plenary on 6 February 2003[16], activity in the Convention was picking up. The first draft articles, including full

---

[14] CONV 421/02).

[15] The debate in the working group on moving from unanimity to QMV focused on areas that were the subject of difficult negotiations in Nice, notably: TEC article 13 to combat discrimination, article 42 on social security for migrant workers and the Union's supporting measures in article 137 paragraph 1 clauses c, d, f and g covering social security and social protection of workers, protection of workers where their employment contract is terminated, representation and collective defence of workers and employers interests, and conditions for employment of third country nationals legally resident in the Union. A bridge or *passerelle* clause already existed for clauses d, f and g to allow the council to move to QMV on a unanimous decision.

[16] CONV516/03 and CONV516/1/03 REV 1 COR 1.

versions of articles 2 and 3, were published on the same day. Not surprisingly, draft article 2 failed to include the additional social values agreed by the group, while draft article 3 only imperfectly reflected its long list of 14 social objectives. But the Convention's social policy enthusiasts at least had an arsenal of proposals to help them submit amendments.

Strong opposition from a minority of group members representing member states stood in the way of agreement on any further move to QMV in social policy. In the following plenary session, Peter Hain for the UK was adamant the UK 'cannot accept any more QMV here'. However, there was consensus that the TEC article 152 on public health should be strengthened to give the Union greater scope to deal with cross-border epidemics and the threat of bio-terrorism. The group also agreed the Convention should consider facilitating EU legislation on 'services of general interest' – EU jargon for public services – as these were perceived by many group members as an important part of Europe's 'social model'. All agreed the constitutional treaty should recognise the role of the social partners – the organised lobbies of employers' and trade unions – in Europe's social dialogue.

Katiforis admitted that the achievements of the group looked modest. But the ensuing debate showed that very many conventionnels wanted to replace unanimity by QMV in the social sphere, with some suggesting a 'superqualified' majority voting system to overcome the blockages. Majority voting in social policy was, as Giscard noted, a difficult issue – and under the watchful eye of Anne Van Lancker, it would stay on the Convention agenda until the very end.

8.6   THE LEGACY OF THE WORKING GROUPS

The working groups drew mixed reviews during and immediately after the Convention's study phase. Hindsight has been kinder.

Those that functioned well produced consensus on issues that had eluded successive intergovernmental conferences, including:

- agreement on a single personality for the Union, which was an important preliminary to completing the skeleton and elimination of the pillars
- consensus on creating the 'early warning system' for national parliaments to police subsidiarity
- an understanding that the Charter of Fundamental Rights should be included in the treaty

- accord on reducing and reforming the array of legal instruments used by the Union to legislate
- an understanding to extend the Community method and qualified majority voting to important areas of internal security, including asylum and immigration.

In the view of Giuliano Amato, the working groups allowed much freer discussion than the plenary debates and this in turn helped positions to change. Working group members found they had to explain their positions – a task rarely necessary in the plenary where contributions were generally three minutes long and virtually unknown in an intergovernmental conference. A 'sovereign no' in an IGC was just that – a rejection with no obligation to explain.

The working groups also helped bring the Convention together and accelerate the process of creating an *esprit de corps*. Amid the pressures of work, the distinction between full Convention members and alternates, which Giscard had wanted initially to emphasise, disappeared.

But the working groups were no panacea. A general problem was that the groups could be unrepresentative of the Convention or the Union as a whole. They were self-selected bodies, where there was no guarantee of balance and where not all members had the stamina or capacity to attend all meetings. Some were very poorly attended.

Amato's working group on simplification contained only one EU government representative (Ireland's Dick Roche) from a membership of 38 despite it dealing with important issues of legislation and procedures and suggesting that codecision, with qualified majority voting in the Council of Ministers, should become the normal procedure for the Union.

The groups were never used for the Convention's biggest challenge – resolving the institutional questions – because governments made clear they would not surrender their bottom lines in such fora where parliamentarians usually formed a majority of active members. For this reason, Giscard, Kerr, Amato and Dehaene never wanted a working group to deal with institutions.

CHAPTER 9
The Institutions

At the end of their bad-tempered summit in Nice in December 2000, the European Union's leaders declared they had 'completed the institutional changes necessary for the accession of new member states'. Less than two years later, institutions were back on the Union's agenda.

They were, however, being kept out of the mainstream of the Convention's discussions. This was not what the conventionnels wanted. But Giscard and Sir John Kerr had decided that the power questions facing the Convention – the 'who does what?' of EU politics – could only be solved if they were left towards its end. Thus, with one or two exceptions, such as the discussion over the Union's foreign minister or the idea of a Legislative Council, the institutional issues that would have to be resolved in the constitutional treaty swirled around the periphery of the Convention sessions for the whole of 2002.

National leaders raised important issues in speeches and in the margins of European Councils. Giscard, in the course of his bilateral diplomacy, met these leaders and discussed their concerns. But none of these contacts informed the Convention's discussions. The Praesidium fell in with the wishes of Giscard and Kerr. It agreed on 28 October there would be no working groups to discuss institutional questions. Instead, the institutions would be discussed by the Convention in plenary sessions. Although the skeleton constitutional treaty of October 2002 outlined no fewer than 13 articles on the institutions, the Praesidium was in no mood to hurry the discussions. The first plenary debate on the institutions was scheduled for January 2003, nearly eleven months after the Convention's launch and barely six months before it was due to end.

The reasons for this reticence were not difficult to discern. Institutional questions had caused an ugly split in the Union between big and small countries at the Biarritz and Nice European Councils in 2000 and again in Seville in June 2002. Their capacity to polarise was undiminished. And yet the big and small country issue was one that Giscard felt the Convention must solve if the Union were to fulfil the Laeken summit objective of becoming more efficient, while expanding to 25 or more member states.

9.1   BIG AND SMALL

It became a constant refrain of Giscard that the agreements reached in Nice may have opened the way to enlargement, but had failed to consider in sufficient depth the political and institutional consequences that would follow from the change of the size and composition of the Union and its greater cultural diversity.[1]

This concern was accentuated by his perception that the Union of 25 would, because of the differing size of its members, be like no other. Its most populated state would have more people than the most populous state in the US, while its least populated would have fewer inhabitants than the least populated state in America.[2]

In a Union of 25 with 452 million inhabitants, the population of the six most populous states with 40 million or more inhabitants each would be 336 million people, or 74% of the total. They would account for 77% of the Union's economic output as measured by gross domestic product. A middle group of eight countries, with between 8 million and 16 million people each, would have a total population of 85 million (just three million more than Germany, the Union's biggest state). These would account for 19% of the Union's population and 17% of its GDP. Eleven Union members, with populations between 400,000 and 5 million each, would have a total population of 30.5 million (less than Poland, the smallest of the six biggest states) and account for just 7% of Union population and 6% of GDP.

The European Union of 25, with the large states in a minority of six, would thus be radically different from the European Economic Community of the 1950s when the founding six member states were evenly split between three big and three medium and small countries. It would be substantially different from the EU of 15, divided between five big members, six medium-sized and four small. Yet the emergence of a Union in which the majority of states would have fewer than 10 million persons each[3] had been accompanied by an enhanced insistence among the medium and small countries on equality of states' rights.

---

[1] See Giscard's remarks to the European Parliament Constitutional Affairs Committee 10 October 2001. Available in the archives section of the Future of Europe page on the Parliament's website.

[2] Giscard – The Henry Kissinger Lecture, Washington, 11 February 2003, filed under speeches on the Convention website.

[3] Thirteen countries in a Union of 25 ranging upwards from Malta with 400,000 people to Sweden with 8.9 million. The 12 states with populations above 10 million each ranged from Hungary with 10.2 million to Germany with 82.4 million.

In Giscard's mind, the difference in member states' size raised fundamental issues for the Union's institutional architecture. How would it be possible to find the right balance between the demands for equality between the Union's citizens and demands for equality of rights between member states, when the latter were so different in size? Was this balance fairly reflected in the institutional structure made up of the triangle of the Council of Ministers, Commission and European Parliament? What about the Commission, which was charged with defining the common European interest and yet from late 2004 would be formed of one member per member state, irrespective of size? And what should be the role of the European Council, the gathering of the EU's leaders, which he, Giscard, had initiated back in 1974, and its president?

9.2   A PRESIDENT FOR THE UNION?

The European Council was also exercising the minds of European leaders. The regular meetings of the EU leaders in the European Council were the Union's principal agenda setter. But the Union's six-month rotating presidencies were variable in performance, depending on the quality of national leaders, their government machines and their domestic political situations. They were frequently hijacked by the specific enthusiasms of the country leader holding the post of president or bogged down by trying to settle problems unresolved by member states in the Council of Ministers. The Laeken declaration put a question mark next to the Union's six-month rotating presidencies. Drawing on his experience of the Belgian presidency, Louis Michel, the Belgian foreign minister, said after Laeken that the system must change. Looking ahead to enlargement, it was easy to see why.

When the European Council first met in Dublin in 1975, the European Communities had just nine member states. With a six-month rotating presidency, each Union leader could expect to arrange its agenda and chair its regular summit meetings every four and a half years. The growing prospect of a 'big bang' enlargement raised two issues. It meant member states would soon be facing a turn in the driving seat only once every 12 and a half years with no prospect of maintaining any institutional memory between outings. Moreover, the already challenging task of keeping in touch with the fellow leaders in a Union of 15 member states to secure consensus would become much more difficult with 25 or more.

There were, of course, ways around the problem. The Seville European Council in June 2002 instituted some useful reforms to make the European Council summits run more effectively. But by this time, the idea of a stable chair for the European Council was firmly in the public domain. It had become known as the 'ABC agenda' after José Maria Aznar of Spain, Tony Blair of Britain and France's Jacques Chirac.

A week after the Convention's launch,[4] Jacques Chirac publicly floated the idea of a 'president for the European Union'. The existing system of rotating presidencies would no longer be viable in the enlarged Union so he envisaged leadership resting with the European Council, consisting of the EU leaders and Commission president. They should elect at their head a person who would hold office for a 'sufficient' period, would represent Europe in the eyes of the world, give the Union the necessary institutional structure to be strong, and 'lean on' a more transparent, better coordinated Council of Ministers which would take decisions by qualified majority voting.

In May, Aznar put his own gloss on the idea in a speech in Oxford.[5] Just over four months of Spain's presidency convinced him that the rotating presidencies would no longer be viable and that a president of the European Council with a longer mandate of five or two and a half years would make the Union's institutions more effective. He proposed the president should not hold national office, should probably be a former head of state or government and could be helped by a 'presidential team' of five or six heads of state or government on a rotation system. The European Council would continue to be 'the political apex' of the Union and could have some extra powers – such as the capacity to dissolve Parliament on an initiative of the Commission.

Tony Blair's support for the idea was broadcast less clearly. But in his first speech to the Convention in March 2002, Peter Hain said Britain wanted stronger political leadership for the EU 'through a radically reformed European Council giving strategic directions'. By May, the British were briefing that the UK too wanted a full-time elected president of the European Council below whom would operate a reduced number of sectoral Councils run by team presidencies. The twin ideas of a 'fixed chair' of the European Council and team presidencies were taken further by Blair in November 2002 in his Cardiff speech on the future of Europe in which the prime minister was sharply critical of the system of rotating presidencies. It had 'reached its limits'. It stood in the way of Europe being taken seriously at international summits and hindered the development of the common foreign and security policy. It was also difficult for the European Council to follow up initiatives such as the Lisbon agenda for modernising the EU economy

---

[4] Speech in Strasbourg on 6 March 2002. Available at http://www.elysee.fr
[5] At St Anthony's College, 20 May 2002.

'across a wide range of sectoral Councils, each with their own hobby horses and vested interests'.

By early 2003, the UK was informally circulating ideas for a very powerful European Council president who should:

- prepare and preside over at least four European Council meetings a year
- undertake a 'tour of the capitals' around all 25 member states at least four times a year
- cooperate with the Commission president in preparing the Union's multi-annual strategic agenda
- chair the General Affairs Council
- supervise the work of sectoral Councils
- represent the Council in inter-institutional meetings with the Commission and European Parliament
- supervise the high representative's work and coordinate foreign policy discussion at European Council level
- oversee the Union's relations with the major world powers
- attend Group of Eight meetings and work with the Commission president on issues including international financial matters, immigration and counter terrorism
- play a 'particular role' in crisis management and defence.

This ultra ambitious job description implied a very powerful figure indeed and was symptomatic of how far discussion on a stable European Council chair had developed outside the confines of the Convention. This was despite strong opposition from small member states, the Commission and federally inclined members of the European Parliament, who feared he or she would be the democratically unaccountable representative of a 'directory' of big nations, would fatally undermine the Commission president as guardian of the European general interest and reduce the Commission to a depoliticised secretariat. Opponents of the long-term presidency pointed out that some of the most effective rotating presidencies were run by small member states (Finland in 1999 and Portugal in the first half of 2000) while the French presidency in the second half of 2000 was an acrimonious shambles. Moreover, the rotating presidencies helped bring the Union to the citizens of the member states. All this was to no avail: the long-term European Council chair was mooted in the skeleton as a possibility.

The issue was finally debated in the Convention after being put forward as one of the main features of joint institutional proposals from France and Germany in January 2003. By this time, certain conventionnels, led by Lamberto Dini and Pierre Lequiller of the Italian and French parliaments and the Liberal caucus leader, Andrew Duff, were suggesting the Union should aim for a single president, who would unify the positions of president of the European Council and Commission. Although mooted for the distant future, the idea proved too bold to be adopted by the Convention.

9.3   THE FOREIGN MINISTER

The idea that the Union should have a more effective foreign and security policy, commensurate with its status as one of the world's great economic and trading powers, was strongly embedded in the Convention from its first day. So too was the realisation that the division of labour between a high representative for foreign and security policy, who reported to the Council, and an external affairs commissioner, who was a member of the Commission's college, was far from ideal. The incumbents, Javier Solana as high representative, and Chris Patten, the external affairs commissioner, had in general cooperated well since the high representative's post was created in 1999. But the structure was inherently unstable. There was a risk of turf wars and large disparities in culture and financial resources between the low-budget, fast-moving operation of the high representative and the very well-endowed but lumbering Commission external affairs directorate. The Laeken declaration asked whether synergy between the two office holders could be reinforced. When the Convention discussed foreign and security policy in July 2002, the question was echoed by many conventionnels.

However, any proposals to change the relationship between the two office holders risked upsetting a delicate institutional balance. The future of the high representative and commissioner for external affairs became a battlefield. On the one hand were the advocates of an enhanced Community method for the Union, who wanted to see external affairs become a responsibility of the Commission. On the other, were the intergovernmentalists who wished to see the high representative reinforced, perhaps by his being able to draw on the diplomatic services of the Commission, but not at the cost of his role being 'communitarised' and thus brought under the Commission's wing.

The Commission fired an early shot in this controversy in its May 2002 paper to the Convention. Arguing that the Community method could make foreign and security policy more effective, it proposed that the high representative should be gradually integrated into the Commission and operate under the responsibility of the Commission president. A Convention debate on foreign policy on 11 July highlighted other, different approaches to the issue. Elmar Brok of the EPP suggested merging the high representative's post into that of external affairs commissioner, but giving the office holder a special relationship with the Council because not all issues in foreign and security policy could be decided by the Community method. The UK's Peter Hain called for the high representative to have a formal right of initiative on common foreign and security policy matters and the right to attend Commission meetings on external policy. But for Hain, foreign policy would remain 'essentially an intergovernmental matter' and talk of it being communitarised was neither realistic nor deliverable. The July debate also saw the first proposals for a 'double-hatted' individual who would carry out the duties of Solana and Patten and yet not be part of the Community method of decision making. Hain was unenthused. 'To which body would that individual answer and be accountable: the Council or the Commission? Who is the master? That is the question. Can you have two bosses?' he asked.

The future of the high representative and the external affairs commissioner was taken up by the external action working group chaired by Jean-Luc Dehaene. In its final report,[6] it outlined four options:

- Keep the roles of high representative and external affairs commissioner separate, while proposing practical measures to strengthen the HR's role and increase synergies between the two jobs.
- A full merger of the HR's functions into the Commission. This radical, federal approach would apply the Community method to external relations and make the Commission responsible for policy initiation, implementation and external representation in all areas of EU external action. Even its advocates accepted that the idea would not fly because there was no consensus supporting it among member states.
- A compromise proposal for a 'European external representative' who would be a member of the Commission, preferably with the rank of vice-president, but who would have a separate mandate from, and be accountable to, the Council for the common foreign and security policy (CFSP). This 'double-hatted' individual would be appointed by a qualified majority of heads of state and government, with approval of the president of the Commission and endorsement of the European Parliament. There would be various provisions to prevent the two roles getting confused: for example, when the external representative used his or her right of initiative on CFSP in the Council, the Commission should abstain from a competing initiative. In the Commission, the representative, as head

[6] CONV 459/02.

of external relations, would be able to make proposals, which would be decided in the college, as now, by majority voting. This double-hatted person would represent the EU and be given a number of deputies to be able to carry out what, by any standards, would be a huge job.

- An 'EU minister of foreign affairs' who would combine the functions of the HR and external relations commissioner under the direct authority of the European Council. Under this option – pushed by the French government – she or he would chair the External Relations Council.

The group reported 'a large trend' in favour of the third, double-hatted option. Dehaene described it as an attempt to bridge the gap between the intergovernmental and Community methods. But, pointing to a potential weakness, he admitted the Union would have to make sure the individual did not come into conflict with himself.

It was this aspect that drew the scorn of Peter Hain during the subsequent 20 December plenary session. Citing doubts about double hatting voiced by none other than Solana, Hain said no one had answered the question who would mediate in a dispute between Council and Commission. Also, who would chair the external part of the External Relations Council if the HR were double-hatted with a Commission college role? And how could a full member of the Commission college chair a discussion on defence issues? It would be 'folly – actually gesture politics' to take such an important institutional step without convincing answers to these questions, he warned. Double hatting should be a matter for discussion in the 'end-game' – the final difficult negotiations in the Convention – when the issue of the long-term presidency of the EU would be addressed.

Nor was Hain alone. De Villepin of France, while backing the idea of a foreign minister, opposed double hatting, as did Lena Hjelm Wallen, the Swedish government conventionnel. Alfonso Dastis, the increasingly active deputy to Ana Palacio, the Spanish government representative, warned that a dual function for a single person 'might create all sorts of institutional difficulties'. However, the double-hatted solution was enthusiastically supported by Joschka Fischer, recently installed as German government conventionnel. Shortly afterwards, the Dehaene working group's third option would surface as the basis for proposals from France and Germany for a Union foreign minister.

9.4   THE COUNCIL OF MINISTERS AND QUALIFIED MAJORITIES

Reform of the Council of Ministers was ongoing Union business when the Convention first met. There were two broad difficulties: one arising from the past and one looming in the future. The problem arising from the past was that the institution, which was intended to represent the member states' interests in the Union's institutional triangle, was no longer functioning well. Giscard liked to observe that inside the Brussels ring road, people spoke of the EU as if it had only two institutions, the European Parliament and the Commission. They neglected the Council even though it was a key decision making body, in which the member states defended their interests and reached common positions to be negotiated with the Commission and Parliament. The problem in the future was enlargement. Germany's foreign minister, Joschka Fischer, pithily highlighted the potential nightmare of Council of Ministers' meetings after enlargement in his Humboldt University speech. 'How long will Council meetings actually last?' he asked. 'Days, maybe even weeks?'

The Council's malaise reflected years of growing complexity in the tasks it faced. There had been the emergence and proliferation of sectoral Councils, which were difficult to coordinate and control. Some of these, such as the Ecofin Council of finance ministers, became extremely powerful and jealous of their prerogatives. Others, such as the JHA Council of justice and home affairs ministers, commanded issues of rapidly growing importance for the Union and yet were prone to the 'hobby horses and vested interests' of which Tony Blair complained. The Seville European Council took the axe to the Council formations, reducing their number from 16 to 9.

The Council of Ministers was still beset by a lack of democratic accountability and untouched by Montesquieu's ideas for a separation of powers between the legislative and executive. It was, as Brussels wags observed, the only legislative body, apart from those of North Korea and Cuba, to pass laws away from the public gaze. For this reason alone, there was a strong intellectual head of steam behind the idea of a separate 'Legislative Council', which would be equivalent to a second chamber of the European Parliament, representing the states.

There was the special problem of the General Affairs and External Relations Council (GAERC), as the General Affairs Council was known after the Seville summit. The General Affairs Council was in a particularly sorry state because the foreign ministers, who took part, showed a marked lack of commitment to the nitty-gritty of running the Union while glorying in the televisual media opportunities offered by its discussions on foreign affairs. Because of bad feelings between the big and small members of the Union, the Seville summit failed to institute a planned reform of the Spanish presidency to separate general affairs from external relations. Although functions were separated within the Council, the GAERC still held responsibility for the management of the Union (general affairs) and for its foreign policy, its nascent defence policy, development policy and trade (external relations). The growing importance that the Convention expected to accrue to Union foreign and defence policies, combined with the growing support for the idea of a Union foreign minister – apparent in the discussions of the external affairs working group – strengthened the arguments for a separate Council of external relations. Meanwhile, the Union needed a more effective General Affairs Council to improve its management.

The challenges that enlargement posed for the six-month rotating presidency of the European Council applied also to the various Council formations and threw up a host of questions. Should they have longer-term chairpersons and if so who? Should this be taken as an opportunity to spread responsibilities for running the Union among member states through team presidencies, and in so doing ease the tensions between big and small, north and south, new and old? Also, should there be special provisions for very important Council formations? If the choice were made to have an External Relations Council and a foreign minister, would it not make sense for the foreign minister to chair that formation of the Council? And who should chair the General Affairs Council?

The voting methods of the Council were a further issue. The question of whether or not to adopt more qualified majority voting as a way of facilitating decision making after enlargement was discussed under the heading of 'simplification', with Giuliano Amato's working group recommending it as a general rule in the Union. But the modalities of qualified majority voting found their way into the debate on institutions.

This issue was supposed to have been resolved at Nice, and it was, but through a compromise that made voting in the Council more complex. Member states are not equal in the Council. They have different voting weights depending on their size. Part of the Nice negotiations concerned the 'reweighting' of member states' votes in the Council to reflect their populations better. The outcome at Nice owed more to negotiating styles than logic, with the toughest negotiators securing the biggest prizes. Thus Germany would have 29 votes from 2005, the same as France, the UK and Italy, even though Germany was more than one-third bigger than each of the three. Poland and Spain would each have 27 votes even though these had less than half Germany's population. The Netherlands with 16 million people had 13 votes, only one more than the 12 votes each of Greece,

Portugal, Belgium, the Czech Republic and Hungary, which had around 10 million inhabitants apiece.

True, Germany was compensated by having more MEPs than any other member state. Germany also secured a clause in the Nice Treaty by which a member state could halt a qualified majority decision if states representing fewer than 62% of the total population of the Union had approved it. But this just increased the complexity of an already complex system. From 2005, a decision by QMV in a Union of 25 would thus have to go through the following hoops. It would need at least 232 votes in the Council from a total of 321: a pass rate of 72.27%. It would have to be approved by a majority of member states, if it was based on a proposal of the Commission – otherwise the threshold would be two-thirds. It could then be blocked by the 62% population rule.

An alternative, supported by the Commission and considered by the Amato group on simplification, was for a system of double majorities by which a qualified majority would represent a majority of member states and a majority (to be defined) of the Union's population. The double majority neatly reflected the EU's dual nature as a Union of states and citizens. It would be easy to understand and not require renegotiation with future enlargements. But acceptance would require some states, notably Spain and Poland, to give up privileged positions secured in the bear garden that was Nice.

9.5   THE COMMISSION

Although the Commission represented the common European interest in the institutional triangle, it stirred national passions in the Convention when its future was considered in the context of the 'numbers questions' posed by enlargement.

The paradox was rooted in a divergence that had grown between the role of the Commission as depicted in the Union's treaties and the perception of its role in many (mainly small) member and accession states. The Commission was conceived as a collegiate body to be the guardian of the treaties and safeguard the European spirit, as well as exercise considerable powers through its right of initiative and administrative duties. To this end, the treaty[7] speaks of a body made up of individuals chosen on merit and 'whose independence is beyond doubt' and who, in the performance of their duties,

---

[7] TEC article 213.

'shall neither seek nor take instructions from any government or from any other body'. Yet during the 1990s, as enlargement to the east developed from possibility to near inevitability, this vision of the platonic, non-national, pan-European commissioner took a knock. Many present and future member states believed each must have *equal* representation in the Commission through their own commissioner to safeguard their national interests.

This was new and would have profound implications. In the original European Community of six nations, there were nine commissioners, comprising two each for the big countries and one for each of the smaller member states, giving the big countries an automatic preponderance which went some way towards recognising their increased weight in the Union. In the Union of 15, the five big countries retained two commissioners against one each for the 10 smaller members, resulting in an even division between big and small in a college of 20.

The problems experienced by the Santer Commission, which was forced to resign en masse in 1999, and the Prodi Commission persuaded many that a large Commission of 20 or more was a weak Commission. However, in the Union of 25, there would be 25 commissioners from 2004 because under the Nice treaty settlement, each member state would have one commissioner until the Union included 27 member states. At that point, the Nice Treaty specified there should be fewer commissioners than member states, with the members of the Commission chosen according to the principle of equal rotation. The Council would work out the details of the system by a unanimous decision at the appropriate time. In the meantime, thoughts tended to concentrate on a two- or multi-tiered Commission with senior commissioners, who would vote in the college, and junior commissioners, who would not. Romano Prodi appeared to favour such a solution, when in the summer of 2002 he floated plans to create an inner cabinet of senior commissioners.[8]

Although the outline of a future reduction was set at Nice, the issue of the Commission's composition shot up the Convention agenda, partly because of the impending unprecedented 'big bang' enlargement and partly because Nice niggled with Giscard. The Commission was a particularly high profile institution for the accession countries because it was their partner in the enlargement negotiations. They argued, with some justification, that each must have a commissioner as the most effective way of learning how to

---

[8] *Financial Times* 3 July 2002.

operate in the Union and to persuade sceptical voters that they were appropriately represented in Brussels.

For Giscard, there was first the problem of whether a Commission of 25 or more could possibly be collegiate and whether there would be sufficient proper jobs in the college for it to operate efficiently in Europe's best interest. But he was also concerned by the political problem of so many small countries making up a body that could vote decisions by a simple majority and also by the eventual implications of equal rotation on the presence of the large member states in the Commission. What legitimacy would the Commission have in the eyes of citizens of the larger member states if their interests could be outvoted by countries with a total population of fewer than 50 million in a Union of 450 million? And would a France or a Germany willingly obey a Commission instruction if, once the Union had more than 27 members, it were excluded from the decision making college of commissioners?

The end of October skeleton referred to the numbers question in a brief description of the proposed article 18. Depending on the future deliberations of the Convention, this 'would envisage the Commission either as a small college or a larger body'. The skeleton was unforthcoming on the other big issue concerning the Commission. This was whether or not to elect the Commission president, and if so how.

It is a common journalistic practice (at least in Britain) to insert the word 'unelected' in front of the word 'Commission'. In fact, the Commission president is selected by a tenuously democratic process in that the (democratically elected) members of the European Council nominate a candidate for president of the Commission by qualified majority voting, who is then approved by a simple majority of the European Parliament. However, the final say on the appointment of the president and the commissioners rests with the European Council.

For its advocates, election of the Commission president by the European Parliament would kill several birds with one stone. It would increase the democratic legitimacy of the Commission and so, it was argued, strengthen it as an institution. Election by the Parliament would enhance its own role, and could generate some positive spin-off in terms of greater voter interest in the European Parliament elections. As a properly elected office holder, the Commission president should also enjoy more clout in the European Council, where he (and it has always been 'he' so far) is the only nonelected leader.[9] All three consequences would be good news for integrationists. It was thus unsurprising that the election of the Commission president was strongly supported by most MEPs and representatives of smaller governments and by Germany, the most federally inclined of the big member states.

The Commission itself favoured election, despite some reservations from Antonio Vitorino. It proposed in its December submission to the Convention on institutional architecture[10] that the existing procedure should be reversed and the Parliament should elect the Commission president (thus ensuring the results of the European elections would be taken into account) before he or she was confirmed by the European Council. There were more radical ideas abroad. John Bruton, for example, suggested direct election by universal suffrage of the Commission president on the grounds this would help create a European *demos*, or political identity, and conform to Montesquieu's separation of powers. The Irish government suggested an electoral college of national and European parliamentarians should do the job.

Others, notably Britain and Spain, needed persuading. There were fears of a politicisation of the Commission that could undermine its regulatory functions, notably in the field of competition policy. Questions were raised over whether Parliament would choose a Commission president of the right calibre and what safeguards should be built into the process of nominating candidates for the post. As a compromise, the centre-right European People's Party at its October 2002 congress in Estoril decided the heads of state and government should nominate the president in the light of the European election results, with Parliament having the power to endorse or reject the nominee.

The question of how to appoint the other Commission members depended largely on the answers to questions over the number of commissioners and the process of choosing its president. If the Convention decided to strengthen the Commission president by making him or her elected, it would be logical to give the president-elect a greater say in choosing the college. But the exact size of the college and the pool of talent on which to draw would depend on the choices made in answer to the numbers question as well as specific issues, such as the location of the foreign minister in the institutional structure.

---

[9] As is the case for all members of the European Council 'club', the personality and ability of the Commission president would also be crucial to his acquiring influence, as opposed to mere acceptance.
[10] CONV 448/02 and COM (2002) 728 final entitled 'Peace, Freedom, Solidarity'.

9.6   THE EUROPEAN PARLIAMENT

While numbers stirred passions over their institutional implications in the Council and the Commission, their impact on the European Parliament tended to be less controversial. The directly elected Parliament operated with a manifest inequality of representation – to the disadvantage of the big member states. But it was ever thus. The system, known as degressive proportionality, meant a member for Luxembourg represented 72,000 citizens while a German MEP represented 829,000. The numbers were renegotiated at Nice but the disparity remained. From 2004, the Parliament, with a maximum of 732 seats, would include 99 MEPs from Germany and six from Luxembourg.

However, there were stirrings to adjust this situation. Before Nice, the Parliament itself had proposed that the MEPs per member state should be determined 'on the basis of populations under a proportional allocation system', adjusted to give states a minimum of four seats and with a maximum of 700 seats in the assembly. The argument in favour of such a system was that the number of MEPs could adjust more or less automatically in line with future enlargements rather than be subject to difficult negotiations as at Nice.

A bigger worry concerning the Parliament was its democratic legitimacy – or the widely perceived lack of it. The Laeken declaration asked whether there should be a review of the way MEPs were elected. In particular, it asked whether there should be a 'European electoral constituency' or whether constituencies should continue to be determined nationally. The European Communities Treaty, as modified in Nice, set the stage for elections by direct universal suffrage 'in accordance with a uniform procedure in all member states or in accordance with principles common to all member states'. This idea was echoed in article 35 of the skeleton, which promised to 'refer to a protocol containing provisions for elections to the European Parliament by a uniform procedure in all member states'. But this was later dropped from the Convention's agenda.

9.7   THE CONGRESS

The 'Congress of the Peoples of Europe' was one of Giscard's pet ideas. He wanted to bring together members of the European Parliament and members of national parliaments from time to time to review the state of the Union. On one hand, it could be seen as innocuous – a sort of bridge to overcome the obvious gaps in understanding between national and European politicians. On the other, Giscard was not averse to giving it some powers.

Article 19 of the skeleton mentioned the possibility of a Congress without providing any details. Most conventionnels were hostile. Debating the skeleton, Poland's Danuta Hübner said it was unnecessary to create new institutions when the existing ones needed improvement. Elmar Brok for the EPP denounced the Congress as a Franco-British inspired ruse to weaken both the European Parliament and national parliaments – the latter by giving their members tasks far away from their national capitals.

9.8 THE COURT OF JUSTICE AND OTHER INSTITUTIONS

The issues concerning the Court of Justice were less politically charged than those relating to the Union's policy-making institutions, but they were difficult nonetheless. A special 'discussion circle', chaired by Antonio Vitorino, met early in 2003. Among its concerns, it considered the procedures for appointing judges, whether to change the titles of the Court of Justice and the Court of First Instance (CFI), whether to shift some laws governing the Court from unanimity to qualified majority voting, whether to extend judicial review to the acts of Union 'agencies and bodies' and whether to make the penalties for non-compliance with Court judgements more effective. Several conventionnels also raised the issue of whether individuals should have better access to the CFI because case law in certain cases could make this impossible. A difficult political issue that crept on to the group's agenda was whether the Court of Justice should have jurisdiction against acts of the common foreign and security policy (CFSP).

As solving these problems turned into a largely separate process from achieving consensus over the main political issues facing the Convention, the results can be summarised here. The Convention ultimately opted for reforms, largely in line with the Vitorino group's recommendations. It was agreed to set up an advisory panel to help member states select the correct candidates to be judges. It renamed the CFI the 'High Court' to reflect the fact the Union was planning to set up further specialised courts, including a patent court, which would also deal with issues 'at first instance'. The creation of the specialised courts, the extension of the Court's jurisdiction to patents and changes to most of the Court's statute were made the subject of laws to be passed by QMV, rather than unanimity. In an important change,[11] the Convention decided the Court should be able to review the legality of acts of agencies and bodies. It adopted simplified wording to help give individuals access to the High Court in carefully defined circumstances. On foreign policy, it stipulated that the Court would have no jurisdiction over

---

[11] Article III-270 of the Convention text. III-365 of the treaty agreed by the IGC.

foreign and defence policy, although it would be able to rule on the legality of sanctions imposed by the Union.

The Convention included the European Central Bank (ECB) among the Union's institutions for the first time, albeit outside the constitutional treaty's main institutional framework.[12] The Convention ignored the efforts of a small minority of left-wing members to have the ECB take account of economic conditions, such as growth or employment, alongside its 'primary objective' of price stability when setting monetary policy. One change, which caused great concern some months later among financiers in the City of London, opened the way for the ECB to be given tasks related to the prudential supervision of banks and other financial institutions, excluding insurance companies, by QMV and codecision rather than unanimity in the Council with Parliament's assent.

Existing rules governing the Court of Auditors were unchanged by the Convention, which took no account of a call from the UK's Peter Hain and other government representatives for a shake-up in the Court's structure. The Nice summit agreed the Court should consist of one national per member state. Hain, who was following up suggestions from the British House of Lords, sought to put the Court under the management of a nine-member board of 'auditors general', who would come from the member states on the basis of strict rotation, and rename it the European Union Audit Office. The UK argued that the Nice arrangements threatened to make the Court unwieldy and ineffective.

9.9   GISCARD AND THE INSTITUTIONAL DEBATE

The institutional debate in the Convention was fraught with hazard. It was so easy to view the institutions individually and as protagonists in a turf war. Yet for the Union to thrive in the 21st century, all three sides of the institutional triangle needed to be strengthened.

This point was made by Giscard. But in the eyes of many conventionnels, he suffered from a credibility problem. He was after all, the man who had invented the European Council and he made no secret of his view that President Prodi's vision of the Commission forming the 'government' of the Union was based on a misunderstanding of history. When Giscard met the European Parliament's constitutional affairs committee in October 2001, he observed that the Union's founding fathers had indeed envisaged that the

---

[12] Article I-29 of the Convention text. I-30 of the treaty agreed by the IGC.

Commission would develop into a European government. But things had changed with the creation of the European Council. That was when Jean Monnet had told Giscard, 'You are right, the future European executive will be the European Council.'

After that, Giscard modified his rhetoric somewhat. At a later meeting of the constitutional affairs committee, a month after the Convention started, Olivier Duhamel, the French Socialist MEP, asked Giscard whether he was a 'Council man' or a 'Communitarian'. Giscard replied that he was a Communitarian at the time of the Treaty of Rome but then became a Council man. He now believed Europe needed a new form of cooperation between the two as well as an identifiable executive. For his listeners, it marked a change of viewpoint, but hardly a conversion.

Giscard faced another problem. He was generally perceived as a 'big country' man – an impression he did nothing to dispel while chairing the plenary. While it was clear that he paid attention when Peter Hain or Joschka Fischer spoke, he would often be seen chatting to Sir John Kerr or Giuliano Amato during the interventions from small member states. Such behaviour rankled and helped exacerbate ill feeling among the 'smalls' as the Convention progressed.

Part III

Changing Dynamics:
From Skeleton to Early Draft Articles

CHAPTER 10
The Member States Awake
and the Commission Confuses

The dynamics of the Convention underwent a radical change during the final months of 2002 and early 2003. As the working groups laboured to put flesh on Giscard's skeleton, the member states' governments woke up to the Convention's importance. Germany and France in particular upgraded their input, drafting in their foreign ministers as government representatives and simultaneously beefing up support staff. By contrast, and through no fault of the two commissioners in the Convention, the European Commission saw its influence erode because of disunity in the college and tactical errors. At the start of the Convention, the Commission had encapsulated the hopes of integrationists and was seen as the natural guardian of the interests of the small countries. Self-inflicted wounds made it largely irrelevant in the final forging of consensus.

10.1   THE INVASION OF FOREIGN MINISTERS

Spain's decision in July 2002 to promote its conventionnel, the MEP Ana Palacio, to foreign minister and keep her in the Convention and its Praesidium appeared an eccentric move at the time. But it set a trend that transformed the Convention. During the autumn, first Germany and then France appointed their foreign ministers to the Convention. Joschka Fischer and Dominique de Villepin were joined later by the foreign ministers of Slovenia and Latvia, and in 2003 by George Papandreou, the Greek foreign minister, who represented Greece in the Praesidium during the Greek EU presidency.

The upgrading of the German and French representations partly reflected the outcome of the two countries' general elections. Pre-election uncertainty – compounded in the French case by the stultifying effects of cohabitation between Lionel Jospin's socialist-led government and Jacque Chirac's right-wing presidency – meant both countries had little to say in the Convention's early months. Germany's Peter Glotz lacked the clout of ministerial office. France's Pierre Moscovici, the minister for Europe in Jospin's left-wing government, lost both office and power-base once cohabitation was swept away and the centre-right Raffarin administration took over in Paris. Moscovici was a semi-detached figure during the autumn of 2002, especially following France's decision during the summer to appoint a new alternate: Pascale Andréani, a precise and petite, bespectacled brunette who was a trusted adviser of President Chirac.

Fischer's appointment, announced in October, also reflected the increased strength of his Green party following a good election performance, which gave Germany's red-green coalition an unexpected further four years in power. Joining him as Germany's alternate and Gerhard Schröder's 'eyes and ears' in the Convention was Hans Martin Bury, a Social Democrat minister of state at the German foreign ministry.

Fischer was Germany's most popular politician and its best known Green. He was a one-time radical firebrand, who as environment minister in his home state of Hessen in the 1980s caused a stir by wearing sneakers in the Wiesbaden legislature. He had become the epitome of silken suited probity since taking over the Auswärtiges Amt after Schröder's first election victory in 1998. When he joined the Convention, Fischer was one of Europe's most respected foreign ministers and one of few who could claim to be an original thinker. He was a passionate European whose idealism was leavened by pragmatism. During Germany's EU presidency in 1999, he played a key part in launching the convention for the Charter of Fundamental Rights and developing Europe's security and defence initiative. His Humboldt lecture in May 2000 was the catalyst that led to the Convention and his decision to take part in its sessions gave it a palpable boost. Aged 54 when he joined the Convention, Fischer was a brilliant speaker who became one of a select band (including Vitorino, Lamassoure and Duff) who was guaranteed an attentive audience on taking the floor. But Fischer was also rather an elusive character, having, like his boss Schröder, re-invented himself several times in a long political career. He was not clubbable. He liked to fix issues behind the scenes and saw his trips to Brussels as occasions for bi-lateral wheeling and dealing rather than open discourse. A true conventionnel he was not.

If Fischer was elusive, de Villepin was showy. He joined the Convention around his 49th birthday, an impressive sight with a slender, tanned alert face and a shock of wavy grey hair. De Villepin cut a dashing figure and he knew it. He was also very cultured and let others know that. His first major speech on Europe[1] was a rhetorical *tour de force* that took his audience in its three opening paragraphs on a whirlwind tour of the continent's culture and history, from its ancient glories to the horrors of Guernica and Auschwitz. As he swept through a pantheon of the continent's cultural icons and inspirational politicians, de Villepin paid homage to Europe's founding

---

[1] 2 December 2002 in Marseilles.

fathers: Adenauer, Gasperi, Monnet and Schuman to whom he added General de Gaulle, who had known 'to combine the essential: Europe's ambitions with respect for its nation-states'. De Villepin had joined the French foreign service in the 1980s and been posted as a diplomat to Washington in that decade. He was a specialist in Asia, Africa and Madagascar before he became Chirac's secretary general in the Elysée in May 1995, a post he held for seven years. He was no expert on Europe when he took over as foreign minister in May 2002. He didn't need to be, with the diligent and efficient Pascale Andréani as his alternate and Pierre Vimont, Andréani's predecessor as alternate and a distinguished former permanent representative in Brussels, at the Quai d'Orsay.

Fischer lost no time in telling the Convention what he expected. In his first appearance on 28 October, he called for a European Constitution without options, which could be adopted without detailed negotiations in the subsequent intergovernmental conference. The Charter of Fundamental Rights would be included as a justiciable part of the text. He also wanted greater democratic legitimacy for the Union, a clear separation of powers at Union level, maintenance of the institutional triangle so that any strengthening of the Council would only be acceptable if the Commission and Parliament were also strengthened, and more integration to strengthen the Union's ability to act after enlargement. The latter point, he stressed, meant no reversal of policies determined by the Community method in favour of intergovernmental decision making. The Union's democratic legitimacy could best be served by having the European Parliament elect the Commission president.

De Villepin was similarly forward-looking when he made his debut in a plenary session on 5 December. He too spoke of a better balance of forces in the institutional triangle, but with a rather different emphasis. De Villepin found it odd that the Commission should only be accountable to the European Parliament and without any reciprocal obligation. He therefore suggested that the Commission should also be accountable to the European Council, which would be able to dissolve the Parliament on a proposal from the Commission. Whereas Fischer stressed the importance of strengthening all sides of the institutional triangle, the European Council bulked large in de Villepin's vision of Europe. It would have the responsibility for setting the strategic guidelines in all areas of Union action. The Council of Ministers' job would be to adopt decisions marked out by the Union's leaders. The Commission would 'imagine, propose and implement'. The Parliament would control, legislate with the Council, vote on the budget and 'perhaps one day, a community tax'. At first sight, Germany and France seemed to have little in common on the institutional front.

It was partly the inertia of Germany and France that had allowed Britain's Peter Hain to shine so much in the early months. Fischer was determined to change this. Hain recalls how at their first meeting in Brussels, Fischer greeted him with the words: 'I hear you Brits are running the Convention, that's why I'm here.' Ironically, the appointment of such heavyweights from the founding members of the original European Community came as Hain was promoted from being minister for Europe to secretary of state for Wales with cabinet rank. Hain stayed as Britain's representative and was as busy as ever. But his promotion left the UK Foreign Office with no direct representation in the Convention. Baroness Scotland, the UK government alternate, was a junior minister in the Lord Chancellor's office – the legal part of the UK government machine.

Hain's retention was a sign that Britain's prime minister, Tony Blair, was taking a keen personal interest in the Convention. But the broader personnel changes in the Convention came at an awkward time for Britain. As the Convention turned to tackle detailed issues, there were ever more questions where the UK had problems being part of a consensus. The working group discussions saw the UK in a minority on aspects of foreign, defence and tax policy, while the UK had difficulties accepting the incorporation of the Charter of Fundamental Rights in the eventual constitutional treaty. As far as Hain was concerned, the Convention's high profile meant he had to be doubly sure that the main UK ministries - the Treasury, the Home Office and the Foreign Office – understood what he was doing and would not work against him. Hain could work a room in Brussels but was in no position to overrule his colleagues in Whitehall.

There were also new faces representing the Netherlands, Portugal, Ireland, and Turkey. The appointment of Gijs de Vries, a former MEP, for the Netherlands, in place of Hans van Mierlo, brought a more active and thoughtful contributor to the Convention floor. The appointment of Dick Roche, the Irish minister for Europe, provided the small countries with a fluent and rugged advocate.

The invasion of the foreign ministers killed off for good the canard that the Convention was just a talking shop. Its profile, as measured by the number of television teams covering its meetings, rose appreciably. The quality of support staff rose in those delegations represented by high-ranking ministers. The foreign ministers, and ministers of cabinet rank such as Hain or Gianfranco Fini, Italy's deputy prime minister, could negotiate and cut deals in the expectation that they would be supported by their governments and parliaments. This was less certain for those countries represented by non-politicians. Finland, represented by an academic, was among the more disappointed member states at its close. Rank was also an important consideration for Giscard. Quite apart from his natural elitism, Giscard was more inclined to take note of a powerful minister representing a country because he or she would be better able to help determine the final consensus and bind their government to it.

There was an immediate inflation of expectations as pundits forecast that the appointments of Fischer and de Villepin would turn the Convention into the locus for negotiations and deal making that would reduce the subsequent IGC into little more than a rubber-stamping operation.[2] This appeared to be Fischer's view in the plenary session of 8 November, when he warned that: 'Anything that is not settled within the Convention will not be settled elsewhere.'

But the appointment of foreign ministers to the Convention was not without risk. They were very busy people with many other claims on their time. Ana Palacio, one of the Convention stars in its early months, was far less in evidence after her promotion in July, and in the late autumn was frequently absent from Praesidium meetings. Louis Michel, Belgium's foreign minister and a Convention representative from the start, hardly shone. Papandreou turned out to be a very spasmodic attendee, which was hardly surprising given the pressures of the Greek presidency in the first half of 2003. Fischer raised eyebrows on his first appearance at the Convention, when he appeared, delivered a speech and left shortly afterwards. In the final plenary session of 2002, which dealt with the important issues of foreign and defence policy, Fischer arrived near the end of the meeting, having been held up by a crucial parliamentary vote in Berlin. De Villepin was not much better, appearing after lunch for the second half of the all day session. The time pressures on the two ministers grew dramatically during 2003 as war loomed in Iraq and Germany started a two-year stint in the UN Security Council. Absenteeism and perfunctory appearances did not go down well with the other conventionnels.

10.2 THE FRANCO-GERMAN MOTOR STARTS TO TURN

The upgrading of the French and German representations was followed by a

---

[2] A trend that Giscard was determined to resist on the grounds that the Convention would lose its democratic legitimacy. See Giscard's article in *Le Monde* 14 January 2003: La Convention européenne à mi-parcours.

revival of the Franco-German partnership inside and outside the Convention room. In his Strasbourg speech of March 2002, President Chirac had called for a 'new founding pact between France and Germany' in January 2003 to mark the 40th anniversary of the Elysée Treaty of reconciliation between the two countries. As the anniversary approached, it became clear that this would also be the occasion for substantial thoughts about the future of Europe. Before the anniversary, however, the two foreign ministers submitted three joint contributions to the Convention on defence policy, justice and internal security and economic policy, which demonstrated shared ambitions for greater integration.

The paper on defence[3] was best timed to influence the debate in the Convention. It was published on 22 November, a month before the plenary discussion on the report of the defence working group, which mirrored many of its ideas. The Franco-German defence paper struck a decisively European (as opposed to NATO) note with a call for a 'solidarity clause' to bind member states in the new Treaty against terrorism and other risks. Its advocacy of reinforced cooperation in defence policy was also reminiscent of long past Franco-German aspirations to form an avant-garde in Europe. But the laudable and heavy stress placed on the need to build up military capabilities, strengthen military research and development, and create a European defence procurement market rang rather hollow in the light of Germany's shrinking military budget and its failure to fully support projects, such as the urgently needed Airbus A400 heavy lift transport aircraft.

The second joint paper on freedom, justice and security,[4] produced at the end of November, was a strongly integrationist document that went beyond the ideas already drafted for the final paper of John Bruton's working group. It urged a step-by-step transformation of Eurojust into a European public prosecutor's office; powers for Europol to carry out investigations, and rules for member state police forces to operate on the territory of other Union members in certain circumstances. It talked of 'harmonising' rather than approximating criminal law, urged 'effective controls' of asylum and immigration at the Union's borders, and called for a target date in the constitutional treaty for creating a European border police. The third pillar would disappear. Qualified majority voting would be introduced after a transitional period for all except coercive measures in the area of police cooperation and for most areas of judicial cooperation. Like Bruton, Fischer and de Villepin suggested that both the Commission and member states should have the power of initiative in policing issues. France and Germany

---

[3] CONV 422/02.
[4] CONV 435/02.

also advocated reinforced cooperation, even when fewer than eight member states supported a given measure in Council. The two countries differed on one detail: the best way of defining minimum standards when harmonising criminal law.

Joint proposals for strengthening the Eurogroup and improving economic policy coordination, published just before Christmas,[5] came too late to influence discussions in the working group on economic governance. But, again, the two countries threw their weight behind integrationist proposals that went beyond the working group's conclusions. Germany shifted its position, which had hitherto stressed the importance of keeping the 15-nation 'Ecofin' Council of EU finance ministers as the forum for economic policy decisions, to backing a 'Euro-Ecofin' Council in which the Eurogroup members could take their own economic policy decisions for the single currency zone. The paper called for recognition of the Eurogroup in a protocol to the constitutional treaty, appointment of its chair for two years and its single representation in international fora such as the International Monetary Fund. The paper also backed QMV for a number of key tax issues, including taxes as they affected the single market and some harmonisation of turnover and consumer taxes, thus posing a significant challenge to the UK, Sweden and Ireland.

10.3   THE COMMISSION AND PENELOPE

As the member state governments were raising their profile in the Convention, the European Commission was having problems. The Commission embarked on the Convention in a sprit of optimism and buoyed by a fund of goodwill, especially from the applicant countries and smaller member states. In addition to having two commissioners in the Praesidium, a large majority of the other Praesidium members could be counted as natural allies of the institution that represented the European interest and sought to preserve and enhance the Community method of decision making in the Union. The three government representatives, Henning Christophersen, a former commissioner, George Katiforis, an MEP, and Ana Palacio, an MEP until July 2002, knew the ways of Brussels and therefore how to appreciate the Commission's role. The same applied to the two representatives of the MEPs, Inigo Méndez de Vigo and Klaus Hänsch. Among the national parliamentarians in the Praesidium, the two from small countries, John Bruton from Ireland and Alojz Peterle of Slovenia, could be expected to sympathise with the Commission's goals. Jean-Luc Dehaene, one of

---

[5] CONV 470/02.

Giscard's two deputies, was an adviser to Romano Prodi, the Commission president, before the Nice European Council. The Commission set up its own task force in its Breydel headquarters building and this would spread its message through briefing notes and background information to inexperienced or sympathetic conventionnels. As an institution, the Commission seemed particularly well-placed to reach out to Convention members from national parliaments and accession countries, while in the Praesidium and plenaries, Michel Barnier and Antonio Vitorino, could draw on the resources of the 'house' to shine.

Words of goodwill came from the unlikeliest of sources. Peter Hain spoke of Britain's desire for a stronger Commission in his first speech to the Convention in March 2002. His sentiments were echoed some months later by Tony Blair in his keynote speech on the EU delivered in Cardiff on 28 November. Yet by early 2003, the Commission had lost much influence in the Convention. Instead of the Commission leading the debate, the Convention's secretariat had established an unchallenged monopoly of initiative.

The root cause was discord in the college on how to play the Convention. The problems started early in 2002 when the Commission was working on a paper to put to the Convention. The document, expected first for April and then early May, failed to appear. Instead, there were reports in April of the college holding an acrimonious seminar in Val Duchesse, the historic house in the suburbs of Brussels where the Commission and the Belgian government held their 'away days'. When the document finally appeared on 22 May,[6] it was a Chinese meal of a paper that left the consumer still hungry for more. Those conventionnels who expected it to structure the debate in the Convention were disappointed. Although entitled 'A Project for the European Union' it was far from comprehensive. It touched only on a few key aspects of the Convention's work: economic policy, CFSP, freedom, security and justice. Its passages on the constitutional treaty and the Union's institutions were discursive and circumspect.

The pattern repeated itself. The Commission was expected to produce a follow up document shortly after the summer break. It failed to appear amid reports and rumours of strains in the college. It was not until the beginning of December that the Commission published its long awaited second contribution[7] to the Convention, which contained its ideas on the EU's future institutional architecture under the title 'Peace, Freedom, Solidarity'.

---

[6] COM (2002) 247 final.
[7] COM (2002) 728 final.

It was a campaigning document rather than one that aimed to bridge the already obvious gap between 'communitarians' and 'intergovernmentalists'. At the heart of the Commission's plan to 'consolidate and develop the integration of Europe' lay an enhanced Community method of agreeing and implementing policy. Intergovernmental cooperation was disqualified as a 'source of inefficiency', while allowing the EU's future to be directed by just a few member states was 'a potential source for tension and dispute'. Unfortunately, hopes that this document might give a boost to the integrationist/small country camp as the Convention moved from the study to the negotiation phase were frustrated by the Commission's inept handling of its launch.

The first week of December saw the release of not just one but two Commission documents. In addition to the formal communication, which was approved after much difficulty by the college, there emerged a more radically federalist, full draft treaty for an enlarged EU in which almost all decisions would be taken by majority votes. Codenamed Penelope and variously described as a feasibility study or working document, this text was produced at Romano Prodi's request by a small group of Commission officials headed by Francois Lamoureux, a close former aide to Jacques Delors. The furore that surrounded Penelope's appearance overshadowed the official text.

Penelope was leaked to the French daily *Le Monde* and leading newspapers in Italy, Spain and Germany. The reports about it appeared on the streets of Paris just as the Convention Praesidium was meeting in Brussels on the afternoon of Wednesday, 4 December for the first of its December meetings. This was just hours before the college of commissioners was due to give final approval to the official document and on the eve of presentations of the formal communication by Prodi to the European Parliament, the press and the Convention.

In the Praesidium, Michel Barnier and Antonio Vitorino found themselves on the spot. They had come prepared to discuss the official document but instead were quizzed about Penelope. Later denials notwithstanding, a reliable source reported that the two disowned any knowledge of Penelope in the Praesidium. It later transpired the two commissioners were aware of the project but were not privy to its imminent, unorthodox disclosure. Giscard was especially peeved, probably because he did not know what to believe. He had obtained a copy of the Penelope text in unusual circumstances. The Convention president was at the Gare du Nord in Paris boarding the train to travel to the Praesidium meeting in Brussels when the individual sent by the Commission to Paris to brief *Le Monde* about the document gave Giscard his copy. It seems that Giscard was under the impression that this was the official Commission document.

The Wednesday night meeting of the Commission was long and stormy with Neil Kinnock, one of Prodi's vice-presidents, cutting Prodi's opening remarks off in mid-flow and demanding to know what was going on. Mario Monti, the Italian competition commissioner and normally a supporter of Prodi's, denounced the leak as unacceptable. According to one official, only four commissioners (Pascal Lamy, Philippe Busquin, Michaele Schreyer and Anna Diamantopoulou) supported the Penelope draft.

The following day, 5 December, Prodi presented the official Commission document to the Parliament, the press and the Convention. He glossed over Penelope, saying this was 'simply a mock-up, a feasibility study, a technical working tool'. It was 'neither discussed by the college nor submitted for its approval'. The college had 'no political responsibility for its content'. Although Prodi said he, Barnier and Vitorino had commissioned it from the group of experts, the pained expressions and uncomfortable body language of the two Commission members of the Convention when the three appeared before the press lent credence to reports that they had agreed to have their names associated with Penelope after its unofficial disclosure only as a face-saving exercise.

The simultaneous appearance of the two documents damaged the Commission's standing inside and outside the Convention. The two commissioners in the Convention were perceived as not having had the full trust of the Commission president. The creation and leaking of Penelope, moreover, reeked of the sort of backroom skulduggery that the Convention method was supposed to have replaced. Most worrying, the obvious disarray of the college of commissioners over Europe's constitutional future pointed to an institution that could at best only follow the Convention and was in no position to lead.

The confusion did nothing to enhance Prodi's credibility. 'I don't think you have done any political favours with this text,' Méndez de Vigo told Prodi after his morning appearance in the Parliament. 'Everyone is now talking about Penelope rather than the good document that you put forward.' As soon as Prodi finished presenting the Commission's formal document to the Convention in the afternoon, Giscard prevented any opportunity for questioning by immediately steering him through the door at the back of the podium. The snub delivered, conventionnels sitting just below the dais were amused to see Giscard return to his seat with a slight smile on his face and rubbing his hands together as if in satisfaction at a job well done.

Giscard's condemnation of the Commission's official contribution and Penelope came the following day. 'One might have thought there would be some emotion' in reaction to the Commission document, 'but no,' he said. He fastened on Penelope's preamble, which took over the text of the European Coal and Steel Community treaty with minor amendments, to deliver the *coup de grace*. Penelope, Giscard sniffed, was 'not current' and had 'an introduction that is 50 years old'. The message was clear. She could hardly serve as a Constitution that should last 50 years into the 21st century.

But Giscard was being unfair to a damsel in distress. Penelope, as a full draft treaty, was of considerable technical importance and, as the Convention's work unfolded, it became a handy source of reference throughout Brussels, not least for Giscard himself.

10.4   BENELUX DEFENDS THE COMMUNITY METHOD

The confusion surrounding the two Commission documents was a setback for those small country representatives who had become fearful that the largely intergovernmental 'ABC' group of Aznar, Blair and Chirac was having its own way in the drive to equip the EU with a powerful president, and that the Community method was in danger of being sidelined in the institutional debates surrounding the Convention.

The integrationists were therefore lucky that the Benelux countries were able to agree a memorandum[8] early in December, which addressed the institutional framework of 'an enlarged, more effective and more transparent Union'. This stated that: 'The Union must have strong common institutions, must favour and extend the Community method, and must strengthen those institutional elements which can best further the common interest'. It came out against new institutions, such as the Congress, arguing that the challenge was to make existing institutions more effective.

The Benelux also favoured keeping rotation for the European Council and specialised Councils. Putting down a marker of sorts, the memo said: 'the Benelux will in any case never accept a president elected from outside Council'.

The memo called for a stronger Commission. Its president should be elected by the European Parliament with a three-fifths majority of members and then confirmed by a qualified majority of leaders in the European Council. Louis

---

[8] CONV 457/02.

Michel, Belgium's foreign minister and representative in the Convention, said this voting system would ensure that the post could not be monopolised by the large countries. The text also provided for censure and dismissal of the Commission, while leaving details vague. The Commission would be 'responsible before the two institutions involved in its appointment and subject to dismissal through censure by one of those institutions'.

It called for sharper legislative procedures with more QMV and the extension of the Community method to the fight against crime and legislation on asylum and migration and judicial cooperation. The Council should meet in public when legislating. Codecision must be extended and the Parliament given equal powers with the Council on spending the EU budget. In the process, the distinction between compulsory and non-compulsory spending would go.

The executive should be improved by giving the Commission clearer powers to adopt secondary legislation, a stronger role in monitoring the stability pact and the extension of the Community decision making to euro-zone economic policy in a special euro-zone Council.

The Benelux countries made one unorthodox proposal intended to enhance the power of the Commission president: that he or she should chair the General Affairs Council. The Commission should also chair the External Relations Councils through the offices of a 'double-hatted' Commission vice-president, combining the roles of high representative and external relations commissioner. The Commission should represent externally other policies of the Union in the same way that it represented the EU at the World Trade Organisation.

The Benelux paper served as a signal that the big countries could not ride rough-shod over the Convention. Gijs de Vries, the Dutch government conventionnel, reported that the Benelux could count on the support of Ireland, Finland, Portugal, Greece, Denmark, Austria, the Czech Republic and Slovenia in calling for the retention of the rotating presidency, which was a principle that guaranteed the equality of member states.

The list of Benelux supporters was a first public reference to a group of government conventionnels from small and medium-sized countries that had begun to organise themselves to protect their interests. The group met first in October 2002 in the house of Gregor Woschnagg, the Austrian permanent representative to the EU, and subsequently over dinner during the two-day plenary sessions in the Brussels Dorint Hotel. Spurred on by Austria's Hannes Farnleitner and Ireland's Dick Roche, the representatives called themselves the 'Friends of the Community Method'. The group would grow to 16 countries and hold the Convention in thrall in the spring of 2003.

10.5   CONCERN OVER THE TIMETABLE

Muscle flexing by the smalls was in the future when the conventionnels returned to Brussels after the Christmas break. A more pressing concern was the tight timetable for completing their work. Tempers were frayed when Giscard refused to present a complete draft text of the constitutional treaty by February despite a request, submitted in the final plenary of 2002, from four MEPs (Alain Lamassoure and Hanja Maij-Weggen of the EPP, and Anne Van Lancker and Carlos Carnero Gonzalez of the PES) which was backed by 53 other signatories.

Instead, the president announced plans to present the first draft treaty articles to the Convention in January for discussion in February. These would cover titles I, II and III of the skeleton treaty on the definition and objectives of the Union; citizenship and fundamental rights and the contentious matter of Union competences and actions. The second set, due in February, would cover titles V, VII and IX, on the implementation of Union action; the Union finances and the relations between the Union and neighbouring states. The really difficult institutional questions would be tackled in the third set of draft articles due in March/April. Titles IV, VI, VIII and X would cover respectively the Union institutions (including the mooted presidencies of the Council and European Council and the Congress); the democratic life of the Union (including voting rules of Union institutions); Union action in the world (and especially the role and status of the high representative) and Union membership (including the issue of withdrawal from the Union).

A general debate on the EU's institutional architecture was scheduled for the January plenary session. But Giscard did little to dispel the conventionnels' fears about lack of urgency: two or three further meetings might be needed before drawing up draft articles, he said. Easter was the target date for the Convention to have a complete draft of the first part of the treaty. The draft articles of part three of the treaty, detailing general and final provisions, would be circulated in April.

Meanwhile, the Convention would begin work on the second, policy-related part of the treaty covering Union policies and their implementation. The Praesidium promised an analysis of existing treaty articles by the end of January, which would specify those needing replacement in the first and second parts of the treaty, and those needing only technical amendment. The Praesidium would prepare articles that needed major amendment, while work on the others would be delegated to the Convention secretariat and experts from the legal services of the Council, Commission and Parliament.

The handling of the draft articles would depend on the plenary discussions. If drafts were broadly accepted in plenary, members of the Convention could submit detailed points in writing. If big differences emerged, the Convention would set up 'discussion circles' with specific mandates and tight deadlines to sort out the problems. The circles would be small but comprise representatives from all the Convention's groups – governments, national parliaments, the European Parliament and the Commission – and so avoid the distortions caused by the self-selecting nature of the working groups.

Would it work or would it all end in tears? Giscard's message to the final session of the Convention in 2002 smacked of caution as well as optimism. He was not sure the Convention had grasped the implications of the 'big bang' enlargement agreed at December's Copenhagen European Council. 'The perception of this enlargement, which is now a reality, has suddenly made me aware of the huge and extraordinarily difficult job we have before us,' he said. On the other hand, he insisted his working methods were the best guarantee of the Convention reaching as large a consensus as possible by the summer. The final product, he added, should be 'precise and lyrical with a certain poetry and strength of expression'. By any standards, there was an enormous amount of work ahead, particularly as the leaders in Copenhagen made it absolutely clear that the Convention must complete its work in time for June's summit in Thessaloniki. There was very little margin for error if the Convention were to meet Giscard's goal of drafting a Constitution for an enlarged EU that would be good for 50 years.

CHAPTER 11
Divisions Among the Member States

In the early months of 2003, the Convention began to run on two tracks, both of which were overshadowed by the build-up to war in Iraq. The split between big and small member states, which had poisoned the Union since the French presidency in the second half of 2000, spread to the Convention and encompassed the accession countries alongside the established member states. At the same time, the Convention's Praesidium embarked on the difficult task of writing the first draft articles of the constitutional treaty. Although it never generated a split in the Convention as such, the division among member states over the conflict in Iraq cast a pall over the proceedings and contributed to delays. These various currents were to come together in April and May when draft articles on the Union's institutions were presented and debated in the plenary. This chapter looks at the tensions between big and small member states and the effects of the Iraq crisis. The next will follow the Convention as the Praesidium drafts the treaty texts.

11.1   FRANCO-GERMAN PROPOSALS ON INSTITUTIONS

The revival of the Franco-German partnership in the final two months of 2002 was welcomed by many conventionnels. Historically, the two countries had functioned as a motor for the Union and it was known that they were working on a significant joint position to mark the 40th anniversary of the Elysée Treaty in January 2003.

When the joint Franco-German proposals on the Union's institutions appeared in January they had a huge impact. They greatly advanced the debate on institutions, albeit in the direction of the 'ABC' suggestions of Prime Ministers Aznar and Blair and President Chirac. This was at the cost of deepening the emerging split between the big and small countries in the Convention.

The first three joint papers, while signalling close cooperation on major policies, had followed rather than led the debate in the Convention. By contrast, the joint Franco-German proposals on the institutions were to prove a key turning point in the life of the Convention. They were published on 15

January 2003,[1] the day after Chancellor Schröder and President Chirac met over a working dinner in the Elysée with their two foreign ministers. The text set the tone of the institutional debate for the rest of the Convention.

As so often in Franco-German relations, a pragmatic deal lay at the heart of the proposals. Chirac was one of the earliest advocates of a stable presidency of the European Council in place of the system of rotating every six months, while Germany, as a federal state and a traditional champion of the smaller member states, backed a stronger Commission with a president elected by the European Parliament. The 15 January compromise papered over these differences by meeting both aims, with plans for a long-term president of the European Council and an elected Commission president. The two countries also proposed a 'double-hatted' foreign minister for the Union, more QMV and codecision, and a restructuring of the formations of the Council of Ministers to cope with increased executive responsibilities in the fields of justice and home affairs, and the common foreign and security policy.

The two countries proposed a full-time president for the European Council of the enlarged Union, who would be elected by European Council members, using QMV for five years or for two and a half years with the possibility of re-election. The European Council would determine the basic political and strategic guidelines of the Union in cooperation with the Commission, and set ground rules and guidelines for CFSP and defence policy. Its president would prepare and chair the meetings of the Union's leaders in the European Council and supervise the implementation of its decisions. He or she would have an external role, representing the Union at meetings of heads of state or government. But the text stressed that the president must not upset the competences of the Commission and its president, and must be aware that the Union's foreign minister would carry out the operational tasks involved in CFSP.

The European foreign minister would be created from the Solana and Patten jobs to boost the coherence and credibility of Union foreign policy. The minister would be appointed by the European Council by QMV with the approval of the Commission president. He or she would have a formal right of initiative on CFSP issues and would take part in Commission meetings both ex-officio and as a special member of the Commission. CFSP matters would not be decided in the college of commissioners. But fulfilling a long-cherished German goal – and a striking novelty for France – the two countries agreed CFSP issues would generally be agreed by qualified majority voting among member states, except for military and defence

---

[1] CONV 489/03.

matters, which would be decided unanimously. The foreign minister would be supported by a European diplomatic service, which would include the Commission's external affairs directorate, the foreign section of the Council Secretariat and diplomats seconded from the member states and the Commission. The Commission's delegations abroad would become delegations of the Union. The Franco-German plan laid down rules in case a member state could not accept a foreign policy decision for reasons of national interest. It would first be the job of the foreign minister to seek a compromise solution. If the minister failed, the chair of the European Council would try. Failing that, the European Council would decide by QMV.

The two countries said the constitutional treaty must strengthen[2] the role of the Commission 'as motor of the European construction, guardian of the treaties and embodiment of the common European interest'. The joint text proposed the nomination of the Commission and its president after the European elections. This would be followed by the election of the president by a qualified majority of MEPs and confirmation by the European Council (also by QMV). The president would appoint the college of commissioners, taking account of geographical and demographic factors, and would be able to make a distinction between commissioners with sectoral, functional or special responsibilities on the basis of equal rotation. After approval by the European Parliament, the European Council would appoint the commissioners by QMV. The Commission president would provide political leadership in the Commission, which, as an institution, would be accountable to both the European Parliament and European Council.

The Franco-German paper proposed greater Commission powers in economic policy, notably the right to determine that an excessive deficit existed under the stability pact. In addition, the Commission must have sufficient powers to execute EU laws and supervise their implementation by the member states. In connection with this, the paper proposed a radical simplification of the Union's complex network of committees.

The European Parliament's powers of codecision would be extended automatically in line with each extension of QMV in the Council. The Parliament might also be given powers over Union revenues in a much simplified budgetary system.

---

[2] With some nuanced differences: the German text said 'muss …stärken' or 'must strengthen'; the French text 'doit confirmer' or 'must confirm'.

The text acknowledged that national parliaments had a role in the Union. It backed the 'early warning system' devised by the subsidiarity working group and said national parliaments should take part in future conventions to revise the treaty. Without creating any new institution, it suggested they take part in a dialogue with the European Parliament, which would include a joint annual debate on 'the state of the Union' in the framework of a 'congress' to be held in Strasbourg and chaired by the European Parliament president.

The Council of Ministers should in future concentrate on essentials, leaving the Commission and member states more responsibility in the execution of decisions. The paper proposed separating the Council's executive and legislative functions, with legislative discussions held in the public domain. Council decisions should, as a rule, be taken by QMV.

There would be a shake-up of chairs of the various Councils, with General Affairs being chaired by the Council secretary general; foreign and defence affairs by the Union foreign minister and Ecofin, the Eurogroup and justice and home affairs each selecting their own chair for two year periods. The other Council chairs would be arranged to give member states as much participation as possible on the basis of equal rotation.

The two countries proclaimed their goal was greater clarity, legitimacy and efficiency through a balanced strengthening of the Union's institutional triangle and its external representation. Their vision was of Europe as a Union of states, peoples and citizens with its institutions operating in a federation of nation-states.

While the Franco-German paper covered the waterfront, it lacked coherence in crucial parts. On detailed issues, the text bore the hallmarks of a fudge – which it was. It was not at all clear, for example, who should nominate the candidates to be the commissioners or the Commission president or whether there should be more than one candidate for Commission president. The paper appeared to hint at a two- or three-tier structure for the Commission, but, again, was not clear. It addressed the problem of a member state being unable to accept a common foreign policy position in the Union, but had nothing to say about potential conflicts of interest between the presidents of the European Council and the Commission, and the Union foreign minister. The lines of command and influence between the European Council president and the sectoral Councils, which were established through the machinery of national governments in the EU's rotating presidency system, appeared not to exist in the Franco-German plan.

The paper was very much a Schröder-Chirac agreement and testified to a strengthening working relationship between two pragmatic, if not opportunist, leaders who were not natural soul mates. It was a relationship in which Jacques Chirac seemed to have the upper hand. The two men had reached an agreement on agricultural policy in the autumn of 2002 that was good for France and bad for the cause of reform of the common agricultural policy that Germany notionally espoused. For Schröder, acceptance of the long-term European Council president was not such a radical step: he had already signalled movement towards supporting the idea, provided the post would not undermine the Commission, and had passed this message to Prodi over dinner at La Truffe Noire restaurant in Brussels in October.[3]

For Fischer the plan was a setback. He made clear his lack of enthusiasm for the European Council president on the day the text was published, commenting that it was 'about the art of the possible'. It transpired that he had proposed combining the roles of Commission president and Council president, but this was rejected by Chirac and Schröder as too complex. Fischer's stance verged on the disloyal in the days following disclosure of the Franco-German plan. When asked in a Frankfurter Allgemeine Zeitung interview[4] what the twin presidents of the Commission and European Council would achieve for the EU, Fischer ignored the question and stressed how he had wanted more, and that the agreement was the only way of bridging the difference between France's intergovernmental and Germany's integrationist approach to the EU.

Andrew Duff was quick to describe the agreement as 'more a barter deal than a genuine compromise'. Hans-Gert Pöttering, floor leader of the EPP in the European Parliament, warned it could lead to a shift of the institutional balance in favour of the national governments. Although the plan for an elected Commission president fulfilled a long held goal of the Parliament, Pöttering warned of a weakening of the Community method and a slide into intergovernmentalism. As if to confirm Pöttering's fears, Denis MacShane, Britain's minister for Europe, described the agreement as a 'good result for Europe and British policy'.[5]

In one special sense, the Franco-German initiative proved counterproductive for Berlin. Since the spectacular row between big and small states at the special European Council in Biarritz in autumn 2000, any coalition of large countries tended to produce an allergic reaction among the smaller EU countries. The strong support of other small countries for the Benelux memorandum in December was one symptom of this trend. Aware of this,

---

[3] *Financial Times* 11 October 2002.
[4] *FAZ* 17 January 2003.
[5] *Financial Times* 16 January 2003.

Elmar Brok had suggested that Germany be a champion of the smaller states. But Brok was a Christian Democrat appealing to a government of Social Democrats and Greens, which was under pressure from Chirac to agree the institutional accord before the celebrations of the 40th anniversary of the Elysée Treaty on 22 January. The German government agreed to the Franco-German institutional proposals without consulting its smaller Union partners. That was a mistake as the following meeting of the Convention showed.

11.2   THE SMALLS REVOLT

The Franco-German paper on the institutional architecture of Europe was meant by the two countries to give new impulses to the Convention as it embarked on the difficult task of addressing power questions in the EU. It did – but in ways that took its authors by surprise.

The paper dominated the proceedings when the Convention met on the afternoon of 20 January for its first discussion of the EU institutions. The tone was set by the first speaker to follow Giscard's introductory remarks. Gijs de Vries, the Netherlands' government representative, condemned the paper, focusing on its proposal for twin presidents. His arguments were echoed by many speakers who followed. The full-time European Council president would encroach on the powers of the Commission president, encouraging acrimony and stalemate. She or he would unbalance the position of the high representative or foreign minister. The plan would not bring the EU closer to its citizens. An EU of 25 needed a stronger, not a weaker, Commission. The rotating presidency was essential for the smaller countries. In fact, all four institutions needed strengthening and not just the Council.

To applause, speaker after speaker, from the smaller member states, applicant countries and the European Parliament joined the refrain. Duff condemned the paper as a 'cut and paste' exercise that accentuated the differences between the presidential and parliamentary Europe. Brok thought there was a risk of two separate European Unions with the Commission subordinated to the Council and confined to managing the internal market, while the European Council focused on foreign and security policy. This could not function in the long term. Dick Roche, the Irish government conventionnel, warned against an 'institutional coup d'etat'. Johannes Voggenhuber, the outspoken Austrian Green, observed sarcastically that 'an evening meal was no system for framing a Constitution' adding that 'the desire of Europeans for a Napoleon IV was limited'. Another prominent rejectionist was Louis Michel, Belgium's Convention member and foreign minister.

Among the rank and file Convention members, the French and Germans were less outspoken in their opposition. But only Hubert Haenel, the right of centre French senator, was enthusiastic. Predictably, another enthusiast for the long-term presidency was Peter Hain, the UK representative. Outside the convention hall, he claimed a 'critical mass' of governments (the UK, France, Germany, Spain, Sweden and possibly Denmark) supported an elected president.

When the French and German foreign ministers took their places in the Convention on the morning of Tuesday, 21 January (having been at the UN in New York the afternoon before) Joschka Fischer gave a singularly lacklustre performance in its support. In the margins of the Convention, Fischer was heard apologising to Brok for having failed to prevent the two countries' leaders agreeing the text. By the end of the meeting at lunchtime, the Dutch Christian Democrat MEP, Hanja Maij-Weggen, announced she had listened to 91 speakers of whom only 12 were for the long-term European Council presidency, 15 had serious reservations and 64 were against.

The revolt appeared to deal the Franco-German paper a serious blow. But the joint proposals were to be the template for all future discussions on the institutional settlement. Ironically, the paper was also the last significant joint contribution from Paris and Berlin as the two foreign ministries became increasingly preoccupied by events in Iraq.

The episode contained some lessons for Paris, Berlin and other governments. First, it showed that the Convention was not yet an Intergovernmental Conference, despite the influx of foreign ministers. Although Peter Hain claimed a critical mass of member state governments supported the long-term presidency and that many national parliamentarians in the Convention agreed with the idea, the strong opposition in the Convention hall suggested otherwise.

Second, the mass condemnation of the proposal for a European Council president showed how well-organised certain groups of conventionnels had become. The main political families – the EPP, PES and Liberals – met before the session on Monday to coordinate their members' interventions. It was around this time that Giuliano Amato, as head of the PES conventionnels, as well as one of the two Convention vice-presidents, established close ties with Brok, the head of the EPP caucus, which were to be of considerable significance when the time came to broker compromises.

Ad hoc groups also played an important role: a 'federalist' breakfast on the morning of the Tuesday, for example, bore fruit in coordinated 'blue card' interventions in support of the rotating presidency and Community method late in Tuesday's session. The conventionnels were learning the advantages of solidarity and numbers.

By early 2003, many Convention members were garnering support for one proposition or another. Examples included Andrew Duff, who gathered signatures from 20 Convention members and 11 alternates (from ELDR, PES and EPP) for 25 proposals on institutional reform; Joachim Würmeling, a Bavarian Christian Social MEP and alternate, who mustered 19 signatories in favour of a reference to God in the constitutional treaty, and Gisela Stuart who was active with Haenel of France in assembling names to ensure national parliaments were not left behind as the institutional debate gathered pace.

11.3   POINTS OF ATTRACTION

While the noisy condemnation of the Franco-German paper dominated the Convention's debate on the institutions on 20–21 January, there were signs of a narrowing of differences in other areas. These were highlighted after the plenary by Giscard and the European Parliament's two Praesidium members, Klaus Hänsch and Inigo Méndez de Vigo.

According to Giscard, the debate had shown 'extremely broad' support for maintaining the institutional balance between Commission, Council and Parliament and for the EU's federal/confederal mix. He claimed consensus was reached on extending codecision, making more use of qualified majority voting, setting up a Legislative Council and the election of the Commission president by the European Parliament. However, he also noted that the details remained in dispute, not least in the case of electing the Commission president by the Parliament. If QMV were adopted (such as a two-thirds vote suggested by the Commission or the Benelux idea of a three-fifths majority) what would happen if no candidate gained the necessary majority? Would the vote go to several rounds and end on a simple majority?

In Méndez de Vigo's view, the Convention was working well with a very positive atmosphere. Hänsch was even more upbeat, declaring that a 'breakthrough' had been achieved. He repeated Giscard's summary of consensus points and added the enhancement of the Parliament's budgetary powers and the creation of a European foreign minister. Hänsch even made some positive noises about the European Council presidency, provided it met certain conditions. These were that the president should have a clear job description with a strict definition of competences vis-à-vis the Commission president; no own administration; the reversion of the European Council to its original role so that it would not be a repair body for other Council formations; and the retention of rotation, with some changes, for other Council formations.

There were other signs of attempts to bridge the gap over the European Council presidency. Britain's Peter Hain went out of his way to call for a strong Commission in the plenary. 'We do not want a president of Europe', he insisted. Instead, circulating a job description to Convention members, he used the neutral term 'chair of the European Council' rather than president.

Giuliano Amato moved further along this line. In the plenary, Amato underlined the desirability of more continuity in the presidency of the European Council to cope with the 'revolution of numbers': the expansion of the EU from the original 6 to 25 members. Amato believed the president should be seen less as the EU's leader as the chairman of the European Council, which was the collective head of the Union. In such a role, a long-term president might help form consensus inside the European Council.

11.4 THE SMALLS ORGANISE

The Franco-German paper on institutional reform shocked the small and medium-sized member states into more action to find common ground against the threat of a *directoire* of big member states. The components of a bandwagon were in place. Calling themselves variously the 'like-minded group' or the 'friends of the Community method', representatives of small countries built on ties forged the previous autumn.

At the end of March 2003, 16 government representatives submitted a paper to the Convention entitled 'Reforming the institutions: principles and premises'.[6] First among the paper's 'key general principles' was maintaining and reinforcing the Community method. It went on to insist on preserving the Union's institutional balance, rejecting the idea of new institutions, stressing as a core principle the equality of member states and demanding the principle of one commissioner per member state 'provided there is full equality'. The group was not completely at one on the issue of the long-term presidency because Sweden and Denmark had, by this time, accepted the idea. But the paper saw retention of rotation 'as the predominant aspect of a

---

[6] CONV 646/03.

new system', particularly for the European Council, General Affairs Council and COREPER, the committee of ambassadors to the EU in Brussels.

Although the paper drew on the Benelux contribution of December[7] with its vision of a strengthened Community method, retention of the principle of rotation and hostility to a long-term European Council president, it was not signed by the Benelux states. Instead, the government representatives of Austria, Portugal, Ireland and Finland signed, as did those of Sweden and Denmark – the latter expressing reservations about the passages on the rotating European Council presidency. It was also signed by ten accession and applicant states: Cyprus, Hungary, Latvia, the Czech Republic, Slovakia, Bulgaria, Lithuania, Estonia, Slovenia and Malta – Poland being the notable absentee.

On 1 April, prime ministers and foreign ministers from Austria, Finland, Ireland and Portugal joined their Benelux colleagues in Luxembourg at the invitation of Jean-Claude Juncker, the Luxembourg prime minister and holder of the presidency of the Benelux group, to discuss institutional reform. The group was immediately dubbed the 'seven dwarfs'. After their discussions, Juncker attacked the proposals of the big countries for a long-term European Council president. The plans, he warned, could make the EU slide towards the intergovernmental method and could 'create a second Commission', reducing the Commission president to being the secretary or assistant of the president of the European Council. The Commission, he said, should keep 'all its rights and all its potential'.

The bandwagon continued to roll through April. On the eve of the Athens European Council on 16 April, the leaders of 18 smaller countries gathered in the ballroom of the Athens InterContinental hotel for a 'Benelux breakfast'. Among points agreed were a call for equality among member states, institutional balance and a refusal to create a new president of the European Council. The seven dwarfs were there as were nine of the accession countries (Poland being absent) and Romania and Bulgaria, which are candidates for membership in 2007. Greece, as holder of the presidency, stayed away to maintain neutrality but it was no secret that its sympathies lay with the 18.

The division between big and small worried many – notably Jean-Luc Dehaene, one of Giscard's two deputies. It appeared also to pose a threat to Giscard's ability to manage the Convention in its final, hectic phase because of his ill-disguised preference for the big country positions. But the unity

---

[7] CONV 457/02.

among the small and medium-sized countries proved fragile. There were differences inside the Benelux and difficulties coordinating its activities because of the volatile state of Dutch politics.[8] As early as February 2003, Guy Verhofstadt, the Belgian prime minister, was privately not at all convinced that a rotating European Council president was tenable and doubted whether there were sufficient proper jobs for a Commission of 25 or more. Furthermore, strong though the group of small countries appeared on institutional issues, there were differences among big and small over Iraq.

11.5   THE IMPACT OF THE IRAQ CRISIS

The Iraq crisis overshadowed the Convention but came nowhere near destroying it. To some extent, the Convention became a haven for the government-appointed conventionnels from either side of the old-new Europe divide diagnosed by US defence secretary Donald Rumsfeld. During Convention sessions, the foreign ministers of France and Germany would go out of their way to chat civilly with their fellow Convention members from Spain and Britain, both within and beyond the range of lurking television cameras. 'I was really struck how little to negligible the impact was that Iraq had on the person to person negotiations, the meetings in the Convention and the outcome for the UK,' Hain said later.

There were few direct references to the split in the debates. The conventionnels instead pressed on with their task of criticising and trying to modify a steadily increasing flow of draft articles from the Praesidium from the beginning of February. A casual observer would have had little sense of the pall cast by Iraq other than to note how Giscard would preface each plenary session from 27 February onwards with a doleful diagnosis of disarray in the continent he was seeking to reform.

The Iraq crisis did have an impact, however. It exposed the weakness of the common foreign and security policy, which, according to the Treaty on Union, obliged the member states to 'work together to enhance and develop their mutual political solidarity'. There was no working together or mutual solidarity in January when France and Germany publicly criticised the US for the Rumsfeld remarks without consulting their partners. There was still less when the leaders of Spain, the UK, Italy, Poland, Hungary, the Czech Republic, Denmark and Portugal signed a letter to the *Wall Street Journal*

---

[8] There were two general elections in the Netherlands during the Convention: on 15 May 2002 and 23 January 2003.

Europe[9] calling for unity with the US in its policy to rid Iraq of weapons of mass destruction without contacting Paris or Berlin. As Giscard noted, the Union seemed to be backsliding from commitments made at Maastricht ten years before.

The split silenced Javier Solana and Chris Patten. In the absence of a common political will, they had nothing to say over Iraq, raising the question of whether a double-hatted Union foreign minister would do much better. However, supporters of a long-term elected president of the European Council argued that such an individual would surely have brought the issue to the notice of EU leaders whereas the existing rotating presidencies had left Iraq off the agenda of successive Union summits.

The Iraq crisis gave new impetus to an idea that had barely surfaced in the Convention's previous discussions – that of 'enhanced cooperation' by which a small number of member states might push ahead of others with policies of greater integration. The interest in enhanced cooperation and, by extension, the possible emergence of a core Europe sprang from the total failure of the EU to hold a common position over Iraq.

For some, the failure of EU foreign policy over Iraq had a positive side. 'In the long term the crisis could become an opportunity for the common foreign and security policy', Elmar Brok told the German newspaper Die Welt on 3 March. Others considered that progress would depend on just a few countries taking the initiative. This idea was taken up by Belgium's prime minister, Guy Verhofstadt, in the course of the European Council of 20–21 March when he proposed an 'avant-garde' of Belgium, Germany and France to develop a common defence and security policy. This would become the 'defence mini summit' of Belgium, France, Germany and Luxembourg in Brussels on 29 April.

While Germany's chancellor, Gerhard Schröder, spoke of the desirability of Britain, the EU's most effective military power, being involved in any defence initiative, his foreign minister, Joschka Fischer, was equally clear that countries, which wanted to push ahead of the rest had a right to do so. 'Europeans must agree greater integration within the EU treaties', he said.[10] 'But if that doesn't work out, then a group of countries must press ahead, if necessary outside the treaties as in the case of Schengen. Whatever they decide can later be moved across into the treaties. There is an old rule in the

---

[9] *WSJE* 30 January 2003.
[10] In *Handelsblatt* 2 April 2003.

EU: Nobody has to wish for something; but those that wish, must also be enabled to act.'

The plans for the four-nation defence meeting split the Benelux and kept alive the divisions exposed by the letter of the eight in January. Early in April, the Dutch prime minister, Jan Peter Balkenende, was quoted as saying European defence without the UK was 'unthinkable'. Jose Manuel Durao Barroso, the Portuguese prime minister and future European Commission president, said any European defence identity must 'not go against our Euro-Atlantic alliance'. On 29 April, the leaders of the four mini-summit countries met and announced plans for a military planning centre in the Brussels suburb of Tervuren, which would be independent of NATO. In so doing, they challenged one of the central planks of British policy on European defence, which was to maintain close links between the EU and NATO. In the short term, the meeting of the four hardened the UK's determination to resist enhanced cooperation in the foreign policy and defence sectors.[11]

The Iraq crisis had other consequences for the Convention. The crisis – or rather French president Jacques Chirac's verbal assault in February on those accession countries that had the temerity to side with the Anglo-American coalition – worked wonders for the accession countries' sense of self-awareness. Partly because of Chirac's strictures that some of the former Communist countries had been 'very rude and rather reckless' in signing a letter of support for the US, and partly because of the liberating effect of having agreed the terms of enlargement at the December Copenhagen European Council, the conventionnels from the accession and applicant countries at last began to play a more prominent role in its discussions.

Less happily, Iraq made it difficult for the foreign ministers, who had joined the Convention in the autumn of 2002, to attend. Fischer and de Villepin would sometimes miss plenaries because of other commitments, including the United Nations' Security Council. Their appearances at the Convention would be brief, limited to a few minutes either side of their pre-planned interventions and alienated further many ordinary conventionnels. George Papandreou, the Greek foreign minister appointed to the Praesidium and Convention after the start of the Greek presidency, was a notable absentee. Spain, which started the fashion for drafting foreign ministers into the Convention drew a sensible conclusion. Early in 2003, foreign minister Ana Palacio became Spain's alternate while her former deputy, Alfonso Dastis, succeeded her as Spain's member in Convention and Praesidium. The promotion of Dastis provided much needed backbone for the government

---

[11] See Chapter 13.6

representatives in the Praesidium, and brought to the fore a formidable negotiator and operator on Spain's behalf.

The crisis added to the time pressure of the final months because the writing, publication and discussion of the draft articles on the Union's external action were postponed. The texts on the common foreign and security policy and defence were missing when, at the end of February, the Praesidium published draft articles 24 to 33 of the first – constitutional – part of the treaty. The two articles, which were foreshadowed in the skeleton, and the detailed provisions relating to the two policies in the second part of the treaty, were instead published in the first plenary after Easter.

Iraq held up the spring review of the Convention's progress by the European Council. The detailed discussion of the Convention, originally scheduled for the spring European Council in Brussels on 20–21 March, was held over to coincide with the signing in Athens on 16 April of the accession treaties for the ten new members that joined the Union on 1 May 2004. That postponement helped delay discussion in the Praesidium and presentation to the Plenary of the all-important draft articles on the Union's institutions.

CHAPTER 12
The Praesidium Produces

The Praesidium started writing the first draft articles of the constitutional treaty in January 2003. The exercise proved more difficult than expected and put the 13-strong steering group on a steep learning curve.

Whereas the working groups were phased to achieve some early 'easy wins' and give the Convention momentum into autumn 2002, the secretariat and Praesidium decided to tackle some of the most challenging issues in the planned constitutional treaty first. The Praesidium began with competences, which were tricky to define and where the working group had got nowhere. Although each Praesidium member was allowed a specialist legal adviser in the meetings, there were whispered complaints from Commission officials about the legal soundness and technical quality of the drafting. As the Convention plenary started on 20 January, Giscard disclosed that two Praesidium meetings reached agreement on no more than three or four articles. Amato admitted that the work was taking longer than expected and that the 'rhythm was not adequate'.

12.1 THE DRAFT ARTICLES: AN OVERVIEW

When Giscard unveiled the first 16 articles in draft form on 6 February[1] he announced that the texts, defining the Union, its values, objectives and competences, would give Europe's citizens the ability 'immediately and simply to grasp the essential characteristics of the Union, why it had been created, what it does and what it seeks to achieve'.

The new texts fleshed out the first three titles of the skeleton draft constitutional treaty, published at the end of October.[2] Giscard explained that the Praesidium had tried to draw up the first seven articles in language that was at once 'simple, forceful and solemn'. Four articles made up the first title, 'the definition and objectives of the Union'. As in the skeleton, they covered respectively: the establishment of the Union; the Union's values; the Union's objectives and its legal personality. The second title, the 'fundamental rights and citizenship of the Union', now comprised three

---

[1] CONV 528/03.
[2] CONV 369/02.

rather than the two articles indicated previously. Reference to the Charter of Fundamental Rights was brought forward to article 5. Article 6, a last minute insertion, barred any discrimination on the grounds of nationality. Article 7 (formerly article 5), defined Union citizenship.

Articles 8 to 16 in title III, 'the Union's competences', sought to bring clarity to a complex area in line with requests raised at the summits of Nice and Laeken. Following the outline of the skeleton, article 8 defined the fundamental principles governing the limits and use of Union competence. Article 9 laid out the rules for their application. Article 10 listed the different categories of competence. Articles 11 and 12 set out to define respectively the Union's exclusive competences and those shared with member states. Articles 13 and 14, a novelty compared with the skeleton, sought to define respectively the coordination of member states' economic policies and their obligations in exercising the common foreign and security policy. Article 15 outlined areas where the Union might help member states with 'coordinating, complementary or supporting action'. Responding to a strong consensus in the Convention, article 16, the so-called 'flexibility clause', updated the existing article 308 of the European Community treaty and gave the Union the capacity to achieve objectives set in the constitutional treaty in cases where it lacked the necessary powers.

The Praesidium's early efforts proved highly controversial. The 16 articles attracted 1,187 amendments, of which 435 referred to the first three articles alone. They were debated in the plenary session of 27–28 February and required extra one-day meetings of the Convention on 5 and 26 March after which many issues still remained unresolved.

In a cover note, the Praesidium paid tribute to the reports of the working groups on legal personality, the charter, economic governance, complementary competences, subsidiarity and external action, as well as guidelines that emerged during the Convention's plenary debates. But in many ways the activity over the preceding 10 months was less than helpful for the Praesidium. There had been no working group to clarify the issues in the first three articles. Only articles 4, 5 and 7 were based on the conclusions of successful working groups: those on legal personality and the Charter. Articles 8 to 16 on competences were prefigured by Henning Christophersen's group on complementary competences, which was the least successful and most contentious of all the working groups.

This lack of clarification in advance, combined with the constitutional significance of the first two titles plus the sheer technical difficulty involved in dealing with competences, helped explain the problems the Convention faced in dealing with the articles. Another problem was that the draft articles had to be taken on trust to some extent. The initial 16 articles were intended to relate to later articles fleshing out the EU's policies, which only appeared at the end of May. The absence of satisfactory background references to the as-yet unwritten policy section of the draft Constitution may have added to the large number of amendments.

The first 16 draft articles were followed by others at each plenary session before Easter. Draft articles 24 to 33 of title V,[3] 'the exercise of Union competence', were unveiled during the plenary of 27–28 February. They dealt with the instruments required to exercise the Union's competences, although details of articles 29 to 31 on common foreign and security policy, defence and police and criminal justice were left for later.

Title VII,[4] 'the finances of the Union', comprised articles 38 to 40 and was released on 17 March. So was the delayed article 31 of part one and 23 articles of part two,[5] laying out the details of the areas of freedom, security and justice.

On 4 April, the Praesidium published draft articles 33 to 37 of title VI,[6] 'the democratic life of the Union', and articles 43 to 46 of title X[7] on 'Union membership' including, for the first time, an exit clause giving the rules for voluntary withdrawal. Another novelty, foreshadowed in the skeleton and published on 4 April, was article 42 making up title IX,[8] which covered 'the Union and its immediate environment' and defined future relations between the Union and its neighbouring states. The Praesidium also published nine articles of what was provisionally called draft part three of the constitutional treaty.[9] These were the 'general and final provisions', which are found in all Union treaties. They defined such issues as legal continuity with past treaties, the geographical scope of the Constitution and, importantly, provisions for its revision, adoption and ratification. The articles on the institutions, as well as the delayed articles dealing with foreign and defence policy, appeared on 24 April, after Easter and less than two months before the deadline for producing the constitutional draft.

In other respects, the first four months of 2003 brought some changes of style to the Convention. As it tackled successive articles, its discussions

---

[3] CONV 571/03.
[4] CONV 602/03.
[5] CONV 614/03.
[6] CONV 650/03.
[7] CONV 648/03.
[8] CONV 649/03.
[9] CONV 647/03.

became more interactive. Those chaired by Giuliano Amato, the former Italian prime minister and one of Giscard's two deputies, often appeared like university seminars.

12.2   DIFFICULTIES WITH FEDERALISM AND GOD

The very first sentence of article 1 [I-1][10] on the 'establishment of the Union' ensured a stormy launch for the draft articles and drove a wedge between the Convention's integrationists and intergovernmentalists. 'Reflecting the will of the peoples and the States of Europe to build a common future, this Constitution establishes a Union [entitled...], within which the policies of the member states shall be coordinated, and which shall administer certain common competences on a federal basis,' it said.

Mention of the peoples as well as the states of Europe was an important modification compared with the skeleton, and in Giscard's words, placed the will of the people 'at the centre of the European construction'. The decision to leave the Union's proper title to be settled later was pure Giscard and bore witness to his hankering after 'United Europe'. But the storm broke over the 'f-word' (federal). Even though it had appeared in the skeleton, it prompted hostile criticism and amendments from a sizeable minority of accession country representatives as well as the UK's Peter Hain and the eurosceptics. It was no recompense that draft article 1 also emphasised that the Union 'shall respect the national identities of its member states'. The f-word was still generating heat during the special session of 26 March.

---

[10] Because the evolution of the articles is integral to understanding the eventual constitutional treaty and the frantic bargaining of the Convention's final phase, this and later chapters deal with the draft articles in some detail. The articles are introduced with the numbers they were given at the stage of the drafting process being discussed. Because the numbers sometimes changed as new articles were created and others deleted, references to the individual articles are accompanied at the first appropriate point in the text by a square bracket, which contains the number of the article as it appears in the final treaty text of 2004. Until the Athens European Council of 16 April 2003, the Convention worked on the assumption that part I of the final text would be the constitutional part, part II would detail policies and legal bases and part III the general and final provisions. This order was modified after the Athens meeting so that the first complete draft on 26 May 2003 designated the Charter of Fundamental Rights as part II of the constitutional treaty, moving the policies and legal bases to part III and the general and final provisions to part IV. The constitutional text stayed as part I. The Intergovernmental Conference that finalised the constitutional treaty in 2004 agreed on continuous numbering of the articles using Arabic numerals. However, to accentuate the division of the constitutional treaty into four parts it also decided that the Arabic numerals would be preceded by a Roman numeral corresponding to the relevant part of the treaty. This system, adopted in CIG 87/04 and the Official Journal of the EU, C310 of 16 December 2004, is used for the articles in square brackets in this book.

By contrast, de Villepin for France and Fischer for Germany were among a broad cross-section of integrationists who wanted a reference to 'ever closer union', which was part of the EU canon but missing from the Praesidium text. Several parliamentarians, notably from France and the Party of European Socialists, wanted mention of the symbols of the Union, such as its flag, money, holiday and anthem. Many conventionnels suggested a reference to citizens rather than peoples. Others wanted a reference to the regions.

The Union's values were dealt with in article 2 [I-2]. It was to be 'founded on the values of respect for human dignity, liberty, democracy, the rule of law and respect for human rights'. This article, Giscard explained, concentrated on the essential values at the very heart of society and was brief so the values could serve as a base for action and sanctions against a delinquent member state if necessary. The later draft articles 43 [I-58] and 45 [I-59], detailing the eligibility criteria for Union membership and the rules for suspension of membership rights, made specific reference to the values in article 2.

Missing was any mention of spiritual values or God in the article, despite heavy lobbying from the Catholic church and its supporters in the Convention. The pros and cons of the religious question bulked large in the amendments to the first articles and was the subject of heated debate in plenaries up to and including the special meeting on 26 March. Conventionnels from the EPP called for a reference to God on the lines of the Polish Constitution.[11] Others fiercely contested the place of God in such a text and sought help from outside. In late February, the Spanish socialist parliamentarian Josep Borrell[12] submitted a resolution signed by 163 MEPs, of whom 80 were from the PES and only nine from the EPP, asking the Convention to assure that 'no direct or indirect reference to any specific religion or belief is included' in the future Constitution. Instead, it called for promotion of the right of freedom of religion and the principle of 'separation and independence between church and state'. The Praesidium's view was that the best place for a spiritual reference was in the (as yet unwritten) preamble. When presenting the draft articles of title VI, the democratic life of the Union, in the early April plenary session, the Praesidium also included, as draft article 37 [I-52], a statement respecting the status of churches and religious associations as well as philosophical and non-confessional organisations.

---

[11] 'The Union's values include the values of those who believe in God as the source of truth, justice, good and beauty as well as those who do not share such a belief but respect these universal values arising from other sources.'

[12] Borrell became president of the European Parliament after the June 2004 election.

Article 3 [I-3] detailing the Union's objectives was less pithy, having expanded in length during the Praesidium's deliberations. A brief opening paragraph, which defined the Union's aim as 'to promote peace, its values and the well-being of its peoples', was followed by a long list of economic, social and technological objectives including full employment, high levels of competitiveness, equality between men and women and even 'the discovery of space'. The various objectives sought to embrace interests as varied as free marketeers and social welfare adherents. Later paragraphs bundled together the Union as an 'area of freedom, security and justice' with respect of cultural diversity. A passage projecting the Union's objectives in the wider world pledged contributions to another eclectic list, including sustainable development, eradication of poverty and protection of children's rights.

Giscard said the text sought not to produce a bewildering full list of EU policies, which would soon lose the attention of the average citizen, but to define objectives in a more forceful and political way. Inevitably the approach triggered opposition. Many conventionnels sought to add more objectives. Some, including representatives of ten governments, wanted a reference to improving the environment. A broad cross-section of the centre-left demanded mention of the 'social market economy' and explicit support for public services. Only in the case of the discovery of space, Giscard's symbol of modernity, were there significant calls to reverse this 'Christmas tree' approach and drop an objective.

The influence of an effective working group was clear in article 4 [I-7]. The single line, 'The Union shall have legal personality', reflected the conclusion of Giuliano Amato's first working group aimed at consolidating the EU and TEC treaties and ending the EU's pillar structure. This, the least controversial of the first articles, stayed unamended throughout.

Article 5 [I-9] said the Charter 'shall be an integral part of the Constitution' and therefore mirrored the conclusion of Antonio Vitorino's working group. Pending clarification of UK objections, it left open whether it should be in the treaty text or a protocol. Article 6 [I-4] barred discrimination on the grounds of nationality and was separated from the following one (article 7) on the grounds that it would also apply to non-EU citizens. Article 7 [I-10] on Union citizenship, said every national of a member state would also be a citizen of the Union, and as such equal before the law. The article repeated rights already defined in the Charter and in the citizenship part of the current European Communities Treaty.

12.3   MAKING SENSE OF COMPETENCES

The Praesidium's draft articles on competences were a blend of the fundamental and the specific and the result of difficult internal negotiations. Drafting treaty texts proved a difficult technical exercise. Parliament's Lamassoure report, the deliberations of the Christophersen working group and the Commission's Penelope draft Constitution all offered different approaches to the problem. Consequently, the Praesidium took four meetings in January to complete the articles on competences.

The Praesidium started work on a secretariat draft, which was concise and relatively simple, and owed a lot to Lamassoure's pioneering work. It immediately upset the Commission and some members of the European Parliament. Reflecting the determination of Commission president Romano Prodi to promote the Penelope document, Michel Barnier tabled an alternative draft, based on the Penelope principles and sought to mobilise the Commission's allies in the Praesidium.

The conflicting philosophies of the secretariat draft and Penelope made for protracted and tense discussions. Barnier and Vitorino were under instructions not to negotiate on the basis of the secretariat's draft articles on competences. The upshot was three days of angry debate in the Praesidium, which cost time, and caused Dehaene and Amato to reconsider their support for the Commission. When it became clear that Barnier's initiative was failing to win sufficient backing the way was clear for the Praesidium, helped by Vitorino, one of the Convention's key problem solvers, to clarify the principles and the categories. The result was a 'first', according to Giscard. He told the Convention that the articles presented the entirety of competences attributed to the Union and the fundamental principles underpinning their application 'in just four pages' without falling into the trap of a rigid catalogue of competences.

Unfortunately, the articles were also confusing in parts. The Praesidium, in embellishing the simpler secretariat text, had allowed some errors to creep in. Hence, the text included the four freedoms as an exclusive competence in article 11, against the advice of the secretariat, while also listing the internal market as a shared competence in article 12. But these were mere quibbles compared with the anger stirred among intergovernmentalists and eurosceptics by the Praesidium's use of language and the surprise that simply spelling out the powers of the Union provoked among many conventionnels and commentators.

Article 8 [I-11] stated that the limits and use of Union competences were governed by 'the principles of conferral, subsidiarity, proportionality and loyal cooperation', the first three points of which should have offered comfort to non-federalists. But in attempting to pin down how powers were conferred on the Union, it stirred a hornets' nest when it said: 'In accordance with the principle of conferral, the Union shall act within the limits of the competences conferred upon it by the Constitution[13] to attain the objectives the Constitution sets out. Competences not conferred upon the Union by the Constitution remain within the member states.' The idea that member states confer powers on the Union was missing.

Article 9 [later incorporated in other articles] defined the application of the fundamental principles in the previous article and was drafted in a similar manner. Moreover, it put down in treaty language for the first time the idea that Union law had primacy over national law. It said: 'The Constitution, and law adopted by Union institutions in exercising competences conferred on it by the Constitution, shall have primacy over the law of member states' [I-6]. Although long established in EU case law, the principle came as a shock to many, including Britain's eurosceptic media. The balancing item that the Union's institutions would apply the rules of subsidiarity and proportionality, as detailed in a separate protocol, when exercising non-exclusive competences went unnoticed.

Article 10 [I-12] contained more surprises for those not steeped in the ways of Brussels when it spelled out the broad categories of competence and the consequences for member states of the Union's exercise of its competences. Leaving no doubt of the significance of exclusive competences, it said: 'When the Constitution confers on the Union exclusive competence in a specific area, only the Union may legislate and adopt legally binding acts, the member states being able to do so themselves only if empowered by the Union'. A bigger surprise came with the definition of competences shared between the Union and member states. Here it said, 'the Union and the member state shall have the power to legislate and adopt legally binding acts in this area' but member states would exercise their competence 'only if and to the extent that the Union has not exercised its'.

Using phrases that would stir the wrath of the UK and the eurosceptics, article 10 stated baldly that 'the Union shall have competence to coordinate the economic policies of member states' and equally 'the Union shall have competence to define and implement a common foreign and security policy, including the progressive framing of a common defence policy'. Again, there was no mention of competences being conferred by member states.

---

[13] Emphasis added.

Article 11 ambitiously gave the Union exclusive competence over the four freedoms 'to ensure the free movement of persons, goods, services and capital, and establish competition rules, within the internal market' [brought forwards to I-4]. It also specified exclusive powers for the Union over the customs union, monetary policy for euro-zone members, the conservation of fish stocks under the common fisheries policy, as well as the 'common commercial policy' [I-13]. The blanket reference to the common commercial policy as an exclusive competence was controversial to the very end of the Convention. It threatened a compromise in the Treaty of Nice that left national governments with a veto over the negotiation and conclusion of trade agreements covering cultural and audio-visual services. Known as the 'cultural exception', this was a fiercely defended French national interest.

Article 12 [I-14] on shared competences provided an illustrative list of 11 policy areas ranging from the internal market (duplicating the reference in article 11), through agriculture and social policy to consumer protection and included energy, which would require a new legal base in the policies part of the Constitution.

The coordination of economic policies and the common foreign and security policy were given their own articles – 13 and 14 – because of their political importance and because they did not involve legislation. Again the texts stirred opposition. Article 13 [I-15] appeared to give the Union greater powers when it said 'the Union shall coordinate the economic policies of the member states'. Using words from the Maastricht Treaty, which were unfamiliar to several government representatives, article 14 [I-16] said 'member states shall actively and unreservedly support the Union's common foreign and security policy'.

Article 15 [I-17] listed employment, industry, education and youth, culture, sport and protection against disasters as areas for supporting action, with the important qualification that legally binding acts in these areas could not lead to harmonisation of member states' laws.

Unlike most of the articles on competences, the flexibility clause, Article 16 [I-18], was relatively uncontroversial despite increasing its scope to all the policies that would be detailed later in the treaty, while the existing article 308 of the TEC applied only to the 'common market'. The flexibility clause allows the Union to act in cases where it has not been given specific powers. To prevent the article becoming an engine for integration, it diverged from the general principle that acts should be taken on the basis of qualified majority voting and codecision between the Council of Ministers and the European Parliament, instead specifying unanimity in the Council on a proposal from the Commission after winning the assent of Parliament. In an important safeguard, member states' national parliaments would be alerted to a flexibility clause proposal.

The articles on competences prompted a large number of amendments although when debated in the 28 February plenary session, they won broad support from MEPs Hänsch (representing the PES) and Lamassoure (EPP). Many conventionnels objected to the lists chosen to augment the articles, with several proposing deletion of the illustrative list of shared competences. Duff for the Liberals thought the classification too rigid while, as champion of Penelope, Commissioner Barnier sniffed that he would have 'preferred a more political classification more in line with what the EU represents'. Predictably, de Villepin and the French parliamentarians sought to maintain the Nice compromise on commercial policy.

The UK's Hain was especially insistent that articles 1, 8, 9 and 10 make clear member states had conferred powers on the Union, and was backed by Dick Roche, the Irish representative. Like Hain, de Villepin of France, Fischer of Germany and Lena Hjelm-Wallen of Sweden sought to change draft article 13 so the member states, and not the Union, would coordinate economic policies. However, there appeared to be a significant difference in Hain's body language to that of most other conventionnels. Clearly angry on the day the articles were released, he behaved at times more like one of the Convention's small group of eurosceptics than the representative of a government that sought to be at the centre of Europe.

12.4   THE PRAESIDIUM UNDER PRESSURE

It is debatable whether Hain, and occasionally other government representatives, would have needed to be so robust in plenary sessions had the government representatives in the Praesidium not been so weak in the first months of 2003. The less integrationist governments had to use the plenary to claw back points conceded in the Praesidium, adding to an atmosphere of rancour. The drafting of the first 16 articles was the first real test of the Praesidium as a body. As the Praesidium's work speeded up – overshooting its self-appointed end-January deadline by a week – it emerged as a more integrationist body than the Convention itself.

This reflected a tendency of Praesidium members to revert to instinctive reactions when under pressure. More than half the members were integrationist by vocation or instinct, including the two commissioners, the two MEPs' representatives and Giscard's deputies, Amato and Dehaene. As the drafting work progressed, the commissioners could call on extra resources from the Commission, which provided 12 officials to help them out.

The three national government representatives were either unable or unwilling to form a strong countervailing force. Spain's Ana Palacio was absent from many sessions from November. Her deputy, Alfonso Dastis, when attending, was not allowed to speak until formally promoted to take her place in March 2003. George Katiforis, until March the Greek representative, was absent from several sessions after a road accident early in 2003. Henning Christophersen, the Danish government representative, was often alone in putting a nation-state viewpoint.

The three national parliamentarians – Gisela Stuart of the UK, John Bruton of Ireland and Alojz Peterle of Slovenia – also punched below their numerical weight. The national parliamentarians were numerically the biggest group in the Convention but less cohesive than others. The three therefore tended to represent only themselves. They also had the additional disadvantage of no great Brussels experience – although Bruton, as a former Irish prime minister, had been a European Council member.

In January, Gisela Stuart was heard to complain of being 'outnumbered and outgunned' as the dynamics in the Praesidium ran in a federal direction. A first draft from the Convention secretariat might be broadly acceptable in her terms. But then a 'mass of amendments' would be presented by the federalist members of the Praesidium and 'the goalposts move'. When reporting to a joint standing committee on the Convention of the two houses of the UK parliament,[14] Stuart contrasted the cohesion of most European parliamentarians with the divisions among national parliamentarians. The debate in the Convention was affected by the ability of the European parliamentarians to overcome their political differences, she claimed.

However, there was an alternative view that the problem lay with Stuart and Bruton, who were handicapped by not being able to represent the disparate bunch of national parliamentarians in the Convention credibly as a whole. Thus when Stuart spoke up for a more stringent 'red card' or veto control over subsidiarity by national parliaments, she was seen as representing Downing Street's interest rather than the views of the biggest group in the Convention. Similarly, when Bruton put forward his idea of a directly elected Commission president, it was viewed as a personal enthusiasm, shared perhaps by two or three other conventionnels.

---

[14] On 12 February 2003.

12.5   THE UNION'S INSTRUMENTS

The Praesidium put up a better show when it presented its second batch of draft articles on 28 February. Having dealt with the *who* and the *what* of competences earlier in the month, draft title V, comprising articles 24 to 33 was concerned with *how* the Union would carry out its tasks. The Praesidium was well prepared after two plenary debates[15] and Amato's successful simplification working group. The result was a low harvest of amendments of just 237 by the time the Convention debated the articles on 17 March.

The Praesidium built on a broad consensus in Amato's working group to reduce sharply the legal instruments from 15 to 6, give them more readily understandable names and, in the process, introduce a hierarchy of legislation in the Constitution. Article 24 [I-33] therefore adopted the names and definitions of the Amato working group, prescribing 'European laws, European framework laws, European regulations, European decisions, recommendations and opinions' and also made provision for some non-standard acts such as resolutions, declarations and conclusions not provided for in the Constitution.

Taking over some of Amato's most important recommendations, Article 25 [I-34] said laws and framework laws would be adopted by codecision, which was renamed 'the legislative procedure'. This meant qualified majority voting in the Council of Ministers. It added that the Council of Ministers and Parliament should meet in public 'when acting under any procedure' for the adoption of laws or framework laws. It made clear, however, that special rules would apply to the common foreign and security policy and former third pillar legislation in the area of freedom, security and justice.

Despite qualms in earlier plenary discussions, the Praesidium tackled the problem arising from the lack of any procedure for secondary legislation in the EU. In article 27 [I-36], it proposed a new type of act – 'the delegated regulation' – by which laws or framework laws could delegate to the Commission the power to enact delegated regulations. Only non-essential, technical elements of legislation would be delegated and strict conditions would apply. These would include 'call back' provisions for the EU legislators, the Parliament and the Council, or 'sunset' clauses in the legislation itself. The delegated act was intended to encourage Parliament and Council to focus on essentials and avoid excessively complex legislation in future.

---

[15] On 23–24 May and 12–13 September 2002.

The plenary discussions on the new articles raised few negative passions. Indeed among the MEPs, Klaus Hänsch for the PES and Alain Lamassoure, speaking for the EPP, were enthusiastic. Hänsch described articles 24 to 33 as 'a major qualitative leap forward' while Lamassoure said the presentation was 'simpler and clearer, reflecting a political and legal hierarchy in line with our vision of the EU'. The eurosceptics were less enthused, with David Heathcoat-Amory warning that non-legislative instruments, mentioned in article 26 [I-35], could lead to 'rule by decree'.

12.6 PROTOCOLS CLARIFY SUBSIDIARITY AND THE ROLE OF NATIONAL PARLIAMENTS

On 27 February, the Praesidium presented a pair of draft protocols, on applying the principles of subsidiarity and proportionality and the role of national parliaments, to the Convention.[16]

The draft protocol on subsidiarity was important, although not as important as suggested by Inigo Méndez de Vigo, the chairman of the subsidiarity working group. Méndez de Vigo, whom Giscard dubbed 'the pope of subsidiarity', told the 18 March plenary that 'nothing of such proportions has been achieved in 50 years'. The protocol detailed how EU institutions would respect the principles of subsidiarity and proportionality and build on the clear proposals of an effective working group.[17] It described a 'yellow card' early warning system by which a national parliament could object to a legislative proposal if it failed to comply with subsidiarity. It also set out the procedures for informing national parliaments of Commission proposals at the same time as the Council and the European Parliament.

The yellow card rules said:

- Each national parliament could activate the early warning system. They would be responsible internally for sorting out which chamber did what, where there were bicameral parliaments or regional parliaments with legislative powers.
- One-third of national parliaments could force the Commission to review its proposal.
- The Court of Justice should be able to rule on infringement actions brought by member states at the behest of national parliaments and regional parliaments and by the Committee of the Regions, in cases where it was consulted.

---

[16] CONV 579/03.
[17] See chapter 7 and CONV 286/02.

Of less constitutional significance, the draft protocol on the role of national parliaments laid down the rules for information on legislation and other documents to flow from the Commission and other institutions. It also promised that the European Parliament and national parliaments would examine how to promote inter-parliamentary cooperation in the EU.

Gisela Stuart proposed having a 'red card', by which two-thirds of parliamentary votes would force the Commission to withdraw a proposal.[18] But this was trounced, with many conventionnels using unusually forthright language. Lamberto Dini poured scorn on Stuart's idea, providing a foretaste of later divisions between these two leading members of the national parliamentarians group. Dini demanded the red card idea be dropped because 'it means giving national parliaments the power of veto over the initiative of the Commission and that we should not do'.

The discussion on national parliaments was notable only because it allowed Giscard, when summing up, to keep alive his idea for a European Congress of MEPs and national parliamentarians. He signalled it would be on the agenda when the Convention finally turned to institutional questions.

12.7   THE AREA OF FREEDOM, SECURITY AND JUSTICE

The articles on 'the area of freedom, security and justice' gave conventionnels a first chance to see how a draft article in the first constitutional part of the treaty would dovetail with the detailed policy provisions of what was then called part two and was to be part III. Comprising draft article 31 [I-42] of part one and no fewer than 23 articles in part two, the new articles were also important because for the first time the Convention could see the practical consequences of doing away with the third 'justice and home affairs' pillar of the Maastricht Treaty.

Presented to the plenary on 17 March, the articles followed closely the conclusions of John Bruton's working group.[19] Article 31 outlined three types of Union action in the area of freedom, security and justice. These 'specificities' prompted a flurry of amendments and much debate in the Plenary session of April 3. The 23 detailed articles showed that the Community method would extend far into areas of government, which, until the 11 September terrorist attacks in the US, had strongly resisted EU influences. Adoption of legislative procedure under the Community method was widespread and would result in a switch to qualified majority voting in

---

[18] Footnote: CONV 540/03.
[19] CONV 426/02.

several articles. Unanimity was retained where new competences would be added.

Article 31 envisaged:

- Community action – 'laws and framework laws' – particularly to approximate national laws in areas such as asylum, immigration and border controls, detailed in part two,
- promotion of mutual confidence between member states authorities 'in particular on the basis of mutual recognition of judicial and extrajudicial decisions'
- operational cooperation between all competent authorities of member states for internal security.

It charted special roles for national parliaments in evaluating JHA policy as a whole and monitoring the activities of Europol, the EU's fledgling police authority. These were detailed in part two in articles 3 [III-259], 4 [III-260] and 22 [III-276]. In a provision unique to this section of the constitutional treaty, article 31 also awarded member states a right of initiative in police and judicial cooperation in criminal matters alongside the Commission's right of initiative. Article 8 of part two [III-264] said this could be triggered by a quarter of member states.

Of the 23 detailed articles, nine in part two [later eight from III-257 to III-264] defined the area of freedom, security and justice, its institutional framework and operations. Four articles [III-265 to III-268] then detailed the policies on border checks, asylum and immigration, specifying in nearly all cases that the 'legislative procedure'[20] would apply to law making. One article [III-269], laid down the Union's policy of judicial cooperation in civil matters, specifying that generally the legislative procedure would apply for adopting measures to approximate national laws. Unanimity would apply to most aspects of family law, however.

Six articles [later five from III-270 to III-274] dealt with judicial cooperation in criminal matters, stipulating the legislative procedure for the approximation of laws and setting of minimum standards in areas such as criminal procedure and crime prevention. Article 17 [III-271] on substantive criminal law included a list of especially serious cross-border crimes, such as terrorism, trafficking in humans, drugs and arms, sexual exploitation of

---

[20] Comprising codecision and QMV in the Council and defined in the final Convention and IGC texts as European laws or framework laws.

women and children, money laundering, counterfeiting, and computer and organised crime, where minimum rules could be set by the legislative procedure. The Council of Ministers would also have the right to add crimes to the list on the basis of unanimity.

In this section, article 19 [III-273] specified the role of Eurojust, the mechanism by which national prosecutors can cooperate in combating cross-border crime. It stated that the European Parliament and Council 'shall' determine its structure, workings, scope of action and tasks by legislative procedure. Controversially, article 20 [III-274] gave the Council of Ministers the option ('may adopt a European law'), acting by unanimity, of setting up a European Public Prosecutor's office within Eurojust to bring to book 'the perpetrators, and their accomplices, of serious crimes affecting several member states and of offences against the Union's financial interests'.

Three further articles [III-275 to III-277], covered police cooperation and specified the legislative procedure for laws relating to information collection, processing and analysis and exchange of staff and equipment. But laws covering 'operational cooperation' among internal security authorities would be subject to unanimity. In the case of Europol, the EU's fledgling police authority, codecision would be the norm for setting laws on its structure, operation, field of action and tasks, while operational action would require agreement of the member states whose territory was involved.

The result highlighted the hybrid community and intergovernmental nature of this part of the Union's activities and inevitably exposed the gap between the strong group of integrationists in the Convention and those of a more intergovernmental bent. This divergence was reflected in the relatively large total of 733 amendments.

Many federalists called for article 31 to be deleted on the grounds that it perpetuated the pillar structure. Elmar Brok gathered 31 signatures from the EPP group and sympathisers for deletion, Olivier Duhamel of the PES 10, and Andrew Duff of the Liberals 20.

Even more Convention members urged deletion of the second of the part two articles, which stated that the European Council 'shall define the guidelines for legislative and operational action within the area of freedom, justice and security'. Brok, probably influenced by the use of the German word Richtlinie, which implies some directive power for guidelines, thundered that was 'not acceptable' for the European Council to issue non-negotiable guidelines to the legislator.

On the other hand, eurosceptics warned that dispensing with the third pillar would lead to excessive centralisation and increase the gap between the EU and its citizens. Jens-Peter Bonde, the Danish MEP, warned that 'policemen and bureaucrats would take decisions instead of elected national representatives'.

The general debate on the articles exposed a gulf between most MEPs and the two commissioners on the one hand and government representatives and some national parliamentarians on the other. Sweden's Lena Hjelm-Wallen argued that the main responsibility for public security should remain with the member states while Hubert Haenel of the French parliament warned: 'We cannot communitarise the entire third pillar and we cannot communitarise criminal law.'

But even the most wary of governments were prepared to move ahead with the Community method in some areas. Hain said the UK government 'strongly believed in effective action' on justice and home affairs and 'fully supported' QMV for asylum and immigration. Accession country representatives, including Danuta Hübner of Poland and Neli Kutskova of Bulgaria, enthused about a provision in article 10 [III-265] that opened the way for laws enacting 'any measure necessary for the gradual establishment of a common integrated management system for external borders'.

As Joschka Fischer noted, the Praesidium's draft articles were 'a step towards integration that would have been unimaginable at the beginning of the Convention'. However, in one important area Germany itself balked at more integration. To the dismay of many, Germany insisted on minimum rules only to cover asylum and immigration that would leave member states controlling access to national labour markets.

The divergence between those in favour of Community method versus national rights was most pronounced over the proposal to create a public prosecutor's office. Integrationist MEPs rallied strongly to the idea. It was also backed by Dominique de Villepin of France and Jürgen Meyer, the German SPD parliamentarian, who pointed out that fraud affecting the Community budget ran at 1 billion euro a year. However, the public prosecutor was strongly opposed by the UK's Hain and both representatives of the British House of Commons, as well as the representatives of the Irish, Dutch and Swedish governments.

Such opposition should have killed the idea. But Henning Christophersen argued successfully that it would do no harm to put the option into the constitutional treaty, particularly as no one knew how conditions might change after enlargement. Recalling that only a small number of offences against the Union were effectively prosecuted, John Bruton suggested that the issue of the public prosecutor would be far less controversial in five to ten years time and it would be right to create a legal base for developing such a post.

12.8   UNION FINANCES

The Praesidium had only limited guidance from the working groups when it came to tackle the Union's finances. It therefore retreated from its previous practice of trying to draft 'ready to use' articles and instead raised questions where it could provide no answers. It set up two discussion circles – one on budgetary procedures and another on own resources – to fill in the gaps for future consideration by the Convention. That the Union's finances were a minority taste was shown by the small catch of 69 amendments, which covered a wide range of issues.

In draft form, article 38 [I-54] on the Union's resources simply reproduced existing article 269 of the European Community treaty (TEC). It stated that the Union's budget 'shall be financed wholly from own resources' and that it was the Council's job, acting unanimously on a proposal from the Commission and after consulting the Parliament, to lay down provisions for a system of own resources which it would recommend to member states. However, in accompanying comments the Praesidium wondered whether unanimity would work in an enlarged union and whether, as some Convention members had suggested, the categories of own resources should not be changed to include a European tax or participation in national taxes.
Article 39 [I-53] detailed the budgetary and financial principles of the Union, drawing on preparatory work by Giuliano Amato's simplification working group. Article 39 enshrined ideas of financial rectitude, such as having revenue and expenditure in balance and implementing the budget 'in accordance with the principle of sound financial management', and was generally well received.

The Praesidium observed bluntly that its draft article 40 [I-56] on the Union's budgetary procedure reflected 'the lowest common denominator of the opinions expressed by the Convention members'. These had favoured a simpler annual procedure for setting the budget and for incorporating the EU's multi-annual financial perspective, with its limits on spending, in the Constitution.

Many of these divisions were still apparent when the plenary on April 4 debated the Union's finances and the discussion circle on budgetary procedure, chaired by Henning Christophersen, concluded its deliberations.

Incorporation of the financial perspective yielded the greatest agreement. The discussion circle called for a new article [I-55] in part one to incorporate the renamed 'mult-iannual financial framework' in the treaty as a binding framework for the annual budget to keep spending under control. Details of the financial framework would be set in part two. These would include its duration with the group suggesting five instead of seven years, and provisions to deal with any failure to adopt a new framework and to ensure the Union could meet its legal obligations. The last point would be important if the Convention decided to scrap the distinction between compulsory and non-compulsory expenditure in the annual budget procedure, as the discussion group suggested.

This idea was one of several elements intended to simplify the annual budget procedure, which brought new difficulties in its train. It ran into problems with France, which wanted existing rules to continue on farm spending.

Christophersen's group also proposed that the Commission should present the draft budget and a simplified codecision procedure for Council and Parliament to turn it into law. The existing rules gave Parliament and Council two readings each on the budget, with the Council having the last word on compulsory spending and Parliament the final word on non-compulsory spending. Getting rid of the distinction between the two types of spending raised the question of which institution would in future have the last word on the budget overall. Because the discussion group was unable to agree, it put forward two options – one beginning with the Parliament and the other with the Council.

A diversity of views on budget procedure was clear in the plenary session on 4 April. A majority, led by the MEPs, called for an end to unanimity in the Council and equal participation of the European Parliament. A bigger role for the Parliament was supported by several government representatives, including Ms Hübner of Poland. However, Peter Hain said he could only accept codecision on the budget if there were mandatory ceilings, which would be set by the European Council.

Big differences also emerged on the issue of the Union's own taxes to replace or augment the present system of own resources. The French, Belgian and Austrian government representatives, and a number of MEPs and national parliamentarians, filed amendments proposing the authorising of European taxes, while in the plenary of 4 April Pierre Lequiller, the French parliamentarian, was one of several conventionnels to suggest 'real' EU taxes would boost the Union's legitimacy and be a new 'conceptual jump' following the euro. However, others including several Scandinavian members expressed strong opposition to the idea.

12.9   THE DEMOCRATIC LIFE OF THE UNION

At the Plenary session of 4 April, the Praesidium put forward a *pot pourri* of articles. Appropriately, Jean-Luc Dehaene presented them as many, especially those concerning the democratic life of the Union, were of particular interest to the non-government organisations grouped under the general heading of civil society for whom Dehaene had been the point of contact since the Convention started.

As Dehaene concluded his introductory remarks, the drafts, which also covered Union membership, relations with nearby countries and part three – the general and final provisions of the Constitution – won high praise from an unlikely source. 'Unusually for me,' announced the UK's Peter Hain, 'I can say all the articles are excellent.'

Boosting the democratic legitimacy and transparency of the EU's institutions was a key element of the Laeken declaration. The seven articles of title VI, numbered from 33 to 37, were intended to show citizens that they could contribute towards framing Union decisions and could follow, and therefore evaluate, the Union's decision making process.

Articles 33 and 34 were both new. Article 33 [I-45], stating 'the principle of democratic equality', established that citizens were equal before the Union's institutions. Article 34 [I-47], on 'the principle of participatory democracy' pledged the Union to a dialogue with citizens which, the Praesidium claimed, was 'largely already in place between the institutions and civil society' through such means as the Internet.

The remaining articles reproduced existing articles in the treaties but with substantial amendments. Article 35 [I-49] described the role of the European Ombudsman, making good an omission from the original skeleton Constitution of 28 October. Article 35a [later expanded as I-46 to describe the principle of representative democracy] briefly described the role of political parties at a European level.

Article 36 [I-50], on 'the transparency of the proceedings of the Union's institutions' echoed article 1 of the present Union treaty when it said 'the Union institutions shall conduct their work as openly as possible'. Not only should the European Parliament meet in public, but so should 'the Council when it is discussing a legislative proposal'. An accompanying note said the reference to such openness was intended to cover discussion of legislation in its entirety from the first discussion of a draft in the Council to its adoption. The rest of the article set out citizens' right of access to documents. Article 36a [I-51] said 'everyone has the right to the protection of personal data concerning him or her' and set out the legal base (legislative procedure) for ensuring data protection by EU institutions.

Draft article 37 [I-52] reproduced the declaration annexed to the Amsterdam Treaty on the status of churches and non-confessional organisations, and committed the Union to a regular dialogue, much as it was committed – in article 34 [I-48] – to dialogue with civil society and NGOs.

However, departing from the October skeleton, the Praesidium held back planned articles on the voting rules of the Union's institutions, which would have defined qualified majorities and the possibility of constructive abstention and a uniform procedure of voting for the European Parliament. It also dropped plans for an article to give constitutional status to the 'open method of coordination' (OMC), the process of benchmarking immortalised in the Lisbon agenda for turning the Union into the world's most competitive economic area by 2010.

The Praesidium, after much mulling, decided the OMC was covered by article 15 on supporting action. The decision to drop the article worried supporters of the Lisbon agenda. It was supported by a curious coalition of integrationists who feared OMC was a way of undermining the Community method and those of a more intergovernmental persuasion, concerned that an article could open the backdoor to meddling in the way it operated by the European Parliament and Commission.

The proposals on the Union's democratic life attracted 235 amendments[21] and one swift protest. Emilio Gabaglio, secretary general of the European Trade Union Confederation (ETUC) and an observer to the Convention complained that the Praesidium had given 'birth to a mouse'. He objected to the absence of any reference to the social partners and the enhanced social dialogue, urged by trade union and employers' representatives among the Convention's observers. Gabaglio's views found a ready echo among conventionnels who put forward amendments to add a reference or a paragraph on the social partners and the social dialogue to article 34. Thus, Elmar Brok gathered 34 EPP signatories and Andrew Duff 22 liberal names for an additional paragraph acknowledging and promoting the involvement of the social partners in the Union's social and economic governance. Anne Van Lancker, the Belgian socialist MEP, rallied 11 PES backers for a separate article on the subject.

---

[21] CONV 670/03.

These group amendments highlighted the growing organisational capacity of the big 'political families' in the Convention's life. Several amendments sought to delete draft article 33 on the grounds that it was covered by the Charter. Another, signed by the three key small state representatives from Austria, Finland and Slovenia, wanted the principle of equality to include member states. Draft article 35 on the Ombudsman prompted massed ranks of MEPs to file or sign amendments specifying that he or she should be appointed by the European Parliament. Many amendments sought to flesh out article 35a on European political parties or substitute the existing article 191 of the TEC to recognise the parties' importance for integration in the Union.

12.10   UNION MEMBERSHIP

The headline-grabbing novelty among the four articles of title X on Union membership was draft article 46 [I-60] laying down the rules for a voluntary withdrawal from the Union. The 'exit clause', article 46, was mooted in the October skeleton. The Praesidium put it forward largely to meet the demands of eurosceptics and the less integrationist Convention members.

A member state wanting to withdraw would notify the Council after which the Union would negotiate and conclude an agreement for withdrawal and the state's future relationship with the Union. The article specified that the Council would act by QMV after obtaining the Parliament's consent. The constitutional treaty would cease to apply to the member state withdrawing once the agreement took effect, or, failing that, two years after the notification of the Council.

The articles attracted 90 amendments[22] of which 35 related to the exit clause. Nine amendments, signed by 41 conventionnels, wanted the article deleted. Duff, backed by 20 Convention members, proposed a new article to create the status of 'associate member' for Union members that leave or countries that have not joined.

Most other amendments sought to toughen the Praesidium draft by limiting the possibility of voluntary withdrawal or make its consequences more severe for the departing state. It was suggested the right of withdrawal be limited to exceptional situations such as a change in the Constitution; that a state be unable to withdraw automatically; that the Council should decide by unanimity, giving other states a veto over withdrawal, and that a waiting

---

[22] CONV 672/03.

period (suggestions ranged from 5 to 20 years) be imposed before a withdrawing state could request to rejoin the Union. Only three conventionnels – the eurosceptics, David Heathcoat-Amory and Jens-Peter Bonde, and the Hungarian PES parliamentarian, Pal Vastagh – called for a softening of the exit terms by reducing the time to one year before withdrawal would automatically take effect.

Article 43 [I-58], giving the eligibility criteria for Union membership, was also new. Opening the Union to all European states whose peoples shared and respected the values of article 2, it incorporated the Copenhagen criteria for enlargement into the constitutional treaty. Some conventionnels sought the deletion of article 43 on the grounds that it duplicated article 1. Twelve amendments, signed by 56 conventionnels including eurosceptics, the representatives of Sweden, Germany and the UK, and Elmar Brok heading a phalanx of 34 EPP-aligned signatories, said the article should state that only European states, and not their peoples, must share and respect the Union's values. This was the line that prevailed in the final text.

Article 44 [merged into I-58] covered how to apply for Union membership and gave a boost to elected representatives by saying the European Parliament and national parliaments should be informed as soon as an application was made. Article 45 [I-59] detailed the procedure for the suspension of membership rights and made no change in substance to existing rules.

12.11   THE UNION AND ITS NEIGHBOURS

Title IX, consisting of draft article 42 [I-57], was another departure from the status quo, although it was foreshadowed in the October skeleton. The objective, as Jean-Luc Dehaene explained, was to establish a neighbourhood policy with near-by as well as adjoining countries. The Union should 'develop a special relationship with its neighbouring states, aiming to establish an area of prosperity and good neighbourliness characterised by close and peaceful relations based on cooperation'. It would be able to conclude specific agreements with the countries concerned, which could contain reciprocal rights and obligations. The Praesidium's covering note said the text would provide for a 'loose but coherent framework' bringing together existing arrangements and create no new obligations.

The article attracted around 30 amendments.[23] Several, including a well-supported amendment from Brok, suggested the EU make full use of the Strasbourg-based Council of Europe in its neighbourhood policy. With countries such as Belarus in mind, other amendments, including one signed by ten PES conventionnels, urged that any special relationship respect basic values, such as human rights, the rule of law and democracy. This proposal, couched in terms of the Union's values, was included in the final text.

12.12   GENERAL AND FINAL PROVISIONS

Nine draft articles, comprising part three or the general and final provisions of the constitutional treaty, were also published on 4 April. To a great extent these articles, which were identified alphabetically by letters A to I instead of by numbers, were not contentious. Later to comprise part IV, they dealt with the necessary business of repealing earlier treaties, establishing legal continuity, defining the geographical scope of the Constitution, permitting regional unions such as Benelux and the Belgo-Luxembourg economic union, defining the treaty languages and stating that the protocols to be annexed to the constitutional treaty would be an integral part of it.

However, two articles were significant. In article F [IV-443] spelling out how to revise the new constitutional treaty, the Praesidium retained the existing procedure of the Intergovernmental Conference for treaty changes. But, in accompanying notes, it suggested that IGCs be preceded in future by more preparatory Conventions.

It also raised the very important issue of how to amend the constitutional treaty. Should this be by the Council or a special conference of member states; by unanimity or QMV and what roles should be played by the Commission, European Parliament, national parliaments and even a Congress, should such a body be created? Another tantalising question was what to do if a member state failed to ratify a revision to the constitutional treaty.

Similarly, article G [IV-447] on the adoption, ratification and entry into force of the constitutional treaty repeated the existing provisions, by which a treaty cannot enter force unless ratified by all member states which sign it. One member state failing to ratify would mean the constitutional treaty could not take effect and the existing treaties would continue to apply.

---

[23] CONV 671/03.

However, the Praesidium added a paragraph calling on the European Council to take up the issue if, two years after the signing of the treaty, four-fifths of member states had ratified it and one or more member states were having difficulties. This would later be turned into a declaration attached to the constitutional treaty.

In the accompanying notes, the Praesidium recalled that some contributions, such as the Penelope document, had suggested the constitutional treaty should take effect once a certain threshold of member states had ratified it. This idea would have given the final text far more the character of a Constitution as opposed to a constitutional treaty. But despite backing in all major party groups, it failed to win sufficient support to be adopted by the time the Convention's mandate to finalise part IV ended.

Of 147 amendments[24] relating to the nine articles, 46 were concerned with article F on revising the treaty and 27 with article G on its ratification.

On article F, Brok and Duff tabled an amendment signed by 48 conventionnels that proposed the European Parliament should have the same right as the Council and Commission to propose amendments to the constitutional treaty. Altogether 71 Convention members supported the idea, including some non-MEPs of whom the most prominent was Joschka Fischer. Many other amendments supported having a Convention prepare future IGCs and several the idea that IGCs should confirm the results of Convention.

Duff and 21 supporters proposed, that in future, the consensus needed to amend the constitutional treaty should be five-sixths of member states, or 21 out of 25 countries, with the European Parliament giving assent by a two-thirds majority. Others suggested four-fifths or three-quarters of member states. Discussion on article G revealed a growing interest in referenda as a route to ratification. Four amendments to article G mentioned national referenda for ratification and three the idea of a European referendum in May or June 2004.

12.13   PRESSURE FOR A REFERENDUM ON EUROPE

The idea of a Europe-wide referendum to approve the constitutional treaty gathered support as the Convention progressed.

---

[24] CONV 673/03.

The case was made by 15 full Convention members and 20 alternates in a submission to Sir John Kerr at the end of March 2003.[25] The signatories argued that referendums on the constitutional treaty should be held on the same day as the European Parliament elections in June 2004. A Europe-wide referendum on European election day would focus the voter's attention on the merits or otherwise of the constitutional treaty rather than other issues. It would give the constitutional treaty 'real democratic legitimacy' and send a signal that Europe was 'about the people' and not governing elites.

> While it is the case that a 'European People' does not exist, it is equally clear that a Europe-wide referendum would create a common political space. It would be a means of bringing the peoples of Europe closer politically; it would ensure that the people were more engaged with and had a greater knowledge of the project.

The attractive idea behind a Europe-wide referendum was that it would force the supporters of the constitutional treaty to get out and sell their product to Europe's voters. If accepted, the Union could no longer stand accused of being a top-down elitist venture. But referendums had a habit of being hijacked by domestic issues – and who was to say that would not happen even in a Europe-wide poll. What would happen if the referendum failed in several countries? Would the constitutional treaty have to be dropped altogether? Given the limited voter appeal of Union issues, a Europe-wide referendum would be a high-risk strategy.

A glance at the signatories suggested some might have mixed motives. They came from a broad cross-section of the Convention and included the constitutional expert, Alain Lamassoure; eurosceptics, Jens-Peter Bonde and David Heathcoat-Amory, as well as such keen integrationists as Olivier Duhamel and Jürgen Meyer.

There were, it was acknowledged, legal difficulties. In cases where countries had no constitutional provisions for referendums, it was suggested they should at least hold 'consultative referenda'. After proposing that a majority of citizens and a majority of states would be necessary to secure ratification, the submission admitted that there would be problems if the constitutional treaty was rejected in a member state. The member state could try again, or seek bilaterally to regulate its relations with the Union. But there would also have to be a clause in the constitutional treaty permitting a member state to withdraw. This was envisaged from the October skeleton onwards.

---

[25] CONV 658/03.

The campaign was taken up by the European Referendum Campaign, a pressure group backed by direct democracy NGOs. By the time the Convention ended, 97 conventionnels had signed the ERC petition for a Europe-wide referendum. By the time the constitutional treaty was signed on 29 October 2004, 10 member states had signalled their intention to hold national referendums on the Constitution.[26]

12.14   UNION LEADERS DECIDE AGAINST DELAY

After a shaky start, the Praesidium and the Convention had achieved a great deal by Easter 2003. As Giscard explained to the special European Council with the accession countries in Athens on 16 April, it had provided answers to the four issues raised by the Nice summit. Thus competences had been clarified with due regard to subsidiarity. The Charter would be incorporated as the second part of the constitutional treaty.[27] The Convention had agreed a radical simplification of the Union's policy instruments. And national parliaments would be more actively involved in the Union's life, notably through controlling subsidiarity.

He also claimed success on four elements of the Laeken mandate. Thus, the Union would have a single legal personality. The Treaties of Union and the European Community would be replaced by a single text. The Union would have a single institutional structure. And the Convention had defined the methods and means for creating a true area of freedom, justice and security.

Some might dispute elements of his summary. Peter Hain, for example, was not yet willing to accept constitutional status for the Charter. It was also doubtful whether 733 amendments to the articles on the area of justice, freedom and security amounted to no more than 'sorting out various editorial matters'[28] as Giscard claimed. Moreover, the Praesidium had not provided a complete draft of the first part of the constitutional treaty by Easter as envisaged late in 2002.

This was not just because of the delays caused by its difficulties with the early drafts and the Iraq conflict. Giscard and Kerr were determined not to

---

[26] The Czech Republic, Denmark, France, Ireland, Luxembourg, the Netherlands, Poland, Portugal, Spain and the UK.

[27] Giscard's announcement meant the section of the constitutional treaty dealing with policies and legal bases would become part III in future drafts and the 'General and final provisions' part IV.

[28] Giscard's oral report to the European Council of 16 April, available in the speeches section of the Convention website.

unveil any drafts dealing with controversial institutional issues before meeting the Union's leaders in the European Council. When Giscard finally met the leaders in April, he instead sought answers on five points, which would dominate the Convention in its penultimate stage before drawing up the draft constitutional treaty.

- How to guarantee the greatest possible continuity in the work of the European Council and other Council formations.
- The future size and composition of the Commission after enlargement to 27 members when, according to the Treaty of Nice, the Commission was due to change from having one commissioner per member state to less than the number of member states.
- The means of appointment and the powers of the Commission president.
- The means of appointment and the powers of a foreign minister for the Union.
- Keeping alive a pet project, the eventual role of a body, call it a Convention or a Congress, to be composed of representatives of national parliaments and the European Parliament.

On one issue, the Union's leaders made progress. After the meeting,[29] Giscard announced 'virtual unanimity' on the appointment of a foreign minister for the EU, who would combine the roles of Solana and Patten. The difficult issues, Giscard admitted, were whether to retain the six-month rotating presidency of the European Council or move to a more permanent arrangement and the composition of the Commission. The Commission, he pointed out, started as a 'very small collegiate body' but had grown and become less collegiate with successive enlargements.

Giscard gave some clues as to how he hoped to resolve these difficulties. He harked back to the numbers problem and its implications. He stressed first the importance of equality of rights of citizens in the Constitution – a principle 'which is perhaps less spoken of in Europe but which is equally important' to that of the equality of states. This meant that when considering institutional issues, such as the long-term presidency or the composition of the Commission, it was necessary to take the size of populations of member states into account.

'The number of people who want one solution or another, that number is important,' he said. 'And at the moment, there is quite a broad majority of the population which is represented and which is in favour of a somewhat

---

[29] Text of presidency press conference 16 April 2003 on www.eu2003.gr

more stable presidency.' Athens also dealt Giscard a harsh blow, however. He had been dropping hints for weeks that the Convention might have to run into July or even past the summer break to finalise a polished text and went to the summit hoping for an extension.

The evening before Giscard gave his progress report to the 25 leaders of the member states and accession countries, the Greek prime minister, Costas Simitis, told him the Union's leaders wanted the final product at their summit in Thessaloniki on 20 June at the latest. Already running late, the Convention was given just two months to complete its task of producing a draft constitutional treaty for the European Union.

Part IV

The Convention End-Game

CHAPTER 13
Institutional Imbroglio

Giscard was not happy with the decision of the European Council in Athens. To his aides, he seemed depressed in the days afterwards, worried about squeezing so much work into so little time before the Thessaloniki summit. His first priority was to push ahead with the draft articles on the institutions that had been promised for the plenary of 24 April. And it was here he had a surprise up his sleeve.

He had been working on a text for six to eight weeks, helped primarily by Sir John Kerr and two collaborators. The work mainly took place in Giscard's study in his house in Paris, well away from the Convention secretariat offices.

When the Praesidium met late in the afternoon of 22 April to start discussions, it was Giscard, the stickler for correct procedure and confidentiality in the steering body, who unashamedly broke the rules. While unveiling his 15 draft articles – printed on paper bearing the imprint of the Convention secretariat – to the 12 other members of the Praesidium, he had his spokesman, Nikolaus Meyer-Landrut, brief the press about them. The impact was immediate. No sooner was the briefing underway, than the mobile phones of Praesidium members began to ring as journalists sought reactions to the unfolding story.

Praesidium members were flabbergasted and furious. They felt betrayed. There was an understanding the previous autumn that the Convention method of debate, working groups and more debate would be unsuitable for preparing the institutional drafts, for fear that Brussels insiders would dominate the process. The idea was that the Praesidium itself would act as a working group and develop a comprehensive approach. Instead, it had been cut out of the loop and presented with a *fait accompli*. Months later, Praesidium members would shake their heads at the events of that afternoon. Giscard's motives remained unclear, although some speculated that he had returned from Athens so convinced that the Convention would fail that he wanted to get his vision of Europe's institutional architecture on record and into the history books. Adding insult to injury, the drafts Giscard and Kerr unveiled were very intergovernmental and appeared extreme and divisive.

13.1   GISCARD'S ARTICLES

Giscard's articles looked like a blueprint for a *directoire* of large member states to run the Union. The European Council, the body he founded in the 1970s, would be the 'highest authority of the Union'. Newly categorised as an institution, it would be in a position to take formal decisions. The system of rotation for its president would go. The European Council would have a long-term chair, elected by the members by qualified majority voting for two and a half years, renewable once. He or she would 'prepare, chair and drive' its work to ensure continuity and would report annually on the state of the Union to a Congress of representatives of the European Parliament and national parliaments. The president would ensure the Union was effectively represented in the wider world.

The president or chair would be supported by a board. Sometimes called the bureau, this would consist of its president, vice-president,[1] two European Council members 'chosen in equal rotation', the foreign minister (in his capacity as president of the Foreign Affairs Council) plus the presidents of the economic and financial affairs Council and the Council on justice and security. The impression of a powerful cabinet was boosted by the provision that this board 'may' (not shall) meet with the presidents of the European Parliament and the Commission to ensure consistency in the Union's activities, implying that it could barrel ahead in making policy without bothering to consult the heads of the other institutions in the triangle. The president or chair would have at least two years' experience as a European Council member. Neither the president nor vice-president would be members of another European institution. Neither the European Council president nor the Commission president, an ex-officio member of the European Council, would vote in it.

The foreign minister would conduct the Union's common foreign and security policy and be a double-hatted figure. This official would be appointed by the European Council by qualified majority after consulting the Commission president, and would remain very much a Council person. She or he would make proposals for development of common foreign and security and defence policies 'which he shall carry out as mandated by the Council'. The minister would also be a Commission vice-president and 'responsible for handling external relations and for co-ordinating the different aspects of the Union's external action'. As Commission vice-president, the minister would be bound by Commission procedures 'in this capacity, and for these aspects alone'.

---

[1] The vice-president was a complete novelty in the institutional debate thus far.

Giscard proposed amending important parts of the hard fought Treaty of Nice. His most provocative article revised the rules for qualified majority votes in the European Council and the Council of Ministers and thus threatened the privileged positions of Spain and Poland, which had emerged from Nice with good deals. Giscard sought to overturn the complicated Nice settlement of weighted votes for each member state by reviving the much simpler concept of the dual majority. QMV was to consist of the majority of member states, representing a relatively high proportion of at least two-thirds of the population of the Union. QMV in the Council of Ministers would be the rule 'except where the Constitution provides otherwise'.

He also proposed to overturn the difficult Nice compromise on Parliament's composition. The number of MEPs should not exceed 700 (against 732 at Nice) and representation of European citizens would be proportional, with a minimum threshold of four members per member state. The word 'proportional' spelled danger for the smalls. The Nice compromise, which was the result of late night horse-trading rather than any mathematical or demographic formula, gave greater weighting to smaller member states.

Also to the alarm of the smalls, his draft article on the Commission envisaged a body much reduced from the present 20-member college or that of one member per member state agreed in the Treaty of Nice until the Union consists of 27 countries. 'The Commission shall consist of a president, two vice-presidents and up to ten other members,' it said. Creating a subsidiary breed of second rank commissioners, it added: 'It may call on the help of Commission Counsellors.' There was no mention of the important safeguard of a 'rotation system based on the principle of equality', as specified in the Treaty of Nice for the time after Union membership reached 27 when there would be fewer commissioners than states.

The text on the European Commission also provoked a storm of protest among the Commission's many supporters in the Convention because of its limp definition of the Commission's role compared with the existing article 211 of the European Communities Treaty (TEC). The Commission was merely 'called on to give voice to the general European interest' and 'monitor the application of the Constitution and steps taken by the institutions under the Constitution'. The article enshrined the Commission's right of initiative 'except where the Constitution provides otherwise' and confirmed the Commission would be completely independent in carrying out its responsibilities but made no mention of the Commission's functions as a coordinator or executive.

Another article gave Parliament power to elect the Commission president by a majority of three-fifths. But the European Council, consisting of national leaders, would decide the candidate by a qualified majority following the European elections. If the candidate failed to gain the requisite support, the European Council would choose another candidate within a month.

The Commission, as a body, would be responsible to the European Council and the European Parliament, *both* of which could pass a motion of censure on the Commission. If the censure motion was passed, all Commission members must resign.

Choice of commissioners would be a shared task of the member states and the president-elect of the Commission. Each member state would submit a list of three people of suitable competence, European commitment and independence, of whom (in a typical Giscardian touch) at least one must be a woman. From these, the Commission president-elect would choose up to 11 persons, taking into account political and geographical balance. The president and the commissioners would be approved as a body by the Parliament. The Commission president would decide on its internal organisation, ensuring it would act consistently, efficiently, and on a collegiate basis, and be able to appoint Commission counsellors on the same criteria as full members. The president would appoint one of the two vice-presidents of the Commission, but not the other, who would be the foreign minister.

Articles on the Parliament and the Council of Ministers made clear that codecision – in future to be known as the legislative procedure – would be the general form of enacting legislation in the Union. The Council of Ministers would also 'carry out executive and coordinating functions, as laid down in the Constitution'. It would consist of a representative of each member state at ministerial level who alone 'may commit the member state in question and cast its vote'.

There would be only five distinct Council formations. The article created a Legislative Council 'to consider and jointly, with the European Parliament, enact European laws and European framework laws'. Each member state's minister in this nascent chamber of states (roughly equivalent to the German Bundesrat) could be assisted by a specialist minister, reflecting the Council agenda.

Taking up an issue hotly contested in the June 2002 Seville European Council, Giscard sought to split off the General Affairs Council (GAC) from the current General Affairs and External Relations Council (GAERC) and give it the coordinating role that it is accorded in the European Communities Treaty. Under the Seville reforms, the two configurations of the GAERC hold separate meetings with separate agendas. Giscard's text proposed that the GAC 'shall ensure consistency in the work of the Council of Ministers' and be chaired by the European Council vice-president.

The Foreign Affairs Council would 'flesh out' the Union's external policies on the basis of strategic guidelines laid down by the European Council and be chaired by the Union's foreign minister. There would be only two other Council formations – economic and financial affairs, and justice and security – although the General Affairs Council would have the power to decide on further formations.

In line with the Seville conclusions, the European Council would meet quarterly. It would be 'convened by its president'. Depending on the agenda, and in line with the Seville decision for delegations to be limited to just two seats, its members could decide to be assisted by a minister and, in the case of the Commission president, a commissioner. The European Council president was empowered to call additional meetings when the international situation required.

As in the TEU, Giscard's text said the European Council 'shall provide the Union with the necessary impetus for its development'. But, using more precise language, it added that it 'shall determine' (rather than define) the Union's 'general political directions' (with directions replacing guidelines). Going into detail absent from the Union treaty, the European Council would 'set out principles and strategic guidelines' for external action and 'give guidance for action, legislative and operational' in the area of freedom, security and justice. 'It shall maintain oversight of the unity, consistency and efficiency of Union action'. Except where provided otherwise, its decisions would be taken by consensus.

The European Council was a monument to Giscard's past achievements as an architect of Europe. The proposed Congress of the Peoples of Europe was his contribution to the present and he envisaged a far greater role for it than anticipated. Starting innocuously, his draft article proposed the Congress should meet at least once a year to provide a 'forum for contact and consultation in European political life'. It would be chaired by the president of the European Parliament, be limited to 700 members and comprise two-thirds national parliamentarians and only one-third MEPs.

The Congress would not intervene in the Council's legislative procedure. But it might be consulted by the president of the European Council or called on by the European Council to 'work up proposals for amendments' to the Constitution. Moreover, if the European Council so chose, it could, by unanimity, turn the Congress into an electoral college to elect the European

Council's president and vice-president. The Congress in turn would decide the appointments by a majority of its members.

13.2   SHOCKED REACTIONS

Giscard's proposals for the European Council mirrored the most ambitious ideas of the 'ABC' group of Spanish, British and French leaders and, combined with his dismissive approach to the Commission, appeared a deliberate snub to the small member states and the Commission. 'As a courtesy' he sent copies of his articles to the Danish, Greek and Italian governments, as holders of the past, present and future six-month EU presidencies and to Romano Prodi, Commission president. If the latter move were to ensure the greatest possible publicity for his ideas, he was not to be disappointed.

The Commission discussed the articles at its meeting early on Wednesday morning, 23 April, and almost immediately published an angry statement in response. By leaving copies of Giscard's articles lying around in its Breydel building, the Commission also ensured they reached a wider public. Giscard's spokesman, when briefing the press the previous evening, had not released the text.

Providing an interesting reflection of its priorities, the Commission chose first to criticise the breach of procedure and the release of the news to the press. On substance, the Commission complained that Giscard's proposals ran counter to the 'orientations of the debate in the Convention and its working groups' and failed to reflect the discussions of the 16 April European Council in Athens where 18 smaller EU countries and accession states rejected the long-term European Council president, calling instead for institutional balance and equality among member states.

The Commission directed much of its fire against Giscard's proposal for a seven-strong board, or bureau. This 'intergovernmental bureau' would, it charged, 'undermine the checks and balances in place between the EU institutions'. It could lead to unequal treatment of member states, jeopardising trust between them, and would undermine accountability, effectiveness and the Community method, the Union's 50-year-old success story. It would duplicate bureaucracy rather than simplify the Union's executive powers.

The Commission acknowledged the Union needed a clearly defined and accountable executive but argued that Giscard's proposals would fall short of this goal and add to institutional fragmentation. It grumbled that no mention was made of the Commission's own executive function, its duties of external representation or its responsibility for executing the EU budget. Privately, Commission officials were apoplectic. According to one in-house analysis, Giscard proposed a completely new institutional structure, based on intergovernmentalism that would leave the enlarged Union dysfunctional. The articles would make the European Council the de facto government of the EU. The revised provisions for representation in the European Parliament plus the new QMV rules would make population the dominant criterion of power in the Parliament and Council of Ministers to the detriment of the small and medium-sized states.

The reaction of European parliamentarians was equally vituperative. Elmar Brok described Giscard's move as 'autistic' and 'unacceptable'. Pervenche Beres and Olivier Duhamel, French members of the Party of European Socialists, denounced Giscard as a *'grand provocateur'*, who had abandoned consensus and produced articles which insulted the small states, the Franco-German contribution to the Convention, the European Parliament, the Commission and its president and the Convention itself.

The anger continued after the Praesidium had substantially modified the text. When Giscard gave details of the revised articles to the Convention, there were loud guffaws in that normally deferential body as he remarked that he had been listening carefully to the conventionnels' contributions for a year. Bringing some light relief to a fraught session, Kimmo Kiljunen, a Socialist member of the Finnish parliament, chided Giscard for 'trying to copy a president from the United States, a Peoples' Congress from China and a Politburo from the Soviet Union'. Issuing a 'personal vote of no confidence' in Giscard, Johannes Voggenhuber, the outspoken Austrian Green, declared that 'the bitter irony of this Convention is that, if it fails it will be because of its president and if it succeeds, it will be despite him'.

13.3   THE PRAESIDIUM REVISIONS

Giscard's articles survived in their entirety for less than 24 hours. The Praesidium met on the evening of Tuesday, 22 April and on Wednesday, 23 April from 09.30 until after midnight, as usual behind closed doors but this time without the members' assistants present. The revised texts of title IV on the institutions were broadly complete by late Wednesday afternoon. The subsequent hours were spent arguing about the Congress and drafting a cover note that made clear there was not unanimous agreement on all issues. The debate was described as heated but not angry. One participant was later to sum up the day as: 'Eighteen hours without a shower – disgusting.'

The most obvious changes in the Praesidium's articles[2] were the removal of the reference to the European Council being the Union's 'highest authority', its demotion to number two in the institutional ranking, the disappearance of the European Council vice-president, the radical slimming down of its board or bureau and deletion of all reference to the Congress becoming an electoral college. Although Giscard's spokesman said all points in the Praesidium draft were supported by strong majorities, the cover note was candid about the disagreements which focused on plans to rewrite the Treaty of Nice. It observed:

> On several major points, two approaches were available: to keep to the provisions of the Treaty of Nice or go beyond them. Following the discussions of the Praesidium on the full range of issues, the proposals put forward concerning the representation of the European Parliament, the definition of qualified majority and the composition of the Commission reflect solutions which go beyond the Nice Treaty. It will be for the Convention to reach a view on this choice.

Two Praesidium members from small countries – the Irishman, John Bruton, and the Slovene, Alojz Peterle – objected to the slimmed down Commission. Alfonso Dastis and Inigo Méndez de Vigo, both Spaniards, objected strongly to the proposed changes to the method for calculating a qualified majority in the Council and the composition of the European Parliament.

The voting arrangements in the Council gave Spain (and Poland) weight almost equal to the Union's four big powers, a deal which Madrid regarded as fair exchange for the loss of a commissioner when the Commission moved to one member per member state after 2004. The Nice decision, amended by the October 2002 Brussels European Council to take account of ten new member states in May 2004, gave Spain and Poland 27 Council votes each from 1 January 2005, compared with 29 each for the big four. Spain, with a population of 40.7 million, would thus have a voting weight of 8.41% against weightings of 9.03% for Germany, with a population of 82 million, and Italy, the UK and France with between 57 and 60 million people each.

At first sight, the proposed redefinition of QMV to reflect population size appeared to favour Spain as its population is 8.94% of the 452 million inhabitants of the soon-to-be enlarged Union and thus higher in percentage terms than the share of the votes decided at Nice. But in addition to issues of prestige, the change would upset the ability of Spain (and Poland) to block unwelcome legislation by giving extra voting power to the four biggest

---

[2] CONV 691/03.

member states, and leaving a multitude of small states each with very little voting weight. Acts passed by QMV under the Nice rules in a Union of 25 would require the support of at least 232 votes, or 72.27% of the total, putting Spain with its 27 votes in a good position to marshal a blocking minority behind its interests. In an enlarged Union with greatly increased recourse to QMV, this would be a valuable asset, especially for a country that never was shy of standing up for its rights.

Although the opposition to revising the Nice treaty was serious, Giscard appeared more concerned in the Praesidium meeting about the reaction of Jean-Luc Dehaene, who was furious that Giscard had leaked his articles before he had seen them. Dehaene was also unwilling to accept the permanent president of the European Council. He feared the post would upset the Union's institutional triangle of Council of Ministers, Commission and European Parliament, and that, with a permanent president, the European Council could be formalised even more as the appellate body for the other Councils and so end up taking all key decisions in the Union. Giscard's ability to overcome Dehaene's reservations prevented a split in the triumvirate and kept the idea of a long-term European Council president in the Praesidium text. That achievement may have been one reason why the president seemed serene when he appeared before the Convention on the Thursday afternoon.

He presented the Praesidium's draft articles as proposals to strengthen all sides of the institutional triangle that were sufficiently flexible to last for the long term – possibly 50 years – in the face of widely different expectations of the future of Europe. They respected three principles that might sometimes seem mutually inconsistent, namely equality before the law of citizens and member states, maintaining the three main Union institutions, and respect for the Community method. He had a word of warning for the Convention. Citizens, he opined, were not too bothered about institutions. They wanted results.

As Giscard outlined the revised texts, it became clear that he had given up a lot. Article 14 [I-19] of the Praesidium text continued to regard the European Council as a Union institution, but took it down a peg, positioning it below the European Parliament.

Reflecting the changed institutional hierarchy of article 14, the European Parliament was covered by article 15 [I-20] in the Praesidium draft instead of article 16 in Giscard's text. This repositioning, Giscard said, was to 'underline the democratic legitimacy of the system'. The Parliament's mission statement was fuller. In addition to legislating jointly with the Council, it would 'exercise functions of political control and consultation'.

The article was explicit in stating: 'It shall elect the president of the European Commission.' The most notable change compared with Giscard's draft concerned the rules for apportioning members. The new draft said representation of European citizens 'shall be degressively proportional' with a minimum threshold of four members per member state. The concept of degressivity was pushed by Bruton to protect the interests of smaller states.

Article 16 [I-21] curtailed the European Council's mission statement as well as cutting out mention of it being the Union's highest authority and the reference to the vice-president. The European Council would still meet quarterly. But the specific Giscardian tasks in relation to external affairs and freedom, justice and security were cut, as was reference to maintaining oversight of Union actions.

Article 16a [I-22] on the European Council chair kept the idea of a full-time, elected president, who would be a former European Council member and hold the job for two and a half years, renewable once. It added that the European Council would be able to end the mandate by the same procedure of QMV 'in cases of serious malpractice'. The job description was similar to that of Giscard's text, retaining the duty of representation in the wider world and adding, by way of more detail, that she or he 'shall endeavour to facilitate cohesion and consensus within the European Council'. However, the president's position was weakened. He or she would report to the European Parliament after each meeting rather than just give an annual report to the Congress. The reference to Congress being able to elect the president and vice-president went. The board became optional ('The European Council may decide by consensus to create a board'). It no longer contained other Council presidents and would be smaller. An important change, which partly reclaimed the principle of rotation, specified it would consist of three European Council members 'chosen according to a system of equitable rotation'.

As revised, articles 16 and 16a significantly trimmed Giscard's ambitions and his presentation to the Convention was correspondingly disingenuous. He pointed to the linguistic difficulties caused by the words 'chairman' in English and 'president' in French. The two words were interchangeable but their meanings were not. The president of the European Council would be a chairman 'and it is in this capacity that he presides and coordinates the meetings of the European Council for which he ensures the preparation and, at the end of the day, presents a report to Parliament'. The president/chairman would not be an executive and potential rival to the Commission president. As for the board, 'many motives have been impugned', he observed. But a large European Council of 25 would need a board. Indeed, town councils needed boards or bureaus.

The Praesidium made few changes to article 17 [I-23] on the Council of Ministers. It would carry out policy making rather than executive functions. In response to the complaints of parliamentarians in the Convention that member states were often represented by unelected officials in the Council, the article specified that they would be represented at ministerial level 'for each of its formations'.

As before, article 17a [I-24] named only five Council formations – General Affairs, Legislative, Foreign Affairs, Economic and Financial, and Justice and Security – although it continued to give the General Affairs Council power to decide more. The General Affairs Council would still ensure consistency in the overall work of the Council, although the disappearance of the vice-president left open who would chair it. A new sentence, stating, 'With the participation of the Commission, it shall prepare meetings of the European Council', gave both the Commission and the General Affairs Council some say in the European Council agenda. Another new sentence gave the European Council power, by consensus, to give the presidency of a Council formation, other than foreign affairs, to a member state for at least a year 'taking into account European political and geographical balance and the diversity of all member states'.

Giscard said the latter provision was one way of ensuring equal treatment of member states in the absence of a rotating presidency. The aim would be to balance the interests of northern and southern, big and small, and old and new members in a non-mechanistic way. He also explained the Legislative Council 'as a kind of second chamber' whose meetings would be public.

In article 17b [I-25] on qualified majority, Giscard's original draft was modified so that QMV in the European Council and Council would reflect a majority of member states and three-fifths (rather than two-thirds) of the Union's population. This, he deemed 'equitable and fair' although he noted that some members wished to retain the Nice Treaty rules.

Article 18 [I-26] on the European Commission retained Giscard's wording on the right of initiative, set the maximum size at 15 members, including the president, and gave it a much fuller mission statement. The Commission, it said, 'shall safeguard the general European interest. It shall ensure the application of the Constitution, and steps taken by the institutions under the Constitution. It shall also exercise coordinating, executive and management functions as laid down in the Constitution.'

Article 18a [I-27], on the Commission president, increased the European Parliament's role in electing the head of the Commission and holding the Commission to account. While Giscard's wording said the European Council would put forward its candidate for Commission president 'following the European elections', the new text gave the process more political significance by obliging it to take notice of the election results. It also stipulated the Commission president would be elected by a majority of Parliament's members rather than three-fifths as in Giscard's draft. The new article retained the procedure of member states submitting lists of three potential commissioners but gave the Commission president-elect the right to select up to 13 Commission members, up from 11. As in the Giscard text, the Commission president and commissioners would be approved as a body by the European Parliament. However, the Commission as a body would be responsible only to the European Parliament, which could censure the Commission, and not to the European Council and Parliament as proposed by Giscard.

The Commission president was given power to appoint vice-presidents (in the plural, rather than just one in Giscard's text) from among the Commission members and 'associate commissioners'. The associate commissioners would not be part of the college of commissioners and would have no voting powers.

Viewed together, the revised articles significantly curtailed the power of the European Council president compared with Giscard's vision. The changes in article 18 and 18a also amounted to a significant enhancement of Parliament's role in the life of the Commission president, compared with the Giscard text, and reflected the effectiveness of Méndez de Vigo and Hänsch, the two MEPs in the Praesidium. The European Council's ability to determine the candidate for Commission president was subtly reduced, and could decline further if European political parties were to get their act together in future European Parliament elections and put forward persons of Commission president material.

Article 19 [I-28], on the foreign minister, contained one notable modification compared with the Giscard text. The minister would still be appointed by the European Council using QMV, but would need the 'agreement' of the Commission president: the Giscard text spoke of a decision 'after consulting' the head of the Commission. As before, the foreign minister would carry out the common foreign and security and defence policies 'as mandated by the Council', and also be one of the Commission vice-presidents and 'responsible there for handling external relations and for co-ordinating other aspects of the Union's external action'. She or he would be bound by Commission procedures 'only for these responsibilities' in the Commission.

The Praesidium took an axe to the proposals on the Congress of the Peoples of Europe, deleting three paragraphs, which would have given the Congress the possibility of preparing amendments to the Constitution and functioning as an electoral college for the president of the European Council.

Both Giscard's text and that of the Praesidium mapped out the responsibilities and, where appropriate, the membership of the Court of Justice, the European Central Bank and the Union's advisory bodies (the Committee of the Regions and the Economic and Social Committee), without triggering controversy.

13.4 FOREIGN AFFAIRS AND DEFENCE

Giscard's presentation of the institutional articles on 24 April overshadowed the introduction by Jean-Luc Dehaene of the Praesidium's draft texts on the Union's external action[3] immediately afterwards. This was a pity because the external action provisions were a meaty part of the draft constitutional treaty and quite radical. They consisted of three articles in part I[4] and 37 articles in the policies section, which, since the Athens summit, was known as part III. The part I texts as published in April gave the provisional numbers 29 to the article on the implementation of the common foreign and security policy (CFSP) and 30 for the common security and defence policy (CSDP), while an article detailing a solidarity clause against terrorism was unnumbered. The draft articles drew heavily on the work of the external action and defence working groups, chaired respectively by Dehaene and Michel Barnier, and gave more details of the planned Union foreign minister.

The April drafts were drawn up in the shadow of the splits among EU and accession countries over the conflict in Iraq, and yet amid evidence that voters wanted common foreign and defence policies for the Union. Article 29 [I-40] of part I therefore took the view that developing CFSP was a process best achieved by encouraging convergence and mutual solidarity among member states. One aim of the constitutional treaty was to provide more effective institutional mechanisms to assist this process. Dehaene was cautious when presenting the texts. 'We are not proposing a miracle solution but are trying to devise procedures and structures which permit more joint action on the part of the Union,' he said.

---

[3] CONV 685/03.
[4] From this point, the Praesidium began to use Roman numerals to distinguish between the parts of the Constitutional Treaty.

Opinion poll evidence encouraged the Praesidium in this approach. A Eurobarometer poll, commissioned at Giscard's request and carried out between mid-February and mid-March, found 63% of EU citizens favoured a common foreign policy (with 22% against) and 71% backed a common defence policy (with 17% against). There was, however, a divergence in enthusiasm between countries such as Luxembourg, Greece and Italy, which were strongly in favour of common policies in both areas, and the traditionally neutral countries like Finland, Sweden, Austria and Ireland, where support was significantly below the Union average. Only in Britain did more people oppose a common foreign policy than support it.

Article 29 on the common foreign and security policy made clear the European Council was to 'identify the Union's strategic interests and determine the objectives' of CFSP while the Council of Ministers framed the policy. Both bodies would adopt the necessary decisions while the foreign minister and the member states would put the policy into effect, using Union and national resources.

The member states were to consult in the Council or European Council 'on any foreign and security policy issue which is of general interest in order to determine a common approach', and also before taking international action or making any commitment which could affect the Union's interests. Using language that alarmed UK eurosceptics, but was already in article 11 of the TEU, article 3 [III-294] in the policies section of the treaty underlined the duty of member states to support CFSP 'actively and unreservedly in a spirit of loyalty and mutual solidarity'. They were also to 'refrain from any action which is contrary to the interests of the Union or likely to impair its effectiveness as a cohesive force in international relations'.

The minister would carry out tasks formerly done by the high representative, the presidency and the Commission and have a right of initiative. The creation of this 'double-hatted' post and the minister's proposed right of initiative were responsible for most of the changes in existing CFSP articles. The April texts assumed the minister would help draw up and be in charge of implementing the Union's foreign and defence policies on a mandate from the Council, and not be subject to Commission collegiality in this area. But he or she would also be a member of the Commission and the rules of the college would apply for external relations issues dealing with traditional Community responsibilities. The minister could seek the Commission's support on CFSP and put forward joint proposals with the Commission. There could be extraordinary meetings of the European Council in case of international crises.

Member states were expected to boost the minister's role: those in the United Nations Security Council were told they should give the foreign minister the right to speak in support of Union positions. Provision was made to provide urgent financing, especially for operations under the CSDP.

Although article 29 stated a general rule that decisions relating to CFSP would be unanimous in the European Council and Council of Ministers, it gave the European Council the power to decide by unanimity to extend QMV to policies that were subject to the national veto. This bridge or *passerelle* clause in draft article 9 [III-300] of the policy section of the treaty was in addition to a controversial provision for QMV in the event of the foreign minister and the Commission producing a joint initiative.

Draft article 9 included rules for abstention, including qualified abstention, which would exempt a country from applying a CFSP decision. The country in question would, however, have to accept that the decision would commit the Union and undertake not to obstruct it. If member states representing more than one-third of the weighted votes in the Council qualified their abstentions, the decision would not be adopted.

Draft article 30 [I-41] described the common security and defence policy (CSDP) as 'an integral part' of CFSP to 'provide the Union with an operational capability' making use of military and civilian means. These, it added, may be deployed 'on tasks outside the Union to preserve peace and strengthen international security in accordance with the principles of the UN charter'.

The tasks, defined more closely in draft article 17 [III-309] of the policies part of the treaty, were an expanded version of the Petersberg tasks and followed the recommendations of the defence working group. To the existing humanitarian and rescue, peace-keeping, crisis management and peace-making tasks would be added disarmament operations, military advice and assistance, conflict prevention, support in combating terrorism at the request of a third country and post-conflict stabilisation.

The high ambitions set for CSDP became clearer in paragraph two, which declared: 'The common security and defence policy shall include the progressive framing of a common defence policy for the Union. This will lead to a common defence when the European Council, acting unanimously, so decides.' But the text then attempted to ease the concerns of those countries, among both existing and future member states, which saw their security anchored in the Atlantic alliance. Reiterating article 17 (1) of the TEU, it said the Union's policy 'shall not prejudice the specific character of the security and defence policy of certain member states and shall respect the obligations of certain member states, which see their common defence realised in NATO, and be compatible with the common security and defence policy established within that framework'.

The article went on to underline how CSDP depended for its capabilities on member states' military and civilian resources and, picking up on defence working group recommendations, urged them 'progressively to improve their military capabilities'. It made provision for a 'European Armaments and Strategic Research Agency' to help strengthen the defence industry and define a European capabilities and armaments policy. Article 30 also said member states establishing multinational forces could make them available to CSDP.

In taking decisions, the Council would unanimously adopt measures proposed by the foreign minister or a member state. The Commission would have no right of initiative in defence.

In one important area, article 30 on defence broke new ground. Largely because of UK objections, the Nice negotiations rejected enhanced cooperation in defence. The draft article, by contrast, broached various forms of 'flexibility' or enhanced cooperation to cope with cases where not all member states would engage in military action together. Thus under paragraph five, the Council would be able to entrust a crisis management task to a group of Union members that would be both willing and able to carry out the task. The Council decision would be unanimous. The nations involved would then agree management of the task among themselves but would have to refer back to the Council if completing the task entailed a new objective or conditions.

Paragraph six envisaged member states with stronger military capabilities establishing 'structured cooperation' and taking on more demanding tasks. The states would be able to use Union structures, such as the political and security committee (PSC) and the military committee, but their operations would not be Union operations.

Most controversial of all, paragraph seven would allow member states to give mutual defence guarantees in case of armed aggression against any one of them. The aim here was to reproduce the mutual defence commitment of article five of the Brussels Treaty of the Western European Union, which bound 10 current member states and allowed them to use Union structures. The article would be a transitional provision until the creation of the 'common defence' envisaged in paragraph two. It fuelled fears that the Union's defence policy could undermine NATO.

The articles incorporated important changes in other parts of the constitutional treaty. They took into account the disappearance of the CFSP 'pillar', which followed acceptance by the Convention of a single legal personality for the Union, and the simplification of its instruments and procedures. The external action articles struck a blow for clarity by bringing the Union's many external activities together into a coherent whole for the first time.

Draft article 24 [III-315] on the common commercial policy contained an important change to bring it into line with article 11 on competences. It categorised trade in cultural and audiovisual services, educational services and social and human health services as an exclusive competence of the Union, and thus subject to QMV and codecision. In article 133 of the TEC, these activities, known as the 'cultural exception' and of huge political importance in France, counted as a shared competence and so were subject to national vetoes.

Dehaene underlined that the grouping of the articles – like the elimination of the pillars – did not mean the harmonisation of procedures or instruments. These, and the roles of the actors involved, would vary according to policy. The Praesidium also made clear that CFSP was not covered by the Court of Justice.

13.5   A BASIS FOR FURTHER WORK?

Despite the sometimes savage changes to his own articles on the institutions, Giscard was in fine spirits when he presented the Praesidium's articles to the Convention plenary on the afternoon of Thursday, 24 April. Elsewhere, the revised texts prompted a good deal of crowing at Giscard's expense. For Hänsch, Giscard's vision now looked like 'a plucked Gallic cockerel' and 'we have the rare case that a plucked foul looks better than one with feathers'. Méndez de Vigo said the Praesidium deserved credit for producing a text that was 'radically different' from Giscard's draft.

Some of Giscard's critics were a little calmer. Brok, for example, said the new text was 'negotiable', although he still criticised the institution of a long-term European Council president for being unaccountable to any parliament. While welcoming the weakening of the board, the long-term presidency was a recipe for power struggles with the Commission and the new Union foreign minister. The slimming of the Commission could lead to small countries turning against the Union in future referendums, he warned.

But ominously, Katiforis, who chaired the government representatives' meetings during the Greek presidency in the absence of George Papandreou, reported 'great unease' at their meeting on the morning of 24 April because the opinions of the 18 small to medium-sized states that had met in Athens the week before were not reflected in Giscard's proposals. These countries feared Giscard's definition of consensus in the Convention 'could be a demographic definition made up by three or four bigger states of the Union'.

The unease was expressed most forcefully by Hannes Farnleitner, the Austrian government conventionnel, who was emerging as one of the most forthright of the small country spokespersons. A former economics minister, Farnleitner shared with his boss, Chancellor Schüssel, a fondness for brinkmanship in negotiation that he put to good use as the Convention progressed. Like his fellow Austrian Voggenhuber, he enjoyed controversy. But whereas Voggenhuber's message would sometimes get tangled in florid, classical metaphors, Farnleitner's style oscillated between the folksy and the frank. On this day, he chose to be brutally frank. He told Giscard that the views of 21 government representatives ranged from 'rejection to very sceptical'. Only two countries in the meeting supported the Praesidium, while two others could not comment because of the absence of their foreign ministers. Farnleitner warned Giscard that the mood among governments had shifted towards drawing up options rather than a single text for the IGC. The threat made, Farnleitner urged Giscard to listen more in future.

In Giscard's defence, Germany's Joschka Fischer, who was absent from the morning meeting, said the Praesidium text was a 'good basis for discussion'. But the government conventionnels of the three Benelux countries sent a stiff note to Giscard rejecting those articles, which 'undermined the Community project and the fundamental equilibrium between institutions and member states'. They pledged they would, with others, draw up alternative proposals.

The events of 22–24 April put the Convention under considerable stress with some members vowing never to trust Giscard again. However, Giscard emerged from the imbroglio with some gains. He secured the Praesidium's backing for the long-term presidency of the European Council while only minor changes were made to his plans for a slimmed down Commission. He brought forward the debate on the most difficult part of the remaining work of the Convention by a good three weeks, which was important given the pressure at the Athens European Council for the Convention to complete its work by 20 June. Giscard and the Convention were also back on the front pages of Europe's newspapers and in the evening television news bulletins.

Some Convention members later spoke of a sense of catharsis that week. Choices were on the table. Time was short. The gloves were off. There were deals to be done. Even as the Benelux representatives were firing off their note to Giscard, there were rumours that Belgium was working towards a compromise. The president, Giscard's aides reported, was happy with the Praesidium's deliberations and was prepared to defend the outcome. At the end of the week, some conventionnels were prepared to credit Giscard with a tactical success.

His easy acceptance of the Praesidium's changes lent credibility to reports that he had loaded his draft articles with dispensable bargaining chips, such as the deputy president of the European Council, and was surprised that so much of his original text survived. It was suggested that by setting his sights high in his initial proposals and drawing opprobrium onto himself, he had bamboozled hostile critics into accepting the Praesidium text as the basis for further work. Giuliano Amato, one of Giscard's two deputies, went so far as to describe the Praesidium proposals as 'a sort of mainstream'.

13.6   ENHANCED COOPERATION AMID CONTINUED DISCORD

For once, Amato's judgement appeared wide of the mark. The Praesidium articles on the institutions attracted 650 amendments and those on foreign policy and defence nearly 850. When the conventionnels gathered in Brussels on 15 May for two solid days of debate on the articles on institutions and external action, it appeared as if the Praesidium's efforts had merely magnified existing divisions in the Convention.

True, there was broad acceptance of the new foreign minister when more than 70 speakers took the floor to debate external affairs on 16 May, although many saw a need to clarify aspects of his double-hatted role in Council and Commission. But on practically all other issues there were divisions.

A wide gulf opened between the keen integrationists, concentrated among members of the European Parliament with the support of Germany and France, who sought far more QMV in foreign policy and a cohort of government representatives, of whom the most outspoken, the UK's Peter Hain, wanted CFSP 'ring-fenced' to maintain its intergovernmental nature and general use of unanimity.

The proposals for various forms of enhanced cooperation in article 30 on defence, and especially that covering mutual defence, revived the split between 'new' and 'old' Europe. While de Villepin for France and Bury of

Germany spoke in praise of the recent defence mini summit and the idea of an avant-garde of more integrationist member states, Hain said bluntly that Britain would not agree to an EU common defence because London supported the NATO guarantee provided to 19 of the soon-to-be 25 member states. From the accession countries, Poland's Danuta Hübner warned a defence guarantee rivalling NATO would risk unnecessary duplication of structures and capabilities. Her concerns were echoed by government representatives from Lithuania, Latvia and the Czech Republic.

The divergence over avant-garde proposals for foreign policy and defence continued to grow. When at the end of May, the plenary discussed a separate article 32b[5] [I-44] setting down the rules for implementing 'enhanced cooperation', Hain, backed by Lena Hjelm-Wallen of Sweden and Rytis Martikonis of Lithuania, rejected outright its extension to defence. Hain remained impervious in the face of a passionate intervention from Lamberto Dini, the former Italian prime minister and foreign minister, that enhanced cooperation was necessary if the UK insisted on continuing restrictions to more QMV in the Union.

Gaining acceptance of enhanced cooperation in the constitutional treaty thus became an important goal of the integrationist conventionnels. Draft article 32b, published in the middle of May, envisaged a significant easing of the restrictions on enhanced cooperation in the enlarged Union by stipulating a minimum threshold of one-third of member states for countries to participate, compared with 8 out of 15 member states under the Treaty of Nice. The Praesidium's view was that enhanced cooperation was a 'last resort' mechanism, which would promote integration by encouraging groups of states to cooperate inside rather than outside the Union and could be useful in the long term in the context of a much bigger and more diverse EU.

When the Convention debated the institutions on 15 May, there was strong opposition to the long-term European Council president, especially from the smaller member states and followers of the centre-right EPP. Many Convention members rejected the idea of the European Council being included among the Union's institutions. Greece, Benelux and the EPP tabled amendments to strengthen the executive role of the Commission. The candidate country Convention members, with strong support from their Irish and Nordic colleagues, pressed for a collegiate Commission with equality of commissioners. There were few backers of the Praesidium draft on the

---

[5] CONV 723/03. The draft articles on enhanced cooperation were published in mid-May and the plenary debate on them two weeks later was a rather curious interlude in a Convention otherwise preoccupied by splits over institutional issues and the first full draft of the constitutional treaty.

Commission's composition. Indeed, most amendments urged one commissioner per member state.

The UK, Spanish and Polish governments, backed in this case by Ireland, rejected the idea of a Legislative Council. In the debate on 15 May, Hain spoke out so strongly against the Legislative Council that it seemed to join the other 'red line' issues, such as tax harmonisation and QMV in foreign policy, which Britain had pledged to resist at all costs. Some amendments, notably from the Benelux countries, explicitly called for retention of the six-month rotating presidency. Reacting to the Praesidium proposal on MEPs' numbers, some small state conventionnels countered by demanding higher minimum thresholds of five or even six MEPs per country. The idea of 'degressive proportionality' in allocating European Parliament seats brought the Spanish and Polish government representatives, as prime beneficiaries of the Nice settlement, onto the same side as many 'smalls'.

The amendments highlighted Spain's outright opposition to changing the Nice decision on votes in the Council. 'My country cannot accept', wrote Ana Palacio, the Spanish foreign minister, about the Praesidium's proposals for a double majority measurement of QMV. Her preference for the Nice formula was shared by government representatives from the UK, Sweden, Denmark, Cyprus, Poland and Slovakia and many national parliamentarians.

The articles on the institutions prompted the conventionnels from the small member states to confer and rally their forces behind the Community method. Just before the Convention was due to discuss foreign and defence policy on 16 May, Henrik Hololei, the energetic alternate for the Estonian government, spoke on behalf of the 16 old and new smaller states that at the end of March had signed a paper on 'principles and premises' for reforming the Union's institutions.[6]

Rattling through his text to pack as many words as possible into his allotted three minutes, Hololei laid out the group's case for maintaining and reinforcing the Community method. Hololei closed the lid of his laptop to the sound of loud applause from his fellow smalls.

But the small and medium-sized countries were not as solid as the 'friends of the Community method' liked to claim. While they could agree on joint statements, they were never able to draw up draft articles together. Moreover, the Benelux countries were no longer aligned with the 16. Early in May, Belgium, the Netherlands and Luxembourg produced amendments

---

[6] CONV 646/03.

to the Praesidium articles, which backed away from one commissioner per member state and moved towards the Praesidium line with a proposal for a college of up to 15 commissioners, supported by an equivalent number of assistant commissioners who would not vote. Their plan[7], however, included the important qualification that the slimmed down Commission would be appointed on an equal and rotating basis.

There were hints of possible compromise elsewhere. Hain took time out from the 15 May plenary to try and persuade sceptical British journalists that a 'historic compromise' was in the offing, based on the Franco-German deal of January. Inside the plenary, he sought to reassure the Convention that Britain, in pushing the long-term presidency of the European Council, was 'not talking about a super-president who is going to be either a rival of, competing with, or dominating the president of the Commission … We just want an effective chairman of the Council to carry out the existing functions, remit or duties far more effectively.'

Despite all the fury about Giscard's handling of the institutional debate, by mid-May positions were beginning to shift. For practical reasons, such as printing and translation, the 20 June deadline for handing over the text to the Union's leaders in Thessaloniki meant the work had to be completed by 13 June, less than a month away. Amato sensed the changing currents, noting: 'Some members of the Convention are realising that if they want to be founding fathers, they will have to move. Otherwise, they will be founding failures.

---

[7] CONV 732/03.

CHAPTER 14
The Revised Draft Constitution

The same choice of being a founding father or a founding failure faced the members of the Praesidium when they met on 21 May for a three-day session to finish the first complete draft of the constitutional treaty. They had to fulfil a promise by Giscard, made in a letter of 8 May that the Convention's members would be able to debate the complete treaty during the plenary scheduled for 30–31 May.

The Praesidium's work rate had already increased compared with the second half of 2002 when there were never more than three meetings a month and few lasted longer than half a day. From 9 January, its meetings lasted all day and were more frequent.

As well as producing new draft articles, the Praesidium had to consider the amendments and feedback in the plenaries to articles it had produced. It also had to keep track of work delegated to a team of six legal experts from the Council, the Commission and the European Parliament who were charged with bringing the policy-related articles and legal bases of the existing treaties into the single text that would become part III of the final draft. Although the experts covered a prodigious amount of ground, they were not mandated to take political decisions. Controversial areas of drafting – such as the part III articles on justice and home affairs, and foreign and economic policy – were left for the Praesidium and the Convention to resolve.

The amendments posed a huge challenge to the Praesidium and the secretariat. Nearly 3,000 were submitted to the draft articles published between February and mid-May. These had to be collated and analysed by the secretariat. When Convention members arrived at plenary sessions, they would find all the amendments piled on their desks and bound with thick rubber bands. Sir John Kerr and his officials would then try to monitor the interventions to see which of the many amendments submitted by a conventionnel really mattered to the individual. If time allowed, or diplomacy dictated, eye contact would be made with the speaker if only to suggest to the conventionnels that their points were being taken seriously. Creating this feel-good factor was important because the amendments put forward often reflected political priorities at home. The secretariat papers analysing the amendments and grouping them into categories were an important public relations tool, because they helped conventionnels to feel that their own amendments were influencing the Convention.

Few really did. Many amendments were of an editorial nature and so politically insignificant and easy to deal with. More controversially, the secretariat disregarded many on the grounds that they were cancelled out by other contrary amendments. The secretariat paid more attention to amendments that carried a lot of signatures, such as those submitted by the party groups, or which carried special weight, such as those from key governments. Processing the amendments showed that not all conventionnels were equal.

While the revised draft articles were being drawn, Giscard's activities outside the Convention turned to massaging important special interests. He stepped up his bilateral diplomacy over a three-week period from 30 April in which he saw Pierre Raffarin, the French prime minister, with de Villepin; German opposition leaders including Erwin Teufel; Joschka Fischer; the Italian Convention members Fini, Dini and Marco Follini; Tony Blair and Romano Prodi. There were fears the Convention could be derailed. Britain appeared insistent that the Convention should not cross its 'red lines'. Prodi had thrown his weight behind one commissioner per member state. The German opposition was pushing hard for a reference to God or Christianity in the constitutional treaty. An important element in these meetings was to tease out the 'bottom lines' which key Convention participants required or could not accept as part of a final consensus.

14.1   THE END-MAY TEXTS

Monday, 26 May was an important milestone in the life of the Convention.

Fifteen months after they started work, the conventionnels were sent a volume of articles containing the revised text of part I of the draft Constitution[1]. A second volume,[2] including the entire Charter of Fundamental Rights as part II of the Constitution, the detailed policies and their legal bases as part III, and the general and final provisions as part IV, was published one day later. Also made public were the draft texts of part II[3] and part IV[4] with explanatory comments, and an overview[5] of those sections of part III which had been modified by the Praesidium, or which were new in relation to existing treaties and which had not so far been discussed by the Convention.

---

[1] CONV 724/03.
[2] CONV 725/03.
[3] CONV 726/03.
[4] CONV 728/03.
[5] CONV 727/03.

The mass of texts was a big media event. It was the first time the press and public had an overview of what the Convention was seeking to produce. However, the Praesidium had failed to meet its target of publishing a fully revised text because it was split. The articles of title IV of part I on the institutions were unchanged from the original version published in April.[6]

In the previous week's marathon, the Praesidium agreed revised articles on economic governance, the budget, the implementation of Union action, justice and home affairs, the definition and objectives of the Union, the treaty's general and final provisions, external action, the incorporation of the Charter, the Union's neighbourhood policy, Union membership and new legal bases in part III that would define policies on energy, civil protection, intellectual property, civil administration, space and sport.

The end-May drafts managed simultaneously to offend supporters of greater European integration, those who wanted a more intergovernmental Union and conventionnels of a religious persuasion – suggesting that Giscard and the Praesidium must have got something right. When part I appeared on 26 May, the impression was that Giscard had persuaded the Praesidium to back away from more integrationist aspects of earlier drafts. Foreign and tax policy remained intergovernmental with unanimity the general rule in these areas.

The assessment swung the other way when volume two appeared on the following day. This revealed a substantial extension of the European Parliament's powers of codecision with the Council (henceforth to be known as ordinary legislative procedure) from 34 to 70 policy areas and the application of qualified majority voting in the Council in place of unanimity in more than 20 procedures.

Giscard and the Praesidium seem to have applied the principle that 'the squeakiest wheel gets the most grease' in response to the thousands of amendments. Reflecting intense lobbying from several countries, but especially the personal intervention of Tony Blair during a visit by Giscard to 10 Downing Street on 19 May, the word 'federal' was dropped from the first article. The well-organised and vocal social lobby gained greater recognition for social and employment policies in the updated drafts.

---

[6] CONV 691/03.

14.2   THE REVISED PART I

With 59 articles, the draft part I now had 13 articles more than promised in the October 2002 'skeleton'.[7] The Praesidium made significant changes, notably to the opening articles, defining and stating the objectives of the Union and clarifying its competences *vis-à-vis* the member states. The first three articles of the Praesidium's first draft[8] had attracted no fewer than 435 amendments, so extensive rewriting was to be expected.

The first paragraph of article I-1[9] entitled 'Establishment of the Union' replaced 'federal' by the ugly, but less politically charged wording 'Community way'. In response to the concerns of the UK's Peter Hain and the Swedish and Irish government representatives, it was made clear that the Union's powers were conferred by member states. The new opening sentences of article I-1 of the draft constitutional treaty were therefore functional rather than majestic.

> Reflecting the will of the citizens and states of Europe to build a common future, this Constitution establishes the European Union, on which the member states confer competences to attain objectives they have in common. The Union shall coordinate the policies by which the member states aim to achieve these objectives, and shall exercise in the Community way the competences they confer on it.

Franklin or Madison, this was not.

Giscard's dalliance with a new name for the Union was stymied when the Praesidium insisted on 'European Union'. An earlier reference to the 'peoples' and states of Europe was changed to 'citizens and states' on the grounds that this reflected the EU's dual legitimacy better.

Several conventionnels, including the French, Belgian, German and Italian government representatives, wanted the goal of 'ever closer union' included

---

[7] CONV 369/02.

[8] CONV 528/03.

[9] Draft articles from the end-May drafts until the end of the Convention were prefixed with Roman numerals denoting the part of the constitutional treaty to which they belonged. The order of articles in part I stayed unchanged from 26 May until after the IGC in 2004, although their contents were revised and the style of numeration was changed again in the final Convention text of 18 July 2003 to article 1, article 2, etc. Articles in parts II, III and IV continued to have prefixes in Roman numerals in the final text. The order of articles in parts III and IV was subject to further change during the Convention, so that references to the individual articles in parts III and IV of the treaty will continue to be followed at the first appropriate point by the number of the article in the final 2004 treaty text in square brackets.

in article one. The Praesidium resisted this and contrary to expectations, Giscard even kept the phrase out of his draft preamble published a few days later. The new article I-1 also omitted any reference to the Union's symbols (its flag, money and anthem) which was an integrationist goal and high on the wish list of conventionnels from France.

Revised article I-2 on the Union's values tidied up the earlier text. The Union was now 'founded on the values of respect for human dignity, liberty, democracy, the rule of law and respect for human rights' which were common to member states and found 'in a society of pluralism, tolerance, justice, equality, solidarity and non-discrimination'. The revised article incorporated the ideas of equality and non-discrimination in response to amendments. As before, there was no reference to God or Christianity as sought by the Catholic and other churches.

Article I-3 on the Union's objectives was extensively rewritten reflecting many amendments. The new version stressed that the area of freedom, security and justice and the single market were benefits for EU citizens. It included a reference to the social market economy and highlighted a high quality environment and linguistic diversity, while deleting 'discovery of space', one of Giscard's pet proposals. The reference to policies 'generating high levels of competitiveness' sought in earlier drafting by Convention observer Unice, the European employers' federation was consigned to part III. The passage on the Union's relations with the rest of the world was rephrased to make it more outward looking and amplified to include such goals as security, free and fair trade and human rights.

A new article I-4, entitled 'fundamental freedoms and non-discrimination' was inserted, partly at the behest of the president of the European Court of Justice. This singled out the four fundamental freedoms of free movement of persons, goods, services and capital, and freedom of establishment, which originally were confusingly included among exclusive competences of the Union, and stressed that they were guaranteed. The second paragraph reproduced unchanged the previous article 6, barring discrimination on the grounds of nationality.

A new article I-5, defined 'Relations between the Union and the member states'. It gave prominence to regional and local self-government, which was an important aim of Giscard's ally, Teufel. Thus the Union was enjoined to 'respect the national identities of its member states, inherent in their fundamental structures, political and constitutional, including for regional and local self government. It shall respect their essential state functions ...' Relocating the idea of loyal cooperation from the title dealing with competences, a second paragraph said 'the Union and the member states shall, in full mutual respect, assist each other to carry out tasks which flow from the Constitution'. Finally, the member states were obliged to 'facilitate the achievement of the Union's tasks and refrain from any measure which could jeopardise the attainment of the objectives set out in the Constitution'. Article I-6 giving the Union legal personality stayed unchanged.

The articles in title II on 'Fundamental Rights and Citizenship of the Union' were little changed. Besides confirming that the Charter was now part II, article I-7 on fundamental rights made clear the Union 'shall seek accession' (as opposed to 'may accede') to the European Convention for the Protection of Human Rights.

Reflecting their painful birth, the articles on competences were substantially revised. On balance, the changes removed much of the original federal flavour of title III, now entitled 'Union Competences and Actions'.

Article I-9 on 'fundamental principles' gave greater stress to the idea that Union competences were conferred by member states following the strong protests from Hain, other UK parliamentarians and Ireland's Dick Roche. Accordingly, the Union would no longer act within the limits of competences 'conferred upon it by the Constitution' but within those 'conferred upon it by the member states *in* the Constitution'. The protocols on subsidiarity and proportionality and the role of national parliaments in the Union were also beefed up somewhat to increase the member states' safeguards against any centralising urges emanating from Brussels.

The editorial changes to I-9 meant article I-10 was much shorter than the previous draft article 9. Renamed 'Union law', it provoked considerable alarm among UK eurosceptics because it made specific reference to the principle of primacy of EU law, which was established by the ECJ in the 1960s but was hitherto absent from Union treaties. However, the reference to competences being conferred by the Constitution was removed, so the article read: 'The Constitution, and law adopted by the Union's institutions in exercising competences conferred on it, shall have primacy over the law of the member states.'

The Praesidium took account of a large number of amendments with a few limited changes to article I-11 detailing the 'Categories of competence'. Compared with former article 10, the most obvious change was to include employment policies with economic policies in the category where 'the Union shall have the competence to ensure the coordination' of member states' policies.

As requested by several conventionnels, including the UK, Austrian, Finnish, Swedish and German government representatives, article I-12 on 'Exclusive competences' dropped the reference to the four freedoms, which became the centrepiece of I-4.

The Praesidium's response to conflicting amendments on article I-13, 'Areas of shared competence', was broadly to leave well enough alone. The illustrative list of competences was tidied up, so that agriculture and fisheries specifically excluded the conservation of marine resources mentioned in article 12. Social policy was to be limited to 'aspects defined in part III', supposedly to ensure that there would be no expansion of Union competence in this sensitive area, and public health, a controversial element in the original text, was changed to 'common safety concerns in public health matters'.

A broad cross-section of member states wanted changes to the original article on coordinating economic policies. The UK, France, Germany and Sweden rejected the idea that 'the Union shall coordinate the economic policies of the member states ...' In response, article I-14 on 'The coordination of economic and employment policies' stated: 'The Union shall adopt measures to ensure coordination of the economic policies of the member states .... member states shall coordinate their economic policies within the Union'. The formula used in the first sentence was also applied in a new PES-inspired paragraph covering coordination of employment policies. Further centre-left amendments added another paragraph saying the Union 'may adopt initiatives to ensure coordination of member states' social policies'.

The Praesidium's original draft on the common foreign and security policy provoked fury on the part of the UK even though it just echoed the Maastricht Treaty in calling for member states' loyalty and mutual solidarity. In the 26 May draft of article I-15 on the 'Common foreign and security policy', the Praesidium not only stuck to its guns, it added that member states 'shall comply with the acts adopted in this area' to strengthen their obligations under CFSP. Reflecting a large number of amendments, a new first paragraph was added to provide an explicit reference to the Union competence in CFSP and a reference to defence. This said: 'The Union's competence in matters of common foreign and security policy shall cover all areas of foreign policy and all questions relating to the Union's security, including the progressive framing of a common defence policy, which might lead to a common defence.'

Article I-16 was renamed 'Areas of supporting, coordinating or complementary action' to reflect better the fact that legislative competence in these areas lay with the member states. The list of such areas was modified to delete employment (now in article I-14) and add 'protection and improvement of human health'. Protection against disasters became 'civil protection'. Article I-17 the 'flexibility clause' was little changed, although the Council of Ministers was to obtain the 'consent' (rather than assent) of the European Parliament for measures taken.

The first part of title V, concerned with *how* the Union would carry out its tasks, was far less controversial than title III about *who* should exercise *what* competence in the Union. Thus the changes to title V, 'The Exercise of Union Competence', generally constituted a tidying up exercise.

Article I-33 on 'Legislative acts' revised the new term for codecision from 'legislative procedure' to 'ordinary legislative procedure' to avoid confusion as the constitutional treaty also provided for a limited number of acts to be adopted differently.

Reflecting many amendments, article I-35 on 'Delegated regulations' was revised to give the European Parliament and Council the power to revoke or 'call back' such legislation independent of each other. The Praesidium also decided to remove sunset clauses from delegated acts on the grounds they could create legal uncertainty.

Title VI on 'The Democratic Life of the Union' was subject to considerable modification. A new article I-45, expounding 'The principle of representative democracy', amplified and replaced the one-sentence article in the original draft providing for political parties at European level. Meeting widespread demands from outside as well as inside the Convention, article I-46 on 'The principle of participatory democracy' was expanded to include a requirement for the Commission to carry out 'broad prior consultations with parties concerned' to ensure the Union's actions are coherent and transparent. Article I-47 on 'The social partners and autonomous social dialogue' was also new and responded to the very large number of amendments that wanted the Union to recognise and promote the role of social partners (trade unions and business umbrella groups) at Union level and facilitate dialogue between them.

The revised title VII, 'The Union's Finances', was noteworthy on two counts. Without specifically mentioning this option by name, article I-53 on 'The Union's resources' left open the possibility of creating European taxes by unanimity. A new article I-54 on 'The multi-annual financial framework' brought the EU's renamed financial perspective into the Constitution, while article III-304 [III-402] set out the details, including a provision that it must last for at least five years. Another important part III article – III-306 [III-

404] – set out a simplified budget procedure in which the distinction between compulsory spending, such as agricultural support, and non-compulsory expenditure was dropped, ministerial decisions would be taken by qualified majority and Parliament would have the final word.

Title VIII, comprising article I-56 'The Union and its immediate environment' was altered in response to a PES amendment to ensure the Union's relations with its near neighbours respected the values detailed in article 2 of the Constitution.

Among the generally little changed articles of title IX on 'Union Membership', article I-59 raised the stakes for 'Voluntary withdrawal from the Union' by subjecting an application for withdrawal to scrutiny by the European Council, rather than the Council of Ministers. However, the Praesidium rejected amendments which suggested penalising any state that later wanted to rejoin the Union. The Union, Giscard observed, 'is after all not a prison'. Instead, the text proposed such countries should apply in line with article I-57 detailing 'Conditions and procedure for applying for Union membership'.

14.3   COMMON FOREIGN AND DEFENCE PROPOSALS AFTER IRAQ

The Praesidium's response to the many amendments on CFSP and the lively debate about them in the mid-May plenary session was broadly to change the rhetoric of the articles to please the integrationists while cutting back the plans for more qualified majority. There was a strong tilt towards the UK position in the revised drafting, reflecting Giscard's visit to 10 Downing Street on 19 May. A notable casualty of this approach was the provision in the April draft for QMV to apply to joint proposals from the foreign minister and the Commission. The involvement of the Commission had aroused British fears of 'communitarisation' of CFSP 'via the back door' and it was deleted.

Rechristened 'Specific provisions for implementing common foreign and security policy', article I-39 of the 26 May draft was couched in rather more forceful language than article 29 of April. Although it looked somewhat fanciful in the light of the Iraq crisis, the revised first paragraph said: 'The European Union shall conduct a common foreign and security policy, based on the development of mutual political solidarity among member states, the identification of questions of general interest and the achievement of an ever increasing degree of convergence of member states' actions.'

CFSP would be put into effect by the foreign minister and member states, using national and Union resources. These provisions were fleshed out in part III. Among detailed changes, article I-39 was tweaked to make sure that the Council of Ministers would frame the CFSP 'within the strategic guidelines established by the European Council' and that the European Parliament would be 'regularly' consulted on CFSP. Article III-200 [III-304] provided for twice-yearly debates on CFSP and defence policy in Parliament, whereas the original idea was for annual debates.

Paragraph seven of I-39 specified that the right of initiative would lie with the member states or the foreign minister. An earlier provision that the minister could act 'alone or together with the Commission' was amended to weaken the Commission's involvement to cover proposals from the minister or 'the minister with the Commission's support'.

The article stated that CFSP decisions would be taken by the Council of Ministers or European Council unanimously, except in certain cases, detailed in III-196 [III-300] where QMV would apply. Although these exceptions were pared back to accommodate the UK and other governments, QMV would apply, as at present, to the implementation of Union actions or common strategic decisions already adopted by unanimity by the European Council and to the appointment of special representatives.

The rules for abstention, including qualified abstention, stayed unchanged between end-April and end-May. Because it posed no risk to the intergovernmental nature of CFSP, the *passerelle* provision by which the European Council could decide by unanimity to allow the Council to act by QMV in other foreign policy areas also stayed unchanged.

In its revised version, the article underlined that QMV in external affairs 'shall not apply to decisions having military or defence implications'.

Article I-40 (article 30 in the April texts) giving the 'Specific provisions for implementing common defence policy' was subject to a few revisions. Reflecting a joint amendment from Britain, France and Germany, the revised 26 May text banished any idea of a European army by underlining that in tackling its CSDP tasks the Union would use 'capabilities provided by the member states'.

In addressing the enhanced Petersberg tasks, the 26 May text beefed up the references to anti-terrorism activity to stress support for 'third countries in combating terrorism in their territories'. At the request of the UK, Irish, Italian, German and Dutch governments, a reference to military capabilities was added to the name of the proposed 'European Armaments, Research and Military Capabilities Agency'.

Although contentious, the three paragraphs of article I-40, which proposed different forms of enhanced cooperation in defence, saw only one substantive change – the addition of a reference to close cooperation with NATO in issues of mutual defence against armed aggression.

Article I-42 [I-43], the 'Solidarity clause', was strengthened considerably. The UK, French and German government representatives obtained tougher language for the fight against terrorism. With support from their colleagues from Ireland, Belgium and Austria, they ensured its scope was extended to natural and man-made disasters in line with recommendations of the working group of defence.

14.4 PART II: THE CHARTER OF FUNDAMENTAL RIGHTS

The Charter, as proclaimed at the December 2000 Nice summit, became part II of the Constitution. Apart from some very minor adjustments, the text was as agreed at Nice. There was, however, a lively debate over the so-called horizontal articles (51 to 54) that were included to prevent any extension under the Charter of the application of Union law at the expense of law of the member states.

For the UK, Hain made clear he would not accept the Charter in the constitutional treaty without an assurance that its social provisions would not undermine Britain's still relatively liberal employment laws. The discussion turned on the status of the so-called explanations to the Charter, which were drawn up in 2000 and clarified the horizontal issue at that time to the UK's satisfaction. In the 31 May plenary, Hain made the UK's acceptance of the Charter conditional on a satisfactory cross-reference to the explanations in the constitutional treaty text, and was supported by Fini of Italy and Roche of Ireland. Commissioner Vitorino said he was working on the issue. Vitorino also made a strong plea for retention of the Charter preamble in the Constitution in addition to its own preamble. 'Aesthetically, it may be odd to have one Constitution and two preambles,' Vitorino quipped. 'But in China they have one country and two systems. So Europe can be different too.'

14.5 PART III: THE POLICIES AND FUNCTIONING OF THE UNION

Although presented to the conventionnels as a technical rather than a political exercise, the part III articles came as a surprise. The decisions to make a rule of 'ordinary legislative procedure' (codecision) between the Parliament and the Council and qualified majority voting in the Council of Ministers resulted in quite sweeping changes.[10] MEPs would have equal legislative powers in 70 rather than 34 policy areas while the national veto would disappear in more than 20 procedures. Some shifts to QMV – such as those covering EU staff regulations – were of minor significance. Others were not. Sensitive areas to be brought under majority voting included the protection of employees' rights for those fired unjustly, social security measures for migrant workers and uniform protection of intellectual property rights in the single market. The communitarisation of the Union's area of freedom, security and justice saw QMV brought in for legislation on border controls, asylum and immigration policies, judicial cooperation and the setting of minimum rules for the definition of offences and penalties in cases of particularly serious cross-border crime. Some of these issues went to the heart of traditional sovereignty.

In seeking to extend QMV and other Union powers, the Praesidium applied a generous interpretation to the results of working groups and earlier plenary debates. Thus, it proposed enabling legislation to create a European Public Prosecutor's Office by unanimity in III-170 [III-274] even though there was no consensus in the Convention. Similarly, in the field of taxation, the Praesidium ignored the protests of the UK, Sweden and Ireland and opened a window to QMV. Article III-59 [III-171] proposed that the Council of Ministers, acting unanimously, could decide that harmonisation measures concerning turnover taxes, excise duties and other indirect taxation related to administrative cooperation or tax fraud. Once taken, that decision would allow it to act by QMV when adopting legislation, laying down appropriate measures to deal with the problem. With article III-60, the same restricted *passerelle* procedure would apply to harmonisation measures for administrative cooperation or combating tax fraud in the case of company taxation, provided such action was necessary to ensure proper functioning of the internal market or avoid competitive distortions.[11]

The 27 May text of part III also contained the first articles covering economic governance in the Union. Again, the Praesidium brushed aside the reservations that had rendered the working group on economic governance inconclusive. The Eurogroup was formally recognised for the first time, to the irritation of the UK. The euro-zone countries were enabled to adopt measures among themselves on economic policy guidelines, budget discipline and multilateral surveillance. A protocol provided for an elected

---

[10] CONV 727/03, ANNEX VIII.
[11] The *passerelles* in III-59 and III-60 were dropped in the late stages of the IGC.

president of the Eurogroup with a two-year tenure. The economic governance articles boosted the role of the Commission, giving it the ability to send an opinion to a delinquent state under the excessive deficit procedure and the power to send a warning to a member state in breach of the Union's broad economic policy guidelines.

Part III consisted of no fewer than 339 articles. Although around three-quarters of the articles were taken over unchanged or only slightly modified from the existing treaties and gathered together into coherent groups, this section of the draft constitutional treaty dealing with policies and legal bases was evidently much more than a 'tidying up' exercise.

14.6 PART IV: GENERAL AND FINAL PROVISIONS

The Praesidium was so obviously satisfied with the Convention's work that it decided in article IV-6 [IV-443] of the general and final provisions that future amendments to the treaty establishing the Constitution should, in general, be studied by a Convention with the same components as the present one. The Convention would make a recommendation by consensus to a subsequent intergovernmental conference of the member states. Only in the event of minor changes would the matter be referred directly to member states' representatives in a mini-IGC.

Despite doubts among the Convention members about the feasibility of securing unanimous support and ratification in all member states for the eventual constitutional treaty and amendments to it, the Praesidium proposed no changes in procedure at this stage.

Thus, article IV-7 [IV-447] stuck to the existing rules for adoption that required all member states to ratify Union treaties in accordance with their Constitutions. However, if, two years after signing the final treaty, one or more countries experienced problems with ratification and four-fifths of member states had already ratified, the problem would then be referred to the European Council.[12]

14.7 GISCARD'S PREAMBLE

After receiving piles of paper in the first two days of the week, the conventionnels were sent a brief missive on 28 May containing the

---

[12] This was to be published separately as a declaration by the Convention and the IGC.

Praesidium's draft preamble.[13]

More accurately, it was Giscard's preamble with his fingerprints all over it, from a quote of Thucydides in ancient Greek at the top (translated as: 'Our Constitution is called a democracy because power is in the hands not of a minority but of the whole people') to a paragraph on the bottom in which the representatives of member states who would sign the text expressed their gratitude to the members of the Convention for having prepared it.

The text sat ill with Giscard's earlier ambition of giving the united Europe of 25 and more member states a lyrical text that eager teenagers would learn by heart. His *oeuvre*, released just before the Ascension Day holiday as he was travelling to Aachen to receive the prestigious 'international Charlemagne Prize' in recognition of his work on the Constitution, was justifiably criticised for being wordy and pretentious.

It was also politically contentious. Rather than include the ringing phrase 'ever closer Union', beloved by integrationists, Giscard's preamble suggested instead that 'the peoples of Europe are determined to transcend their ancient divisions, and, united in *an ever closer fashion*, to forge a common destiny'. Despite pressure from the Christian wing of the European People's Party and the Vatican, Giscard pointedly omitted a reference to Christianity or any other specific religion in his text. Instead, it made just passing reference to Europe's 'cultural, religious and humanist inheritance' and the 'spiritual impulse always present in its heritage'. Starting with its quote from Thucydides, the preamble was very much a hymn to humanism and democracy. In seeking to encapsulate 2,000 years of European history, it omitted all reference to the dark ages, the middle ages and the centuries when Christianity suffused Europe's politics and culture. There was no mention of the world wars, dictatorships and genocide of the 20th century.

Skipping as it did from the 'civilisations of Greece and Rome' to the 'philosophical currents of the Enlightenment', Giscard's preamble told its readers more about the author's perception of himself than the historical roots of the constitutional treaty. Here was Renaissance man, putting his own stamp on Europe. However, it was far from clear at this stage whether the preamble would ever be used because agreement on the constitutional treaty looked remote.

---

[13] CONV 722/03.

CHAPTER 15
Managing the Splits

15.1   CRISIS IN THE PRAESIDIUM

The Convention was in crisis because of a split in the 13-strong Praesidium, the very body that was supposed to steer it to success. At the end of May, consensus on a constitutional treaty appeared remote indeed.

The crisis came to a head on 22 May, in the middle of the three-day Praesidium session to finalise the revised drafts. Heartened by the mid-May plenary session, Spain's Alfonso Dastis balked at the proposals to scrap the Nice Treaty provisions on voting weights in the Council of Ministers. His revolt prompted other Praesidium members to object to other proposed changes to the Nice Treaty as presented by Giscard to the 24 April plenary.

The Spanish problem had festered since Giscard first proposed a double majority system for qualified majority voting in the Council, a slimmed down Commission and a somewhat reduced European Parliament. Stepping up the rhetoric, Dastis warned in the 15 May plenary session that reopening the Nice settlements on voting weights in the Council and seats in the Parliament would lead to 'no agreement in the Convention' and a 'long and difficult Intergovernmental Conference' afterwards. Reinforcing these threats and stiffening Dastis with frequent phone calls was José Maria Aznar, Spain's prime minister. Under pressure from the Socialist opposition at home because of his support of the war in Iraq, the last thing Aznar needed was a decision in the Convention that would undermine his success in Nice of securing Spain's position as one of the Union's big powers.

To make matters worse, the Presidium's discussion on the institutions during its three-day session in May was badly orchestrated, allowing Dastis to rally other members against changing the Nice agreements. The meeting began by looking at the proposals to restructure the distribution of seats in the European Parliament. At this point, Dastis complained about the bid to alter Nice and unveiled his implacable opposition to the proposals on Council votes. By linking the two issues, he prompted Henning Christophersen and John Bruton to query the plans to overturn the Nice settlement on the Commission. The already fragile consensus behind the late April institutional articles threatened to unravel. Doubts about the composition of the Commission raised questions about the foreign minister and the minister's role in the Commission. This in turn prompted questions about the long-term presidency of the European Council and the entire institutional architecture contained in the Praesidium draft. With the Praesidium split, and two government representatives openly opposing the draft provisions on the institutions, the decision was taken to leave the existing institutional chapter unchanged in the revised part I of 26 May.

The move not only exposed the Praesidium's divisions. The do-nothing decision offended conventionnels who had submitted amendments to the original drafts. But by this stage, both the plenary and the Praesidium were becoming side-shows. When the Praesidium met again on 28 May, it decided that the plenaries of Friday, 30 May and Saturday, 31 May should focus on enhanced cooperation, economic governance, the Union's budget and own resources, and give conventionnels a chance to comment on parts II and III. The Praesidium would meet again after the Saturday session for another discussion of the institutions. But it was also decided that Giscard and his two deputies should set aside Wednesday, 4 June for consultations with the Convention's four component groups.

The decision of the leadership to consult the *'composantes'* showed just how dramatically the dynamics of the Convention were changing. Activity was moving into the corridors and back rooms. The structure agreed at Laeken was falling into disuse. The end-May plenaries were lacklustre affairs. As Amato observed: 'The plenary is discussing important topics, but attention is already on future deliberations.'

Dastis, meanwhile, had pulled off a coup. He had widened the appeal of his crusade to retain the Nice Treaty agreements to include the 16 small and medium-sized countries that, as 'friends of the Community method', had been campaigning against the long-term European Council president and for one commissioner per member state. He also persuaded eight government representatives, including fellow Praesidium member Henning Christophersen of Denmark, to join in a signed appeal[1] to the Convention not to tamper with the Nice institutional package.

The nine were a strange bunch. They included the representatives of the UK, Poland, Sweden, Austria, Ireland, Lithuania and Cyprus, and, as Duff remarked, signed the letter 'for different and contradictory reasons'. Christophersen objected to the plan to cut the number of MEPs from 732 to 700 because it meant problems for certain small member states. Those with coalition governments, for example, would not be able to have enough seats

---

[1] CONV 766/03.

in the Parliament to ensure a suitable share-out of committee posts among the political parties.

Ireland's Dick Roche was primarily concerned about the proposals for the slimmed down Commission and the absence of the Nice Treaty assurances that the reduced college would be 'chosen according to a rotation system based on the principle of equality'. Poland signed because it was in the same position on voting weights as Spain. The UK's position was the result of a deal between Peter Hain and Dastis to secure Spain's support for maintaining the national veto on tax and social security policies. As members of the coalition of 16 small to medium-sized countries, the other signatories were deeply suspicious of Giscard and his perceived tendency to back the interests of the big EU members. The accession countries, in particular, did not want to reopen the Nice agreements, which were part of the membership agreements they negotiated with the Commission and were being put to their electorates in referendums.

The letter of the nine was circulated among conventionnels on 30 May. While acknowledging that Nice 'was not perfect', they warned that reopening the Nice settlement would result in the Convention having to submit options to the following Intergovernmental Conference, with the inevitable consequence of limiting its influence over the IGC.

15.2 THE EUROPEAN COMMISSION: MISSING IN ACTION

There were some important absentees from the battlefield as the crisis gathered. Many conventionnels pinned their hopes on a compromise from the original six member states amid reports that they were hatching a text that would bridge the differences. The idea was politically appealing. The original six contained member states that were big and small, and from north and south, and politically from left and right. Yet the efforts came to nothing.

Also striking was the absence of any attempt by the Commission to broker a compromise in the fevered activity of the Convention's final weeks. Such a move would have been expected of the Delors Commission a decade earlier. But the Prodi executive had its own corner to fight as the Convention's close drew near.

The Commission never recovered from the bungled launch of Penelope the previous December. Its problems grew rather than declined in the weeks that followed that fiasco. Barnier and Vitorino suffered setbacks in the college, which weakened their standing in the Convention and Praesidium when the news seeped out. The tide of sympathy for the Commission in the Praesidium ebbed.

Its ability to mould the final outcome of the Convention declined sharply after it backed the 'small country' side over the future size of the Commission and the permanent president of the European Council in the row between big and small member states. During March and April, the representatives of the small and medium-sized governments appeared to be the coming force in the Convention and, as 'Friends of the Community Method', included in their platform a demand for one commissioner per member state[2].

The Commission's position on the size of the college was ambiguous during 2002. Romano Prodi and the college had backed one commissioner per member state as the correct way of dealing with the 'big bang' enlargement. But Prodi also floated the idea of an inner cabinet of senior commissioners in the summer of 2002 and the Commission's official document of December appeared to favour a small Commission in the interests of efficiency. Both Barnier and Vitorino believed a small Commission would be a strong Commission.

But when Giscard presented his April drafts on the institutions, the Commission came out clearly for one member per member state. The two commissioners supported this position in the Praesidium meeting of 23 April, when the Praesidium opted for a smaller Commission with a maximum of 15 members. On 30 April, the Commission discussed the Praesidium's proposals on the institutions at length. It reported[3] that 'the college expressed its preference to have one commissioner per member state' but also made clear that a large Commission could only function as a team by allowing its president to make the necessary divisions of responsibility in its internal organisation. It also opposed the stable presidency of the European Council.

From this point, Prodi was publicly identified with policies diametrically opposed to those adopted by the Praesidium and there was no chance that the Commission could ever play a mediating role in the final crucial weeks of the Convention. The Commission's problems grew when the protagonists of one commissioner per member state among the member states began to fall away. In mid-May, the Benelux countries switched to supporting the

---

[2] See the end of March contribution from the representatives of 16 small and medium-sized countries entitled 'Reforming the institutions: principles and premises', CONV 646/03.
[3] Commission press release IP/03/611.

Praesidium.[4] Albeit reluctantly, a majority of the other small and medium-sized member states fell into line with the Praesidium plans for a smaller Commission in the final stages of the Convention in June. That was when the Praesidium agreed that the Commission appointed in 2004 would be constituted in line with the Nice agreement and have one member per member state, and that from 2009 the future 15-member Commissions would work on a system of equal rotation. When the government representatives in the Convention met on 12 June for the last time before Thessalonki, only five still insisted on one commissioner per member state with full voting rights.

After Thessaloniki, an unrepentant Prodi vowed to carry the fight for one commissioner per member state to the IGC[5] and, as the intergovernmental conference got underway, appeared to be staging a successful fight back. But the consensus that emerged on 13 June marked an unhappy end to an unhappy Convention for the Commission president. In the opening session of the Convention, Prodi promised the Commission would 'make a full and enthusiastic contribution, drawing on all its own experience and its expertise'.[6] Instead, the Commission had been reactive rather than proactive and was left outside the June consensus as far as its own future structure was concerned.

So what went wrong? The Commission certainly suffered no lack of resources. The number of Commission staff working on the Convention was greater than the Convention secretariat. But they were split into different groups. Some worked with the commissioners in the Convention, others were among Prodi's staff, others in the Commission's group of policy advisors headed by Ricardo 'Ricky' Levi while, operating in secrecy, was the group around Francois Lamoureux that produced Penelope. These groups seemed unable to work together.

Matters were not helped by a clash of personalities between Giscard and Prodi. Giscard had little time for Prodi and made no attempt to conceal his feelings. Prodi repaid the compliment. They conducted a dialogue of the deaf. For much of May 2003, the two were embroiled in a well-publicised squabble over where, when and how to stage a public debate over the institutions which, in the end, never took place.

---

[4] CONV 732/03.
[5] 'Europe and the Constitution: Letting the people have their say'. Speech/03/346 at the University of Bologna, 5 July 2003, available among Prodi's speeches on his webpage on the Commission website at www.europa.eu.int
[6] Speech/02/88, 28 February 2002, CONV 4/02.

In one important respect, the Commission appears to have misread the small member states' analysis of what constituted a better deal for them. A 15-strong Commission looked less unattractive to several of the small member states once the Convention Praesidium conceded the principle of equal rotation for membership of the college. Such a system promised the smalls a fair shot at the top Commission jobs, whereas they would have no such guarantee in a large Commission in which the Commission president would choose how to divide responsibilities.

Indeed, Prodi may have been the author of his own misfortune through publicly coupling the idea of the large Commission with an insistence that its president be a powerful figure who would take responsibility for allocating portfolios, designating vice-presidents and asking for the resignation of Commission members.[7] Although elected by the Parliament, the Commission president would, under the terms of the Praesidium's proposals, be nominated by the European Council 'deciding by qualified majority'. From the viewpoint of some small member states, it was all too easy to imagine the successful candidate for the Commission presidency, once installed, selecting the inner circle commissioners from the large countries, which had voted in the European Council to nominate him or her for the post. Such a course would, it is true, run counter to the spirit of the constitutional treaty, but it would be in line with the practices of the European political market.

15.3   BRITAIN OPTS FOR A SINGLE TEXT

Hain's signature on Dastis's round robin was deeply disappointing for Giscard. He convinced himself after his first meeting with Blair that the prime minister was pro-European in a way that no recent UK leader had been. Giscard had been solicitous of Hain and the UK position throughout the Convention. On the few occasions that Hain did not attend a plenary, Giscard could be heard asking Kerr: 'Où est Hain?' As he once told *Le Monde*:[8] 'I am doing my best so that our text of the Constitution is compatible with the demands of Britons desirous of participating in the life of Europe.' When Giscard met Blair in London on 19 May to sort out the UK's non-negotiable positions, the double majority in the Council of Ministers was not among them. Giscard, however, had a promise to remove the word 'federal' from article 1 up his sleeve. During the three-day

---

[7] IP/03/611.
[8] Edition of 14 March 2003.

Praesidium meeting that followed, Giscard got rid of the 'f-word' and retained unanimity in foreign policy. He had delivered and he felt betrayed.

In fact, Hain did the deal with Dastis without Blair's knowledge. Hain reasoned that as long as the Convention delivered the stable European Council presidency and respected the UK's other 'red lines', it did not matter much to the UK whether it opted for the Nice treaty agreements or Giscard's institutional proposals. Hain's own feeling was that reopening Nice was akin to opening Pandora's box. The price for securing an ally against a very unwelcome extension of QMV appeared low.

Looking at conditions in Britain, it is easy to understand why Hain wanted an insurance policy. After long quiescence and neglect, the British tabloid press had discovered the Convention. The right-wing, middle class *Daily Mail* was first off the blocks. 'A blueprint for Tyranny' screamed its front page on 8 May. More worrying for the government was the stance of Rupert Murdoch's *Sun*, the daily with the biggest circulation in Britain. On 15 May, with 'Save our country' emblazoned across the UK's Union flag, and pictures of Queen Elizabeth I, Admiral Lord Nelson and Winston Churchill across the top of its front page, the *Sun* summed up Britain's achievements of the past five hundred years. '1588 we saw off the Spanish. 1805 we saw off the French. 1940 we saw off the Germans.' Below, next to an unflattering picture of the prime minister, the headline read: '2003 Blair surrenders Britain to Europe'.

Hain, in Brussels for the mid-May plenary, dismissed the press coverage as 'hogwash'. For the government in London, the tabloid fury resulted in unwelcome political pressure for a referendum on the outcome of the IGC following the Convention. In the Convention, however, the furore probably helped Hain's negotiating position.

UK 'bottom lines' proliferated. In mid-May, they included the elected long-term president of the European Council; national parliaments policing subsidiarity; incorporation of the Charter in such a way as not to change domestic law; foreign policy subject to unanimity with governments in control; tax and social security legislation subject to unanimity; no Legislative Council and no European public prosecutor. In the end-May plenary sessions after publication of the revised part I and parts II, III and IV, Hain added more red lines. He rejected reinforced cooperation in foreign and security policy. Debating economic governance, he insisted the Commission and European Parliament should have no additional powers to coordinate economic policies; that there was no reason to strengthen the Eurogroup and that control of the Union's own resources should remain with the member states.

'All agree that QMV and codecision should be the norm,' Hain declared to a startled plenary session. He then bluntly ruled out QMV for legislation under article III-18 [III-136] on social security for migrant workers and articles III-59 and III-60 on tax. On social policy, he charged that proposals to scrap the national veto in III-99 [III-210.3] went 'way beyond the consensus' in the social affairs working group. Accordingly, he rejected QMV for minimum standards for the protection of workers when their employment contract ended, codetermination in the workplace and conditions of employment for third country nationals on the grounds that the Nice treaty, which retained the veto in these areas, had yet to be tested. Moreover, Hain 'still had problems' with article III-166 [III-270] prescribing QMV for legislation on judicial cooperation in criminal matters. It could change the fundamental principles of the British legal system, including *habeas corpus*.

Hain was supported on social and tax issues by Ireland's Dick Roche. But he fell foul of the many MEPs from the EPP and PES who felt that the moves to QMV in part III did not go far enough. Anne Van Lancker, the Flemish Socialist MEP and tireless battler for the social component of the Constitution, complained bitterly. Brok, as leader of the Convention's EPP caucus, called for more QMV in foreign policy and accused Britain alone of stymieing the ambitions of the French and German governments. Commissioner Barnier called for the restitution of QMV for joint proposals in foreign policy of the foreign minister and the Commission.

Hain's remarks provoked outrage – both real and feigned – among many conventionnels. The Austrian government's Farnleitner charged that the UK's insistence on a veto in foreign policy 'could blow up the Convention'. As Farnleitner would later indulge in high profile brinkmanship on behalf of the smalls, his remarks served only to highlight how confused conditions were. The Convention had become a negotiation that was being conducted at many different levels: in numerous bilateral 'confessionals' and group meetings outside the plenary hall, and over mobile phones with the aides of national leaders who were attending the 300th anniversary celebrations of the Russian city of St Petersburg. Events in Brussels were no longer transparent. All statements were suspect. Dissembling and double-speak were now the norm. The Convention seemed to be turning into an IGC, with the same propensity for blockages, deadlock and breakdown. Optimism was at a low ebb.

Anybody listening to Hain's plenary statements would conclude that the UK was a major threat to consensus in the Convention. But he was also sending out different, more positive signals. From around the middle of May, Britain was signalling its preference for a single text at the end of the Convention.

At the end of the month, Hain's message was that the UK would not make common cause with any group to wreck the Convention. Its decision to eschew options would be an important background factor in achieving consensus. For the Netherlands' Gijs de Vries, Hain's indication to the government representatives' meeting during the 30–31 May plenary that London would prefer a deal at the Convention was 'the one positive element of the week'. De Vries was speaking after the 31 May plenary, just as Praesidium members were preparing to devote their Saturday afternoon to yet another discussion on the institutional articles.

15.4   GISCARD PREPARES TO BREAK FREE

Giscard was prepared to play hardball. He regarded the backers of the Nice agreements as an opportunist coalition, supporting an intellectually untenable agreement for diverse and selfish reasons. 'If we stick with Nice, the constitutional part of the Convention is pointless,' Giscard told reporters on the margins of the 31 May plenary session. He was not prepared to dress up failure as consensus. 'I will go to Thessaloniki in any case. I will tell them this is what we proposed but there was stalemate in the Convention.'

There was no progress on the specific Nice issues when the Praesidium reconvened on Saturday, 31 May. Yet, despite its ongoing split, the Praesidium was able to produce a revised text of part I on the institutions[9] that was issued two days later and which signalled some capacity for compromise and movement.

One of the most important changes came in article I-25, which now provided an assurance that the system of one commissioner per member state would be maintained for the life of the Commission to be appointed in 2004. By specifying that a slimmed down Commission consisting of a president and just 14 voting members 'will not take effect before November 1 2009', the revised article went some way to addressing the concerns of the applicant countries which had rallied behind Dastis and Nice.

The wording of article I-21 on the European Council chair was changed to assuage worries about an overmighty European Council president encroaching on the international activities of other top officials. The article now specified that he or she would ensure the external representation of the Union 'without prejudice' to the responsibilities of the foreign minister and Commission president.

---

[9] CONV 770/03.

Those opposing the Legislative Council because it fitted awkwardly with the needs of coalition governments, or because its members would quickly lose touch with political developments at home, were promised in article I-23 that the ministerial representative could be accompanied by 'one or two representatives at the same level with relevant expertise' to tackle sectoral issues. Articles I-19 and I-22 respectively made clear that the Parliament and Council of Ministers were responsible for the EU budget.

Without fanfare, the text dropped Giscard's idea for a congress of national parliamentarians and MEPs. This deletion of one of the president's pet projects was a very important signal to the Convention. It showed Giscard could change his position. The big question was whether he could compromise further in the make or break consultations with the Convention's component parts that would determine its outcome.

CHAPTER 16
Countdown to Consensus

The Convention entered its final phase, with its Praesidium paralysed over the ages-old question of how to share out the power of the member states in the institutions of the European Union and with just 10 days to reach consensus on the constitutional treaty ahead of the European Council meeting in Thessaloniki.

The conventionnels were asked to be in Brussels for two periods of three days each between 4–6 June and 11–13 June for a more interactive phase. There would be meetings of the political and component groups to identify and solve problems. Plenaries would be more ad hoc, with breaks into the smaller groups. The president and his two deputies would 'be involved in consultations and contacts, enabling the Praesidium to evaluate progress towards consensus as events unfold'.[1]

16.1   WEDNESDAY, 4 JUNE

The decision of Giscard and his two deputies to approach the Convention's component groups marked a new and decisive phase in the life of the Convention. After its shaky start, the triumvirate had welded itself into a strong and interdependent team. There were only two occasions when its unity appeared threatened: once when Giscard cast doubt on the feasibility of Dehaene's idea of the double-hatted foreign minister and the time when Dehaene objected so strongly to Giscard's leak of his institutional articles. When the crisis enveloped the Praesidium, the three could take over as an effective steering group. Towards the end of the Convention, they were meeting more frequently than the Praesidium – with Sir John Kerr in attendance – and always before each meeting of the Praesidium.

That said, the chances of the Convention agreeing a single text for the IGC appeared bleak when its members converged on Brussels for a three-day session starting on Wednesday, 4 June. That day, flanked by Jean-Luc Dehaene and Giuliano Amato, Giscard met in turn with the representatives of the national parliaments, the national governments, the European

---

[1] Giscard's letter of 8 May 2003 to Convention members. CONV 721/03.

Parliament and the Commission's two conventionnels with the aim of listening rather than negotiating.

Meeting with national parliamentarians

The day started well. The trio found the national parliamentarians, which constituted the biggest group in the Convention, in an unexpectedly constructive mood. The group – so often portrayed by its representatives in the Praesidium as an inchoate and incoherent body – had produced a 'non-paper' outlining a potential package deal.

René van der Linden, a Dutch Christian Democrat senator, Lamberto Dini, the Liberal Italian senator, and Jürgen Meyer, a Social Democrat member of the German Bundestag, had organised an ad hoc working group, which came out strongly in favour of safeguarding the Community method of decision making in the Union while giving the big countries a stable presidency of the European Council. Their paper envisaged an integral draft Constitution with no options, the use of the Convention method for future changes, QMV as a general rule, integration of the Charter of Fundamental Rights in the Constitution and enhanced cooperation in defence. It proposed to 'strengthen all sides of the institutional triangle'. Thus, the Commission president would be elected by the European Parliament and all member states would be represented in the Commission until 2009 (i.e. for the full life of the Commission to be chosen in 2004). After 2009, there would be representation of member states based on an equal system of rotation.

While 'acknowledging the merits' of the EU's rotating presidency, the national parliamentarians were prepared to accept a longer term chair of the European Council, on condition that he or she would be elected by two-thirds of the member states, the European Council would not be a separate institution or have its own bureaucracy or executive powers, and rotation in other Council formations would be maintained. The chairperson could be a member of another EU institution or hold a national mandate. The paper also backed the idea of a separate Legislative Council for law-making and stated that the Council's legislative powers should always be exercised in public.

The caucus had therefore produced an integrationist document that confirmed what Giscard and his staff had begun to suspect: that Praesidium members Gisela Stuart and John Bruton were not representative of the national parliamentarians as a whole. The paper also reflected the increasingly close ties of its authors with like-minded conventionnels from the European Parliament, which had been fostered through the big political families.

Dini reported that Giscard left his meeting with the national parliamentarians 'elated'. No wonder, therefore, that his session with the government representatives afterwards came as a rude shock.

Difficulties with government representatives

The mood of the government representatives was somewhere between the grumpy and the ugly. Dastis had done a good job of pulling together support for the Nice arrangements among the nine signatories of the letter and the 16 friends of the Community method.

In the circumstances, it was unfortunate that it fell to George Katiforis, the Greek government alternate, to chair the meeting with Giscard and his two deputies in the absence of George Papandreou, the Greek foreign minister and senior Greek conventionnel since earlier in the year.

The meeting got off to a bad start when Giscard requested a restricted session with the senior representatives. He was told that he came as a guest and that alternates and assistants would stay in the interests of transparency. Katiforis then failed to encourage a more constructive tone. He first allowed participants to sit behind cards bearing the names of their countries rather than own names, breaking the habits of the Convention and reinforcing their identity as government representatives rather than individual conventionnels. He then polled the participants for their views on key issues, breaking with the Convention's taboo against voting and emphasising the disagreements with the proposals on the table. Finally, he organised a *tour de table* of the more than 20 countries present that was still in progress when a visibly irritated Giscard left the meeting after one and three-quarter hours to join the MEPs, leaving Amato and Dehaene in the lions' den.

The divergences between Giscard and the governments were substantial. In a letter to 'Mr President' faxed later that day on his own initiative, Katiforis reported to Giscard that:

- 18 government representatives backed the six-months rotating president of the European Council against five supporting a full-time elected chair
- 18 were against reopening the Nice agreements on the weighting of votes in the Council of Ministers, the number of European Parliament seats and the structure of the Commission. If the Commission had to be downsized, equal rotation among member states should apply
- only two voices were in favour of a Legislative Council

- there was 'virtual unanimity for qualified majority voting' except for two wanting the veto on taxation and one for the veto on the 'the strategy of foreign policy' and on social security.

Some members of the group were later to quibble over details of Katiforis's head count. But the negative implications of the meeting for eventually reaching consensus with Giscard were clear and highlighted in a press conference of the 16 'friends of the Community method' that evening. The most serious threat to hopes for a successful conclusion of the Convention came from Hannes Farnleitner, the Austrian representative, who again called for options instead of a single text in the final draft. He claimed that several colleagues had argued for 'good options' rather than 'a bad compromise'.

Ireland's Dick Roche asserted, with some justification, that neither the Nice nor the Laeken European Council mandates authorised the Convention to deal with institutional issues. For Finland, Teija Tiilikainen expressed doubts over whether a long-term European Council chair could be constrained from becoming a rival to the Commission president. Pointing to the Union's economic power, Farnleitner maintained that one commissioner per member state was not excessive. Roche and Henrik Hololei, the Estonian representative, likened re-opening Nice 'to opening Pandora's box'. Tellingly, however, Hololei added: 'None of us think that Nice is good. It is just that no one has come up with anything better.' He went on: 'The double majority is more transparent. But we can't have Nice *a la carte*. It is illogical to scrap something which was created with so much sweat and tears.'

Although Latvia's Sandra Kalniete began the press meeting claiming the 'group of 16 is more united than ever', Hololei's remarks pointed to a fundamental weakness in their position. The group of 16 was a negative coalition, united only in its opposition to Giscard's institutional proposals. It was never able to come together to produce a comprehensive set of draft articles in their place.

Common ground with MEPs

While the 16 were fulminating in the European Parliament's ground floor pressroom, Giscard was sitting several stories higher and enjoying a much cosier chat with the Convention's MEPs. He found that most European Parliament Convention members were interested in a deal not confrontation. Publication of draft part III of the Constitution at the end of May showed that the European Parliament stood to gain a great deal by the extension of 'codecision', its right to legislate as an equal partner with the member states in the Council of Ministers.

The MEPs, like the integrationist caucus of national parliamentarians, wanted a single text with no options. True, they proposed further extensions of QMV to include tax and foreign policy and, echoing ideas put forward by Dini, proposed super-qualified majority voting instead of unanimity elsewhere. But they also signalled a willingness to compromise. Like the national parliamentarians, they suggested that the Commission retain one member per member state until 2009 but with the eventual constitutional treaty laying down the rules for the period afterwards. In return for having the European Parliament elect the Commission president, most MEPs could live with a long-term president of the European Council provided his or her powers were constrained and limited to providing strategic impulses and coordination. 'This component is not dissatisfied,' declared Klaus Hänsch, the German Social Democrat MEP and Praesidium member, after the meeting.

Giscard and his aides had started the day expecting a relatively easy meeting with the MEPs, some difficulty with the government representatives and chaos among the national parliamentarians. The meeting with the government representatives was far worse than anticipated. But by the time they were heading for their final meeting with the two commissioners in the Convention, they realised that the majority positions and willingness to find solutions of the national parliamentarians and MEPs could provide an alternative route to achieving consensus in the Convention as a whole. As he left the MEPs' room, Giscard was asked about his earlier meeting with the government representatives. That component, he sniffed, 'is a minority in the Convention'.

Despite widespread despondency in the corridors of the Parliament building, the day spent by Giscard and his deputies among the Convention's component parts had been unexpectedly positive. It pointed to ways he might circumvent the hostile position on the institutional architecture of the government representatives. Until that Wednesday, it had been assumed the Convention's final days would see the governments gaining the upper hand and the MEPs marginalised as negotiations increasingly foreshadowed the power balance in the IGC to follow. Instead, the MEPs and their integrationist allies among the national parliamentarians – linked through the political families – continued to strengthen Giscard's hand to the final day of the Convention. The Convention had passed a decisive turning point.

16.2   THURSDAY, 5 JUNE

After Wednesday's hectic activity, Thursday, 5 June looked set to be relatively quiet. The Praesidium reconvened during the morning. A plenary session was scheduled for the afternoon but, reflecting the Convention secretariat's determination to keep the initiative in the last weeks of negotiation, was not intended to deal with institutions. Giscard still had to deal with the split in the Praesidium but this was put to one side during the morning. Instead, the Praesidium tackled some of the less controversial issues that had been raised the previous day.

Concessions in the Praesidium; warnings from the Plenary

Responding to the mood of the Convention, the Praesidium decided to drop some of the more intergovernmental features of its previous institutional proposals. It abandoned the 'board' or 'bureau' to support the longer-term president of the European Council. It also agreed the European Council president could hold office in another EU institution, while keeping the restriction that he or she could not hold a national mandate. It therefore took on board the hostility of most national parliamentarians, MEPs and the Commission towards having a new bureaucracy attached to the European Council presidency post, while keeping open the (admittedly distant) possibility of this being double-hatted with the Commission presidency.

The subsequent plenary was supposed not to deal with institutional issues. And indeed its discussions ranged over other disputed issues, such as whether or not to include references to Christianity or God in the final text and the reinstatement of competitiveness among the Union's objectives. But the Convention's mind was elsewhere. There was no way of preventing the previous day's events spilling into the plenary. Recognising this, Giscard adroitly exploited his position as chairman to put the government representatives at a disadvantage.

He did this by giving the floor first to Olivier Duhamel, the French socialist MEP. Duhamel had the air of a '68er', that generation of student protesters who shook France in 'the events of May' 1968. He was one of the few conventionnels with an ability to deliver highly emotional, tub-thumping rhetoric. Although very different, the two men had ties that went back a long way and were often to be seen chatting in the margins of the Convention. Duhamel did not disappoint. 'We are deadlocked', he declared. 'Certain people are trying to stop us. Don't let them sabotage our work!' To retain the Nice institutional arrangements was, he said, 'totally absurd'. To propose them as an option was 'equivalent to suicide'. The Convention was not an IGC: it existed for the general European good. It was not set up to 'arbitrate petty quarrels among member states over the number of their commissioners, their MEPs or their votes in the Council'. Such petty details were the preoccupation of IGCs and explained their failure.

Echoing Giscard's point, Duhamel underlined that the government representatives were a minority of 28 out of 105 full Convention members. They might have the final word in an IGC, but the Convention should not allow them to make a mockery of its work. It was the Convention's duty to press on with its task of reforming the Union and the Convention members should make absolutely sure that governments took the blame if they wrecked its work now, or later. Duhamel's carefully structured outburst was loudly applauded and echoed by others, including commissioner Michel Barnier, EPP caucus leader Brok and Ben Fayot of the Luxembourg parliament. Supporters of the Nice settlements, such as Ireland's Roche and Austria's Farnleitner, were put on the defensive.

Earlier that day, the UK's Peter Hain, who was absent from the plenary because of a cabinet meeting in London on the UK's government's impending decision to stay out of the euro, opined that a deal was 'in reach', which would secure a full-time chair of the European Council, an elected president of the Commission and a foreign minister for the Union. According to Hain, it was 'make up your mind time' for the other governments that continued to oppose these policies in the Convention.

Isolating Dastis in the Praesidium

Further progress now hinged on the Praesidium overcoming its differences. It met on Thursday evening after the plenary finished at 20.30. De Villepin contributed to the eventual success of the meeting by taking Giscard out to dinner. That left Dehaene in charge at the beginning of the meeting. In what one participant later described as 'Jean-Luc's finest hour', Dehaene set out to broker deals that would end the deadlock in the Praesidium over the institutions.

The negotiations started slowly. Dastis presented a text that would have put off all discussion about the Nice related issues until 2009 when it would be up to the European Council to start negotiations on the weighting of votes in the Council of Ministers, the structure of the Commission and the number of seats in the European Parliament. This proposal would, in effect, have delayed a solution long beyond 2009. After this discussion went nowhere, it was decided instead to look at the institutions in turn, starting with generally uncontroversial issues such as the European Court. Giscard arrived from dinner in time to deal with the Commission. While making clear his doubts about the idea, he conceded that places in a slimmed down Commission should be given on the basis of equal rotation, as specified in the Nice Treaty.

This concession won over Bruton and satisfied Papandreou. Among Praesidium members, Bruton had always been the most critical of the drafts on the Commission. Papandreou, anxious to secure a successful Thessaloniki summit later in the month, realised that equal rotation of commissioners would be a key element in winning over a significant number of government representatives in the Convention.

Christophersen's resolve began to weaken when the meeting turned to the number of seats in the European Parliament. When Giscard suggested keeping the Nice total of 732 after 2009, Christophersen realised that he would be able to report a success to his own and similarly concerned governments.

At this point, the alliance between Dastis and Christophersen began to weaken. Nor could Dastis count on Alojz Peterle, the Slovenian parliamentarian and sole representative of the accession countries in the Praesidium. Peterle, a former Slovenian prime minister was already set to top the EPP list of Slovene candidates for the 2004 European Parliament elections and so had an interest every bit as strong as existing MEPs in steering the Convention to success.

Dastis was therefore alone when the discussion turned to QMV and the proposal for replacing the complex allocation of votes per member state, detailed in Nice, through a double majority of half the member states and at least 60% of the population.

That discussion, as Giscard said later, was 'long, until late at night'. It was agreed that the Nice formula should apply until 1 November 2009. There was also some discussion about an enabling clause by which the move to double majority would only be triggered by a unanimous vote in the Council. But this was dropped in favour of a provision by which the double majority system could be delayed for three years, provided two-thirds of member states supported the idea. Despite these concessions, Dastis was heard to declare he would pursue a policy of non-cooperation for the rest of the Convention if the Praesidium held to the double majority on QMV and threatened there would be no further extension of QMV to other areas of policy. The meeting finished some 90 minutes after midnight.

Giscard's victory in the Praesidium left some issues still unresolved. But it marked an important breakthrough after an exhausting 48 hours of complex and emotionally charged negotiations at many different levels in and around the Convention. The Convention by this time had mutated into a mass of interlocking networks. The meetings on Wednesday between Giscard, Dehaene and Amato with its component parts were followed by a welter of meetings and contacts inside the components, among the political families and in the many informal dining and contact groups that had sprung up in the Convention over the previous 15 months, turning the corridors and bar near the plenary hall into hotbeds of gossip and speculation.

16.3   FRIDAY, 6 JUNE

The component parts reconvened separately on the Friday morning to debate the outcome of the Praesidium while waiting for briefings from Giscard and his aides. At 11.00, the three fanned out to separate meeting rooms in the European Parliament. Giscard returned to the group of national parliamentarians in recognition of the crucial change that Wednesday's meeting had brought to his and the Convention's fortunes. Dehaene went to brief the MEPs. It was left to Amato to tackle the most difficult group: the government representatives. To the pleasure of several, he appeared more solicitous of their views than Giscard had two days before.

Giscard outlines the deal

Giscard entered the national parliamentarians' room to applause and proceeded to give an oral report, taking them through the Praesidium's decisions. These were more extensive than the compromises needed to isolate Dastis.

- For the Council of Ministers, the Praesidium proposed a General Affairs and Legislative Council to overcome the strong hostility of member states to the idea of a special Legislative Council. Giscard explained that this was not quite equivalent to the German Bundesrat, or second chamber representing the states, because it would have an additional function: in liaison with the Commission, the General Affairs Council would also prepare the European Council meetings. As already planned, there would be a Foreign Affairs Council chaired by the Union's foreign minister. No other Council formations were specified although Giscard said Councils such as Ecofin would be detailed in part III. Whereas the early June draft empowered the General Affairs Council to authorise other formations, this task would now fall to the European Council. The presidency of other Councils would be held by member state representatives on a basis of rotation for at least a year. The European Council would lay down the rules for this annual rotation, which Giscard indicated, could lead to team presidencies.

- As envisaged since the end of April, the European Council would be a separate institution, would meet every three months and have its own president elected by QMV among its members for two and a half years, renewable once. But, confirming the previous morning's Praesidium decisions, there would be no board. The president, however, could hold an EU office. Giscard said national mandates were not to be permitted, because this would be incompatible with the common European interest. National foreign ministers would no longer have an automatic right to attend European Council meetings.

- Qualified majority voting would be the general rule for decisions in the Council of Ministers, except where specified in the constitutional treaty. In line with the previous night's decision, QMV would be a majority of member states representing at least 60% of the Union population and take effect on 1 November 2009. In his oral account, Giscard also said the Praesidium was proposing a 'super-QMV' of two-thirds of member states and four-fifths of the population for issues such as CFSP decisions where the European Council or Council of Ministers did not act on a proposal of the Commission or foreign minister. It appeared at first as if the Praesidium was taking up a Lamberto Dini suggestion for an alternative to unanimity. But this proved not to be the case.

- Giscard also outlined for the first time the controversial idea of a *passerelle* or bridging clause by which the European Council, acting unanimously, could decide thereafter to apply QMV to areas still governed by unanimity in part III of the constitutional treaty. Although unanimity would be a huge hurdle in a Union of 25, the *passerelle* offered greater scope for change in the future than unanimity plus ratification in line with the national Constitutions of the member states.

- The new provisions strengthened the Commission and the Commission president by way of far more detailed job descriptions. They made clear, for example, that the Commission would oversee the application of Union law, ensure the Union's external representation 'for areas falling within its responsibility' and initiate the Union's 'annual and pluriannual programming'. The latter provision gave the Commission some leverage over the Union's long-term strategy and was an important concession to opponents of a strong longer-term European Council president. Before selecting a Commission president, the European Council would have to hold 'appropriate consultations' as well as take the results of the previous European Parliament elections into account. Giscard also confirmed that equal rotation among member states for filling places in the college of 15 (including the president and foreign minister) would take over from the Nice formula of one commissioner per member state from 1 November 2009.

- The article providing for an EU foreign minister was left unchanged from the early June draft, in spite of complaints, notably from the UK, that the title 'minister' was inappropriate because the Union is not a state.

- The European Parliament would, Giscard confirmed, keep the Nice total of 732 seats beyond 1 November 2009 when it would introduce the principle of degressive proportionality for the allocation of seats, with a minimum threshold of four per member state. The distribution of seats set at Nice would apply in the 2004 elections, while details of the new regime would be agreed unanimously by the European Council, on a proposal of the Parliament, before 2009.

The national parliamentarians responded positively with only one or two exceptions, such as the British Labour peer Lord Tomlinson who sought in vain to persuade Giscard that the integrationist bandwagon was not representative of the group as a whole. The MEPs also welcomed the proposals, while Amato reported a much better atmosphere in the governments' meeting than on Wednesday. Joschka Fischer said it was a 'day of hope', before characteristically warning that the 'devil was in the detail'. For the EPP's Elmar Brok, the changes to the proposed European Council president were important. There would be no board or bureau, no formal procedure for steering work in other Councils and the possibility of a double-hatted presidency with the head of the Commission.

When Giscard appeared before the press, he forecast the Praesidium would be able to produce a single proposal without options for the EU leaders in Thessaloniki. He made light of the Spanish problem, quoting in jest a 'famous French thinker'[2] who once said 'what is truth on one side of the Pyrenees is error on the other'. On a more serious note, he pointed out that Spanish parliamentarians were not notably hostile to the Praesidium's proposals. Indeed, the new proposals were 'supported by a significant number of representatives in the Convention' and would therefore 'form the basis of a final consensus'.

---

[2] Blaise Pascal 1623-1662.

The Praesidium's package ended the efforts of the six original member states to produce their own proposals. Jean-Claude Juncker, the Luxembourg prime minister, was trying to arrange a meeting of the six leaders early in June and several meetings were held at senior official level. But Germany and France called the venture off after the breakthrough.

Some rumblings of discontent remained, however. Reflecting discussions in the preceding day's plenary session, Brok was one of many MEPs to want QMV to apply to foreign policy. The absence of a specific reference to Christianity continued to exercise many conventionnels from the Christian Democrat centre-right. Federalist MEPs were especially critical that the *passerelle* should be unlocked only by unanimity in the European Council. The Thursday plenary also witnessed growing pressure, notably among MEPs, for the eventual Constitution or constitutional treaty no longer to be ratified by unanimity. Elena Paciotti, an Italian Socialist MEP pointed out that the final text should not be ratified by unanimity 'if we want a Constitution worthy of its name'. Unanimity would mean the end result was a constitutional treaty rather than a Constitution. 'If there is no change in procedure we will have a treaty which cannot be called a Constitution. We cannot lie to the citizens,' she said.

There were also new problems in the Praesidium on Friday afternoon. Giscard had promised that texts of the revised articles would be provided later that day. They were not. The problem was the *passerelle*. Although outlined in some detail by Giscard earlier in the day, there had been no previous discussion of a text in the Praesidium. In a move, apparently to 'bounce' the less integrationist members of the Praesidium into agreement, Sir John Kerr produced the first draft texts on the *passerelle* for approval in the closing minutes of the afternoon Praesidium meeting. In reaction, Gisela Stuart and John Bruton angrily walked out to catch evening planes home.

16.4   COUNTDOWN TO CONSENSUS: WEEK TWO

The hazards of late night negotiation and oral reporting became apparent the following week as conventionnels re-converged on Brussels for the final days before the 13 June deadline. Conflicting accounts of the detail of the Praesidium proposals and the absence of a text until the afternoon of Wednesday, 11 June, fuelled suspicions that Giscard and the secretariat might be seeking to renege on deals done. Equally, the lack of clarity sustained hopes in all segments of the Convention that more might be extracted from the last rounds of negotiations.

It was in the latter spirit that the leaders of the big three party caucuses – the EPP's Brok, the Liberals' Duff and the Socialists' Amato – met on the evening of Tuesday, 10 June to put their names to two amendments. This first such concerted action by the leaders of the three political families aimed at enabling the Constitution to enter into force if not all 25 member states were able to ratify it and provided for a 'lighter' revision procedure where no shift in competences was planned.

Brok, meanwhile, alerted his party colleagues to 'serious problems' arising from apparent anomalies between the previous week's oral accounts of the Praesidium's agreement and the text due on Wednesday. Duff too was concerned that the Praesidium, when it produced its revised articles in written form, would seek to recover powers for the European Council president at the expense of the Commission.

16.5   WEDNESDAY, 11 JUNE

The Convention's component parts met during Wednesday morning. There were again calls from integrationists in the national parliaments and the European Parliament for more QMV and a stronger Commission vis-à-vis the proposed European Council president to maintain the Union's institutional balance. While several government representatives were reported as willing to accept the Praesidium's proposals, the UK's Peter Hain said they were 90% acceptable, and the rest would have to be negotiated in the IGC. The UK, he warned, would speak out against the *passerelle* clause, which was opposed by 'six or seven' countries in the government representatives' meeting.

Revised articles unveiled

When, on the afternoon of Wednesday, 11 June, Giscard unveiled revised articles for the whole of part I and the preamble,[3] Duff and Brok called for an early adjournment so the Convention's members could discuss the texts in their component groups.

The Praesidium's revisions went beyond the institutional articles in title IV. Thus, the preamble was modified to excise its cursory and eccentric account of Europe's history as a near seamless progression from the glories of ancient Greece and Rome to the wonders of the Enlightenment. But while it retained the reference to Europe's 'cultural, religious and humanist

---

[3] CONV 797/03.

inheritance', it made no concessions to the powerful Vatican-backed lobby that sought a specific reference to Christianity or Christian values. Nor did the federalist goal of 'ever closer union' make a come-back in the preamble, preference being given instead to the concept of a Europe determined and 'united ever more closely, to forge a common destiny'. One oddity in the preamble was the inclusion of the phrase describing Europe as 'united in its diversity' in inverted commas. This device, Giscard was later to admit, was a way of floating a possible slogan for the new, enlarged EU.

Another inclusion was the idea in article I-3 on the Union's objectives that Europe's social market economy should be 'highly competitive'. The objective of economic competitiveness had yo-yoed in and out of successive drafts. Its restoration, after deletion from the late May draft, reflected interventions by several conventionnels in the previous week's plenary, as well as protests from Unice, the European employers' body.

In title VII on the Union's finances, article I-54 was amended to make clear that the Council of Ministers would act unanimously when adopting the first multi-annual financial framework following the Constitution's entry into force. This was construed by some as giving Spain an arm-lock over regional fund negotiations well into the future.

Inevitably, the main interest focused on the precise institutional texts. Here there were some surprises. The concept of Super-QMV, requiring support reflecting four-fifths of the Union's population, had disappeared. Instead, draft article I-24 restated existing treaty provisions for Council decision making in cases where there was no Commission proposal. The majorities here would be two-thirds of states and three-fifths of population. In an attempt to draw a distinction between the two types of commissioners, those with votes and in the college were to be called 'European commissioners' and the others, without votes, simply 'commissioners'.

A flurry of interventions before the adjournment showed there were still several issues to clear up. Duff, putting the integrationist argument, raised the issue of easier treaty revision and called for more QMV. Ireland's Dick Roche and the Netherlands' Gijs de Vries argued that the passage on equality of member states was not clear enough in the texts on the Council of Ministers and also called for further clarifications to preserve the Commission's competences. The UK's Peter Hain, Sweden's Lena Hjelm-Wallen and the Danish eurosceptic MEP Jens-Peter Bonde opposed the *passerelle* with Bonde complaining that this 'revolutionary clause' had never been debated in the Convention. Erwin Teufel, the Christian Democrat prime minister of Baden-Württemberg, rejected the *passerelle* on behalf of the German *Länder*. He also called for Christianity to be reflected in the preamble. Testifying to what had developed into a close working relationship between the two men, Teufel's plea on Christianity was backed by Joschka Fischer, Germany's Green foreign minister.

To Giscard's approval, Alain Lamassoure, the French centre-right MEP, tabled a proposal that was first promoted by Jürgen Meyer, the German Social Democrat parliamentarian, for a citizens' right of petition to the Commission to be included in title VI on the democratic life of the union. The idea was that a petition signed by one million citizens from at least eight member states could induce the Commission to take a legislative initiative.

Earlier the French government's normally clipped and cautious alternate, Pascal Andréani, surprised many when she told of her 'regret and astonishment' at the draft's failure to ensure that trade policy relating to cultural services, education and health were an area of shared competence and so subject to unanimity. She warned that without suitable clarification, 'this Constitution will stand no chance of being ratified in France'. But such discordant notes were few. One other came when Hain reminded the Convention that whatever they decided was not an end in itself. Hain's observation that 'we have a very good basis for negotiation in the Intergovernmental Conference' provoked hisses and murmurs of dissent.

The hisses that greeted Hain were a sign that the integrationist parliamentarians in the Convention felt the wind still running in their favour. By dint of careful planning, they were about to play a dominating role in the Convention's final 48 hours.

National parliamentarians and MEPs make common cause

Those national parliamentarians who had not jumped aboard the integrationist bandwagon organised by van der Linden, Dini and Meyer were the first to find out how well-organised their colleagues had become. Shortly after the national parliamentarians group had reconvened, an irritated Lord Tomlinson rose to warn of the dangers to parliamentary rights of such innovations as the *passerelle*. He was cut short by the chair, Marietta Giannakou of the Greek parliament, who told him that the group was about to decamp to another room for a joint session with the Convention's MEPs. In vain did Tomlinson protest 'we have agreed to meet but not what we are going to say'. As the meeting degenerated into ill-tempered squabbling, the redoubtable Ms Giannakou – herself a former MEP – led her troops over the bridge[4] linking the third floors of the European Parliament's two main buildings in Brussels to a prearranged appointment with the MEPs.

When the plenary reconvened that evening, Inigo Méndez de Vigo, one of the two MEPs in the Praesidium, spoke up for both the MEPs and the national parliamentarians in the Convention. They wanted the Convention to extend QMV and codecision, maintain the institutional balance and examine both the possibility of a less onerous revision in future of the Constitution and the right of citizens to petition the Commission. A visibly pleased Giscard could not resist a touch of irony. Referring to his own idea for a special Congress of national parliamentarians and MEPs, which he had abandoned because of lack of support from the Convention, Giscard complimented Méndez de Vigo for having set up 'a kind of Congress of your own' before handing the floor to Ms Giannakou.

Picking up from where Méndez de Vigo left off, she then proposed strengthening the Commission and role of the European Parliament in appointing the Commission president by authorising the nominated Commission president to reject certain commissioners proposed by member states, and by allowing the Parliament, after two rejections of a candidate nominated by the European Council, to nominate its own candidate for Commission president.

For Johannes Voggenhuber, the Austrian Green MEP, the afternoon's meeting of the two groups of parliamentarians was 'one of the happiest moments of recent months because it created a chance that the Convention would not simply become an IGC'.

Voggenhuber's hopes appeared fulfilled when George Katiforis reported on the government representatives' meeting. Where the parliamentarians had presented a united front, Katiforis reported a mix of views. 'Points of doubt and disagreement remain', he acknowledged. His group was 'virtually unanimous' in asking for 'strictly equal rotation in the presidencies' of the Council formations. 'Some, but not all' wanted deletion of the *passerelle* clause. 'Some' wanted a threshold of five, not four members, for national representation in the European Parliament. 'Some raise the question of qualified majority, preferring to stick with Nice.'

The integrationist bandwagon rolled further as Brok, Barnier, Duff and Duhamel called to extend the scope of QMV. In response, Giscard was obliged to warn that the Convention, with perhaps 12 hours of real work

---

[4] Appropriately called a *Passerelle.*

ahead of it, should not go back over old ground but should focus on three or four key issues to achieve consensus. The most important was the issue of qualified majority voting and whether it should be determined by the double majority system proposed by the Praesidium, or the Nice formula. In addition, Giscard singled out the issue of economic governance in the euro-zone and the *passerelle* from unanimity to QMV. It was up to the component groups to iron out their differences on these issues.

He received unexpected backing from Peter Hain who declared: 'We all have some things we are not happy with.' Hain warned that re-opening basic compromises on the election of the Commission president and the election of the chairman of the European Council could 'blow the whole thing up and we will have wasted the whole of our 15 or 16 months spent getting this together'. It was agreed that the Convention's component parts should again meet the following morning, preceded by meetings of the political families. Giscard, Dehaene and Amato would attend the meetings of the '*composantes*', splitting up as before, after which the component groups would submit a last batch of amendments.

These would be considered by the Praesidium on Thursday afternoon and the results presented to the Convention as a whole in a plenary meeting that evening. The Praesidium imposed one important condition on the amendments: that they should be unanimous submissions of the respective component groups. The change of rules was to benefit the better organised caucus of integrationist MEPs and national parliamentarians who by now had effectively muffled the more nationally inclined members of the national parliamentarians' group. The dominance of the integrationists in the national parliamentarians group was complete the following day, when they disowned Gisela Stuart and John Bruton, their two representatives in the Praesidium.

16.6   THURSDAY, 12 JUNE

Thursday's meetings of the Convention's component parts replicated Wednesday's pattern. The national parliamentarians and MEPs were willing to compromise and able to forge joint positions, which became the basis of amendments submitted to the Praesidium. Meeting as usual behind closed doors, the government representatives were split, grumpy and resentful.

Divisions among government representatives

The government representatives were also faced with a rather different Giuliano Amato than in previous sessions. Several complained afterwards that Amato was reluctant to take on board amendments, even when they reflected the views of 18 governments, on the grounds that they were not unanimous. Accounts of the meeting indicated little inclination to change. The UK's Peter Hain strongly attacked the idea of the *passerelle*. Germany's Joschka Fischer, attending his first ever meeting of the group, repeated his plea for super qualified majority voting on foreign policy issues.

Highlighting the underlying divisions between incoming and existing, and big and small member states, the representatives of 16 small and medium-sized countries (including all ten accession countries) put their names to a joint statement. But rather than convey unity, the four-point statement, from the representatives of Austria, Cyprus, the Czech Republic, Estonia, Finland, Hungary, Ireland, Latvia, Lithuania, Luxembourg, Malta, Poland, Portugal, Slovakia, Slovenia and Sweden, made clear there were additional divisions among the members of this group.

MEPs and national parliamentarians agree common amendments

Because of the divisions among the government representatives, the national parliamentarians found Giscard in an unexpectedly downbeat mood. Although the Convention had made advances that an IGC would never have achieved, the result was not sufficiently ambitious, he complained. The overall result was disappointing.

He did not understand why there had been such resistance to a stable president of the European Council, when this person would have no more power than Greece's Costas Simitis or Denmark's Anders Fogh Rasmussen, the two incumbents in the present and previous rotating presidencies. The insistence of the smaller and accession countries for perfect and equal rotation in the Commission was a mistake and would lead to conflict, he warned. It was inconceivable that the Commission should have a college without the participation of big member states for an extended period of time. Giscard had also been disappointed at the reluctance of so many *conventionnels* to reopen the Nice compromises on QMV, the Commission and the Parliament. Taking the example of the Parliament, he said an assembly of 732 members was much too big to be effective.

In his meeting with the MEPs, Dehaene heard again the now familiar calls for more QMV, especially in foreign policy; unlocking the launch of the *passerelle* from the requirement of unanimous agreement among member states; an 'easier' procedure for ratifying and modifying the eventual Constitution and the incorporation of a right of petition to the Commission by citizens. It was fortunate that the MEPs had Dehaene, a true federalist who nonetheless had a keen sense of the possible, in their midst. Dehaene underlined the great progress made on spreading QMV and codecision, and the potential for future progress inherent in the existing proposals for more QMV in combination with the *passerelle*. To press for an easier revision clause at this stage would 'open a can of worms', he warned.

The two sets of parliamentarians agreed on a joint position, covering seven points. Picking up the joint amendments for a revision clause agreed by Amato, Duff and Brok at the beginning of the week, they called for a 'more flexible procedure' to change the Constitution in cases where there would be neither a shift of competences nor a change in the Charter of Fundamental Rights. Approval in these cases, which would be in part III, by five-sixths of member states 'would deliver the Union genuine constitutional status'.

They were prepared to accept a permanent president of the European Council, provided the president-elect of the Commission could reject candidates for the Commission proposed by the member states; the (junior) commissioners be subject to the same selection procedure as 'European commissioners' and the functions of the European Council president would not prejudice those of other Union institutions. QMV should be the general rule, also for common foreign and security policy. *Passerelle* decisions should be taken in the European Council by super QMV. They also proposed that QMV should apply in CFSP to joint proposals from the foreign minister and the Commission and that the Convention should be able to decide individual cases of moving from unanimity to QMV in part III after the Thessaloniki European Council.

In addition, the General Affairs and Legislative Council should decide on further Council formations. The scope of the European Court of Justice should be extended to the whole Constitution. European citizens should have a right to petition the Commission along the lines proposed by the Bundestag's Jürgen Meyer and the European Parliament's Alain Lamassoure. And no European laws should be agreed without approval of the European Parliament.

The joint position was turned into seven specific amendments that were approved by a 'large majority' of the two groups and submitted to Giscard. At the last minute, the joint sponsors, Inigo Méndez de Vigo and Marietta Giannakou, decided not to submit an amendment for a revision clause and instead called for this issue to be considered in the July sessions after the Thessaloniki summit. Giscard later indicated that he would allow this. The groups of parliamentarians then despatched their representatives to that afternoon's Praesidium session. In the case of the national parliamentarians, this was an opportunity for long-repressed frustrations to rise to the surface. Stuart and Bruton, according to eyewitnesses, were openly attacked by name for having failed to represent the views of the group accurately in the Praesidium. To applause from the majority of the group, Lamberto Dini told the two that they were expected either to defend the amendments or stay quiet, but above all not to be disloyal.

The Praesidium's final offer

Uncertainty persisted until the final night. Just before the penultimate plenary session on the evening of Thursday, 12 June, Hannes Farnleitner, the Austrian government delegate warned of failure.[5] Waving the paper with the demands of the 16 governments on the Union's institutions, Farnleitner threatened that the festive lunch promised by Giscard for the next day would 'become a last supper' unless the president compromised.

The excitement among the conventionnels was palpable when Giscard presented the Praesidium's final batch of amended articles[6] to the plenary at 19.45 on Thursday, some 100 minutes later than promised. There were detailed but significant changes to the articles on the European Council, its chair, the Council formations, the Commission and QMV, which met demands from the Convention's various component groups.

Responding to demands of integrationist parliamentarians and smaller member states, article I-20 now specified that the European Council 'shall not exercise any legislative function'. In article I-21, the role of the European Council chair was further constrained by a stipulation that the job of ensuring preparation and continuity in the European Council's work would be 'in cooperation with the president of the Commission, and on the basis of the work of the General Affairs Council'. Reacting to one of the key demands of the group of 16 small and medium-sized countries, article I-23 now stated that the presidencies of the Council formations, other than foreign affairs, would be held by member state representatives on the basis of 'equal' rotation for periods of at least a year.

Many conventionnels worried that the institutional balance of the Union would be upset unless the dates for new measures taking effect were brought into line. Thus, Article I-24 on QMV retained the double majority

---

[5] Farnleitner also took steps in preparation for failure. He scheduled a press conference of the smalls for 11.00 on Friday, 13 June to coincide with the start of the session of the Convention that established consensus on the constitutional treaty. The event was publicised among the meetings displayed on the European Parliament's monitor screens during Friday morning. Farnleitner had second thoughts, however, and took part in the week's closing plenary session.

[6] CONV 811/03.

arrangements favoured by all Praesidium members except Spain's Dastis, but provided greater precision in stating that these would 'take effect on November 1 2009, after the European Parliament elections have taken place.' Similarly, article I-25 on the Commission made clear that the arrangements replacing the Nice system of one commissioner per member state 'will take effect on November 1 2009'. Article I-19 on the European Parliament specified that the new distribution of seats that would replace that agreed in Nice for the 2009 elections would apply 'for further elections'. Later Giscard claimed that the decision to delay application of these changes until 2009 played a key part in securing the support of the accession countries for the Convention's final draft text.

The article on QMV no longer contained the possibility of member states agreeing by a two-thirds majority to extend the Nice arrangements on QMV for an extra three years from 2009. In addition, the hopes of the two groups of parliamentarians that the *passerelle* would be unlocked by super QMV, rather than unanimity, were frustrated.

In article I-25, the duties of the Commission *vis-à-vis* the European Council and foreign minister were made even clearer with inclusion of a sentence saying: 'With the exception of the common foreign and security policy, and other cases provided for in the Constitution, it shall ensure the Union's external representation.' In the same article, any doubts about the composition of the college of commissioners were eliminated by declaring that it would consist of 'its president, the minister for Foreign Affairs/vice-president and thirteen European commissioners'.

Article I-26 rectified an earlier omission by making clear that those nominated 'as non-voting commissioners' would be submitted for approval by the European Parliament in a body with the president and other members of the college, including the foreign minister. No change was made to the foreign minister's role. But a footnote was added to article I-27 promising the establishment of a 'Joint European External Action Service, to assist the minister'. Germany's Joschka Fischer – who at the time was widely seen as a candidate for the foreign minister's post – had pushed the idea of an EU diplomatic corps.

Jürgen Meyer was rewarded for his persistence with a new paragraph four in article I-46 creating the legal base for citizens' initiatives in the Union. 'A significant number of citizens, not less than a million, coming from a significant number of member states' would be able to 'invite the Commission' to submit a proposal for a law to implement the Constitution. The Praesidium continued to set its face against pressure for a specific reference to Christianity in the Constitution, opting only for a minor revision of the preamble to make clear that the 'values' of the cultural, religious and humanist inheritance of Europe 'are always present' in its heritage.

To rectify grievances voiced by conventionnels from Romania and Bulgaria, the Praesidium produced a draft declaration to deal with the impact on the distribution of parliamentary seats and votes in the Council of Ministers of the two countries possibly joining the Union during the period of the Nice arrangements before 2009. For technical reasons, this necessitated a last minute change to article I-19: this now set the permitted maximum of seats in the European Parliament at 736 against 732 previously.

To the deep irritation of many MEPs and national parliamentarians, the Praesidium also acted to meet a specific UK request for additional assurances that the Charter of Fundamental Rights would not impact on UK labour and social security laws. Peter Hain had called for a cross-reference to the so-called explanations to the Charter, which were drawn up in 2000, to ensure that the Charter could not lead to any extension of the application of Union law at the expense of those of the member states. Hain got his wish with a sentence added to the preamble of the Charter. Harking back to the work of the EU's only previous convention, it said 'the Charter will be interpreted by the courts of the Union and the member states with due regard for the explanations prepared at the instigation of the Praesidium of the Convention which drafted the Charter'.

The anger among the integrationists partly reflected the realisation that the UK had secured a rather good deal out of the Convention. By dint of repeatedly underlining the 'red lines' over which the UK would not go, Hain had prevented the spread of QMV to foreign and defence policy and all areas of taxation, except by way of a very limited *passerelle* for cases dealing with tax fraud that threatened the single market. The UK had secured its main goal of a long-term president or chair of the European Council.

16.7   PEACE BREAKS OUT

Brok and Duff, the first speakers to respond to the revised articles, were cautious and emphasised in turn the Praesidium's failure to spread QMV to foreign policy and its decision to keep the 'padlock' of unanimity on the *passerelle*. But it quickly became clear that the package of amendments, while full of disappointments for many, contained sufficient to please most conventionnels. Marietta Giannakou, chair of the national parliamentarians group, caught the mood. 'What is done is probably as much as could be done', she declared.

The prospects for consensus brightened when government representatives from very different philosophies came out in favour of the compromise. Ireland's Dick Roche, who was one of the most outspoken of the group of 16, noted with approval how Amato had taken on board the demands of the small and medium-sized countries for equal rotation in the Council formations and more precise job descriptions for the Commission and European Council presidents. Germany's Fischer emphasised how the Praesidium had tackled issues raised in the government representatives' meeting and the resulting drafts allowed the Convention members to meet 'in the middle of the bridge'. Hain appealed to the Convention to think of 'the bigger picture' arguing that the Praesidium's work would enable the Convention 'to attain an historic achievement in coming together and creating the first new single constitutional treaty for Europe'.[7] The texts were approved by the political families and the Convention's component groups the following morning. The way was clear for the Convention in its final session before the Thessaloniki summit to establish consensus: a remarkable and unexpected achievement when compared with the bleak scenario ten days before.

Friday, 13 June

In fact, Giscard chose not to use the word 'consensus' in the plenary of 13 June. He did not have to. Convention members, who only 24 hours before had appeared irreconcilable, rose to praise the outcome of nearly 16 months of hard work and Giscard's chairmanship. In the end, everybody compromised. 'All of us will find certain elements that we are not keen on and others that we very much support,' Giscard told his fellow conventionnels.

First to speak was Méndez de Vigo for the European Parliament. Standing up to praise the 'historic moment', he signalled to the hall that the time for disputing the constitutional part of the final text was over. He was followed by René van der Linden for the national parliamentarians. Two hours before, in the meeting of the EPP group, van der Linden had opened his remarks with an appeal: 'Let us not make this result a triumph for the president of this Convention because in the last two to three weeks he has set out to destroy the Convention method,' he said. In the plenary hall, these words were forgotten as van der Linden hailed the Convention as a success, offered thanks to the secretariat and congratulations to Giscard, saying how 'very happy' he and his fellow conventionnels were to have had 'such a president'.

---

[7] Hain's enthusiasm may have reflected an important diary date. He was determined not to miss his own wedding, which took place on 14 June.

Very few conventionnels expressed reservations or set down markers for the IGC that would follow. One was Ana Palacio, Spain's foreign minister. She made clear Spain had a 'basic reservation', but nonetheless hailed the text as 'a legal revolution without precedent' that 'put an end to 19th century diplomacy where we signed such things behind closed doors'. Another was Hannes Farnleitner of Austria, the second to last to speak from the floor. After giving Giscard a backhanded compliment for his 'authoritarian, purposeful and determined' leadership, Farnleitner said he could defend 95% of the outcome with his 'lifeblood'. But there was 5% – the section on the institutions – which he would not have voted for, had votes been allowed. By contrast, Poland's Danuta Hübner raised no specific objection to the double majority system for the Council.

An extraordinary coalition of conventionnels representing governments, parliaments and the Commission, from left, right and centre of the political spectrum endorsed the text and the work of the Convention. A palpable sense of satisfaction suffused the plenary hall of the European Parliament building in Brussels as Convention members outbid each other to hail their achievement with statements as contrived as they were sincere. 'Today is Friday 13,' declared Alojz Peterle, the Slovenian parliament conventionnel and Praesidium member. 'But it is not black Friday. Indeed, it is one of the brightest days that Europe has ever seen.'

For Germany's Joschka Fischer, the outcome symbolised the success of an enlarged, united Europe that could look the US in the eye. 'We have worked together here, old members and new members, big and small from all parts of Europe,' he said. 'This Convention has demonstrated that, differences notwithstanding, there is not an old and a new Europe but a Europe of citizens and states, a Europe of freedom, a Europe of justice and a Europe of democracy: our Europe!'

Even Johannes Voggenhuber, the outspoken Austrian Green who had made it his business to criticise and clash with Giscard for the past 15 months, was fulsome in his praise: 'Mr President, you have accomplished your task,' he declared. 'In the end, and against my expectations, you were not the Jupiter of this Convention but acted as its midwife. I thank you and offer you my respect.' Only Jens-Peter Bonde, the Danish MEP representing a small group of eurosceptics who had submitted a minority report for a 'Europe of democracies', rejected the outcome. But he earned a round of applause as he thanked 'everyone for all the new friendships which have been made in this Convention process.'

After all the plaudits, Giscard stepped down from the dais to address the conventionnels from the Parliament's 'lectern of honour'. 'The result is not perfect, but it is unhoped-for,' he said. The Convention had come far since receiving its mandate from the December 2001 Laeken European Council. After 15 and a half months, the assembly comprising 105 Convention members and 102 alternates from both sides of the former Iron Curtain had, Giscard judged, drawn up 'the basis of a future treaty creating a Constitution for Europe'. He would, he said, present their 'joint opus' to the Union's heads of government in Thessaloniki on 20 June with a word of warning for the 25 existing and new member states in the Intergovernmental Conference (IGC) that would follow. 'The closer you stick to our text, which has been discussed at great length, the lighter will be your task.'

Unexpectedly, the strains of the EU anthem – Beethoven's *Ode to Joy* – filled the hall. Ushers bearing trays of warm Bollinger champagne followed. The conventionnels could toast their success in producing a single constitutional text without options to put to EU leaders at their summit in Thessaloniki a week later.

16.8   VERDICTS AT THESSALONIKI

The initial response of the leaders of the enlarged EU at the European Council in Thessaloniki was to welcome the draft 'Constitution for Europe'[8] and judge it 'a good basis for starting negotiations in the Intergovernmental Conference' to be convened in October.[9]

But the celebrations were accompanied by some discordant notes, prompted largely by the Convention's institutional proposals. Poland and Spain made clear their strong opposition to the introduction of a double majority system for QMV in the Council of Ministers. Austria stuck by its assessment that the final product may be 95% acceptable but the remaining 5% of institutional proposals disadvantaged the small member states and needed to be changed. Although Britain's Tony Blair spoke warmly of Giscard, the UK government underlined that the national veto on issues of tax, social security, foreign policy and defence constituted 'red lines' which could not be crossed. Four countries signalled that they wanted a specific reference to Christianity in the Constitution. Poland's Leszek Miller was outspoken on both the Nice issue and that of Christianity in the Constitution. It was 'incomprehensible' that the voting system should be changed as 'nothing has happened since Nice' to justify this. As for the preamble, it 'should be a

---

[8] CONV 820/03.
[9] Presidency Conclusions: Thessaloniki European Council SN200/03.

reflection of the European legacy and an element of that legacy is Christianity', Miller said.

Luxembourg's prime minister, Jean-Claude Juncker, who had launched a blistering attack on the Convention's text and methods in its final days,[10] continued to be hostile, focussing his criticism on the proposed long-term European Council president. Although Juncker's tone in Thessaloniki was less strident, he, with Poland's Miller and Austria's Wolfgang Schüssel, put diplomatic evasions to one side and chose to broadcast their concerns openly at the summit.

The Thessaloniki summit gave Giscard's draft a fair wind despite these, and other less explicit, reservations. Some leaders, such as Germany's Gerhard Schröder and Denmark's Anders Fogh Rasmussen said they could accept the text more or less as it was written.

But it became clear that agreeing the constitutional treaty at the IGC would be no shoo-in. The IGC, the leaders agreed, should complete its work and agree the treaty 'as soon as possible and in time for it to become known to European citizens before the June 2004 elections for the European Parliament'. The treaty, they added, 'will be signed by the member states of the enlarged Union as soon as possible after 1 May 2004'. So that the final treaty text could be translated into all the languages of the enlarged Union, the IGC would have to conclude some weeks before 1 May, although some countries, notably Germany, were pushing in Thessaloniki for the IGC to finish by the end of 2003.

Two sessions of the Convention remained – on 4 July and 9–10 July. According to the Thessaloniki conclusions these were required to complete 'some purely technical work on drafting part III' detailing the Union's policies and their legal bases. The mandate meant parts I and II of the constitutional treaty were henceforth sacrosanct, while there could be no significant constitutional changes to part IV.

---

[10] Published in *Der Spiegel*, the German news magazine, during the weekend after 13 June.

CHAPTER 17
The Convention after Thessaloniki

17.1   TIDYING UP PART III

After the heady emotions of 13 June, it was difficult to escape a sense of
anti-climax when the 'conventionnels' returned to Brussels on 4 July for the
first of the two extra sessions approved by the EU's leaders at their summit
in Thessaloniki.

There was, however, some serious work to do. The Convention members,
who had submitted 1,687 amendments to the articles in part III, found them
piled high and bound by thick rubber bands on their desks. Numerous
though the amendments were, Giscard ruled that many cancelled each other
out and that none would be accepted which threatened the consensus of 13
June over parts I and II of the constitutional treaty. This meant the
Convention was to focus on only a score of issues. The one issue addressed
most forcefully in the plenary concerned the extension of qualified majority
voting (QMV) beyond areas already agreed. The alliance of national
parliamentarians and MEPs that played such a crucial role in securing
agreement by 13 June was again in evidence.

In a 'key points' paper, Andrew Duff, the Liberal caucus leader, and
Lamberto Dini, who now chaired the national parliamentarians by dint of
Italy having the EU's rotating presidency, revived their campaign for more
QMV in foreign and security policy, and areas of fiscal and social policy.
The text had been carefully coordinated with Elmar Brok, leader of the
European People's Party caucus, and reflected informal soundings with the
Commission and the French and Belgian governments. The final touches had
been agreed late on 3 July by a cabal including Méndez de Vigo, Brok,
Hänsch, Dini and van der Linden.

The paper demanded no retreat from the consensus achieved over parts I and
II of the Constitution, and no dilution in part III from the status established
under the existing EU treaties. Other goals included majority voting in CFSP
in cases where the initiatives of the foreign minister would be supported by
the Commission, and in the two contentious tax articles for harmonising
measures to aid administrative cooperation or the battle against tax fraud or
evasion. On an issue that stirred passions among constitutionalists and those
wanting a more 'social Europe', the key points paper urged QMV for article
III-5 [III-124] covering policies against discrimination on grounds such as

sex, race, age and religion, and in social policy for the protection of workers who had been fired. The paper also suggested a bigger role for the Court of Justice in CFSP, more flexible procedures in part IV for future revision of the Constitution and an assurance that the Parliament must give its consent if member states wanted to hold an intergovernmental conference to change the Constitution without first setting up a convention.

The Duff-Dini paper broached other contentious issues, which would play a big part in the Convention's discussions before its final session on 10 July. One of the most sensitive was the German government's insistence that access of third country nationals to the labour market should stay subject to unanimity. It was difficult not to feel a sense of *Schadenfreude* at the uncomfortable position that Germany's Joschka Fischer found himself in. He had been a passionate supporter of more QMV throughout the Convention, lecturing all and sundry on how the Union would seize up unless unanimity was swept away. But rising unemployment at home was reflected in strong support for national immigration controls across a broad cross-section of German political opinion. Retaining the veto was a key political goal of the prime ministers of the *Länder*, most of which were controlled by the centre-right opposition. They had made their position clear to Chancellor Schröder. Subsequently, Fischer, Erwin Teufel, the Christian Democrat representative of the German *Länder* in the Convention, and Jürgen Meyer, the Social Democrat Bundestag conventionnel, had written to the Praesidium pressing for unanimity.

Fischer began his remarks on 4 July with a strong appeal to the Convention for more QMV in tax and foreign policy. But with campaigning underway for September's state elections in opposition-controlled Bavaria and Teufel sitting close by, he took a radically different line just seconds later. 'Immigration policy is one of the most sensitive areas of home affairs,' he said. 'A generalised shift to QMV is not possible at present for Germany.'

France, another advocate of QMV, also had an area where it wanted to keep the national veto. In an earlier session, Pascale Andréani, the French government alternate, had warned that ratification of the constitutional treaty would be a lost cause in France without retention of unanimity for granting negotiating mandates to the Commission for trade negotiations that concerned the 'cultural exception'. With a phalanx of French conventionnels, she again pressed for changes in the draft text, which envisaged QMV for international trade agreements covering services in the cultural, audio-visual, health and education sectors. Her call, she declared, was backed by some 30 Convention members from 11 countries who had submitted amendments for the 'cultural exception' to be treated as a shared competence between the Union and member states, and subject to unanimity.

The plenary debate also saw a new effort by the political left to obtain greater support in the Constitution for 'services of general interest' – Brussels jargon for the public services which many politicians, notably in France and Belgium, enthusiastically support because of their powerful trade union links.

Conventionnels of all political backgrounds from the euro-zone wanted the 'Eurogroup' nations to have a greater control over their economic governance. Several integration-minded Convention members urged that the Constitution refer to the Union's symbols such as its flag and anthem. A new push was made by Joschka Fischer and the Netherlands' representative, Gijs de Vries, to strengthen the role of the proposed, but disputed, post of European public prosecutor.

The session was in fact a busy one for Fischer, who was one of few senior government representatives to have come back to the Convention after Thessaloniki. His presence testified to a backlog of lobbying on his agenda to shift decisions in Germany's favour. Fischer rarely raised issues of national concern in the Convention's plenary, preferring to influence the Praesidium and key players by direct contact in the small VIP rooms dotted throughout the Parliament building or by letter from the foreign ministry in Berlin. His intervention on immigration came after these techniques had failed. He had another aim – to support a declaration which he had encouraged the Praesidium to add to part III, providing for the future creation of a 'European External Action Service' to assist the planned Union Minister for Foreign Affairs 'under the minister's authority'. This EU diplomatic corps would be composed of officials from the Council secretariat, the Commission and member states' diplomatic services.

The draft declaration caused problems for Brok and other integrationist MEPs. Ever fearful that the Convention was tipping the institutional balance too much towards the member states, they insisted the service should be located within the Commission. Fischer expressed his personal sympathy for Brok's proposal but warned it would not have the backing of those member states which wanted the minister's power base in the Council.

The UK was now represented by the British government's alternate, Baroness Scotland, because Peter Hain was fully occupied taking charge of new responsibilities as leader of the House of Commons. Warning the Convention against moving the goal posts, she underlined Britain's determination to retain national sovereignty over tax, foreign policy, defence and criminal law procedure. The Swedish, Estonian, Irish and Italian government representatives also called for continued unanimity on tax policy.

But it was Giscard and Amato who defined the limits to the further expansion of QMV. Giscard invited Amato to outline ways of moving to agreement. Taking issue with the idea that extending QMV was a purely technical matter, Amato said the passage from unanimity to majority voting implied a different institutional balance and was also an emotional question. 'On a number of issues, several member states, national public opinion in several countries and several of our colleagues feel that their identity is at stake, their diversity is at stake, some of their vital interests are at stake. That is a fact of life.'

The cases where more QMV could be compatible with the Thessaloniki mandate for the Convention were therefore limited. As the conventionnels prepared to leave for the weekend, Giscard warned that moving much further towards QMV would 'shatter the consensus', adding: 'I know many cases among different European partners where moving to QMV would provoke very negative reactions.'

17.2   THE LAST TWO DAYS

The Praesidium met on Tuesday, 8 July to draw up amendments in the light of the previous week's discussions and Amato's guidelines. It made some progress. But, in what Giscard conceded was a 'mixed bag' of proposals, it agreed no significant changes towards QMV in foreign or tax policy. It left open the issue of the cultural exception after an hour of wrangling in order, it was said, to gauge the opinion of the plenary.

Its key decision favoured Germany, and proved that Fischer's presence in Brussels the previous Friday had been worthwhile. The relevant article, III-163 [III-267], prescribed QMV for the Union's planned common immigration policy. But Germany secured national control over the access of immigrants to the labour market with the addition of a sentence, making clear that QMV 'shall not affect the right of member states to determine volumes of admission of third country nationals coming from third countries to their territory in order to seek work, whether employed or self employed'.

Euro-zone countries were given, in III-85a [III-194], their own powers to strengthen budgetary discipline and surveillance in the single currency area and specify their own economic policy guidelines.

To take account of concerns of some neutral countries over the defence articles, the Praesidium changed the rules applying to 'structured cooperation' in III-208 [III-312], by which member states forming coalitions of the willing could carry out demanding military tasks. These were made subject to the same safeguards, which apply to 'enhanced cooperation' in other policy areas.

To please integrationists, a new article, III-324a [III-422], opened the way for countries practicing enhanced cooperation to decide, by a unanimous vote, to move from unanimity to QMV in a manner similar to the bridging clauses or *passerelles* agreed before 13 June for part I. For some less integrationist countries, this decision raised the spectre of the Constitution authorising the creation of an *avant-garde* or core group of countries within the Union.

Other amendments were tidying up initiatives. A clause in article III-196 [III-300] would engage the foreign minister in trying to resolve a dispute should any member state invoke the 'vital reasons of national policy' to block a decision in one of the few areas of common foreign and security policy subject to QMV. The Praesidium also opened fractionally the capacity of the European Court of Justice to rule on foreign policy matters by giving it jurisdiction to review sanctions against individuals under CFSP. The Praesidium gave the Parliament the right to be consulted in article III-133 [III-240] over measures against discrimination in the area of transport and in III-210 [III-313] for cases where the Union seeks rapid access to funds to finance urgent foreign policy measures. Also, the Parliament would be informed about agreements between management and labour at Union level in III-101 [III-212] and, should the Union ever have to implement the solidarity clause, in III-226 [III-329] in the case of a terrorist attack or natural or man-made disaster. Other changes would encourage young people to take part in the Union's democratic life in III-177 [III-282] and enable European researchers to cooperate across borders in III-141 [III-248]. The latter decision gave some heart to supporters of the 'Lisbon agenda for making Europe more competitive.

In reaction, there was widespread discontent among Convention members from the national and European Parliaments and the Commission. After the document[1] detailing the changes was distributed, MEPs turned on Klaus Hänsch and Inigo Méndez de Vigo, their two representatives in the Praesidium, accusing them of having failed to press Parliament's case. So bitter were the complaints that Hänsch had to ask his colleagues 'not to get physical'. As chairman of the meetings of Convention MEPs, the EPP's Méndez de Vigo had always tried to give himself manoeuvring room by

---

[1] CONV 847/03.

shying away from formulating firm conclusions after discussions in the European Parliament group. This time, he drew up a list of points and pledged to fight for them in the plenary.

The alliance of integrationist national parliamentarians and MEPs also responded vigorously. After meeting Amato to discuss the Praesidium's decisions, Duff, Dini and Brok reworked their 'key points' paper of the previous week, listing seven demands 'of pivotal importance'. These were:

- QMV in foreign policy when the foreign minister's initiatives were supported by the Commission
- the External Action Service as a single administration within the Commission
- QMV for setting minimum standards in article III-5 on non-discrimination
- QMV for legislation under III-59 harmonising indirect tax measures relating to administrative cooperation, tax fraud and tax evasion
- greater scope for the Court of Justice regarding CFSP, particularly with respect to agencies such as the proposed European armaments agency
- clarification of the European Parliament's role in international commercial agreements – the proposed article III-222.7 failed to make clear whether its consent was needed
- a requirement in part IV article 6 that the European Parliament must consent should a future European Council decide *not* to call a convention to revise the Constitution.

A succession of speakers took the floor in the afternoon plenary session to hammer home these points. Singing from the same hymn sheet were Dini for the national parliamentarians, Méndez de Vigo for the MEPs, Duff, Brok, the Belgian Socialist MEP Anne Van Lancker and the Austrian Green Johannes Voggenhuber for the big political families, and Commissioner Antonio Vitorino. Some Convention members also reminded Giscard of their call for the Constitution to refer to the Union's symbols. Others wanted it to mention the open method of coordination.

But the Convention's integrationists did not have things all their own way. The government representatives were largely opposed to significant change and made their position clear. 'It is now time to stop with ambitions,' declared Ireland's Dick Roche. The UK's Baroness Scotland expressed surprise at the 'non-technical changes' in the latest text, including the proposals for structured and enhanced cooperation and the role of the Court. 'We simply cannot support them,' she said.

Henrik Hololei, Estonia's representative, spoke out against attempts in the plenary 'to insert fundamental changes' in the Constitution and urged the Convention instead to stick to the Thessaloniki mandate. A hush fell over the plenary when Fischer spoke. Here, despite his insistence on national control over Germany's labour market, was the most prominent of the integration-minded government representatives. His remarks were sobering.

Fischer told the assembly that he encountered problems persuading the cabinet in Berlin to accept compromises reached in the Convention. With the forthcoming Intergovernmental Conference in mind, he warned the conventionnels, Giscard and the Praesidium 'not to open up compromises that have been reached to extract a final centimetre'.

Fischer went on to plead for solutions to 'two small matters'. One was the cultural exception, for which Pascale Andréani made another robust plea, with the support of several French conventionnels and Latvian, Polish and Austrian members. Fischer's other preoccupation was the status of the Euratom Treaty *vis-à-vis* the Constitution. The Convention had been unable to reach an agreement over Euratom. Giscard and his secretariat always wanted to leave it alone, arguing that to deal with the 46-year-old treaty would be too difficult and was outside the mandate of the Convention.

In the plenary, Fischer, playing on his status as Germany's foreign minister and the Convention's most prominent Green politician, asked for a minor amendment so that Euratom would retain its own legal personality. This demand had earlier been adopted by the Convention's Greens to keep open the option of their amending or killing off Euratom at a later date without having to revise the Constitution. It was accepted by the Praesidium in its final meeting, late on Wednesday, 9 July.

17.3   THE PRAESIDIUM MEETS FOR THE LAST TIME

The final meeting of the Praesidium nearly ended in failure over the cultural exception. The Convention initiated a quiet revolution when it agreed – against French objections – that article I-12 should list the common commercial policy, without any qualifying clauses, among the Union's exclusive competences. This decision invalidated those parts of article 133 of the Nice Treaty, which placed 'agreements relating to trade in cultural and audiovisual services, educational services and social and human health services ... within the shared competence of the Union and its member states' and subjected them to unanimity.

Consensus on article I-12 made it impossible to solve the problem by reproducing the Nice treaty text in the Constitution, as demanded by many, mainly French, conventionnels. This logic was reflected in draft article III-212 [III-315] which ranked trade in services alongside goods as part of the common commercial policy that would be implemented by European laws or framework laws, and therefore by QMV. On the other hand, the Praesidium could hardly ignore the clamour from parts of the Convention for the cultural exception or the behind-the-scenes lobbying by the French government. Paris's call on national loyalties had prompted Commissioner Michel Barnier to support unanimity in the previous Praesidium meeting, even though the Commission's policy was for trade in goods and services to be decided by QMV.

Before Giscard joined the Praesidium, he met Amato, Dehaene, Duff, Méndez de Vigo, Dini and Brok; a group he called 'the elite'. He had taken to consulting this group after his first successful meeting early in June with the national parliamentarians. He made clear that there could be no further extension of QMV on tax or foreign policy and that a way must be found in the final consensus to satisfy the French and German demands. As a compromise, the elite agreed that the Convention should send a letter to the member states in the IGC to underline how a large majority of Convention members wanted more QMV for tax policy and foreign affairs.

The government representatives also met, for a rather more ill-humoured session. There was considerable criticism of the Praesidium for exceeding the Thessaloniki mandate, and of German and French demands for unanimity in their special areas of interest. No German was present. Pascale Andréani arrived late and did not take the floor.

Before tackling the cultural exception, the Praesidium set about meeting the demands of others. This was both necessary and shrewd in view of the widespread impression that the Convention leadership was doing little else but bend over backwards to deal with the problems of France and Germany. The Praesidium took about 30 seconds to decide on a new article [I-8], creating official symbols for the Union. This was placed in part IV because there was no way of reopening part I, but with a recommendation that the IGC move it forwards to the 'constitutional' part of the text. The constitutional treaty would thus recognise the Union's flag of twelve golden stars on a blue background, its anthem based on Beethoven's *Ode to Joy* and the euro as its currency. The day in 1950 when Robert Schuman started the process of European integration with his proposal for a European Coal and Steel Community, 9 May, would henceforth 'be celebrated throughout the Union as Europe day'. The Union would also have as its motto 'United in diversity', the phrase highlighted by Giscard in the preamble to part I.

It agreed to amend article IV-6 to give the European Parliament the right of approval over whether the European Council in future should decide *not* to call a convention to revise the Constitution. This important amendment meant, in effect, that heads of government would never again be able to call an IGC without first having Parliament's approval. By changing references in article IV-2 [IV-438] from European 'Communities' to 'Community' and deleting the first article from the protocol annexed to the Constitution, which amended the Euratom Treaty, the Praesidium met the demands of Fischer, Voggenhuber and the environmental lobby, and ensured that Euratom retained its own legal personality.

The Praesidium went only part of the way to deal with Brok's worries about the Union foreign minister's planned European diplomatic corps. It added some words to the declaration on the 'European External Action Service' at the end of the Constitution. This now read[2]: 'To assist the future Union Minister for Foreign Affairs, introduced in article 1-27 of the Constitution, to perform his/her duties, the Convention agrees the need *for the Council and the Commission to agree, without prejudice, to the rights of the European Parliament*, to establish under the Minister's authority one joint service (European External Action Service) composed of officials from relevant departments of the General Secretariat of the Council of Ministers and of the Commission and staff seconded from national Diplomatic Services.' As the declaration also said necessary arrangements for establishing the joint service should be made within a year of the Constitution's entry into force, the Praesidium effectively left the Union's institutions to sort out whether the service should be based in the Commission or the Council at a future date.

The Praesidium also went halfway in response to the strong demands of parliamentarians for QMV to apply to article III-5 on anti-discrimination legislation. Taking account of a strong wish by Britain to retain the national veto, it decided unanimity should apply in the Council of Ministers for anti-discrimination laws. But they were to be subject in future to the Parliament's consent rather than consultation. Existing legislation already provided that incentive measures in support of anti-discrimination legislation should be decided by QMV. The Praesidium decided the same procedure could also be used to establish basic principles as well.

A further 'halfway house' solution concerned the open method of coordination. Although adopted with great fanfare at the March 2000 Lisbon European Council for the Union's economic competitiveness programme,

---

[2] Additional text in author's italics.

this system of benchmarking had been kept out of the constitutional treaty by purists who feared it could undermine the 'Community method' of decision making in the Union. Rather than take the contentious route and draft a special article for the Constitution, the Praesidium decided to allude to the open coordination method without actually naming it in four articles: III-102 [III-213], III-143 [III-250], III-174 [III-278] and III-175 [III-279], dealing with social policy, research, health policy and industrial competitiveness.

Where each article enjoined the Commission to promote the policy in question, the Praesidium added that its actions should cover 'in particular initiatives aiming at the establishment of guidelines and indicators, the organisation of exchange of best practice, and the preparation of the necessary elements for periodic monitoring and evaluation. The European Parliament shall be kept fully informed.' Not for the first time, the Praesidium opted for language that was practical rather than elegant to resolve a problem.

17.4   BACK FROM THE ABYSS

With the 'all must have prizes' phase of the Presidium's deliberations complete, it turned to the difficult issue of the cultural exception.

The Praesidium was divided. Although the majority appeared to favour retaining QMV, it was clear Giscard wanted to accommodate France. First soundings showed that Amato supported unanimity with the tactical aim of solving the issue before the IGC. Dehaene, who was absent, was counted as backing France: he had expressed his support and backing the cultural exception was a traditional Belgian policy. Hänsch and Méndez de Vigo were non-committal.

Barnier had been reined in by the college of commissioners and was now counted as favouring QMV. As a commissioner, the absent Antonio Vitorino could also be counted as a QMV supporter. Alfonso Dastis backed QMV, partly out of displeasure that the Praesidium was making such efforts to appease France and Germany, when it had done nothing the previous month to help Spain in its opposition to the double majority system for determining a qualified majority. Earlier in the plenary, Alojz Peterle, the Slovene, had described the existing text with its provisions for QMV in trade policy as 'well-balanced and acceptable'.

John Bruton asked for a better definition of the issue. He pointed to article I-3 on the Union's objectives, which stipulated that: 'The Union shall respect its rich cultural and linguistic diversity, and shall ensure that Europe's cultural heritage is safeguarded and enhanced.' Earlier in the plenary session, Bruton drew a distinction between cultural issues and the audio-visual industry. The latter, he pointed out, was 'big business'. Did the Convention 'really want to put the Commission in a position where, when it goes to negotiate on a wide range of issues, it cannot do a package deal that includes something on the media?'

Henning Christophersen, the Danish representative, had a different preoccupation – transport. Speaking also on behalf of George Papandreou, Greece's representative who was absent, Christophersen wanted to retain the language of the Treaty of Nice, which prescribed the national veto in the area of maritime transport. The Christophersen problem was addressed by insertion of language,[3] obscure even by EU standards into article III-212 on the common commercial policy. The wording linked trade negotiations on maritime transport to the section of part III dealing with transport policy and convinced the Dane that unanimity in maritime transport was secure. With Christophersen satisfied, the dynamic of the meeting changed. He was now prepared to back the French position and could throw the absent Papandreou into the scales on Giscard's side.

But two things happened to sour the atmosphere. Giscard put pressure on Peterle by wondering aloud whether he was entitled to be part of the consensus in the Praesidium. The Laeken declaration specified that the accession countries could take part in the Convention's proceedings in the same way as member states, 'without, however, being able to prevent any consensus which may emerge among the member states'. This condition had been forgotten in the life of the Convention as the enlargement negotiations were completed and the accession country conventionnels came to play a full role in its proceedings. But Giscard, desperate to have a Praesidium decision in his favour, now revived the Laeken condition in an attempt to remove Peterle from the ranks of opponents to the cultural exception. His move backfired. Méndez de Vigo, who was Peterle's mentor in the centre-right EPP, upbraided Giscard for treating Peterle so unkindly and came off the fence to join the supporters of QMV.

The other disturbing moment came when Gisela Stuart decided to tease the French. She asked for the opinion of the Commission and, on hearing it, said she would be against any change away from QMV if that was the Commission's position. Stuart's intervention made Giscard very angry, not

---

[3] The relevant sentence reads: 'The negotiation and conclusion of international agreements in the field of transport shall be subject to the provisions of section 7 of chapter three of this title and article III-222.'

least because, against his own convictions, he had always respected the UK's right to resist the Commission's drive to have tax policy determined by majority voting. Giscard, backed by Amato, countered by asking her whether she wanted the opinion of the Commission on QMV for tax matters and whether she would accept this.

A worried Sir John Kerr crept round the table and passed Stuart a pencil-written note 'seriously advising' her not to irritate the president any further. Stuart obliged but the impasse remained. Giscard declared the meeting was over and there would be no amendment to solve the problem of the cultural exception. The Praesidium had failed to agree – leaving the Convention without consensus on an issue, which would certainly become a bone of contention in the IGC. But nobody stood up or made to leave the room. There was a pause. Hänsch broke the silence. 'We have to have a compromise,' he said. Slowly the Praesidium began talking again. It looked again at Bruton's points about cultural diversity. The crisis was over.

Thanks largely to Bruton, the Praesidium devised a compromise that managed both to satisfy the proponents of QMV in trade policy and the backers of the cultural exception. It agreed a text that opened the way for unanimity in the cultural and audio-visual sectors, but narrowly defined its scope thus ensuring QMV should be the general rule. By stating that the Council of Ministers 'shall also act unanimously for the negotiation and conclusion of agreements in the field of trade in cultural and audiovisual services, *where these risk prejudicing the Union's cultural and linguistic diversity',*[4] the text made unanimity a safeguard and shifted the burden of proof to member states to determine if it is warranted.

The success of this formula was illustrated a few days later in the French daily *Le Figaro*, when in separate articles on the same page, Jean-Jacques Aillagon, the French minister for culture, and Pascal Lamy, the trade commissioner, hailed the new accord. During the lengthy discussions on the cultural exception, Lamy had never allowed his French nationality to weaken his support for QMV on trade issues. In *Le Figaro*, Lamy now argued that the new text was a qualitative leap forward for trade policy because the 'logic of initiative and movement' replaced that of 'veto and retreat'.

---

[4] Author's italics.

THE TRIUMVIRATE
From left to right - Amato, Giscard and Dehaene on the Convention's opening day
Source: European Convention

GISCARD AND SIR JOHN KERR
Absorbing reactions to the first draft articles on 6 February 2003
Source: European Parliament

GISCARD GREETS SPAIN'S NEW FOREIGN MINISTER
A warm welcome for Ana Palacio during the July 2002 plenary as Andrew Duff looks on
Source: European Convention

AMATO MAKES A POINT
As Gisela Stuart (background) reports on the National Parliaments working group
Source: European Parliament

ELMAR BROK
Denouncing the Praesidium at an EPP press conference, 27 May 2003
Source: EPP-ED

INIGO MÉNDEZ DE VIGO
Praesidium member, 'Pope of subsidiarity' and Brok's rival in the EPP
Source: EPP-ED

NEW KID ON THE BLOCK
Joschka Fischer (left) catches up with Klaus Hänsch on Fischer's first day at the Convention
Source: European Parliament

THE ONE MAN IDEAS FACTORY
Alain Lamassoure assesses the Franco-German deal on institutions, January 2003
Source: EPP-ED

EUROSCEPTICS GRIT THEIR TEETH AND SIGN
Jens-Peter Bonde and David Heathcoat-Amory (right) add the words 'minority report'
Source: Bonde.com

PICADOR AND BLOGGER
Olivier Duhamel during the plenary of
4 July 2003
Source: Ambroise Perrin, GPES

TIRELESS BATTLER FOR
'SOCIAL EUROPE'
Anne Van Lancker finds time to relax in
the 4 July 2003 plenary
Source: Ambroise Perrin, GPES

GISCARD ADDRESSES THE CONVENTIONNELS
At the Parliament's 'lectern of honour' during the 13 June 2003 plenary
Source: European Parliament

THE BUSY NETWORKER
Britain's conventionnel Peter Hain (right) meets Pat Cox, European Parliament president
Source: European Parliament

A JOB WELL DONE
The Taoiseach Bertie Ahern (right) and Irish foreign minister Brian Cowen in celebratory
mood after member states agree to the constitutional treaty on 18 June 2004.
Source: www.eu2004.ie

SECURING BRITAIN'S 'RED LINES'
UK prime minister Tony Blair (right) and foreign secretary Jack Straw in the
Intergovernmental Conference, Brussels, 17 June 2004
Source: Council of the European Union

NO AGREEMENT TODAY
Silvio Berlusconi, Italy's prime minister and president of the European Council, glosses over the failure of the December 2003 summit in Brussels
Source: Council of the European Union

RETURN TO EUROPE
Spanish prime minister José Luis Rodriguez Zapatero (right) confers with EU high representative Javier Solana (centre) and Spain's foreign minister Miguel Angel Moratinos (left) during the Intergovernmental Conference, Brussels, 17 June 2004.
Source: Council of the European Union

17.5 THE SHIP REACHES PORT

The compromise on trade prepared the way for a triumphant end to the Convention. Revised texts of parts III and IV[5] incorporating the Praesidium's amendments were circulated the following morning. But well before that, the conventionnels converged on the plenary hall in a carnival spirit. They had been given small bound versions of the penultimate draft the day before. These became autograph books, as, like children at the end of their first summer camp, the Convention members began rushing round seeking signatures from each other.

Any fears that the frustrations of the previous day would spill over into the final session were finally dispelled after Giscard began to outline the Praesidium's amendments. Shrewdly, he mentioned the symbols first and was rewarded with applause from across the hall. The stage was set for a re-run of the enthusiastic, congratulatory speeches that marked the consensus on parts I and II a month before.

Hänsch was asked to speak first for the European Parliament. Throughout the Convention's 16 and a half months, Hänsch had always seen the glass as half-full rather than half-empty. He did not disappoint. 'The European Parliament delegation says "yes" to this draft treaty for a European Constitution and we say "yes", not with caveats or reservations but full of conviction and wholeheartedly because we want our draft to be the Constitution of the European Union.' True the draft was made up of compromises, but these did not represent the lowest common denominator. Instead, the Constitution, as agreed, was 'a single coherent whole'.

Dini followed with a pointed challenge to the government representatives in the hall. They had 'a moral responsibility to support, together with their respective heads of government, the work that we have collectively agreed upon in the Convention'.

Bruton spoke next 'as one of the elected representatives of national parliaments in the Praesidium'. That component, representing 550 million people, 'gave an unambiguous welcome to the work we have completed'. The challenge now was 'to go out from here and explain this Constitution to our people; to ensure that our people feel part of our work and part of our achievement'.

---

[5] CONV 848/03.

Not even Jens-Peter Bonde, the veteran eurosceptic, could break the spell. There were grumbles as Bonde began with the words, 'Mr President, congratulations on the new superstate'. But these turned to laughter, when his final plea 'for referendums alongside the next European elections' was applauded by just one Convention member. 'Well, that was a sort of referendum,' Giscard observed, to yet more laughter.

Twenty speakers later, it was the turn of the vice-presidents to take the floor. For Giuliano Amato, the Convention had reunified Europe. It had achieved far more than an IGC. In an IGC, a 'no' was a 'sovereign no' and there was no need for the government representative to explain. The Convention, by being transparent, forced anyone saying 'no' to engage in democratic debate. That in turn produced results.

Jean-Luc Dehaene recalled how many had considered the Convention a 'mission impossible' at the time of the Laeken summit. It was now 'mission accomplished'. As advisers to the Belgian prime minister ahead of Laeken, both he and Amato had fretted over whether they should use the word 'Constitution' for fear that it was too provocative. Now, people could speak about a 'European Constitution, as the most normal thing in the world'. Switching from Dutch to French, Dehaene predicted that the Convention would soon be seen as a decisive step for Europe. He then turned to Giscard, without whose personality 'this Convention would not have been what it was'. Giscard, he said, had presided with authority but without being authoritarian. He had listened and created the consensus. He called on the president to become the defender of the Convention's decisions *vis-à-vis* the Union's heads of state and government.

It was Giscard's turn to speak. Balancing his microphone precariously on a pile of EU Treaties, he turned to the polyglot and heterogeneous crew before him: 'I am proud to have been your president and to have piloted our vessel, sometimes through the mists, sometimes through the cold and sometimes through the waves. But the important thing is our ship has reached port.' Their voyage had been a journey into the unknown. Now their vessel would embark on a second journey, one less perilous, but not without risk, into the IGC. It was the duty of all conventionnels to watch over its journey and ensure that the Constitution remained as intact as possible.

The Constitution was coherent and without options, Giscard said. It was the product of trade-offs between frequently contradictory demands: between federalist and non-federalist, between more and less populated member states, between richer and poorer and between the different institutions. The Convention succeeded because its members accepted that their preferred solutions were not always acceptable to others. The result was a consensus that was balanced in its details. 'Anyone wanting to change this Constitution and the balance achieved could risk distorting, even dismembering our work. In that case, public opinion, and one day perhaps historians would say a fantastic opportunity had been lost.'

Giscard switched into English, 'a language all can understand', to thank the Convention members and Amato and Dehaene, Sir John Kerr and Annalisa Giannella, Kerr's deputy in the secretariat. 'We have succeeded because we have learned from each other,' he said. 'I have learned from all of you, at an age that is normally not propitious for learning.' Admitting to a 'touch of melancholy', Giscard added: 'In one's life, if one is lucky, one is permitted once or twice to make a difference, to touch the hem of history. Together we have had that chance. Together we have taken that chance. We should all be proud of that.'

He invited the Convention members to sign the document, which would be handed over with the Constitution to Italy's President Ciampi and Prime Minister Silvio Berlusconi in Rome the following week. The Convention was over. The Constitution was now the responsibility of the Italian presidency and the intergovernmental conference.

17.6   FOUNDING FATHERS

The final plenary session of the Convention was a time to reflect on more than 16 months of hard graft. Its members had met on 26 occasions in plenary sessions covering 52 days. The Praesidium had come to Brussels on 50 separate occasions with an increasingly time-consuming schedule in 2003. The conventionnels made more than 1,800 interventions in the plenary, produced 386 written contributions to the Convention and a further 773 to its working groups and discussion circles. The Praesidium's draft articles generated some 6,000 amendments.

Giscard, as the plaudits during Convention's final sessions recognised, deserved much credit for steering such a diverse body to agreement on a single text. He did not start with a blueprint for the constitutional treaty. But he certainly had a compass for the Convention. He was able to exploit developments, because he had very clear ideas on a number of policy issues and could count on:

- a flexible hard working secretariat (which was better organised than the Praesidium)
- a concentration in his office of information from all key sources, including the fruits of his bilateral diplomacy

- a well-honed personal perspective of what could be achieved, for example, realising the limits to qualified majority voting in the foreign policy area
- an ultimately pragmatic approach, highlighted by his willingness to junk pet ideas, such as the Congress of MEPS and national parliamentarians
- personal authority, so that he was never really challenged by the 'conventionnels'
- a keen sense of timing
- an exclusive understanding of the consensus needed to bring the Convention to its close.

The big political families (the centre-right European People's Party, the Party of European Socialists and the European Liberal Democrats) were also crucial to the Convention's success. They provided bridges between MEPs and national parliamentarians. The party frameworks fostered links that became quite close – such as those between the EPP's Brok and the socialists' Amato, or between Dini and Duff in the Liberal group. In addition, informal cross-cutting dining clubs of movers and shakers enabled ideas to flow, policies to crystallise and consensus to form. Much of the Convention's business was conducted over meals during its frantic final weeks. 'I had at least two breakfasts and two dinners almost every day,' Andrew Duff recalled later.

All the leaders of the big political families (Brok, Duff and Amato) wanted the Convention to be a success. All three reached out to the national parliamentarians in the process of gathering support for amendments to the draft articles produced by the Praesidium from February 2003. From there it was a short step to using the political families as a conduit for transferring know-how and back-up resources from the well-organised and well-endowed European Parliamentarians to their like-minded but less well-resourced colleagues from national capitals.

Many conventionnels helped shape the consensus. Some, like Andrew Duff, Lamberto Dini, Alain Lamassoure, Peter Hain and Antonio Vitorino, were active both inside and outside the plenary hall. Others, such as Elmar Brok, Inigo Méndez de Vigo and Joschka Fischer, were more active behind the scenes.

Some conventionnels were driven by idealism. Some by the feeling that failure would be poor recompense for 16 and a half months of travelling back and forth to Brussels. For those conventionnels of the accession countries, who could look forward to advancing their careers as officials of members of the Union, it was obviously better to have membership of a successful Convention on their résumés.

Even the eurosceptics could not resist associating themselves with the Convention at its close. Four eurosceptic Convention members and four alternates, headed by Jens-Peter Bonde[6], produced a minority report proposing a 'Europe of Democracies' which was forwarded by Giscard to the Italian presidency[7] with the completed constitutional treaty. But, when on the final day in July, the conventionnels were signing the text at the front of the plenary hall, the eurosceptics were placed in a dilemma. Should they sign, and be accused of betraying their position, or not sign and be forgotten by history? Lord Stockton, a British Conservative MEP, who was not one of the minority report signatories, offered a way out of the dilemma: 'I signed the document but didn't sign up to it,' he said.

Bonde and his associates took a deep breath and signed, placing the words 'minority report' in brackets after their names. They had come to the conclusion that it was better to be remembered among the Europe's 'founding fathers'.

17.7   A PROBLEMATIC CONSENSUS

But fathers to what? The Convention consensus turned out to be fragile. The tensions that surfaced at the June 2003 European Council in Thessaloniki remained. Some of the institutional questions, which dominated the Convention's final weeks, as well as some of its proposals for shifting decision making in the Council from unanimity to qualified majority voting, continued to stir up passions.

These were issues that impinged on national sovereignty and had never been thoroughly aired using the Convention method. The Praesidium produced only one 'reflection paper' on the functioning of the institutions.[8] There were no detailed papers from the Praesidium; no working groups, not even a reflection circle. The institutional issues were raised in plenary sessions, but towards the end of the Convention and when time was short. The

---

[6] In addition to Bonde, the following signed the minority report: William Abitbol MEP (alternate); Per Dalgaard, Danish parliament (alternate); John Gormley, Irish parliament (alternate); David Heathcoat-Amory, UK parliament (member); Esko Seppanen MEP (alternate); Peter Skaarup, Danish parliament (member); Jan Zahradil, Czech parliament (member).
[7] Annex III CONV 851/03.
[8] CONV 477/03 of 10 January 2003.

institutional provisions of the constitutional draft were hard-wired into the Convention by the interventions of the large member states, modified only modestly through chaotic procedures inside the Convention and always tempered by the insights of Giscard and Sir John Kerr into what Germany, France and the UK would accept.

The broad support given to about 90% of the draft constitutional treaty in the Intergovernmental Conference vindicated the 'Convention method' of deliberation and decision by consensus. The process of discussion, refinement of issues in working groups and formulation of draft articles, which were subject to further discussion on the basis of amendments, was successful as the later negotiations in the IGC bore witness.

The Convention method contrasted with the approach taken for the institutional questions where gamesmanship was at a premium from the moment Giscard leaked his own draft articles in late April 2003. It was with gusto that Sir John Kerr resorted in the Convention's closing weeks to tricks learned through decades of negotiation in smoke-filled rooms. The secretariat focused on keeping control of the agenda, holding back documents, never letting opposition groups consolidate, and creating a climate in which the most enthusiastic partisan among the conventionnels would eventually settle for a compromise.

Although entertaining to watch, the secretariat's handling of the institutional issues produced a consensus that was less convincing and therefore flawed. The tactics owed nothing to the 'Convention spirit', which Giscard demanded in his opening address.

One of Giscard's earliest decisions was to allow no votes in the Convention. It appeared a stroke of genius. He alone would determine what consensus was and consensus remained a riddle even after the Convention members had cleared the hall on 13 June 2003. The day before, the group of MEPs tried to find out from Dehaene what consensus might mean. 'What is consensus?' Dehaene mused. 'My answer is that the day you define consensus, you'll never again find it. It is really something you can't put your finger on. We shouldn't try to translate it into mathematical equations.' Giscard didn't even use the word consensus during the final session, reserving for the press afterwards his judgement that support for the draft was 'virtually unanimous'.

But nebulous consensus could only translate into virtually unanimous support if all participants felt they were treated fairly. Giscard took great pains to meet British objections. He made a major effort in the July session to settle Germany's difficulties over immigration and France's insistence on the 'cultural exception', with the result that France and Germany put themselves in the vanguard of countries willing to accept the final draft, virtually unchanged. Giscard was far less solicitous throughout the Convention of the smaller states and accession countries.

The consensus in June 2003 came at the cost of some hurt feelings and bruised egos. It was damaging for the Union that the split between big and small member states, that entered the EU's bloodstream during the French presidency in the second half of 2000, persisted and got worse during a Convention chaired by a former president of France and continued into the IGC. It was scant consolation that small and medium-sized countries from either side of the former Iron Curtain could make common cause in the big-small country dispute and so reinforce the image of the Convention as 'the first constituent assembly on a European scale'.[9]

Giscard's consensus was based on a coalition of parliamentarians. The good news here was that the constitutional treaty could be described as reflecting a Europe of citizens. However, the political reality was that the Intergovernmental Conference which followed was a negotiation among governments, reflecting Europe of the states.

---

[9] Giscard's description in his speech accepting the Charlemagne Prize, Aachen 29 May 2003.

Part V

Member States Agree a Constitution

CHAPTER 18
The Intergovernmental Conference

18.1   THE ITALIAN PRESIDENCY

Giscard had appealed to governments not to tamper with the Convention's work. That proved a vain hope. But although Britain's foreign secretary, Jack Straw, calculated afterwards that 80 separate sets of amendments were agreed in the Intergovernmental Conference (with 39 advocated by Britain),[1] the text agreed by the Union's heads of state and government in June 2004 was clearly based on the Convention's draft.[2]

The IGC turned into a game of two halves. The Italian presidency, which was in charge of the negotiations in the second half of 2003, began hopefully with the aim of wrapping up the talks in December. But it had to deal with a hardening of attitudes in several member states against some of the Convention's proposals. It was left to the Irish presidency in the first half of 2004 to bring the negotiation to a successful conclusion.

Although the formal completion of the EU's 'big bang' enlargement was not due until 1 May 2004, several months after the start of the IGC, the eight former Communist countries of eastern and central Europe plus Cyprus and Malta participated fully in the negotiations. The other three candidate countries – Bulgaria, Romania and Turkey – took part as observers.

By the time the IGC began on 4 October 2003, the small member states had regrouped, led by Austria and Finland, under the banner of 'the like-minded countries' to press for one commissioner per member state. Poland – in tandem with Spain – had strengthened its determination to oppose the double majority system for qualified majority voting in the Council. With other Catholic countries, Poland was also pressing hard for a reference to Europe's Christian heritage in the final text.

---

[1] Article in *The Economist* 10 July 2004.
[2] Giscard claimed that of 14,800 words in the original document, 13,500 words or about 90% were retained in the final version. See Peter Ludlow: The IGC and the European Council of June 2004. EuroComment Briefing Note, No 3.2 bis. 14 July 2004.

As the negotiations progressed, the UK government, which in September 2003 had welcomed the Convention's outcome as 'good news for Britain',[3] became increasingly insistent that its special interests, or 'red lines', be observed in full. EU finance ministers in the Ecofin Council attacked the Convention's proposals to give the European Parliament greater powers over the EU budget. The flouting by Germany and France of the euro-zone's stability and growth pact and the pact's de-facto suspension by Ecofin further added to tensions as the December summit of the IGC approached.

These pressures notwithstanding, the Italian presidency made progress on the IGC's agenda. Franco Frattini, the foreign minister, headed a competent team of officials who cooperated closely with the Council secretariat. They spent the months before the start of the IGC canvassing the views of all parties to ensure a relatively smooth start to the negotiations.

Thus, the foreign ministers immediately got down to substance after the conference's ceremonial opening in Rome. They started, during their afternoon session of 4 October, by scrapping the Convention's idea of a combined Legislative and General Affairs Council. This move was widely expected because the combined Council had swiftly been recognised as an unsatisfactory compromise. Amato, who prided himself on being the inventor of the Legislative Council, disowned the combined Council at the end of the Convention as 'the walking dead' and a 'terrible mistake'.

The presidency set up a working party of legal experts from the member states, accession countries, the Council and the Commission to carry out a legal verification of the Convention text and weed out provisions that had become obsolete from existing protocols, accession treaties and texts of EU primary law. Chaired by Jean-Claude Piris, director-general of the Council legal service, the experts presented a 'cleaned up' draft treaty at the end of November, which became the basis of the IGC negotiations.[4]

After despatching the Legislative Council, the foreign ministers addressed institutional and non-institutional questions in a series of meetings. A successful conclave of ministers in Naples on 28–29 November temporarily encouraged hopes that the IGC might conclude by the end of the Italian presidency.

---

[3] White paper entitled 'A Constitutional Treaty for the EU: The British Approach to the European Union Interogvernmental Conference 2003', CM5934.
[4] CIG 50/03 and CIG 50/03 ADD1.

Ahead of the December IGC at the level of heads of state and government, there was broad agreement that the sectoral Councils should, in future, meet in two parts, dealing respectively with legislative and non-legislative acts, and in public when discussing and voting on draft legislation. The foreign ministers also moved the debate on future Council formations in the direction of team presidencies of three member states, which would run the Council configurations, other than foreign affairs, for 18-month periods. The presidencies would be determined according to the principle of equal rotation.

Following strong UK lobbying, the Italian presidency decided drastically to restrict the possibility of changing the Constitution by way of the general *passerelle* clauses, devised in the Convention's final weeks. The *passerelle* idea (which was moved from article I-24 of the Convention draft to part IV of the constitutional treaty) gave the European Council scope to shift decision making in part III of the treaty from unanimity to qualified majority voting by way of a unanimous decision of EU leaders, avoiding lengthy ratification procedures. Whereas the original *passerelle* clause provided for consultation of national parliaments, the UK intervention ensured a single national parliament would be able to block such a move.

Parallel to the IGC, Britain, France and Germany ironed out their differences over defence so that the European Council could reach an agreement to settle relations between the Union and NATO. The EU would set up a strategic planning cell in its military headquarters in Brussels while also creating a presence at SHAPE, the Atlantic alliance's strategic headquarters in Mons, Belgium.

However, there was widespread concern that the IGC was not sufficiently advanced on the difficult institutional issues. After a meeting early in December of former conventionnels, Giscard told the IGC: 'We would rather do without a Constitution than have a bad one.' A sixth foreign ministers' meeting on 9 December was inconclusive. Nonetheless, when the presidency published a 70-page 'consolidated set of proposals' to help the EU's leaders 'reach an overall agreement' at their meeting on 12–13 December,[5] its supporters claimed that Frattini and his team had registered agreement on 82 points, or about 90% of the IGC agenda, in just over two months.

The problem was that the unresolved issues were as intractable as ever. This became abundantly clear as the December meeting dawned. Although Silvio

---

[5] CIG 60/03 and CIG 60/03 ADD 1 of 9 December 2003.

Berlusconi, Italy's prime minister, boasted that he had a 'secret accord in his pocket', few commentators or other leaders took him seriously. The Polish government – weak at home – stepped up its opposition towards the double majority in the Council. Gloom mounted in other national capitals in the absence of any clear idea over how to solve the differences over voting methods in the Council, the extent to which QMV should be used in the Council and the future shape of the Commission.

Although the failure of the Brussels summit was widely anticipated, its rapid collapse on 13 December after less than 24 hours still caused surprise and shock. Failure was brought on by Polish and Spanish insistence on the Nice system of weighted votes in the Council. But the Italian leader's appalling chairmanship also proved a severe handicap. Berlusconi threw the proceedings into confusion by scrapping the pre-planned agenda. He then distinguished himself at Friday's working lunch by inviting his fellow leaders to talk about 'women and football'. Other sexist remarks followed as did a series of futile bilateral meetings in which it became apparent that Berlusconi had no idea how to bring the negotiation to a successful conclusion. As the talks headed towards breakdown, there was an obvious lack of will among the leaders of France, Germany and Britain to push for a compromise.

Observing the debacle, Peter Ludlow[6] attributed the failure to a 'rich mix of incompetence, obduracy and deviousness'. But it was also 'an accident waiting to happen' that reflected the cumulative effect over many years of tensions between small states and large states, and old and new EU members, as well as differences and rivalries among the largest states, with the specific problems of Poland and Spain on top.

The summit's downward spiral revived thoughts of a 'core Europe', with Jacques Chirac again propagating his idea of a 'pioneer group' of countries that would press ahead with integration. As failure loomed, there was a flurry of rumours that France, Germany and other founding members were planning a declaration that would signal the creation of a 'core group'. The speculation proved groundless at the time, although it prompted a scramble among accession country representatives to ensure they would not be left out, with the Czechs and Hungarians making clear their determination not to be put in the same league as the Poles.

---

[6] The European Council and IGC of December 2003. EuroComment Briefing Note, No.2.8. 9 January 2004.

Despite the summit's shambolic end, the heads of state and government avoided mutual recrimination. Nor did they abandon the constitutional treaty. Instead, a brief annex to the conclusions of the meeting asked Ireland, which took over the EU's rotating presidency on 1 January 2004, to carry out consultations and 'make an assessment of the prospect for progress and to report to the European Council in March'.

18.2   IRELAND TAKES OVER

The Irish presidency wasted no time. Led by Bertie Ahern, Ireland's *Taoiseach* or prime minister, the presidency embarked on an intense and wide-ranging series of contacts with all of the Union's existing, acceding and candidate states, as well as with the European Commission and Parliament. Some of the contacts were informal talks at the highest level. Others were at foreign minister level and among senior officials. In the meantime, the legal and technical experts led by Piris continued the process of refining the texts that began under the Italian presidency.

It is doubtful, however, whether such careful preparation would have yielded results had not Europe's political landscape changed dramatically by the time Ahern reported to his fellow EU leaders on 25–26 March.

Al-Qaeda terrorists attacked commuter trains in Madrid during the morning rush hour of 11 March with devastating loss of life. The following weekend, José-Maria Aznar's Partido Popular lost a general election it was expected to win. The new Spanish socialist prime minister, José Luis Rodriguez Zapatero, who had based his campaign in part on a slogan of 'Return to Europe', immediately called for 'accelerated adoption' of a new text. Although some time elapsed before Spain's willingness to negotiate the double majority became clear, Zapatero lost no time in aligning Spain's foreign and EU policies with France and Germany.

The change in Spain had an immediate impact in Warsaw. During the week after the Spanish election, Leszek Miller, the Polish prime minister, made clear he did not want his country to be isolated. 'For an individual loneliness is a very unpleasant mental state,' he told visiting Brussels-based journalists. 'For a country it would be very dangerous.'[7] Following talks with Gerhard Schröder, the German chancellor, on 23 March, Miller said compromise on the constitutional treaty was both necessary and possible.

---

[7] *Financial Times*, 19 March 2004.

In his report to the March Council,[8] Ahern said he believed there was 'a strong shared sense of the desirability of concluding negotiations as soon as possible'. His soundings told him that the 'great bulk of the provisions' of the draft constitutional treaty were not in dispute and that many of the Italian presidency proposals set out in the document of 9 December 'would be the subject of a broad positive consensus in the context of an overall agreement'.

Most of the remaining issues, he felt, 'could be resolved without due difficulty'. Consensus over the minimum seat threshold in the European Parliament could, for example, be reached through a 'modest increase' in the threshold from four seats per member state. But this still left as the 'most difficult issues' the definition and scope of QMV and the size and composition of the Commission. An overall solution would require political will and flexibility.

Ahern made clear that a consensus on the definition of QMV 'must be based on the principle of double majority' in the Council, must allow for greater efficiency and have due regard to balance among the member states and to their specific concerns. Shortly before midnight on Thursday, 25 March, the European Council instructed the Irish presidency to resume and complete the negotiations on the constitutional treaty by the 17 June summit meeting of EU leaders at the latest.

Three days after the EU's 'big bang' enlargement on 1 May 2004, officials from the 25 member states and the three applicant and candidate countries gathered in Dublin to resume work on the constitutional treaty. Dubbed the 'focal points' group, they began working from a document[9] based on the main Italian text of December 2003,[10] which dealt with the less sensitive political questions. Thus began a negotiating procedure based on two sets of texts. One set, placed in the public arena for the first time on 13 May,[11] ventilated issues where the presidency felt consensus was likely in the context of an overall agreement and which could be taken off the negotiating table. The other set, kept out of the public eye until June, contained issues which remained to be resolved. As the talks progressed at different levels, the text where the presidency thought agreement existed grew steadily in bulk and that where problems remained slowly shrank in size.

On 20 May, Ahern completed a third round of discussions with the other European leaders. He underlined that 'only a dual majority outcome can

---

[8] CIG 70/04.
[9] CIG 73/04.
[10] CIG 60/03 ADD 1.
[11] CIG76/04.

command consensus' but indicated adjustments were possible to the QMV formula approved by the Convention. Without making a proposal, Ahern outlined his ideas in a note to foreign ministers ahead of a meeting they would hold on 24 May.

The note[12] contained ideas that had been circulating for some time. It warned that agreement would only be possible by raising the population threshold of the double majority formula from the 60% agreed in the Convention. And because some small states wanted parity or as small a gap as possible between the member state and population thresholds, Ahern concluded that the member state threshold should be increased from the 50% agreed in the Convention 'so as to ensure, at minimum, that the gap between the two is not increased over that proposed by the Convention'.

Ahern pointed to other possible areas of compromise. He noted that existing voting rules in the Council meant abstentions had the same impact as a negative vote and he wondered whether this might not be changed so that abstentions counted as neither positive nor negative. He also reported that the presidency's consultations had thrown up 'interesting suggestions', including some relating to the definition and operation of blocking minorities. A few days before his note, the first reports circulated of an 'emergency brake' that could help the UK and other countries insisting on the retention of unanimity to accept more qualified majority voting.

The scene was thus set for the end-game of the IGC. True, there were at times serious outbreaks of tension, not least in the negotiations among the British, French and German foreign ministers. The issue of the British 'red lines' became far more vexatious after London, in a striking policy U-turn that shocked its EU partners, announced on 20 April that ratification of the constitutional treaty in the UK would be by referendum.

But work continued at 'focal point' and foreign minister level on narrowing differences among the 25 on the less sensitive issues. There were also intensive discussions behind the scenes on more difficult matters. In May and June, Bobby McDonagh, head of EU affairs at the Irish foreign ministry, held two clandestine meetings with senior officials from Britain, France and Germany, which explored ways of achieving a compromise between competing demands for unanimity and more QMV in Council voting.

Ahern embarked on yet another round of visits to sound out the other 24 national leaders ahead of the June summit that was scheduled to wrap up the

---

[12] CIG 77/04.

IGC. His aim too was to narrow down the number of outstanding issues. It was no easy task. When Ahern met Blair over dinner in Downing Street at the beginning of June, he warned that there were around 12 issues outstanding and that if he went to the summit without that number reduced, he would leave Brussels with 20 unresolved. 'As presidency, it is for us to try to find, in a balanced way, compromises that can get everybody on board,' he said after his meeting with Blair. 'Obviously where there are conflicting issues, we have to dissuade people from pursuing them.'

It helped that Ahern loved doing deals. He mastered the details of the negotiation. He had his own ideas on how to solve problems. He listened, proposed, chided and joked – and kept everything very close to his chest. He understood how to run a negotiation on the principle of balancing interests. Thus when pressed to include a reference to Christianity or God in the constitutional treaty, he freely admitted that he too would like to see this in the text. But, he pointed out, one member state (by which he meant France) had a revolution to remove God from its own Constitution and was not prepared to risk another.

While Ahern was cajoling his fellow heads of government, Brian Cowen, Ireland's foreign minister, was making progress. A presidency paper, issued a few days before the General Affairs and External Relations Council of Monday (GAERC) on 14 June in Luxembourg,[13] included 49 items where the presidency believed consensus was possible compared with 43 items in May. During the weekend ahead of the GAERC, the presidency issued a second paper,[14] which suggested compromises for those areas where a shift from unanimity to QMV was proving very difficult. It also put forward new wording on a number of economic questions and proposals for making the Charter of Fundamental Rights acceptable to the UK. Ideas for solving the institutional questions – the definition of qualified majority voting in the Council, the future structure of the Commission and the minimum number of seats per member state in the parliament – were left for later.

The second paper from Cowen's office contained several ingenious proposals to secure consensus on the future scope of QMV. Some of these reflected ideas considered earlier in McDonagh's secret discussions with British, German and French officials. To win UK support for qualified majority voting in the case of EU legislation concerning social security for migrant workers, the presidency proposed an 'emergency brake' provision that would allow a member state facing fundamental problems to halt

---

[13] CIG 79/04.
[14] CIG 80/04.

discussions in the Council for four months and refer the matter to the European Council for arbitration. As if to emphasise the Irish philosophy of balance, similar emergency brakes were coupled with 'accelerator' provisions in the articles dealing with cross-border judicial cooperation and the definition of serious cross-border crime, to speed the enhanced cooperation procedure if at least a third of member states decided they wanted to press on with integration in these areas.

As another carrot for Britain, the presidency proposed dropping the very limited *passerelle* from unanimity to QMV for legislation covering administrative cooperation or combating tax fraud in company taxation. It indicated that the similar measure proposed for turnover taxes, excise duties and other indirect taxation could also be dropped 'in the context of an overall balanced agreement in which all delegations demonstrate some flexibility'.

In the same document, the efficient, no-nonsense Irish presidency dealt a blow to enthusiasts of Europe's classical tradition. Without fanfare, it removed the quotation in ancient Greek by Thucydides that Giscard had placed at the top of the treaty's preamble.

The foreign ministers made good progress on 14 June. Accordingly, the brakes and accelerators appeared in a greatly expanded set of texts, which, in the presidency's view, could form the basis of consensus.[15] This document, published on 16 June, the day before the leaders assembled in Brussels for their summit to complete the IGC, covered 57 topics and ran to 89 pages. At the same time, the presidency produced yet another paper to guide the leaders' negotiations.[16] This, for the first time, broached possible solutions for the disputed institutional issues.

The presidency suggested a qualified majority in the Council should reflect at least 65% of the EU population and no fewer than 55% of the member states. To deal with the objection of small member states that the big countries could gain too much power, a blocking minority would require at least four member states. To help Poland give up its favourable position secured at Nice, it also suggested a special provision to accommodate situations where a group of member states constituting 'somewhat less than a blocking minority was opposed to a particular measure'.

---

[15] CIG 81/04.
[16] CIG 82/04.

Drawing inspiration from a compromise agreed by an earlier generation of EU leaders in Ioannina, Greece, in March 1994, the idea amounted to a cooling-off period in which the Council would do everything in its power to achieve a settlement satisfactory to all. The presidency left open how a reworked Ioannina compromise would operate. It also invited debate on the idea that abstentions should no longer count in calculating a qualified majority.

On the issue of parliamentary seats, the paper proposed a minimum of six per member state. To ease compromise, it suggested possibly raising the number of seats in the parliament from the 736 agreed by the Convention to 745 or 750 and fixing a maximum number per member state.

To balance conflicting demands over the composition of the Commission, it proposed retaining one member per member state until 2014 after which the Commission would consist of 18 commissioners, including the president and foreign minister. This compared with a Commission of 15 in the Convention draft. The 18-strong Commission would be 'chosen according to a system of strictly equal rotation'.

Matters of economic governance accounted for three of the non-institutional issues on the leaders' agenda. The presidency paper proposed giving euro-zone member states the right to recommend new members for the single currency. It contained a reworded treaty article plus a declaration to bridge the differences between France and Germany on the one hand and the Netherlands on the other over the battered stability and growth pact. It also included language, urged by Britain, to emphasise the member states' role in coordinating economic policies.

To satisfy the Dutch government and other net contributors to the EU budget, the presidency proposed that the multi-annual financial framework be agreed unanimously in the Council until such time as the European Council decided to use a *passerelle* and move by unanimity to QMV. The Convention text had provided for QMV after 2014.

The presidency also sought to soothe lingering British concerns that the Charter of Fundamental Rights would undermine UK law. Its document claimed there was consensus on the content of the Charter, on its legal status as part of the Constitution, and 'on the need for the courts when interpreting the Charter to give due regard to the explanations', which the British believed offered protection against any extension of Union powers at the expense of the law of the member states. The presidency therefore proposed wording for the Charter preamble, the constitutional treaty text and a declaration to accompany the treaty that it hoped would boost the status of the explanations in cases of any legal dispute in such a way as to win the support of the UK and the acquiescence of other member states.

The negotiations among the EU leaders began on 17 June under far better auspices than those of December 2003. Spain and Poland were more open to persuasion after the change of government in Madrid. Germany and France signalled early in the round that they wanted agreement, not least to repair some of the damage done to the EU's image in the previous weekend's European elections, which were marked by falling turnout across the Union and antipathy towards incumbents. Unlike December 2003, there was a feeling that success was imperative and failure no longer an option.

But the talks were not easy. Despite goodwill, the main protagonists – and many of the lesser ones – needed tangible gains to take home to win over public opinion. The presidency paper did not offer a complete solution to the question of defining QMV because there were quite sharp divisions in underlying preferences, with many small states wanting the member state and population thresholds to be the same. In addition, some issues that the Irish thought practically resolved had to be discussed anew, mainly because of UK sensitivities.

There were some practical difficulties, linked mainly to the need to translate complex texts during the negotiation into the working languages of the expanded Union of 25 member states. More worrying, the summit was punctuated by a blistering row during Thursday's dinner over who should be the candidate for Commission president to follow Romano Prodi. The discussion, which saw the eclipse of the candidacy of Guy Verhofstadt, the Belgian prime minister, was marked by some deeply unpleasant exchanges, especially between Blair on the one hand and Schröder and Chirac, who supported Verhofstadt, on the other.

Paradoxically, the bad blood over the Commission candidacy[17] helped promote agreement on the constitutional treaty when the IGC negotiations resumed on the following day. One official described how the French and German leaders were 'eerily' subdued, perhaps because they reckoned that the EU could not easily live down a double failure at the summit.

The presidency produced a new document for the talks,[18] which, for the first time, included draft articles defining the double majority method of voting in the Council and the rules for the system of blocking minorities. It also

---

[17] Which resulted in the leaders putting off a decision until later in the month.
[18] CIG 83/04.

bumped up the number of annexes dealing with non-institutional issues from 7 to 14. A two-hour meeting of the IGC at summit level in the morning and over lunch was followed by six hours of bilateral and trilateral 'confessionals' between Ahern and the other leaders. Much of the late negotiation was taken up by UK demands for tighter wording in the constitutional treaty on the Charter and economic policy coordination.

In the evening, the presidency drafted its 'final' offer,[19] which, it said, constituted 'the basis for an overall and balanced agreement which should allow for the adoption of the draft treaty establishing a Constitution for Europe'. The expansion of this text to include 19 non-institutional annexes also reflected the UK's concerns on energy policy, Eurojust and other internal security issues that had resurfaced over the day.

When the document was presented to the plenary session of heads of state and government shortly before 22.00 on Friday, there was – unusually – an ovation for Ahern. 'We knew we were there,' one official recalled afterwards, 'because no member state would dare to unlock the deal after that.' Three declarations were added to the text to satisfy outstanding British and Dutch concerns. At around 22.30 on 18 June 2004, the leaders agreed a final version of the presidency document.[20] The IGC negotiations were over. Europe's constitutional treaty had crossed another hurdle. It was time to open the champagne.

18.3   THE CHANGES WROUGHT BY THE IGC

Compromise in the IGC came at the cost of extra complications to the draft constitutional treaty. This was especially the case for the rules covering qualified majority voting in the Council on which the December 2003 IGC at head of government level had foundered.

The double majority, as agreed by the Convention, was a simple concept that captured the EU's essence as a Union of states and peoples. The double majority remains central to article I-25[21] of the treaty. But, if it takes effect

---

[19] CIG 84/04.

[20] CIG 85/04.

[21] To avoid confusion and assist the reader cross-refer to the constitutional treaty text. This and following chapters use the article numbers adopted in the final official version of the constitutional treaty, published as C310 of the Official Journal of the EU on 16 December 2004. These are the numbers used in square brackets earlier in the text. At the time of the negotiation, the leaders were using provisional numbering based on documents CIG 50/03 and CIG 81/04.

as planned on 1 November 2009, the double majority will require minimum thresholds of 55% of member states and 65% of the Union's population, compared with 50 and 60% respectively in the Convention text. In cases where the Council will not act on a proposal of the Commission or the Union foreign minister, the minimum qualified majority will be 72% of member states representing at least 65% of Union population compared with two-thirds and three-fifths previously.

A late intervention by Wolfgang Schüssel, the Austrian chancellor, added a rider that 'at least 15' member states will be needed for a qualified majority. This condition will narrow the gap between the two thresholds should EU membership stay at 25 after the constitutional treaty takes effect. The presidency had earlier ensured that a blocking minority would need at least four Council members. The presidency's idea that abstentions should no longer count as 'no' votes, which would have simplified procedure in the Council, foundered on German objections at the June 2004 summit.

The Ioannina-style 'cooling off' compromise that was designed to help member states belonging to a minority resolve their special problems is tortuous in its detail. A separate declaration says member states with less than a blocking minority but representing three-quarters of such a minority in terms of population or numbers of member states will be able to call on the Council 'to do all in its power' within reason to find an answer to their problem.

The emergency brake that will allow a member state to delay a contentious issue by referring it to the European Council appears in three articles – covering social security for mobile workers [III-136], laws on cross-border police and judicial cooperation in criminal matters [III-270] and minimum rules for the definition of serious crimes and penalties [III-271]. In the latter two cases, the IGC approved the accelerator to allow at least one-third of member states to adopt the stalled measure by way of enhanced cooperation after a year's procrastination.

These new arrangements stripped the Convention text of its simplicity compared with the arcane Nice system of weighted votes in the Council. But they still mean the EU will be able to enlarge without having to revise the Council voting rules each time. How far they will pose an operational problem is unclear because voting in the Council has so far been rare.

By contrast, the IGC improved the Convention's proposals for the composition of the Commission, which were criticised as complex and unworkable by many, including the Commission itself. The final compromise modified the Irish presidency proposals for a reduced college of commissioners so that, according to article I-26, the number of commissioners will correspond to two-thirds of the number of member states from 1 November 2014 unless the European Council decides to overturn this solution by unanimity. The compromise retains one commissioner per member state for the first Commission appointed under the constitutional treaty – in other words, until 2014.

From 2009 there will be a maximum of 750 members of the European Parliament, with no member state having fewer than six. This concession to the small member states in article I-20 was helped by Germany giving up three of its existing seats and agreeing to a maximum of 96 seats per member state – a decision that could be of considerable importance if and when Turkey joins the Union.

In some cases, the IGC reversed Convention provisions for decisions by QMV and reinstated unanimity in the Council in response to objections by Britain and its allies.   The IGC completely scrapped the Convention proposals for limited *passerelles* in tax policy (III-62 and III-63 of the Convention text), thus cementing the idea that taxes would remain a national prerogative in the EU. Marking a success for the UK Treasury and City of London, the Council will need unanimous agreement before the European Central Bank can be given the job of prudential supervision over banks and other financial institutions under article III-185. The final wording of article I-54 preserved unanimity for the UK's EU budget rebate won in fierce negotiations in the 1980s by Margaret Thatcher.

By accepting Dutch demands that decisions on the multi-annual financial framework [I-55] must be decided by unanimity, the IGC has ensured that Union member states will be periodically plunged into extremely difficult negotiations on a very important issue. However, Jan Peter Balkenende, the Netherlands' prime minister, added a unilateral declaration to the treaty making clear that The Hague will support a *passerelle* to QMV once its excessive net contribution to the EU budget has been corrected.

The IGC also agreed that unanimity will apply in the common commercial policy [III-315] where trade agreements in the areas of social, education and health services 'risk seriously disturbing the national organisation of such services' and could upset the responsibility of member states to deliver them. This clause reduced the scope of QMV in favour of the principle adopted for France's cultural exception in the final hours of the Convention.

On balance, however, the constitutional treaty will increase the scope of qualified majority voting in the Council and provide for much greater involvement of the European Parliament as a co-legislator, with rights equal to those of the Council.

According to a European Parliament report on the treaty[22], the text as agreed by the IGC will move 17 legal bases[23] to qualified majority voting in the Council from unanimity. More than half [articles III-263, III-265 to III-267, III-270 to III-273, III-275 and III-276] are related to the EU's area of freedom, justice and security, and include such important issues as asylum and immigration.

QMV will apply to 26 legal bases, which are new. These include policies on sport, tourism, civil protection, human health, services of general interest and the exploration and exploitation of space, where the constitutional treaty defines scope for EU action for the first time. Six cover aspects of the EU's policies on external action, including the location and statute of the European Defence Agency [III-311, paragraph 2] and details of structured cooperation in EU defence policy [III-312, paragraphs 2, 3 and 4].

The treaty includes 86 legal bases where decisions will be taken by the ordinary legislative procedure (hitherto known as codecision). In about half these cases, which involve QMV in the Council and approval by Parliament as an equal partner, the legal base is either new or has been changed to give Parliament equal powers. The nine articles covering freedom, security and justice in part III that, in future, will be decided by QMV, include many specific provisions where Parliament will be involved as an equal co-legislator instead of just being consulted by the Council. Parliament also gains equal rights as co-legislator in article III-231 for setting the rules of the common agricultural policy.

The EU's annual budget [article III-404] will be determined by an ad hoc procedure akin to codecision. In five areas, the Council will decide by unanimity but with Parliament's consent. In 17 cases, unanimity will prevail among member states with Parliament being consulted.

About 70 legal bases remain subject to unanimity among the member states, according to Parliament's report. Countries such as the UK, Sweden and Estonia held out against dilution of national sovereignty over tax and social policy. Foreign policy will stay overwhelmingly intergovernmental and almost entirely subject to unanimity. Among new policy areas, unanimity

---

[22] Report on the Treaty establishing a Constitution for Europe. Ref A6-0070/2005.
[23] The technical term for articles that give the Union the right to act and which describe the type of decision making and voting procedure used.

will apply to decisions of the Council to create a European public prosecutor's office [III-274] to deal with financial crimes against the EU and to any eventual decision of the European Council to broaden the office's powers to deal with serious cross-border crime.

On the other hand, the treaty should allow greater flexibility through enhanced cooperation and the various *passerelle* clauses. These provisions should partially offset the tendency of the IGC to opt for more unanimity compared with the Convention.

A potentially significant article, approved by the IGC, is III-422, which allows a group of countries in enhanced cooperation, that are pursuing a policy normally subject to unanimous decision making, to shift to decision making by QMV. This change is a radical step that could promote the emergence of pioneer groups of countries integrating far faster than the rest, even in taboo areas such as taxation. However, it will require unanimous agreement among the member states concerned and cannot apply to decisions with military or defence implications.

The IGC agreed small but significant changes to some important articles in part I. Article I-2 on the Union's values was amended to add a reference to equality between women and men, while Hungary won inclusion of a reference to the rights of minorities. Price stability was added to the Union's objectives in I-3, meeting a request of the European Central Bank. Article I-5 on relations between the Union and member states underlined the equality of member states before the Constitution. Details of the Union's symbols were brought forward from part IV to article I-8. As a result of UK pressure in the final round of negotiations, articles I-12 and I-15 put member states more firmly in the saddle when coordinating economic policies. The importance of 'ensuring the continuity of the Community acquis' was underlined in the preamble in response to integrationist demands.

The IGC tidied up the language of the Convention draft. Article I-1 no longer contained the rather odd reference to the 'Community way'. Instead, its all-important first paragraph said: 'Reflecting the will of the citizens and States of Europe to build a common future, this Constitution establishes the European Union, on which the member states confer competences to attain objectives they have in common. The Union shall coordinate the policies by which the member states aim to achieve these objectives, and shall exercise on a Community basis the competences they confer on it.'

Despite heavy lobbying from the church and Europe's Christian parties, the IGC did not include any reference to God or Europe's Christian heritage in the final text. However, Giscard's preamble was rewritten to include a mention of Europe's past 'bitter experiences' to counter criticism that the original gave a one-sided, positive account of its history.

CHAPTER 19
The Challenge of Ratification

19.1   BRITAIN AND THE IGC

Just as Giscard made it a priority to secure UK support for the Convention's work, a major pre-occupation of Bertie Ahern was to ensure Britain obtained satisfaction in the IGC. It was no easy task as Britain's 'red lines' tended to grow as the negotiations progressed.

It was the view of most participants and observers that Britain had a successful Convention. The UK used the Convention to promote and protect its interests. Peter Hain, the government's conventionnel, was able to resist pressure for a communitisation of tax, social and foreign policy while Giscard made a special effort to keep the UK within the consensus – as when he agreed to the dropping of the word 'federal' from article 1 at a meeting with Blair in May 2003.

Britain secured its goal of a stable president of the European Council, albeit with limited powers compared with London's early ambitions that would have turned the individual into a 'boss of bosses' in the Union. Conversely, Britain appeared to accept the Charter of Fundamental Rights after securing assurances that it could not be used to undermine the UK's laws covering the labour market, tax and social security.

Indeed, Britain won grudging respect from mainstream Convention members by playing a defensive game without resorting to alliances with the eurosceptics among the conventionnels or supporting those small states, led by Austria, which at one point were threatening to push for options in the final text rather than a single recommendation. In general, the UK played the Convention game fully and fairly.

Blair's government appeared to recognise that the Convention results were, on balance, favourable for the UK in its White Paper [1] outlining the British approach to the intergovernmental conference. 'Let me be clear,' Blair wrote, 'the Convention's end product – a draft constitutional treaty for the European Union – is good news for Britain.'

---

[1] 'A constitutional treaty for the EU', September 2003, CM5934.

But UK caution was also evident in Blair's follow-up observation: 'The Convention text spells out that the EU is a union of nation-states and that it only has those powers which governments have chosen to confer upon it. It is not and will not be a federal superstate.'

On the one hand, the White Paper listed several positive features of the Convention draft. It would 'build an efficient, transparent and accountable EU, equipped to meet the challenges of the 21st century'. But the document concluded on a downbeat note when it said 'the government will not sign up to any treaty which does not, in its view, advance Britain's interests'.

There were some specific reservations, many of which would become 'red lines' across which the UK was not prepared to budge. The White Paper signalled concern about the Convention text on the EU's own resources, which UK officials saw as a ruse to undermine the British budget rebate. The paper was adamant that national parliaments should have their say over treaty change – a position threatened by the Convention's *passerelle* proposal. Unanimity should be the general rule for common foreign and security policy and was vital for tax and social security. It was wary about creating the title of foreign minister for the combined Patten and Solana job. It was sceptical about the Charter of Fundamental Rights and promised a final decision on its incorporation into the draft constitutional treaty 'only in the light of the overall picture at the IGC'.

To some extent, this downbeat tone was a sign that the foreign office, under the leadership of a more euro-wary Jack Straw, had regained control of the negotiations and UK news management in the IGC. But it was also consistent with a wider lack of support in the UK government for the result that Hain brought back from the Convention.

Gordon Brown, the chancellor, took to sniping at the draft treaty and rallying his Ecofin colleagues in opposition to it. Apparently forgetting that she, as a member of the Praesidium, was partly responsible for the draft treaty, Gisela Stuart, the Labour MP and House of Commons conventionnel, wrote a polemical critique of the Convention and its outcome.[2] Published just before the December IGC, it said she was not convinced the proposed Constitution 'will meet the needs of an expanding Europe'.

Unease grew in the City and among business leaders as examination of part III, which had been rushed through the Convention, threw up areas of concern. The idea that the European Central Bank should be given powers to

---

[2] The Making of Europe's Constitution, the Fabian Society, December 2003.

supervise banks and financial institutions by QMV reminded many of earlier French government plans for an EU-wide financial regulator that could pose a threat to Britain's financial services business. The Convention proposals for a Union policy on energy were widely interpreted as a thinly disguised ploy by other member states to gain control of North Sea oil in a crisis. Britain's eurosceptic press and a well-organised and persuasive 'no' campaign had a field day, cherry-picking the Convention text to highlight supposed threats to the British way of life posed by the new European 'superstate'. Frequent reference was made to article II-88 of the Charter, which included the right to strike, but usually without mention that this had to be 'in accordance with Union law and national law and practices'.

The government was notably silent in the face of this hostility. It appeared quietly relieved by the failure of the Brussels summit in December 2003. For Tony Blair, who had once deemed the constitutional treaty more important than Iraq, an increasingly difficult issue had been kicked into the long grass – without Britain having to shoulder any blame.

But any sense of calm was quickly dispelled by the Madrid bombings and the election of the new Spanish government on 14 March. The draft Constitution moved back onto the UK's domestic political agenda. There was mounting pressure on the government from the eurosceptic press, the Conservative opposition and pressure groups to allow a referendum.

'I can only go one way. I've not got a reverse gear,' Blair told the annual conference of his governing Labour Party on 30 September 2003. Just over six months later, he discovered his reverse gear on the constitutional treaty. On 20 April 2004, he announced Britain would hold a referendum on the planned treaty after parliament had debated and decided upon it.

It was a remarkable turnaround. The September 2003 White Paper said a referendum was not necessary because the reforms proposed by the Convention did 'not alter the fundamental, constitutional relationship between member states and the Union'. The prime minister's new message was: 'Let the people have the final say.'

Blair now said the government needed 'to confront head on' what he described as a 'partially at least, successful campaign to persuade Britain that Europe is a conspiracy aimed at us rather than a partnership designed for us and others to pursue our national interest properly in a modern, interdependent world'. But there were also short-term considerations in play. He wanted to deprive the Conservatives of the referendum issue in the campaign for the June 2004 European elections.

Also important was the weakening of Blair's own political position at the time. His decision came against a background of opposition inside the parliamentary Labour party to his domestic UK reform agenda and ongoing problems in Iraq, which weakened his authority. More eurosceptical colleagues inside the government gained in strength. Straw, it emerged afterwards, played a key role in persuading Blair to opt for a referendum.

There was also an impulsive side to the prime minister's change of mind. His decision was made without great discussion or consideration. Blair didn't bother to consult his cabinet before having his intentions leaked to the eurosceptic Murdoch press: indeed he had to begin the cabinet meeting that gathered after the news became known with an apology.

Blair's announcement produced some short-term gain. It blunted the opposition Conservative party's attacks on the government in the run-up to the European elections. But those elections also showed the danger of taking a defensive stance on Europe. The Labour party experienced its lowest support in an election for decades while 16% of those who decided to vote opted for the United Kingdom Independence Party. UKIP – which returned 12 of Britain's 78 MEPs – is committed to taking the UK out of the EU.

Blair's abrupt *volte face* had an impact on the conduct of the IGC. The negotiations became more abrasive. The term 'red lines', once banned by the UK foreign office as too confrontational, became accepted shorthand for the UK's negotiating position. In May, Joschka Fischer, the German foreign minister, accused the UK of using 'salami tactics' to slice off more concessions from its partners. French and German officials complained that the UK was using the referendum to make new changes to the text.

There was, of course, some special pleading on their part. The UK, which claimed it secured all its key negotiating goals in the June 2004 session of the IGC, would not have done so without the help of other member states. Like the UK, many new member states did not wish to cede sovereignty over core areas of government, such as taxation, social security and defence. They were suspicious of Franco-German pretensions to lead the EU. The UK was also lucky that Ireland held the presidency in the crucial months of the negotiation. Although it had to observe the rules of balance and neutrality, the Irish presidency had a vested interest in the UK securing its aims on tax and social policy.

But to a large extent, the UK was engaged in a different negotiation than its EU partners. It was neutral on the key issue of double majority voting in the Council. Blair's statement to the press at the end of negotiations on 18 June 2004 made only passing reference to the changes in the way the EU would work. Its main message was that 'in those areas where it is essential that we retain the ultimate power, we retain that power'.

Blair's account of the conference was interesting for the narrowly partisan way he reviewed the UK's membership of the EU. In tone, his remarks were a world away from the speeches on the EU that he delivered in Warsaw in October 2000 and in Cardiff in November 2002.

> So for example, in relation to economic policy, that remains in the control of the nation-state. The veto on tax is kept, so taxes cannot be harmonised. The veto on social security is kept, foreign policy and defence is still subject to unanimity. We retain, of course, full control of our armed forces. We retain our veto over our budget rebate and the negotiations about the future financing of the Union. And the Charter of Rights is expressed specifically in such a way that it means that the industrial relations law of our country cannot be altered by the European Court of Justice through the Charter of Fundamental Rights.

The prime minister went on to claim that:

> It is absolutely clear that those countries that have come together to make this treaty recognise that for us and for others it is essential that Britain, and the British view of Europe, remains in place, that this is a Europe of nation-states cooperating with each other, it is not some federal superstate.

Some elsewhere in Europe agreed with him. 'Whatever people say, this text remains a British victory,' commented *Le Monde* of France after the final negotiations. The Belgian daily *Le Soir* described the constitutional treaty 'as a text in the service of Her Majesty'.

Perhaps the biggest compliment came from Laurent Fabius, the former French socialist prime minister, who launched a campaign to turn the French Socialist party against the constitutional treaty on the grounds that it was too supportive of liberal 'Anglo-Saxon' economic policies.

19.2   THE UK REFERENDUM

Blair's government has decided the British referendum will be held in 2006. The electorate will be asked: 'Should the United Kingdom approve the treaty establishing a Constitution for the European Union?'

To some extent, the timetable reflects pressure of other events: a general election and Britain's presidency of the Group of Eight nations in 2005, and of the EU in the second half of the year. But the plan for the UK to be among the last to decide on the constitutional treaty is also a measure of how risky Britain's referendum is in the face of strongly entrenched euroscepticism.

When announcing the referendum, Blair indicated that he wanted the poll to be a plebiscite over UK membership of the EU. He told the House of Commons on 20 April: 'The question will be on the treaty. But the implications go far wider. It is time to resolve once and for all whether this country, Britain, wants to be at the centre of European decision making or not; time to decide whether our destiny lies as a leading partner and ally of Europe or on its margins.'[3]

But even if the prime minister can define the debate in these terms to circumvent widespread public ignorance about the finer points of the treaty, there are daunting hurdles ahead.

The UK has not held a national referendum since 1975 when the vote was on the clear and relatively simple issue of whether Britain should remain a member of the European Communities, which it had recently joined. That plebiscite – the first and only national referendum so far in UK history – resulted in a 'yes' vote. But the position for the pro-Europe lobby was in many ways more favourable than today.

In 1975, Britain had much to learn from Europe in economic terms. At that time, the UK was clearly the economic 'sick man of Europe' with inflation of more than 25% and the International Monetary Fund about to impose a stringent economic austerity programme in return for much needed credits. Although the rest of the EC, like Britain, was suffering the effects of the 1973 oil shock, it had a track record of economic success.

Thirty years on, and the economic picture is largely reversed. Parts of the euro-zone lag behind Britain's economy, with growth and employment in Germany, Italy and France comparing unfavourably with that in the UK. Why, the argument goes, should the UK, which has prospered outside the single currency, be more closely aligned with countries that are less successful?

Political conditions are also very different. The Conservative party, which took Britain into the EC, will campaign against the constitutional treaty. A constant barrage of negative reporting about the EU in a large section of Britain's press has left its mark on British public opinion. The eurosceptic

---

[3] Statement to Parliament on the EU White Paper and the EU Constitution. www.number-10.gov.uk

bias of the influential British print media has grown, especially among the tabloids.

The visceral opposition of the *Sun*, the UK's most powerful tabloid, to the EU is especially problematic for Blair. Traditionally right-wing, it supported the prime minister before his first landslide election victory in 1997. Britain's Labour government has since made it a high – if not overriding – priority to stay in the good books of the Murdoch press which owns the *Sun*, the *Times*, the *Sunday Times* and the *News of the World*, limiting the government's will and ability to combat eurosceptic myths.

In the *Sun*'s view, the constitutional treaty threatens the achievements of a thousand years of British history. The newspaper's tendency to hark back to Britain's past glories points to a special facet of British euroscepticism. It is able to feed on historical exceptions and perceptions of potent force of which three are especially significant.

One is the Second World War. Until the Soviet Union and the US entered the war, Britain stood alone against Hitler. It emerged on the winning side. It was never occupied. It never suffered the brutal loss of sovereignty that occupation entails and that most other EU member states have suffered. Although worn out and effectively bankrupt in 1945, Britain never took the view that it was as much a loser from that conflict as any of the other European belligerents.

Even after making allowance for special circumstances, such as the 60th anniversary of the end of the war in 2005, the Second World War remains a remarkably strong feature of British cultural life. It is embedded romantically in the collective memory as the nation's finest hour – a triumph of good over evil. The war is re-fought almost daily in the broadcast media. The important consequence for the constitutional treaty and the referendum is that issues of sovereignty (and the feared loss of it) play a much bigger role in British politics than in many other EU member states.

A second historical exception concerns the timing and circumstances of British entry into the Union. Britain was rejected when it first applied to join the club in 1961. When the UK did finally join the EC in 1973, the years of early, strong economic growth had given way to stagnation, inflation and rising unemployment. Unlike the founding nations and most of the later joiners, entry into the EU was not associated with a 'success experience' in the UK.

For citizens of the original six, membership of the EC meant rising prosperity and more choice in the shops. In Greece, Spain and Portugal, which joined after Britain, it offered the prospect of catching up with a higher level of prosperity and a guarantee against the return of dictatorship. For the former Communist countries of eastern and central Europe, the EU holds out hope of prosperity and provides security.

In the UK, membership of the EC brought complaints about rising food prices, which were not stilled by Harold Wilson's artfully managed 'renegotiation' of membership that culminated in the 1975 referendum. Indeed, Wilson's renegotiation turned out to be a sham. It left serious issues, such as the excessive UK budget contributions, unaddressed. These were tackled by an altogether more abrasive prime minister – Margaret Thatcher – in the 1980s in a bruising campaign that accentuated the difference in attitude between Britain and other members of the European Communities.

A further important and enduring historical influence has been the failure of the UK political class to make clear the political nature of the EU to the British people since joining the EC. The EC was always known in the UK as the 'Common Market' – indicating an overwhelmingly economic purpose. When other member states pursued a political agenda, commentators were quick to cry foul and raise the spectre of a 'superstate' that sought to trample on ancient liberties.

The myth in the UK of the European Union as a superstate in preparation has proved impossible to eradicate. There are good grounds for arguing that the superstate has been in retreat as a realistic scenario for the EU since the Maastricht Treaty of the early 1990s. But the myth lives on and helps explain the hostility of many Britons to the constitutional treaty.

The superstate myth gives the opponents of the constitutional treaty an immensely strong platform from which to operate. If provisions in the treaty are evaluated in the context of a Europe moving towards a superstate or 'ever closer union', they appear far more of a threat to the status quo in Britain than if they are evaluated in the light of the EU as it is: a confusing hybrid of the federal and the intergovernmental in which governments pool some powers and retain others to cooperate on policies, and which draws its legitimacy from the member states and the citizen. The superstate myth informs much of what passes for debate on the constitutional treaty in the UK and government appears powerless to rebut it.

Indeed, Eurobarometer polls point to a British electorate that is at best ignorant and, more often, alienated from the EU. A flash survey on the eve of the 2004 European elections found that only 14% of Britons knew that 25 countries now belonged to the EU. A more in-depth poll of the-then 15 member states earlier in 2004 found Britons the least trusting of EU institutions and the least supportive of EU membership.

Eurobarometer surveyed 25,000 EU citizens in the 25 member states in November 2004[4] just after the signing ceremony in Rome and found that only the citizens of Cyprus knew less about the constitutional treaty than Britons. In the UK, 50% of those polled had never heard of the Constitution. A further 44% knew about it but very little of its contents. Only in Britain was there a majority opposing the text among those expressing a view for or against the Constitution.[5]

Securing a 'yes' vote in Britain's referendum will be difficult. The level of understanding about EU matters suggests the need for a vigorous information campaign about the constitutional treaty. Yet there was no sign of any such effort after the UK's successful defence of its 'red lines' in the IGC, just as there was no orchestration of support for the Convention text following Hain's successful negotiations in Brussels.

It will not be easy for the UK government to instil in the British people the enthusiasm necessary for a positive referendum vote after a defensive negotiation in which Britain accentuated the risks to its way of life posed by draft treaty texts. In his post-IGC press conference on 18 June 2004, Tony Blair was asked how he would turn round British public opinion. The question was left unanswered.

19.3 THE RATIFICATION CHALLENGE

According to article IV-447, the constitutional treaty is due to enter force on 1 November 2006. That, however, presupposes that all 25 signatories will have ratified it.

Ratification will not be easy. Ten countries - the Czech Republic, Denmark, France, Ireland, Luxembourg, the Netherlands, Poland, Portugal, Spain and the UK - have signalled they will hold referendums on the treaty and several of these will be problematical. Other member states will rely on parliamentary votes, where an upset is less likely.

---

[4] Eurobarometer Special 214 'The future Constitutional Treaty' published January 2005.
[5] UK: opposed 30%, for 20%, no response 50%. EU 25: opposed 16%, for 49%, no response 35%.

The first referendum took place in Spain, a strongly pro-EU country, on 20 February 2005 and produced mixed tidings for the Constitution's supporters. While 77% voted in favour of the constitutional treaty, only 42% of voters bothered to go to the polls. A glitzy campaign failed to make up for widespread ignorance about the Constitution.

By the time the Spanish voted, three other countries had ratified the treaty by parliamentary votes. Lithuania was the first, approving it in November 2004 by 84 votes in favour to 4 against, with 3 abstentions. Hungary followed in December with 322 votes to 12 and 4 abstentions. Slovenia approved the treaty on 1 February 2005 by 79 votes to 4 with 7 abstentions.

All referendums have an element of risk because they offer an opportunity to voters to ignore the subject under scrutiny in favour of a general protest against whoever is in power. While the British referendum outcome is the most in doubt, the Polish and Czech polls are also uncertain. When, in January 2005, members of the European Parliament approved the constitutional treaty by 500 votes to 137 with 40 abstentions, only a minority of MEPs from each of the three countries were in favour of it.

In Poland, however, there was an improvement in public support for the EU during 2004, reflecting an inflow of foreign investment since accession and the arrival of EU funds for Polish farmers. But uniquely in Poland, the referendum must attract a turn out of at least 50% to be valid. This could prove difficult in the light of the Spanish experience.

The Czech Republic is expected to be one of the last to hold a referendum in 2006. Although the Eurobarometer poll carried out in November 2004, suggested that nearly twice as many Czechs support the constitutional treaty as oppose it,[6] only 19% said they would be certain to vote. Adding to the uncertain outlook is the position of the Czech president, Vaclav Klaus, who has said of the Constitution: 'I am not critical. I am 100% against.' A vitriolic eurosceptic, Klaus has charged that the treaty would create a 'superior entity that will make us abandon our national democracy, sovereignty and political independence'.[7]

Among the other referendum nations, there are two – Denmark and Ireland – where voters have previously voted down important EU decisions.[8] In July 2004, Jacques Chirac very reluctantly bowed to pressure for a referendum in

---

[6] Eurobarometer Special 214: 39% in favour against 20% opposed.
[7] Financial Times, 22 February 2005.
8 Danish voted against the Maastricht Treaty in June 1992 and membership of the euro in September 2000. Ireland rejected the Treaty of Nice in June 2001.

France following the UK decision.[9] The political picture in France is clouded by high unemployment, popular disenchantment with President Chirac and the country's centre-right government, and widespread opposition to the prospect of Turkish membership of the EU. Although the prospects for a 'yes' vote brightened after Laurent Fabius failed in December 2004 to make opposition to the constitutional treaty official Socialist party policy, opinion polls pointed to growing support for opponents of the constitutional treaty in the early weeks of 2005.

The Dutch referendum will be the first national referendum in the country's history and will come after several years in which that country's once enthusiastic support for the EU has waned. The referendum in Luxembourg will be the first since 1937 but is unlikely to bring any upset.

Officially, there is no 'plan B'. But even before the constitutional treaty was signed on 29 October 2004, foreign ministries across the EU began weighing scenarios in case it is rejected by one or more member states. If there is one thing officials can agree on, it is that all the options so far identified carry heavy political costs, while some aired in public are illegal or impractical or both.

The final declaration attached to the treaty makes the European Council responsible for a rescue effort if, two years after signing, four-fifths of the member states have ratified the treaty and one or more 'have encountered difficulties in proceeding with ratification'.

Although, in theory, all member states are equal, the response to any rejection would depend on many variables, including the size of the member state, whether more than one state has rejected the treaty, the length of EU membership and whether rejection reflects popular disapproval of too much or too little integration. The response to any 'no' vote in a referendum would have to take account of the scale of the rejection and whether the campaign focused on the details of the constitutional treaty or the broad issue of EU membership.

There are precedents for reversing negative referendum votes. Denmark in the case of the Maastricht Treaty and Ireland after its 'no' vote against the Nice Treaty held fresh polls which passed the measures after diplomatic efforts in the EU to ease popular concerns, and more energetic and effective

---

[9] As of mid-March 2005, referendums were fixed for the following dates: France, 29 May 2005; the Netherlands, 1 June 2005; Luxembourg, 10 July 2005; Denmark 27 September 2005.

campaigning at home. But such action is only feasible in small countries and where rejection is an isolated phenomenon in the Union as a whole. It would be politically inconceivable for the UK or France to embark on a new referendum if the constitutional treaty is rejected by voters.

Another option could be to allow the constitutional treaty to enter force provisionally while renegotiating the parts that prompted rejection in one or more countries. The problem here is that the new negotiations would need the goodwill of all countries, including those that had ratified the treaty in full and would be unwilling to unwind often hard-fought agreements.

An alternative plan to stay with the Nice Treaty, while introducing aspects of the constitutional treaty, would require the consent of those countries that had rejected the treaty. The solution would be difficult to operate, hard to sell politically in the rejectionist states and, at best, only limited in scope.

A variation on this theme could see integration-minded countries using the enhanced cooperation provisions in the EU treaty to advance certain policies. However, the existing enhanced cooperation rules agreed in the Treaties of Amsterdam and Nice have never been used because they are so complex, while a special dispensation would be required to use the more flexible rules in the constitutional treaty.

One superficially appealing idea would be for some member states to go ahead and adopt the constitutional treaty, which others have rejected. But in the view of many experts, this 'treaty within a treaty' option would be legally and practically impossible. So too would the idea of a forced withdrawal of rejecting countries, which would plunge the EU into a deep, if not terminal, crisis.

A more hopeful option would be for dissenting countries to withdraw voluntarily from the EU, leaving member states accepting the Constitution to forge ahead. This approach would be legally possible but would require the cooperation of the departing country or countries. The only territory to have withdrawn from the EU so far is Greenland.

The copper-bottomed legal option in the event of a rejection is to accept the rule that ratification has to be unanimous among the member states and drop the constitutional treaty. This, however, would alienate the European Parliament, the Commission and the member states that had ratified the treaty and be sure to leave the Union in a deep crisis.

It is likely that ideas for creating a 'core Europe' or a pioneer group of countries would come to the fore in the event of an unenthusiastic member state such as Britain rejecting the treaty. Core Europe has a fairly lengthy pedigree in France and Germany and has spawned ideas of a union between the two countries.[10] Although there is no legal base for such a move, the flurry of interest in core Europe that surfaced when the December 2003 IGC summit failed suggests there could be considerable political momentum behind launching core Europe initiatives as a pragmatic response to crisis.

As a general rule, the bigger the country saying 'no', the more difficult a solution will be. A rejection by France in its referendum would be a crisis for the Union as a whole and could kill off the constitutional treaty. A rejection by the UK in 2006, at the end of the ratification process and following approval by all or nearly all other member states, would be a crisis – but a crisis for Britain, and for its relations with the rest of Europe.

---

[10] For example, in a paper by Pascal Lamy and Günter Verheugen, respectively French and German commissioners, in January 2003.

CHAPTER 20
'A Constitution for Europe'

20.1   AN ACCIDENTAL CONSTITUTION

The negotiations that resulted in the 'Treaty establishing a Constitution for Europe' were a tale of the unexpected. The Convention's chemistry was always volatile. Many of its turning points were unpredictable. The 'cliff-hanger' ending to the Praesidium meeting late on 9 July 2003 was just the last of many events that could have ended differently – and in failure. The Intergovernmental Conference that followed had its fair share of drama and farce and changed course dramatically after the appalling terrorist attacks on Madrid.

The draft constitutional treaty that Giscard handed to the Italian presidency in Rome on 18 July 2003 was in many ways an accidental Constitution. It was far from preordained. The Laeken declaration envisaged a less ambitious final document 'which may comprise either different options, indicating the degree of support which they received, or recommendations if consensus is achieved'. The Convention's first big surprise came in the opening ceremony, when Giscard announced his goal of a 'broad consensus on a single proposal' for a 'constitutional treaty for Europe'.

There was nothing inevitable about the Convention's other key turning points. Work on the first 'skeleton' draft began because of pressure from impatient rank and file members of the Convention, led by the Austrian alternate, Maria Berger. Sir John Kerr was inclined to leave such drafting until early in 2003, by which time the Commission's Penelope document would have shaped discussions.

There was nothing predestined in the autumn 2002 'invasion of the foreign ministers', an event which changed the dynamics of the Convention, although not quite turning it into an IGC. Would Joschka Fischer of Germany and Dominique de Villepin of France have joined the Convention in the late autumn of 2002, had not Britain – of all countries – taken the Convention seriously from the beginning and posted Peter Hain, an effective politician as its conventionnel?

Another important turning point was the January 2003 Franco-German paper on institutional reform, in which Germany accepted a stable president for the European Council in return for France backing a Commission president elected by the European Parliament. This was not the preferred solution of Joschka Fischer, Germany's representative in the Convention. But the deal was done at a higher level than foreign ministers by Jacques Chirac and Gerhard Schröder, with the German chancellor, not for the first time, deferring to the president of France.

The paper determined the structure of all subsequent debate on the institutional issue, even providing the base for Giscard's far more radical ideas at the end of April 2003. Its proposal for a stable presidency of the European Council provided common ground for the big countries, otherwise divided by Iraq, won support from Sweden and Denmark among the smaller nations, and even had some appeal for the Belgian government. Although most small and medium-sized countries continued to press for a rotating presidency, the focus of the debate began to shift towards the future composition of the Commission. This was an issue where federalists and small country representatives were not necessarily in agreement. For many federalists, a small Commission meant a strong Commission, while a Commission of one member per member state risked being weak.

The Franco-German institutional reform paper marked the high-water mark of Franco-German cooperation in the Convention. Afterwards, the foreign ministers were preoccupied with another unpredictable event – war in Iraq.

Giscard's proposals for the Union's institutions in late April 2003 were another unexpected turning point. It looked for all the world as if he was attempting to set up a *directoire* of the big member states to run the Union. These proposals provoked immense shock and anger in the Praesidium and among the integrationist Convention members from the European Parliament and the smaller member states. Yet the Convention did not break apart. Instead, Giscard's proposals acted as a kind of catharsis, paving the way for compromises between integrationists and intergovernmentalists.

Although Giscard's proposals survived in their extreme form for only a day, enough remained after the Praesidium meeting of 23 April to put the Convention on a new course over the two months to the Thessaloniki summit. Most significant was his idea that a 'double' majority should determine a qualified majority in the Council of Ministers. This challenge to the institutional settlement of the Nice Treaty was completely unexpected and transformed the Convention's final weeks.

A late-breaking, wholly unexpected development was the alliance in early June 2003 between the integration-minded national parliamentarians and the members of the European Parliament that gave Giscard the opportunity to reach and determine consensus on the draft Constitution. It was generally expected that the Convention would become an intergovernmental conference in its final weeks with the parliamentarians marginalised. The outcome then would probably have been failure because Spain, driven by its opposition to revising the Nice treaty, had immobilised the Praesidium and forged its alliance of convenience with the 16 small Convention states. Giscard was not bluffing when he talked at the end of May of possibly having to go tell the European Council in Thessaloniki of 'stalemate in the Convention'.

Other factors helped the Convention produce the result that it did. Non-events can play an important part in shaping history. One of the most important – and a rather sad tale – was the failure of the Commission to play a leading role in the Convention as it moved towards a conclusion. By spring 2003, Giscard and the Convention's secretariat had established a virtual monopoly over the power of proposal.

Another important non-event was the UK decision, made known during May 2003, to work for a single text rather than options. France, too, contributed significantly to the eventual success of the Convention by quietly dropping its previous insistence on equal voting rights with Germany in the Council of Ministers. This was one factor that made Nice such a difficult negotiation. France's change of heart, which has to be seen in the context of the two countries drawing closer to protect their interests in a union of 25, meant the double majority idea had a chance of acceptance.

But would the double majority have proved acceptable to Spain without the unexpected defeat of the Aznar government in the weekend elections after the Al-Qaeda attacks on Madrid? The election of the Socialist government in Spain triggered a radical realignment of forces in the IGC. After the loss of its ally, the Polish government had little option but to modify its hard line stance on the double majority, paving the way for the final compromise.

20.2   THE CONSTITUTIONAL TREATY AND THE CITIZEN

The EU's leaders, during their Nice summit in December 2000, identified a 'need to improve and to monitor the democractic legitimacy and transparency of the Union and its institutions, to bring them closer to the citizens of the member states'. A year later, in Laeken, they decided the Union was 'at a crossroads'. They agreed it needed to become 'more democratic, more transparent and more efficient'. How far does the constitutional treaty measure up to these goals? In terms of transparency, the Convention draft and final treaty text mark a huge advance on the treaties that have gone before. True, it is doubtful whether they would appeal, as

Giscard hoped, to the average intelligent secondary school pupil. But the constitutional treaty has a beginning, a middle and an end that an ordinary mortal can follow.

That is still true despite the complexities introduced during the IGC. Taken together, part I (the 'constitutional' part of the treaty) and part II (the Charter of Fundamental Rights) give a clear idea of what the EU does and what it stands for. The overall result far outshines anything produced by the intergovernmental conferences that resulted in the Treaties of Amsterdam and Nice.

Thanks to the Convention, the text meets the mandate set in the Nice declaration on the future of the Union in full. It delivers a clearer definition of who does what that will make the Union more accountable to its citizens, parliaments and governments in member states. The political approach towards policing subsidiarity offers hope that the idea of taking decisions as close to the citizen as possible will, more than a decade after first being written into the Treaty on Union, at last be taken seriously. The article and protocol on subsidiarity also promise to involve national parliaments constructively in the Union's affairs. By incorporating the Charter of Fundamental Rights in the treaty, Europe's citizens have a bill of rights, which is necessarily hedged to take account of the laws and practices of the member states as well as those of the Union.

The constitutional treaty does an important service by making clear how much a role the Union now plays in the lives of Europeans. The primacy of Union law has been a fact of life since a European Court judgement in 1964 but was never written down in any treaty. Article I-6 makes clear what sort of Union the member states have joined and helped create.

Similarly, the implications for member states of competences shared with the Union are now clear. The discovery in article I-12 that 'the member states shall exercise their competence to the extent that the Union has not exercised, or has decided to cease exercising, its competence', may, on reflection, be a statement of the obvious. But for those beyond the Brussels beltway, the reach of Union power has the capacity to surprise, if not shock, when on the printed page.

Such clarity is welcome. It promises, in the words of the Nice declaration, to improve 'the democratic legitimacy and transparency of the Union and its institutions'. It may even 'bring them closer to the citizens of the member states'. But the Convention's mixed record on getting its message across shows there is still much to do. Although it operated more transparently than any previous IGC, the Convention failed to generate the public interest that its organisers hoped.[1] Also striking was the lack of interest shown by business in the Convention.

If the Convention and the constitutional treaty are to mark the start of a new relationship between the Union and its citizens, the Union's many actors must rise to the challenge, and explain and justify what they are about. This applies especially to the Brussels institutions, but also to the member states.

The European Parliament must take this challenge seriously after turnout has fallen in every European election since 1979 to a low of less than 45% in 2004. The Union's member governments must improve on their own past conduct. How often has an unpopular policy been blamed on 'Brussels' without any acknowledgement that the country in question has approved and often willed it? The clarity provided by the constitutional treaty may eventually limit such behaviour.

The constitutional treaty places new responsibilities on national parliaments, giving them opportunities to play a role in the life of the Union that go beyond the policing of subsidiarity. They will be involved in monitoring Europol and Eurojust and evaluating the implementation of Union policies in the area of freedom, security and justice. Article I-18 now orders the Commission to draw the attention of national parliaments to proposals under the so-called flexibility clause, by which the Council of Ministers acting unanimously can shift action not specified in the constitutional treaty from the member states to the Union. Article IV-444, the generalised bridging or *passerelle* clause, gives national parliaments still greater power: a single national parliament can block a unanimous decision of the European Council to remove the national veto from areas of legislation in part III of the constitutional treaty.

Increased responsibilities will only work, however, if national parliaments improve their scrutiny of what is happening in the Union. If the constitutional treaty is to deliver the Laeken declaration's goal of bringing its citizens closer to Europe there must be deeper understanding and more discussion of the Union and its impact in national and regional legislatures. Some elements of the constitutional treaty should help promote a more informed debate about the Union in its member states. Although the final text merits only a middle grade for jargon busting, the constitutional treaty

---

[1] The Convention website had an average of 47,000 visits a month, rising to 100,000 in June 2003. The Eurobarometer Special 214 survey, published in January 2005, reported that 11% of the 25,000 EU citizens polled in the 25 member states in November 2004 said they had a good overall knowledge of the constitutional treaty against 56% who said they knew very little about it and 33% who had never heard of it.

will, if adopted, end the Union's confusing pillar structure and provide the Union with a legal personality. Giuliano Amato and his second working group successfully re-christened and rationalised the various acts by which the Union legislates. These steps, although seemingly remote from the preoccupations of everyday life, should, over time, clear away much of the mystery and confusion surrounding 'Brussels' for the ordinary citizen.

Other gains in this area include opening the Council of Ministers to public scrutiny when legislating, and the commitments to dialogue and transparency in the new section of the treaty dealing with the democratic life of the Union. Special interest groups have already discovered the potential of paragraph 4 of article I-47, which will enable one million citizens, provided they are scattered across several member states, to petition the Commission to propose EU legislation on their behalf.

Also important for connecting with the citizen will be practical results in policy areas where the Union gains more responsibility. The end result is more than just the 'tidying up exercise' that Peter Hain once claimed it to be. The decisions making it easier for the Union, with the member states, to deal with asylum, immigration and cross-border organised crime should, once transposed into law, lead to easily comprehensible benefits for Europe's citizens.

Whether provisions for stepping up cooperation on foreign and defence policy with the support of the new Union foreign minister will have a rapid impact on the general public or world affairs is less clear. Although public opinion polls suggest a more active Union role in these areas would be welcomed, the constitutional treaty sets out to facilitate rather than act. Common foreign and defence policies will only play a bigger role when there is sufficient political will. The role played by the EU in late 2004 in support of democracy in Ukraine demonstrated its capacity to exercise 'soft' power effectively. But the divisions over Iraq in 2003 showed how difficult it can be to generate a common political will among 25 member states.

The willingness to embrace more qualified majority voting was what distinguished the approach of the Convention and IGC to the justice and home affairs agenda from that on common foreign and defence policies, where unanimity remains the general rule.

The European Commission has complained that the constitutional treaty's extension of qualified majority voting is too timid to cope with the management challenges of a Union expanded from 15 to 25 member states.

The text agreed by the IGC created 26 new legal bases where QMV will apply to decisions in the Council on specific policies. It shifts decisions in the Council from unanimity to QMV in the case of 17 legal bases compared with 31 in the Treaty of Nice. There will still be about 70 areas of decision making subject to unanimity among the member states. The authors of the European Parliament's report on the treaty[2] declared it 'regrettable that the opportunity was not taken to do more' in the field of qualified majority voting.

Inside the Brussels beltway, QMV may appear essential for reasons of efficiency in an enlarged Union. But it can look very different from outside Brussels. Every past extension of qualified majority voting has made the next move to QMV more difficult as legislators come closer to core issues of sovereignty. Joschka Fischer's insistence in the Convention's final days on national government controls over third country nationals entering the labour market showed how even an enthusiastic federalist had to trim his sails to match domestic political realities. QMV can also have its downsides. As has been the case with some financial services legislation, it can result in compromises that are so far removed from their original goal as to be wrongheaded and damaging.

Although the Convention was a broadly integrationist body, it – and the IGC – operated in a political environment where integration was not notably popular. Sweden's September 2003 vote against euro membership was a reminder of this. But within these constraints, the constitutional treaty has provided mechanisms that should enable countries that want to integrate to forge ahead.

After two false starts at Amsterdam and Nice, the Convention and IGC may have devised rules for enhanced cooperation [I-44] that should encourage groups of countries to adopt this 'last resort' mechanism for working together in the furtherance of their own objectives in line with the rules of the Union. Such compromises will be more necessary following the Union's enlargement. Provided participants avoid the trap of creating exclusive 'core groups', they should add substance to the motto of the constitutional treaty: 'United in diversity'.

---

[2] Richard Corbett and Inigo Méndez de Vigo.

20.3   A MORE EFFICIENT UNION?

At the ceremony in Rome on 18 July 2003 when Giscard handed over the Convention draft to the Italian presidency,[3] he extolled the constitutional treaty for providing Europe 'with stable, democratic and effective institutions'. The European Parliament became 'the Union's main legislature'. The Council would 'have a face and a measure of durability' with a president who 'will organise states' work and will be able to plan for the future and think ahead'. The Commission 'organised so as to fulfil its European role' would 'act as a driving force and the main executive' and 'embody the common European interest'.

The constitutional treaty does indeed promise to strengthen the European Parliament's power and influence considerably. The Parliament's report on the treaty mentioned that codecision, or the ordinary legislative procedure, would apply to 86 areas of legislation compared with 37 previously.

But do the Convention's results, after amendment by the IGC, strengthen the other sides of the triangle? Despite the complexities added in the IGC, the double majority system for measuring qualified majorities in the Council [I-25] promises to be more efficient than the tally of weighted votes negotiated at Nice. For Giscard, the stable presidency of the European Council, the slimmed down Commission and the Union foreign minister counted as significant improvements. The first two achievements were among the first aims he disclosed after being appointed Convention president.

The European council chair or president, on which the big member states expended so much political capital, is a significant institutional innovation. He or she is meant to drive forward and 'ensure the preparation and continuity' of the European Council's work, according to article I-22. Appointed for two and a half years, with a possible second term, the president will be judged on whether he or she can sustain the body that provides the EU's collective leadership. In an EU of 25 or more, the system of six-month rotating presidencies can no longer bring continuity or institutional memory to the task of running the Union.

But with the job's scope restricted by successive waves of amendments in the Convention, it is unclear how the European Council president will exercise adequate authority. He or she will be able to draw on the resources and talents of the Council secretariat. But how will the president interact with other Council formations, which, as specified in article I-24 and a

---

[3] 'The Rome Declaration', 18 July 2003.

declaration attached to the treaty, will be run by team presidencies of member states 'on the basis of equal rotation'? The constitutional treaty provides no chain of command akin to that provided by cabinet government and a national bureaucracy for national leaders exercising the role of European Council president under the rotating system.

Another challenge will be establishing effective relations with the double-hatted Union minister for foreign affairs, who in turn will have to define a new role. The European Council 'shall define the general guidelines for the common foreign and security policy' including defence [III-295]. The foreign minister shall have the power to make proposals and ensure the implementation of decisions taken by the European Council and the Foreign Affairs Council.

As article III-296 makes clear, the Union foreign minister is another notable innovation and endowed with considerable clout. He or she (and, barring an upset, the first holder of the office will be a he: Javier Solana, the Union's high representative for foreign and security policy) will chair the Foreign Affairs Council, which alone among the sectoral Councils will not come under a rotating team presidency. The minister will be supported by a 'European External Action Service' made up of officials from the Council, Commission and national diplomatic services. And he or she will also be a vice-president of the Commission and responsible for the Commission's external relations role.

There is also a question mark over how the president of the European Council will interact with the president of the Commission, who, after a fight back by the smaller member states and the European Parliament, emerged from the negotiations in the Convention with considerably more power than Giscard originally envisaged. 'I have defended the two-headed Europe,' Amato remarked on the day the Convention ended, 'but no animal can live with two heads for too long'.

Given human nature and institutional jealousies, there is a risk that the president of the European Council, the Commission president and the European foreign minister will become involved in demarcation disputes and turf wars, which will do nothing to enhance the Union's standing abroad or efficiency at home. The double-hatted foreign minister, with power based mainly in the Council but also a Commission vice-president, may have to resolve conflicts within him or herself.

The inescapable conclusion is that the personal qualities of the individuals elected to these high posts by qualified majorities of the members of the European Council will be crucial. Yet the European Council has a mixed record in choosing senior officials for the Union. All can agree that Javier Solana has been a success as EU foreign policy supremo. But how many would make the same claim for some of the European Council's recent choices for the post of Commission president?

The institutional arrangements in the constitutional treaty leave much to chance. It remains to be seen whether the details of sharing out Parliament's seats according to the 'degressively proportional' approach of article 1-20 can be resolved without tension. The mechanics of reducing the Commission's size after 2014 to two-thirds of the number of member states [I-26] could cause problems. And once slimmed down on the basis of equal rotation, how will a country without a commissioner respond, say, to the Commission fining one of its leading companies over a competition case or imposing a fine for an illegal state aid? The risk, as Giscard acknowledged, is a college whose legitimacy 'would be challenged, which would weaken the Commission's moral authority accordingly'. However, these caveats cannot detract from what was achieved over two and a half years by the IGC and the Convention that went before it.

The treaty that emerged from the IGC modified, rather than overhauled, the draft produced by the Convention during its 16 and a half months of work. About 90% of the Convention text survived the negotiation among the member states. Where there were significant amendments, they usually involved issues where the Convention consensus was less than solid or the rushed negotiations of the Convention's final weeks left too little time to reach a sound conclusion.

In the end, it was not surprising that important elements of the institutional package agreed in the Convention were challenged by the IGC. The double majority system, the two-tier Commission, the low minimum threshold for seats in the European Parliament and the Legislative Council were 'power' questions *par excellence*. It is moot whether Giscard or the Convention had a mandate to decide in favour of a double majority in the Council, as there was no mention of the Council's voting system in the Laeken declaration. Although the Convention was undoubtedly innovative and inventive in the solutions it proposed, it was hardly likely that sovereign states would accept them without a second thought.

The fact remains. The Convention text successfully formed the basis of an agreement among 25 member states on a document encompassing 448 articles. Reflecting that success, article IV-443 justifiably specifies the convening of similar Conventions to prepare significant reform of the constitutional treaty in the future.

20.4   A TREATY ROOTED IN DUALITIES

Europe's constitutional treaty is, as Giscard admitted at the close of the Convention, not perfect. It certainly lacks the majesty and simplicity of the US Constitution. But this should be no surprise because the product of the two and a half years of negotiation that followed the Laeken summit is not a Constitution in the US sense, and never could be. It is not a compact between the Union and its citizens – unlike the US Constitution, with its ringing opening line of 'We, the people'. Instead, Europe's constitutional treaty reflects a dual legitimacy based on the will of the Union's member states and citizens.

The constitutional treaty lacks the brevity of the US Constitution and has been much criticised for its length and detail. But as its very first article [I-1] makes clear, the EU is a complex entity 'on which the member states confer competences to attain objectives they have in common'.

The members of the Convention and the IGC that followed were not mandated to be revolutionaries. Nor did they start with a clean slate. They had to create one treaty out of several, pulling together complex texts developed over more than 50 years of EU law and treaty making.

The constitutional treaty is a big document because in Part III it details the legal bases under which the Union exercises its competences. These detailed provisions, which attract much scorn from eurosceptics, limit the powers of the Union and prevent it from becoming a superstate. Anthing less could, as the Convention Praesidium argued in 2002, pose a threat to legal certainty and 'prove a permanent source of conflict'.

The Convention's work survivied the IGC. But it is still unclear whether Europe's constitutional treaty will survive the ratification process. In particular, Britain's decision to hold a referendum on the treaty has created great uncertainty over whether all 25 member states will approve it.

The text deserves better than to be sent to oblivion. It is more than the usual European Union compromise. Giscard described the Convention's outcome as a 'synthesis', something that strikes 'the necessary balance between peoples, between states old and new, between institutions and between dream and reality'.

The Convention's text, as modified by the IGC recognises that the EU is rooted in dualities and sets out to reconcile these. It is a Union of states and citizens; a Union of the federal and intergovernmental where states both pool sovereignty and cooperate on policies. It is a Union that has emerged in a bewildering and often accidental manner into something that is less than perfect, often infuriating and capable of great improvement. But capable of improvement it is, and the constitutional treaty produced by the Convention and the IGC is, both in terms of process and product, evidence of that.

.

Index

Peter Norman's 'The Accidental Constitution' occupies a unique position in recent writings about the European Union. Fluent, witty and accessible, this highly acclaimed book, published by EuroComment of Brussels, remains the only authoritative account of the European Convention and the controversial draft Constitution that it produced.

Peter Norman has now taken the story of the EU's 'Accidental Constitution' further. Subtitled, 'the making of Europe's constitutional treaty', the new edition explains the text that must now be ratified by all the Union's 25 member states. It sheds light on the complex political and constitutional issues that the EU's leaders set out to solve and explains why the subsequent negotiations among the member states came close to disaster before ending in agreement.

Knowing how the European Union's constitution came about is crucial to understanding a text that could have a profound effect on the lives of 500 million European citizens for decades to come. This book, written by a former bureau chief of the Financial Times in Brussels, draws on a wealth of documentary evidence, the insights gained from talking to key participants in the creation of the EU's constitutional treaty and the author's expert knowledge of EU affairs.

Aimed at the lay reader as well as the specialist, the book is essential reading for all who want to understand the European Union of today. It is a tale of people and politics. It is also a tale of the unexpected. That is why the book is called 'The Accidental Constitution'.

Peter Norman is uniquely qualified to explain the making of Europe's constitutional treaty. He attended all the Convention sessions from its launch on 28 February 2002, got to know many Convention members, and reported on the Convention's development in detail for EuroComment of Brussels. He brings to the book deep knowledge and wide-ranging experience of the European Union, gained during 35 years as a political and economic journalist. Peter Norman was a foreign correspondent for a total of 22 years, based at various times in Frankfurt, Bonn and Brussels for Reuters, the Times of London, the Wall Street Journal-Europe and the Financial Times. The most recent of his three assignments to Brussels was as the Financial Times Bureau Chief and Chief Correspondent between November 1998 and March 2002. He currently works in London as a journalist and author and is a regular contributor to the Financial Times.